Cultural and economic reproduction in education

Routledge Education Books

Advisory editor: John Eggleston
Professor of Education
University of Keele

Cultural and economic reproduction in education

Essays on class, ideology and the State

Michael W. Apple

Routledge & Kegan Paul

London, Boston & Henley

First published in 1982
by Routledge & Kegan Paul Ltd
39 Store Street, London WC1E 7DD,
9 Park Street, Boston, Mass. 02108, USA and
Broadway House, Newtown Road,
Henley-on-Thames, Oxon RG9 1EN
Set in IBM Press Roman by
Columns, Reading
and printed in the United States of America
Selection and editorial matter copyright © Michael Apple 1982
Contributions © Routledge & Kegan Paul 1982
No part of this book may be reproduced in any form without permission from the publisher, except for the quotation of brief passages in criticism

Library of Congress Cataloging in Publication Data

Cultural and economic reproduction in education.
(Routledge education books)
Includes index.
Contents: Reproduction and contradiction in education / Michael W. Apple – Education and class formation / David Hogan – Education, economy, and the state / Martin Carnoy – [etc.]

1. Education – Social aspects – Addresses, essays, lectures. 2. Education – Economic aspects – Addresses, essays, lectures. 3. Social evolution – Addresses, essays, lectures. 4. Social control – Addresses, essays, lectures. 5. Social structure – Addresses, essays, lectures. I. Apple, Michael W. II. Series.
LC191.C77 370.19 81-15884

ISBN 0-7100-0845-7 AACR2
ISBN 0-7100-0846-5 (pbk.)

Contents

Acknowledgments

Edited volumes are always difficult to do. The trials of deadlines, co-ordination, etc. are just that – trials. Yet for all of that, volumes of this type help both to create collective bonds where none existed before and strengthen those that existed previously. The very task of trying to bring together individuals who are doing some of the best work on education and cultural and economic reproduction helped to establish bonds between what are too often two separate communities. Lines of communication and the possibility of collective conceptual and political work are established. This is important not just for the authors of the individual chapters in this book, but for the reader as well. As a community is formed, we can learn from each other; new lines of action can be identified; and, just as significantly, a step can be taken to overcome the historic divisiveness within those groups of people who are so deeply concerned for a non-exploitative society.

A number of people have contributed significantly to my efforts of thinking through this volume and refining it. All of the contributors have taught me a good deal. Some – such as Roger Dale, Michael Useem, and Philip Wexler – were instrumental in enabling me to recognize important areas that I might otherwise have ignored. Other friends and colleagues provided necessary criticism and suggestions, sometimes even unknowingly perhaps. Among them were Jerry Karabel, Michael Olneck, Paul Willis, Joel Taxel, and the membership of the *Social Text* editorial collective in Madison. David Godwin of Routledge & Kegan Paul suggested the volume originally and provided much needed encouragement and assistance when the 'trials' got to me. Rima D. Apple contributed important editorial advice and so much more. Bonnie Garski's secretarial excellence was demonstrated once again.

Authors

Michael W. Apple is Professor of Curriculum and Instruction and Educational Policy Studies at the University of Wisconsin, Madison. He has written extensively on the relationship between education and economic and cultural reproduction. His most recent volume is *Ideology and Curriculum* (Routledge & Kegan Paul, 1979). His new book, *Education and Power*, will be published by Routledge & Kegan Paul soon.

Basil Bernstein is Professor of the Sociology of Education and Director of the Sociological Research Unit at the University of London Institute of Education. He is the author and editor of many volumes on culture, class and education including *Class, Codes and Control*, Volumes I, II, and III. He is presently finishing work on a new edition of Volume III in this series.

Martin Carnoy is Professor of Education and Economics at Stanford University. He has written extensively on the political economy of education and on alternatives to capitalist production. His most recent works include *Education as Cultural Imperialism* (1974); *Segmentation of Labor Markets* (1980); *Desarrollo economico y reforma educativa en Cuba* (1980); *Economic Democracy: the Challenge of the 1980s* (1980). He is currently completing the *Dialectics of Education* with Henry Levin.

Roger Dale is a Lecturer in the Sociology of Education at The Open University. He has contributed to several courses in the sociology of education there and published a number of articles in the field. He has co-edited *School and Society*, *Schooling and Capitalism*, and *Education and the State*. His new book, *The State and Education*, is to be published by Routledge & Kegan Paul. His current interests are education and the state in the peripheral countries of Europe and the influence of international organizations on national educational policies.

Paul DiMaggio is Assistant Professor in the Institution for Social and Policy Studies, the Department of Sociology, and the School of Organization and Management at Yale University. He is a contributing editor of *Working Papers for a New Society*, has written on the arts, education, and cultural policy, and is co-author, with Michael Useem and Paula Brown, of *Audience Studies of Museums and the Performing Arts: A Critical Review* (National Endowment for the Arts, Research Division, 1977).

Todd Gitlin is Assistant Professor of Sociology and Director of the Mass Communications Program at the University of California, Berkeley. He is co-author of *Uptown: Poor Whites in Chicago*, author of *The Whole World is Watching: Mass Media in the Making and Unmaking of the New Left* (University of California Press), and has written on popular culture, social theory, and politics for *Theory and Society*, *Nation*, *Social Problems*, *Social Policy*, *Village Voice*, *College English*, *Commonweal*, *Progressive*, *Film Quarterly*, the *Columbia Journalism Review*, and other journals.

David Hogan is an Assistant Professor in the Graduate School of Education at the University of Pennsylvania. He is completing a manuscript tentatively entitled *Education and the Making of the Chicago Working Class, 1880-1930*. In the fall of 1979 he commenced, with Michael Katz, a research project on the social history of work, family life, and schooling in Philadelphia between 1830 and 1930. In 1977 he was awarded the Henry Barnard Prize of the History of Education Society and in July 1980 was made a Spencer Fellow for 1980-3.

Gail P. Kelly is Associate Professor, Department of Social Foundations of Education at the State University of New York at Buffalo. She is author of *From Vietnam to America: A Chronicle of the Vietnamese Immigration to the United States* and co-author of *Education and Colonialism*. She is Associate Editor of the *Comparative Education Review* and has co-edited a special issue of that journal on the Education of Women in the Third World. Gail Kelly has written extensively on research on women's education cross nationally and is currently co-authoring a book, *Feminism: Its Impact on the Disciplines*.

Ann S. Nihlen received her PhD in Anthropology and Education from the University of New Mexico in 1976. Her dissertation was an ethnographic study entitled *The White Working Class in School: a Study of First Grade Girls and their Parents*. Dr Nihlen is currently at the University of New Mexico as an Assistant Professor in the Department of Educational Foundations and as the Coordinator of the Women Studies Program. She has taught courses in the area of sexism in education for nine years and is currently doing research for a book on the history of women in education.

Michael Useem is Associate Professor of Sociology at Boston University. With general interests in the field of political sociology, he has written on political protest, the financing of social research, culture and education, and the upper class. He is completing a study of large corporations and corporate leadership in America and Britain, and he has recently published 'Corporations and the Corporate Elite', *Annual Review of Sociology* (1980).

Philip Wexler teaches education and sociology at the University of Rochester. He is the author of *Sociology of Education: Beyond Equality* and the forthcoming *A Critical Social Psychology*. His interests include critical theory and the relationship between the commodification process, ideology, and interpersonal relations.

Chapter 1

Reproduction and contradiction in education: an introduction

Michael W. Apple

Introduction

Much of the current discussion about the role of schooling in advanced industrial societies has been stimulated by a large quantity of scholarship that is critical of what educational systems may do. In essence the disagreements have centered around four interrelated issues: (1) Do schools primarily reproduce the social division of labor or are they avenues for lessening the existing inequality of power and knowledge in our society? (2) Are schools 'strongly determined' by ideological, economic, and cultural forces outside of them or do they have a significant degree of autonomy? (3) Do theories of economic reproduction adequately respond to the cultural and ideological roles played by education? (4) What actually happens within the school (the curriculum, the social relations, the language and culture considered legitimate) that may provide answers to these questions?

There can be no longer any doubt that schools do seem to be institutions of economic and cultural reproduction. However, the way this goes on within educational institutions is exceptionally complex. A number of the recent theories of the relationship between education and an 'external' society miss important aspects of this complexity. One cannot fully understand it using many of the models of analysis which dominate research on these four original questions *in isolation from the others.*

For example, most scholarship on the question of the effect of schools in economic reproduction treats elementary and secondary schools as 'black boxes.' It uses input/output measures of achievement and mobility without engaging in in-depth analyses of how these effects are created in the school (Apple 1978). Further, it neglects the fact that (as recent research in France, England, Sweden, and the

United States has shown) schools are cultural as well as economic institutions. Hence, an analysis of the formal and informal culture of schools and other educational institutions, and the knowledge that gets in and is taught in them, is quite important, for as this research has documented, both the curriculum and the culture of schools have a profound impact on students' life chances and can illuminate the ties schools have to the surrounding social order. Unfortunately, however, a good deal of the research on cultural reproduction has neglected the concerns and insights of those scholars investigating economic reproduction. Thus, both groups often speak past each other. In many ways this is quite unfortunate since beneath the overt differences many aspects of each of these positions clearly complement each other.

Added to this problem of isolation is another. The relationship between economic and cultural reproduction and education is not 'merely' one found in the formal institution of the school. The cultural apparatus of a society is much broader than that covered either by the formal corpus of the school curriculum or the more tacit hidden curriculum. We need to understand other aspects of a society's modes of communicating and creating what Raymond Williams (1977) has so felicitously called an 'effective dominant culture.' Because of this, analyses of mass media, popular culture, and the role of the arts become critical if we are to fully comprehend how education and reproduction are linked beyond the classroom as well.

In essence, what we are beginning to see is a profound shift in our very notion of culture, one which 'rescues it from elitist or narrowly literary or artistic usages'. At the same time, we are witnessing a break with mechanistic theories about people and their consciousness. These shifts themselves rest on a marked alteration in the relationship between intellectuals and working people (Clarke, Critcher, Johnson 1979:58) for we have had to take seriously the real everyday experiences and objective conditions in which people find themselves.

Yet even with this shift, all too many theorists of both economic and cultural reproduction in education focus on the economy and culture in abstract 'received' terms and categories. They have not developed adequate tools that would enable them to specifically analyze the actual and concrete cultural, political, and economic meanings and practices of various groups within our social formation. This is especially unfortunate in education since here the everyday meanings and practices constitute the warp and woof of reproduction, contradiction, and contestation in important ways. As I have argued at length elsewhere, in schools, for example, the form and content of the curriculum – both hidden and overt – are clearly significant in this regard, as are the forms of social interaction that dominate such institutions (Apple 1979a). The same claims can be made about the family, the state, the media, the workplace, and elsewhere.

This neglect of the concrete meanings and activities of culture and people as they interact in our institutions is unfortunate in another way. It limits the very ability we have to think about how these institutions may reproduce the relations of domination and ideological conflicts in which we are interested. That is, many of our 'received' categories are not totally sufficient for analyzing the actual processes and sites where the creation and recreation of the hegemony of dominant classes and class segments goes on. For this hegemony is *not* something abstract. It is not something that exists merely at the 'roof of our heads', so to speak, nor can it be fully encompassed by concepts such as control, manipulation, or indoctrination (Williams 1977:110). Rather, as Williams so nicely puts it (1977:110):

> [Hegemony] is a whole body of practices and expectations . . .: our senses and assignments of energy, our shaping perceptions of ourselves and our world. It is a lived system of meanings and values – constitutive and constituting – which as they are experienced as practices appear as reciprocally confirming . . . . It is, that is to say, in the strongest sense, a 'culture,' but a culture which has also to be seen as the lived dominance and subordination of particular classes.

Hegemony is not found in one's head, then, but made up of our day-to-day cultural, political, and economic (ideological) practice, a set of practices which help create us. As both Gramsci and Althusser remind us, 'ideology is a practice producing subjects' (Mouffe 1979:187).

To primarily focus on culture – either in its lived or commodified forms – as we have done here for the past few pages can itself be awfully limiting, however. For in the process we may tend to neglect the crucial issues related to mode of production and objective class structure that the investigators of economic reproduction have so rightly brought to our attention. We may forget how very important and real the connections among the economy, ideology, culture and other aspects of a society are.

Given this, any serious analysis of education and reproduction must account for a number of complex interconnections. It must concern itself with the role of the educational apparatus in roughly reproducing a labor force stratified by sex and class. It requires a concomitant investigation of the way education functions in the process of class formation and struggle, capital accumulation and the legitimation of the privileges of dominant groups. But schools do not exist in a political vacuum. They are structurally limited by the power of the state, an area which has remained systematically underdeveloped theoretically in the literature on education. Hence, the role state intervention plays in legitimating and setting limits on the responses that education can make to the processes of stratification, legitimation, and accumulation is essential. These are, of course, not only questions of current interest. The processes of reproduction have a history, a history that needs to be uncovered if we are to know the possibilities of action today.

These previous issues tend to be oriented toward an appraisal of the role of education in economic reproduction. However, as I noted, the educational apparatus of a society is also an important set of agencies in the cultural reproduction of class relationships. In order to understand this we need to respond to the role of the arts and mass media outside the school, to the actual social relations and the knowledge within the school, and finally, to the way people respond to the ideological and cultural messages these institutions are presenting. For we may find that 'simple' reproduction is not the only thing occurring. Cultural forms may have some autonomy or may be much more contradictory than we might have supposed. Thus, cultural reproduction (and how it relates back to economic reproduction) needs just as thorough an analysis as the role of education in class formation, and in reproducing and legitimating economic stratification and capital accumulation.

Answers to these kinds of problems have usually required that one take seriously both the questions and the techniques that have arisen out of the Marxist tradition. Yet aside from some important work in the last ten or so years, this tradition has been markedly absent in educational investigations. Though it has been kept alive with remarkable tenacity by individuals in, say, England and elsewhere, it is only recently that serious work has again emerged in the United States.

The chapters included here, and the volume as a whole, represent attempts to come to terms with the influence of Marxist approaches to educational analysis. While not all of the authors will agree on the specifics of the efficacy of certain elements of a Marxist program, all of them speak from a joint interest. This is a concern with the structural roots of domination and exploitation. Thus, something is taken as already well documented by these authors. Society is structurally unequal and this inequality by race, gender, and class *is* truly structural.[1] That is, it is not a fixable maladjustment in the social machinery, but is rooted in and reproduced by the economic, political, and ideological forms which currently exist. The question is not the reality of differential power, but how that power is made manifest, in which spheres it operates, and who ultimately benefits.

I want to stress that this does not mean that answers to these questions are pregiven. It does mean, however, that the fundamental problematics the reader will encounter here are engaged. They seek to understand how the economic and cultural practices involved in education contribute to the reproduction of these structural relations, to contradictory tendencies within these relations, and to possibilities for organized action upon them.

Hence a particular conceptual apparatus will be employed in this volume, one which depends on terms such as class, gender, hegemony, ideology, capital, the State, reproduction, contradiction, division of labor, and so on. No simple definition is sufficient to convey the richness of these concepts if they are used in an undogmatic way. Therefore, I shall not attempt to provide any such definitions here. Instead, the meaning of these terms and their conceptual and political grounding will emerge from their use. The test of their fruitfullness is in their applicability to the interrogation of concrete situations. I believe that the essays collected here can go a long way in providing for both the building of a consistent framework that may be applied to the specificity of real conflicts and practices in education, as well as providing instances of such application.

This sense of engagement is coupled with a particular kind of tension, a tension that will be evident to those readers who are familiar with the larger controversies within current scholarship on the relationship between culture, politics, and the economy on the one hand and the (somewhat more derivative) investigations of the social and ideological 'functions' of education on the other. In simple terms, there are major tensions and controversies within *each* of these traditions. In very many ways, the chapters which follow are both responses to and/or influenced by both sets of tensions. To make this clear, it might be wise to briefly examine some of these major disputes within the literature. In so doing, we shall then want to relate these to the more complex and general issue – the relationship 'between' base and superstructure – that lies behind nearly all of these controversies.

Culture and economy in education

At the outset of this introductory chapter, I noted that two unfortunately relatively disparate traditions have come to the fore in scholarship on reproduction in education. Clearly, these are really only ideal types since many individuals have been influenced by both.

A primary concern with culture and power, with the form and content of the knowledge and symbols found in education and the relations of domination and exploitation found outside these institutions, is evident in the very titles of many of the major volumes that have had an impact during the past decade. *Knowledge and Control*, *Education as Cultural Imperialism*, *Education and Social Control*, *Class, Codes and Control*, *Explorations in the Politics of School Knowledge*, *Reproduction in Education, Society and Culture*, and many others speak to these concerns.[2] The interest in education, power, and economic results – a somewhat different problematic – is just as evident in titles such as *Inequality*, *Schooling and the Rise of the Corporate State*, *The Sorting Machine*, *Schooling in a Corporate Society*, *Schooling in Capitalist America*, and *Who Gets Ahead?*[3] Rather than culture, the focus in these volumes has been primarily on the relationship between education and the individual or class composition of the occupational structure, as well as on economic power.

Obviously, there have been serious attempts to bring these two perspectives together in the past. Karabel and Halsey's (1977) timely volume represents a valuable effort to both give a sense of the state of the field and to synthesize the varying economic and cultural approaches then extant. Basil Bernstein's (1977) continuing efforts to show how economy, class and culture are interwoven in education and the Open University materials on Schooling and Society (Dale *et al*. 1976; MacDonald 1977) provide other examples. My own studies over the last decade or so, published in *Ideology and Curriculum* (1979a) present one more instance of a consistent attempt to bring together the dual concerns of the political/economic and the cultural/ideological outcomes of education. Let us look at some of the issues each of these concerns raises in somewhat more detail.

We are coming to know a good deal about the relationship between the economic reproduction of class relations and education. As Erik Olin Wright (1979:xxi) has recently demonstrated, for example, class is a primary explanatory device in any account of the evident differential returns to education for blacks and whites, and between men and women. In fact, the differences in economic benefits gotten from education that separate economic, racial and gender groups are strongly related to where one stands in the class structure. This is not to say that racial and sexual oppression are not real and powerful forces. Rather, it is to say that they are dynamically interconnected with the relations of economic domination and exploitation that exist.

Wright documents some rather interesting findings. Even after controlling for age, occupational status, family background, and so on, the economic returns one gets from education are much greater for managers than for members of the working class (Wright 1979:138). As Wright states (1979:162):

> Class [defined as one's position in the social relations of production] consistently and significantly mediates the income determination process. People occupying different class positions but with the same level of education and occupational status, the same age and seniority on the job, the same general social background, and working the same number of hours per year, will still differ substantially in their respected incomes. And people in different class positions can expect to receive different amounts of additional income per increment in educational credentials, even if they do not differ on a variety of other characteristics.

Furthermore, this differential income return is even greater when one compares employers and workers. That is, ownership of property and 'real economic control over the means of production' does seem to count a good deal in power and benefits, including the returns gained from one's education (Wright 1979:224).

Of course, it is not only the economic return from education that has interested researchers in this area. Education's role in the reproduction of the social relations of production and the control and division of labor has been an overriding interest. The evidence suggests that the educational system, in concert with other aspects of a social formation, plays a fundamental part in such reproduction, though the importance of education in this, the way it is accomplished, and the 'functions' it will perform may clearly differ among countries and over time.[4] Further evidence also indicates that school systems may also reproduce class, status, and racial relations through a system of urban segregation and through their integration into a marketplace of credentials (Castells 1980; Collins 1979; Ogbu 1978), while at the same time being an important agency for the production of the technical/administrative knowledge needed for capital accumulation (Apple 1979a, 1979b). Just as importantly, the place of education in recreating some of the conditions necessary for the continuation of a sexual division of labor and patriarchal power structures has become even more evident (Eisenstein 1979; Kuhn and Wolpe 1978; MacDonald 1981, 1980).

From all of this we can see that education needs to be viewed as *part of* a larger economic and ideological configuration. The real issue is not what education alone does, but how it is related to class, race, and gender and the control production, and distribution of economic (and cultural) power.

Yet even given the growing statistical and conceptual sophistication of the analyses of the nexus between education and the economic structure, there has recently been an overemphasis on the power of 'the economy' as a fundamental and unmediated determinant in the literature on education and social reproduction. One paradigm case can serve as an example here. Few theories of the role of schooling in contemporary society have had such a major impact on educational argumentation as that postulated by Bowles and Gintis in *Schooling in Capitalist America* (1976). Their analysis points to a relation of 'correspondence' between modern forms of capitalism, the functional requirements of the division of labor, and modern forms of schooling.[5] On the one hand this kind of research is provocative. It takes us light years beyond many of the apolitical and non-structural theories of education and is certainly needed to shake educators out of their more self-congratulatory perspectives. On the other hand, while correct to a point,[6] a correspondence theory can not do complete justice to the complexity of either school life, the actual and often contradictory conditions which tie education to an unequal society, or to the struggles and contradictions that exist in the school, the workplace, and, as we shall see in a number of the chapters in this volume which take over where Bowles and Gintis leave off, in the State.

First, it underemphasizes many of the points about lived culture that I mentioned earlier. It assumes, rather than investigating in detail, the internal characteristics of educational institutions. Second, it tends to assume that students are fully 'determined,' that they passively accept what the school teaches them – hegemonic teaching that prepares them ideologically for life in an unequal labor market. In this way, it seriously undertheorizes the complex issues surrounding class cultures and the dynamics of working-class and gender resistances in and out of schools. As recent Marxist ethnographies of working-class students have so clearly shown, this simply will not do. The correspondence between the needs of the social division of labor and the real meanings that students act on in schools is not all that clear. Male and female students often expressly reject or contest the overt and covert messages of the institution (Everhart 1979; McRobbie 1978; Willis 1977). Reproduction and contestation go hand in hand. Therefore, one cannot assume that institutions are always successful in reproduction. No assemblage of ideological practices and meanings and no set of social and economic arrangements can be totally monolithic. As Gramsci, for instance, was adamant in pointing out, there will be countervailing tendencies and oppositional practices occurring within and 'reproduced by' these institutions as well.[7] This is doubly significant given the school's role as a state apparatus, a role which makes it a location where serious conflict is to be expected (Dale, Esland, Furgusson and MacDonald 1981).

Finally, and just as crucially, by focussing most of our attention on the place of schooling in economic reproduction – on how an 'economic base' reproduces, and is in turn partly reproduced by, the 'ideological superstructure,' if you will – correspondence theories have often neglected a vital arena in which education operates. This is its activity in what Basil Bernstein and others have called the *cultural* reproduction of class relations, its role in recreating and legitimating the form and content of the communicative and symbolic resources, the 'cultural capital,' of dominant groups (Apple 1979a; Bernstein 1977; Bourdieu and Passeron 1977).[8]

Thus, a good deal of the most impressive literature on the political economy of education – literature whose importance must not be denied – has been challenged because of its overly deterministic outlook, its lack of examination of the internal qualities of schools, and its neglect of the cultural sphere and the lived responses of class and gender actors. As we shall see in the next section of this chapter, these problems are by no means limited to education.

Base and superstructure in reproduction

A number of issues immediately spring to the surface from the foregoing discussion. How do we think about culture? About the way a mode of production 'determines' education? About reproduction and non-reproduction going on at one and the same time? These are general issues that are not at all simple, ones which point to the tensions and controversies within a much wider range of scholarship on culture, politics, and the economy. In fact, the major problem facing all of those concerned with the relationship between education and the economic and cultural reproduction of class relations is not unique to education. It is one confronting every person who attempts to unpack the complex ties connecting economics and culture together. As Althusser, Hall, and others have suggested, the problem is 'how to think the specific relations between the relations of production and the political, juridical and ideological forms in such a way as to grasp, simultaneously, the "determination of the economic in the last instance" and the "relative autonomy" or effectivity of the superstructures' (Hall 1977: 54).

Within Marxist theory, the debate over the relationship between base or infrastructure and superstructure has been transformed over the past decade or so. Rather than an acceptance of economistic formulations – where mode of production and class position totally determine at every individual point everything else – there has been a rapidly expanding body of work which has taken the study of this relationship as a problem still to be worked out. While there are serious disagreements among the participants of this debate, all seem to agree on one thing, an opposition to reductive forms of determination.

It is important to state, however, that this is not new or a radical shift. In fact such arguments have quite a long tradition. For instance, Marx himself consistently employed the ideas of base and superstructure in a complex way. Rather than calling for an economistic perspective where 'the economy' produces everything else, we find a much more substantive usage. As Barrett *et al.* (1979:20) put it in their discussion of the inadequacy of economistic metaphors of production:

> We have to be clear from the start that the notions of 'base and superstructure' (the apparent obviousness of the 1859 'Preface' notwithstanding) were used as metaphors, as condensed and shorthand devices. . . . If we move away from the much quoted 1859 'Preface' and examine . . . *The Eighteenth Brumaire* or the draft and text for *The Civil War in France*, we find it impossible to sustain the normal base/superstructure distinction and its direction of 'causality' as the basis of Marx's analysis.

Others have made similar points. In his own analysis of the way Marx used the concepts of base and superstructure, Stuart Hall goes on to claim even more strongly that had Marx expanded his notions about the relations between mode of production and, say, ideology, politics, culture, the law, and so on, beyond what he said in Book One of *Capital*, 'the one thing it would *not* have exhibited is a simple law of correspondence between the material base and the forms of the superstructure' (Hall 1977:58).

The point here is not to take the rather silly position that since Marx said it, it must be true. Rather it is to reassert a more dynamic 'relational' position, one that unfortunately has been sometimes lost, given a propensity to search for the 'laws of history', or to reduce all history to the automatic workings out of a specific mode of production, divorced from the classes of people and struggles that produce that very same history (Hibben 1978; Mouffe 1979; Ollman 1971).

In regard to this we are beginning to see breaks with the more conventional sociological and Marxist approaches, 'where culture and ideology are theorized as superstructural reflections of class contradictions at the economic level' (Barrett *et al.* 1979:10). Thus, a number of authors have begun to examine the specifics of cultural production as a process of production itself, not as a mere reflection of something external to it. As Barrett *et al.* argue, for example, cultural practices have their own specific relations of production. These are related to the political economy of a given society in some very important ways, but are not reducible to it. Because of this sensitivity to the specific conditions of existence or determinations which set limits on and produce real cultural products and practices a whole range of new terms and approaches to cultural analysis is being developed. Discourse analysis, relative autonomy, subjectivity, signification – in addition to those with a longer history such as culture, ideology, and consciousness – have appeared and have been quickly (some might say all too quickly) taken up. New journals have begun to be published in Europe and the United States – such as *Ideology and Consciousness* and *Social Text* – specifically devoted to analyses based on these approaches and problems, with others such as *Screen* and *Screen Education* deeply involved in examining the relationship between ideological and cultural production and reproduction and education even more specifically.

While the language used in these cultural analyses has often been rather dense and highly theorized, we should remember how complex the issues are that these people are grappling with. For the culturalist problematic includes such questions as 'How are meanings made?', 'Whose meanings are they?', and 'What are the ties between these meanings and the economic and cultural reproduction (and contradictory non-reproduction) of sexual, racial and class relations in our society?'. Clearly these are not easy to answer and often require a conscious attempt to develop what are sometimes rather involved modes of analysis, as do the following further questions.

How are we to understand the character of the 'determinations' surrounding cultural meanings and practices? Clearly the cultural sphere has a degree of relative autonomy; yet what does this autonomy entail? To what extent are, say, cultural elements such as literary or textual meanings and practices autonomous from economic practices? While one must not ignore the material conditions of existence surrounding the production of culture – its economic and political groundings so to speak – recent analyses of culture and ideology have stressed the legitimacy of focussing on the internal structure of cultural products like texts themselves, 'to examine how texts (film, books, etc.) work as meaning-producing practices in their own right. It may be thus possible to indicate ways in which textual practices may operate "unconsciously" in contradiction with their own conditions of existence.' This may seem quite abstract but its import lies in the claim that some texts and other cultural products in the media for example, which on the surface appear to present clear ideological meanings that do not allow for anything else, may in fact be filled with internal contradictions which 'subvert their apparent ideological closure.' They may embody a number of mutually contradictory positions which could actually act against reproductive forces (Barrett *et al.* 1979: 17-18). Something else is important here – the stress on ideological *production*. Ideologies are actively constituted. They do not appear fully blown out of thin air, but need to be ongoingly built in a variety of specific places.

That is, once again we need to be careful of being overly reductive here. For cultural products such as texts and the mass media do not only express ideologies; they are 'actually constitutive of ideologies,' as well. For ideologies are not merely one of the elements that need to be detected in, say, texts and the media. They are also products of it (Hill 1979:115). Speaking about mass media, John Hill makes this latter point rather well (1979:116).

> The ruling ideology is not just 'entrenched' in the media; it is actually produced. For there is no general or abstract system which is the ruling ideology: rather the ruling ideology is only constituted in and through the concrete. 'Ideology is there and yet it is not there. It appears indeed as if the general structure of a dominant ideology is almost impossible to grasp reflexively and analytically as a whole. The dominant ideology always appears, precisely, in and through the particular.' Indeed . . . the task of the media as part of the state may indeed be to create an ideological unity where none before existed. 'Far from expressing or reflecting an already given class interest, television, [as with other aspects of mass media], is one of the sites where ideological elements and positions are articulated into a specific type of political class discourse.'

This more 'internalistic' analysis proposed by Hill and others can be taken too far, of course. It is still essential to locate cultural production back into the wider system of ownership, control, and production (Barrett *et al.* 1979:23). Thus, the political economy of culture, and of the knowledge found within education, is quite consequential to our work. For to only focus on ideological production within texts and media is rather limiting. The production of these cultural products themselves – *as commodities* – is neglected at our own risk. They are commodities 'manufactured for sale' and, as part of the culture industry, need to be analyzed as such. For just this reason, texts, knowledge, and media need to be located within the political economy of corporate production as well (Golding and Murdock 1979:220). Without this combination of a serious political economy of culture and just as serious an appraisal of the way cultural products themselves help produce hegemonic ideologies, we will remain unable to understand what sign systems, codes, and styles are available with which authors, students, and audiences can actually make meanings (Barrett *et al.* 1979:23).

These issues – how cultural practices and products relate to the production of hegemony, the existence of contradictions within texts and cultural forms themselves, the relationship between cultural forms and the commodification process, and the intricate connections between class, economy, and culture – provide a good deal of the background against which current educational scholarship can be seen. They provide the impetus behind a number of chapters in this book, in particular those by Wexler, Gitlin, Bernstein, DiMaggio and Useem, and myself.

Others take up different themes that reflect other aspects of the larger debates going on. For example, at the same time that this kind of anti-reductionist debate over culture goes on, another repeatedly comes to the fore – that between the culturalists and the structuralists, between people such as E. P. Thompson and Raymond Williams on the one hand and Louis Althusser on the other. It is a debate that is strikingly similar to that found in education between those who focus on the actual knowledge and culture in schools and those whose primary interest is in the political economy of and economic returns from schooling. Both culturalism and structuralism developed out of a particular climate – the political opposition to both Stalinism and the oppressive tactics of some state socialist regimes and, just as significantly, a theoretical opposition to an overly deterministic economism (Johnson 1979:56).[9] Unlike some of the more vulgar analysts of education, however, they both insist on seeing culture and ideology as having some real autonomy, with consciousness being more than 'a mere reflex of economic relations.' Yet neither would deny that there are indeed serious connections between culture, ideology, and consciousness, and economic processes. These agreements do not keep the positions from being in strong disagreement, however. The structuralist critique of culturalist assumptions – one that seems quite powerful at times – does in fact point to the relative neglect within culturalism of class as an objective economic as well as cultural category. In its focus on the real everyday experience of class actors, culturalism does often undertheorize 'the connection between classes and the relations of production.' Class *is* too often seen as a category of experience and consciousness, as what might be called a political rather than an economic and structural category. The processes by which classes are constituted, how and why these classes come to be in a basically antagonistic relationship – it is these kinds of questions with which culturalism may have trouble dealing (Johnson 1979: 64-6). With all this said, though, there is real power behind studies in education which have been influenced by some of the best of the culturalist analyses. This is especially the case in investigations of the history of education and reproduction, a point that will be clearly brought out in David Hogan's chapter on the relationship between education and class formation in the United States.

For all of the power of the structuralist criticisms of culturalism, structuralism has not been immune to some important criticisms itself. Unlike the interest in the real lives and knowledge of concrete classes of actors that one finds in the work of culturalists such as Thompson, structuralist investigations have tended to be quite abstract. Even in a literature noted for its involved theoreticism, such as the theoretical discussions involving the way base and superstructure interact, they have tended to carry the abstractness to another level, though this may have been required at times. Furthermore, structuralism has been involved in an even more serious dilemma in that it has often reduced a good deal of the complexities of a social formation into a kind of functionalism. In a way, it has similar problems to the correspondence theories in education. That is, ideology and culture – while having a degree of relative autonomy to be sure – 'are subsumed within a single function: the reproduction of the conditions of capitalist production' (Johnson 1979:69; see also Connell 1979). Like some of the aforementioned work of the political economists of education, it ultimately undertheorizes struggles, disjunctions, and contradictions. As Richard Johnson nicely puts it, in structuralist analysis: 'the overriding concern with outcomes – "reproduction" – suppresses the fact that these conditions have continually to be won – or lost – in particular conflicts and struggles' (Johnson 1979:70).

This relationship between structuralist analysis and contradictions and struggles specifically in education is taken up in this volume by Carnoy and Dale in their chapters on the State. Their studies are of considerable moment since it is not just the relative autonomy of the cultural sphere that concerns recent theorists of reproduction. The political sphere, in particular the State, has also received an immense amount of attention lately in the wider literature.[10] Does the State only serve the interests of capital or is it more complex than that? Is the State instead an arena of class conflict and a site where hegemony must be worked for, not a foregone conclusion where it is simply imposed? Are schools – as important aspects of the State – simply 'ideological state apparatuses' (to quote Althusser), ones whose primary role is to reproduce the ideological and 'manpower' requirements of the social relations of production? Or, do they also embody contradictory tendencies and provide sites where ideological struggles within and among classes, races, and sexes can and do occur? Notice once more that these kinds of issues imply a questioning of reductive and totally functionalist theories. If one reduces the State to an epiphenomenon, to a reflection of class contradictions at an 'economic base,' then the entire political sphere is reduced as well. Economic action, defined rather narrowly, is all that is required. Political action as part of an ideological struggle against the hegemonic practices of dominant classes is made much less significant (Mouffe 1979). As Carnoy and Dale will make clear in their essays, if we think carefully of the school's 'functions' as a state apparatus current developments on the theory of the State are essential to our understanding, and action, in education.

Even though it is not fully represented in this book one other related and hotly contested area needs to be mentioned in this summary of some of the major conflicts within the larger body of scholarship in reproduction. The debate about the relative autonomy of culture and politics, about the nature, power, and scope of 'economic determinations,' can be seen as well among those individuals who dispute the fact that there must be any *essential* connection between economic class relations and, say, ideology and politics. Thus, refusing to accept a fundamental 'received' premise, individuals such as Paul Hirst and Barry Hindess have argued on epistemological grounds that most current Marxist investigations of culture, politics, and economy (in particular Lukács, Poulantzas, and Althusser) are themselves still too reductive. Even given their interest in the question of relative autonomy, they are ultimately teleological and contradictory. Even though these writers (i.e. Poulantzas *et al.*) strive to go beyond simplistic base/superstructure models and are overtly concerned with the power of politics and culture, their final result is little more than the production of 'a more or less complex economism involving both the recognition and the denial of the autonomy of politics and ideology vis-à-vis the economy' (Hindess 1977:102-3; Hirst 1979). In essence, they ultimately become too deterministic, since their logic still points to the interrelationships between various aspects of a social formation – however complex they may be – that in the end must serve to reproduce a specific mode of production. The raising of this point opens up a whole terrain that is rather controversial as you would imagine; yet its exploration over the next few years will undoubtedly contribute to the growing flexibility, subtlety, and sophistication of our research.

I could go on, documenting the arguments about how we are to 'think through the relations between the relations of production and the political, juridical, and ideological forms' *within* each of these 'contending positions,' for these too are often quite intense. All I have done here is to provide an outline of a number of the most lively disputes. One thing these disagreements do put to rest is the inaccurate stereotype that investigations within or influenced by the Marxist tradition are merely sterile applications of an economic formula. This is clearly not even remotely the case. If anything, this relatively brief presentation of the range of controversies lying behind the reproduction literature gives a sense of ferment. It is a time of intense theoretic argument and turmoil both within and without the literature on education. But it is also a time of rapid advance in our understanding both of the intricate nature of the nexus which provides the connections and contradictions among the economic, cultural, and political spheres and of the possibilities for organized action in each of these spheres.

Out of all this turmoil a number of significant points are being recognized. First, and most important for analysis and action, while it is critical for us to more fully know how reproduction is accomplished, we are beginning to see that there are serious difficulties with the very concept of economic and cultural *reproduction*. The over-use of the perspective embodied in this concept tends to 'produce in its wake its own distortion: that of an endlessly successful, functionally unfolding, reproduction of capitalist social relations without either end, contradiction, crisis, or break' (Hall 1977:71).

Second, and inextricably related to the first, any concrete social formation cannot be totally understood in terms of its mode of production and the ideological and political elements which support it, as a simple problem in, for example, the abstract control of culture and education by the economy. There will always be aspects of a society that are 'articulated to the mode of production and may be transformed by it, but cannot, without a loss of complexity and a return to functionalism, be subsumed within it.' A primary example here is the dominance of patriarchal relations in the family. The issue of gender relations cannot be fully subsumed under the 'needs' of an economy; nor can it be completely assimilated to a class analysis; nor, again, as Kelly and Nihlen will imply in their own chapter here, can we assume that women will be passively controlled by ideologies deriving from an economy. To do so would be to ignore what is specific to gender relations, as well as to neglect the impressive feminist criticisms of traditional Marxist concepts (Johnson 1979:72; Women's Studies Group 1978).

The debates and questions I have introduced here are not merely of academic interest. They are essential as part of our continuing attempt to think through appropriate *political and educational practice*. Different analyses will lead to different kinds of struggles in different places. A paradigm case here is again sexual oppression. If one sees gender relations in the family, the school, and elsewhere as fitting directly within a mode of production, then the terrain of the struggle will not necessarily be specifically feminist. The struggle will be carried out on the terrain of class politics. If, on the other hand, one sees a relatively strong separation between relations of sexual domination and capitalism, then forms of separatist action would seem much more powerful (Bland, McCabe, and Mort 1979:80). While these need not be either/or options, the case is similar in education. If, for instance, culture and the State are seen as totally determined by a mode of production, then action in those arenas is relatively inconsequential. However, if culture has some degree of relative autonomy and indeed can act in contradictory ways from economic form and can be not necessarily functional to reproduction, then actions on that terrain may be critical. As Gramsci might put it, cultural and political struggle become an essential part of a 'war of position,' a war on many fronts. And one of these fronts involves the transformation and rearticulation of dominant cultural and educative practices (Mouffe 1979:191-2).

In part, the implications of this perspective are reiterated in exceptionally clear terms in a recent statement in a major American journal on the left (Editorial Collective 1980:13).

> Any significant left politics in this country will have to be built everywhere. It will require a sustained, deliberate involvement [in the State] ; engagement in the labor movement; and creative activity throughout cultural and social life. The forms of intervention will vary according to where they occur. *At particular times, activities in one sphere will be decisive for the outcomes of struggles in others.* Yet these questions cannot be settled *a priori*. The problem is how to relate these different types of activity within a broad movement, not which to validate as the site of socialist virtue.

As we shall see in this volume, many of the authors take these debates over theory and practice in education and the wider arena as their starting point. For all of them there is agreement that one must avoid simple base/superstructure models to explain education and engage in action. Thus, just as when Hogan in his chapter argues that class formation is the outcome of the *totality* of economic, political, and ideological forces and struggles, so too is it incumbent on all of us not to succumb to the all too easy tendency to reduce education to an unalloyed expression of economic needs. Yet to be wary of such reductionistic tendencies also means that we must be sensitive to controversies in the literature, even if we cannot resolve them.

This last point is certainly true of the authors in *Cultural and Economic Reproduction in Education*. All of these tensions and debates – culture 'v.' structure, economy 'v.' culture, determination 'v.' relative autonomy, functionalism 'v.' contradiction, and so on – will be found in the pages of this volume. The authors have been influenced by these tensions, and while they do not fully settle the issues (no one volume could hope to do this), they do take us part of the way in showing how serious work can go on while the debates continue. They also bring this wider range of debate home to education, surely not an inconsequential step to any of us interested in creating the conditions necessary for the development of more economically and culturally equal institutions.

How each of the individual chapters included here respond to these debates and how each specifically interrogates the role education may play in economic and cultural 'reproduction' will be the substance of the concluding section of this introductory chapter.

Class, ideology and the State

Any analysis of class structure must be historical. This may seem like a relatively commonsensical point, yet it speaks directly to the very conceptual grounding of an appraisal of reproduction. Class structures are *never* completely static. They are not simply struggles between antagonistic social classes, but are struggles over class relations themselves. What this implies is rather consequential. Class structures are 'continually transformed by the very class struggles which they determine.' Because of this dialectical relationship between class structure and class struggle, we need to see the conflict between classes as constantly reshaping the composition of the class structure. And as this conflict alters the structure of classes in our society, this restructuring itself acts back. It then alters the terrain of the conflict (Wright 1979: 22-3). This is something David Hogan takes quite seriously in his essay in this volume.

Hogan wants to go beyond both the social explanations of the status attainment researchers in education and the recent work of the theorists of cultural reproduction. Both accounts fail to generate fundamental questions about the role of schooling within a class society. As he puts it:

> Current research glosses over the distinction between the intergenerational reproduction of inequality (the reproduction of classes) and the reproduction of class relations in accounts of the relationship between education and social reproduction, and universally fails to consider the overwhelming significance of historically specific processes of class formation for processes of social reproduction.

While criticizing some of his framework, Hogan draws heavily on the theoretical and historical categories of E. P. Thompson in his discussion of the effect of education on class formation and class culture. He distinguishes between three aspects of the over-all process of class formation: (1) class production – this refers to the expansion of capitalist property relations and the creation of a market in labor power, e.g. the basic process of proletarianization; (2) class development – this refers to the creation, scope, and density of working-class institutions like trade unions, parties, intellectual traditions, community patterns, and working-class 'structures of feeling;' and (3) class reproduction – this refers to two general processes, one which distributes people into positions in the social division of labor (this is what is refered to in the quote above as the reproduction of intergenerational inequality) and a second which relies heavily upon cultural and ideological processes (what he refers to above as the reproduction of class relations). The latter of these two processes concerns class cultures and the contested reproduction of bourgeois hegemony.

Notice that Hogan's insistence on these three aspects requires us to take account of both culture and economy. Yet neither culture and economy nor the above aspects of class formation are really separate except analytically. Each of these three aspects interact continually in complex ways and need to be understood historically. And this is exactly what he sets out to do – to outline the general characteristics of the process of class formation in America and to consider the impact of these historically specific processes of class formation on the relationship between social reproduction and education. This is accomplished by tracing out the dynamic interplay among class production, class development, and class reproduction. His primary focus for explicating these relationships will be on the determination of working-class and ethnic educational behavior and the connections between schooling and work.

Martin Carnoy takes the idea of education and the changing elements of class struggle and applies it to the current situation. Carnoy interrogates the Marxist tradition to illuminate its main positions on education. By surveying Marx, Engels, Gramsci, Althusser, Poulantzas, Baudelot and Establet, and Bowles and Gintis (as well as non-Marxists such as Bourdieu and Passeron), he shows the similarities and differences among these major figures in their analyses of the role of education in the reproduction of capitalism. Drawing primarily from Poulantzas, education is seen as not only part of a class struggle – a position fundamental to the Marxist tradition – but part of a class struggle that constantly changes as a result of previous struggle.

Education plays a significant role in this reproduction and struggle, by being not simply an instrument through which the bourgeoisie effects its domination over other groups, but also by being the *result* of struggle between dominant and dominated groups. Education is a state apparatus that is both the result of social and economic contradictions and the source of new contradictions at one and the same time. In describing this, Carnoy provides an interesting discussion of some of the weaknesses, as well as the strengths, of a number of current Marxist analyses of education such as Althusser, Baudelot and Establet, and Bowles and Gintis. He goes on to suggest the principal kinds of contradictions facing schools today, posing the question of what the impact of these contradictions may be on the process of reproduction. In essence, the argument presented differs from a number of previous Marxist approaches in that it suggests that action in the 'superstructure' – that is, in the schools themselves – can exacerbate serious contradictions in the 'base.' Thus, action in education – in and outside of formal school settings – can in fact potentially make a positive contribution to labor's position in the current situation due to the close relationship that presently exists between struggle in both base and superstructure.

In his discussion of a Gramscian educational strategy, Carnoy argues that a key element in such action is the creation of counter-hegemony outside the schools. In a war of position, the state apparatus needs to be surrounded by counter hegemonic apparatuses. This counter hegemony can be used to develop organic intellectuals from the working class. It can 'mobilize disillusioned bourgeois intellectuals and those traditional working class intellectuals who have become separated from their class origins.' Furthermore, these counter hegemonic forces can be important tools in enabling, say, working-class youth to resist the use of schools in 'maintaining and extending bourgeois dominance.'

In a related vein, Roger Dale examines even more closely the contradictions confronting education. Dale mounts a serious challenge to both micro and macro approaches which currently dominate the study of education. He argues that neither one is adequate for understanding the source and nature of educational stability and change. Only by grappling with the various roles performed by the State can we begin to fully comprehend the assumptions, intentions, and outcomes of educational change in capitalist systems. As a state apparatus, educational systems are confronted with a number of basic problems. These problems are strongly related to the basic issues faced by the capitalist state in general. These three 'core problems,' as Dale calls them, consist of supporting the capital accumulation process, guaranteeing a context for its continued expansion, and legitimating the capitalist mode of production, including the part of the State itself plays in it.

However, solutions to these problems are each mutually contradictory. It is this assemblage of mutual contradictions that provides a good deal of the driving force behind the dynamics of educational systems. Yet, as Dale notes, we cannot pre-specify either the means or the outcomes of the process by which the State may intervene to 'solve' each of these core problems. We need to analyze the role of the State in *both* its specificity at that historical moment and the possible resistances which may be engendered by its attempt to resolve these contradictory problems. Thus, the history of an individual state apparatus (compare, say, the different systems in the United States, England, and France), the extent and type of bureaucratization, the forms of control of employees within the state apparatus, the attempts by state workers and others to preserve 'autonomy,' and the struggles by groups to resist the hegemonic functions of the State, all of these need to be taken into account if we are to see how different educational state apparatuses deal with the core problems they face.

Dale concludes that by the very fact that educational systems are part of an inherently contradictory state apparatus, that since education is as much an aspect of the political as well as economic sphere this provides for the very real possibility for effective resistance and action.

Schools are deeply involved not 'just' in the contested reproduction of class relations, but in race and gender reproduction as well. Kelly and Nihlen focus on the relationship between the educational system and the reproduction of patriarchal social relations. Unlike many other researchers, however, they insist that too much of our evaluation of the school's role in reproducing the division of labor is 'framed in terms of wage and workforce status of women versus men.' This has caused the neglect of the import of the family in patriarchal society since it tends to ignore the question of whether schools prepare women for the same 'public' or workforce roles as men. They propose that a thorough evaluation of the issue must include an analysis of the creation of inequality in private or domestic life and how this affects relations between the sexes (and between races within sexes as well).

A second area they treat is one that has been and will be a significant element working through a number of the essays in this volume, the fact of resistance and contradiction. As they say, research on the education of women has systematically assumed that schools teach a unitary and relatively uncontradictory set of messages surrounding what the appropriate division of labor between the sexes should be. But this is not all, for it has also been assumed that students are passive agents who take in what the school 'wants' to teach in an unmediated way. Kelly and Nihlen argue, however, that the education of women is filled with contradictory messages. Women do often partially reject or filter knowledge, or even use it to their own advantage. This renegotiation and contestation needs to be taken much more seriously if we are to comprehend changes in women's public and private lives and the role schooling plays in this. In their discussion of these points, Kelly and Nihlen review a good deal of the literature on the economic and educational status of women and present a number of questions that are in need of further research.

The question of the renegotiation of knowledge, and the dynamics and control of culture, contestation, and ideology leads us into the next essays published here.

We can think of culture in two ways: first, as a lived experience, a set of meanings and practices that are constituted by our day to day life; or, second, as a set of commodities. The first focusses on cultural production, the second on cultural products. Both are necessary, for while the first tells us how hegemony is produced (and contested) by our everyday cultural practices in and out of education, the second inquires into the reasons why particular products are made available for our use in everyday interaction.

Paul DiMaggio and Michael Useem examine the latter sense, the control and distribution of cultural products. Drawing from both the literature on 'cultural capital' (in particular that of Pierre Bourdieu) and on changing class structures, their chapter provides an analysis of the role of high culture in the reproduction of the class structure from generation to generation. They emphasize the function of art in maintaining existing structures of domination. As they claim, the 'high arts – reproduced and consumed in schools, museums, and live performing arts settings – facilitate class reproduction through their legitimation and screening value for the upper and upper-middle classes.'

As a form of cultural capital, the high arts have acted as a screen, maintaining the cultural tastes and membership of élite groups. Yet, this screening role is complimented by, and in fact is being replaced in part by, a legitimating function. That is, we are witnessing a shift from élite control to corporate control of the arts, a shift which signals the use of the arts by large companies to enhance their declining public images. This will have a major impact both on the traditional form of class domination of the arts and on the ideological limits set on the content of the art that is presented to the public. Once again by focussing on the cultural apparatus outside of formal school settings, a number of significant ways in which cultural and economic reproduction occurs can be illuminated.

The question of 'high culture' does not exhaust the issue, as we know. No analysis of education's role in reproduction can afford to ignore popular culture. However, popular culture too can be both lived and commodified. Important aspects of it are bureaucratically and commercially organized and mass produced. As Todd Gitlin documents in his chapter on television, 'Television is the culminating institution of the culture of corporate capitalism, invading and reshaping the private space of the home, filling it with an unending procession of mass-produced images.' Yet mass culture also registers transformations in dominant ideologies, ideologies which are never static, abstract entities. It signifies resistances to and departures from hegemonic meanings and practices. These are often self-contradictory, but they exist none the less.

Drawing upon the work of Gramsci and many of the British analysts of popular culture such as Hall, Williams, and Willis, Gitlin demonstrates how the form and content of television 'entertainment' and the way it is produced and organized are transformed over time. Television constantly reproduces hegemonic ideologies and attempts to resolve ideological tensions in imaginative ways by selectively re-absorbing aspects of alternative or oppositional ideologies. In this way, the mass media provide a site where hegemonic ideologies are kept up to date. Television encompasses disparate messages that are sufficiently pluralistic to attract a wide array of audiences, 'while transposing social conflicts into a key where hegemonic ideology is re-legitimated . . . *in all its contradiction and instability*.'

Gitlin focusses on many of the most popular television shows. He examines the way the format, formula, genre, setting, character type, and the way these television narratives set out problems and point to solutions, all attempt to incorporate competing class, ethnic, and sexual communities into the dominant discourse. In so doing, he enters into the argument over structuralist and culturalist analysis and proposes a number of conceptual and methodological avenues for resolving some of the debate in practice. He argues, as well, that the study of popular culture must become increasingly ethnographic so that we may understand the ways in which real actors 'consume,' reinterpret, resist, and act on the ideological messages with which the culture industry seeks to 'educate' us.

When we return to the more formal institutions of education such as the school similar kinds of considerations about ideology and control come to the fore.

In my own chapter on curricular form, I explore the way ideology, culture, and economy intersect in the school by examining recent alterations in the process through which teaching and knowledge are organized and controlled. Schools are seen as sites where ideological subjectivities are partially formed and as places that are currently undergoing transformations based on changes in both the control of labor and the commodification process. By drawing upon recent studies in the labor process – studies which show how mental labor is separated from manual, conception separated from execution, and how workers in nearly all levels of employment are involved in a complex process of rationalization, deskilling, and reskilling – I illuminate how these processes, and the changing ideology of control they embody, enter into the everyday life of schools.

In both the economy and the State particular methods aimed at increasing productivity, rationalizing, controlling and dividing labor, and reducing resistance, have had a long and changing history. While schools have often been resistant to these logics of control and to some of the influences of capital – in part because of the dominance of patriarchal social relations of authority and contradictory ideologies within the institution – there has recently been a significant influx of the rationalized procedures of 'technical control' into them. Here the forms of control are built directly into the 'machinery' of the job itself. In schools, this is evidenced by a transformation of curriculum (and the social relations these engender). Thus, as more and more curricula are prepackaged with goals, procedures, evaluation, and even student responses prespecified, and as more and more curricula are constructed around the principles of a student's 'individual' rate and skill level, conception is separated from execution in the teacher's job.

In the process, as in other workplaces, teachers are deskilled, while at the same time being reskilled in the techniques and ideological visions of management. The curricular forms can have a profound impact on students as well since their organization is ideally suited to reproduce an ideology of possessive individualism. This process and these outcomes are not the result of a corporate conspiracy, but result from the political economy of corporate publishing, from the internal needs and pressures within the school, and the contradictory functions of the school in its role as a part of the state apparatus.

There are contradictions being reproduced here as well, however. If men's and women's jobs are being increasingly deskilled, if even 'professional' jobs such as teaching are being more thoroughly rationalized, then we would expect that, like other places of work, this will create resistances as well, thereby opening up the possibility of political intervention and political education. As Wright (1978b) has claimed, since teachers have what might best be called a 'contradictory class location,' such action is made even more possible. By placing the curricular forms that dominate schooling and the teachers themselves back into alterations in both class structure and the labour process and into the processes involved in the commodification of culture, we can begin to find appropriate avenues for such action.

Philip Wexler tends to look at the other side of the issue of culture, focussing his attention less on the control distribution, and commodification of culture than on the processes of cultural production and ideology. Wexler examines the current research on the sociology of school knowledge and argues that its very categories make it difficult for it to go beyond the existing ideologies that dominate capitalist societies. Class, reproduction, socialization, ideology, the hidden curriculum, each of these and more tends to 'surrender in advance the human capacity for appropriation and transformation to the needs of a system for which individuals are merely structural supports.' They, thereby, can enhance political apathy and act as reproductive forces themselves.

Wexler presents a research program based on a view of knowledge as a process of transformative social activity. Here, instead of assuming in advance a reduction of culture and knowledge to the needs of reproduction, one's analysis must deconstruct and reconstruct those social processes that go into the production of knowledge, be it curricula, film, literature, and so on, per se. Basing his arguments (though not uncritically) on recent advances in structuralism and semiotics, he suggests that we can understand the production of knowledge, and its relationship to economic and cultural reproduction, by looking at it as a chain or series of 'transformative activities.' These activities range from the social organization of text industries, to the activities of the people who produce the text, through 'the symbolic transformations of the text itself,' and to the 'transformative interaction between text and reader, or school knowledge and student.' In this way, the symbolic practices which provide the constitutive categories of class consciousness can be grasped. In the same way, the processes by which 'signification' is commodified can be unpacked as well.

Each of the last four chapters attempts in its own way to deepen our understanding of different aspects of cultural products and cultural production and reproduction. Basil Bernstein goes one step further. He returns us, in essence, to our original problematic. How do we theorize the general relationship between the economic and cultural spheres at the level of class actors? What 'rules' govern this relationship?

Bernstein's chapter provides us with one of the first systematic attempts to articulate a coherent theory of the relationship between power and control. Based as it is on his previous work and on an integration of structuralist, semiotic, and cultural scholarship, it is concerned with systematizing his prior theoretical and empirical investigations of the connections among class, the division of labor, symbolic practices, and cultural and economic reproduction. Fundamentally, it is the latter, the relationship *between* economic and cultural reproduction (and production) that is his interest. He focusses on the process by which 'basic classifications' such as class relations 'are transmitted and acquired by codes which differentially, invidiously and oppositionally position subjects with respect to both discursive and physical resources.' These codes are specific semiotic grammars or forms of discourse which regulate one's acquisition and reproduction of social rules and by which and through which 'subjects are selectively created, positioned and oppositioned.' While these codes may originally have come from the division of labor, the principles of such cultural codes are not directly related to the social relations of production.

Yet Bernstein is clearly conscious of the fact that a static model of reproduction is insufficient. He also wants to inquire into how the distribution of power and control are partly transformed at the level of the subject in ways which both position people and yet create the possibility of change in the way these people are positioned. In order to do this, his analysis must, and does, refer not only to class reproduction but to the issue of ethnic and gender relations as well. As he claims, even though his model of education and the processes of cultural reproduction is abstract, the codes and rules which he has set out to identify have inherent within them significant possibilities for variation, opposition, and change.

As the reader will soon see, these are themes – stability and change, reproduction and contradiction, culture and economy – that all of the chapters included in this volume deal with.

Notes

1 The state of our economic knowledge on these affairs is summarized by Carnoy and Shearer (1980:17) in the following rather succinct statement: 'As numerous academic and governmental studies have demonstrated, the distribution of wealth and income in the United States has changed little in the direction of greater equality since the turn of the century, and hardly at all since World War II.'

2 See Bernstein (1977), Bourdieu and Passeron (1977), Carnoy (1974), Sharp and Green (1975), Whitty and Young (1976), and Young (1971). These are, of course, only a limited selection of a much wider array of scholarship.

3 See Bowles and Gintis (1976), Carnoy (1972), Jencks *et al.* (1972), Jencks *et al.* (1979), Spring (1972), and Spring (1976). Again these volumes are only a small sample of a significantly larger range of Marxist and non-Marxist investigations, from stratification research to human capital theory, to studies of education and class reproduction.

4 Among the literature on these points are Bowles and Gintis (1976), Karabel and Halsey (1977), Littlejohn *et al.* (1978), Meyer (1977), Persell (1977), and Young and Whitty (1977). Historically, it may be helpful to examine Kaestle (1973), Kaestle and Vinovskis (1980) and Lazerson (1971) among others. Interesting comparative analyses can be found in Altbach and Kelly (1978), Altbach, Arnove and Kelly (1981), and Levin (1978).

5 Such arguments by 'homology' have their counterparts in cultural and textual analyses too. See Goldmann (1976).

6 A number of writers have challenged the empirical as well as conceptual apparatus and results of Bowles and Gintis, however. See, e.g., Apple (1979a, 1980a, 1980b, 1981), Collins (1979), Gorelick (1977), and Olneck and Bills (in press). See also Bowles and Gintis (1978).

7 I have argued this more fully in Apple (1979a, 1980b, 1982). See also the exceptional essay by Richard Johnson (1979).

8 Gintis himself has begun to make some very interesting excursions into the issues of communication and social discourse. See Gintis (1980).

9 Johnson's essay is a fine introduction to the structuralist/culturalist debate. See also Clarke, Critcher and Johnson (1979), Thompson (1978), Williams (1977), and Willis (1977).

10 Among the growing literature on the State are Hibben (1978), Holloway and Picciotto (1978), Littlejohn *et al.* (1978), Mouffe (1979), Wright (1978a), and the seminal work of people like Althusser and the late Nicos Poulantzas. Some of the major work is summarized nicely in Jessop (1977).

Bibliography

Altbach, Philip, Robert Arnove, and Fail Kelly (eds) (1981), *Comparative Education*, New York: Macmillan.

Altbach, Philip and Gail Kelly (1978), *Education and Colonialism*, New York: Longmans.

Apple, Michael W. (1978), 'The New Sociology of Education: Analyzing Cultural and Economic Reproduction,' *Harvard Educational Review* XXII (November), 495-503.

Apple, Michael W. (1979a), *Ideology and Curriculum*, London: Routledge & Kegan Paul.

Apple, Michael W. (1979b), 'The Production of Knowledge and The Production of Deviance in Schools,' in Len Barton and Roland Meighan (eds), *Schools, Pupils and Deviance*, Driffield, England: Nafferton Books, pp. 113-31.

Apple, Michael W. (1980a), 'Analyzing Determinations,' *Curriculum Inquiry* X (Spring), 55-76.

Apple, Michael W. (1980b), 'The Other Side of the Hidden Curriculum,'

Journal of Education CLXII (Winter), 47-66.
Apple, Michael W. (1981), 'Class, Culture, and the State in Educational Interventions,' in Robert Everhart (ed.), *The Predominant Orthodoxy: Education and the State in American Society*, Cambridge, Mass.: Ballinger Books.
Apple, Michael W. (1982), *Education and Power*, London, Routledge & Kegan Paul.
Barrett, Michele, *et al.* (eds) (1979), *Ideology and Cultural Production*, New York: St Martin's Press.
Bernstein, Basil (1977), *Class, Codes and Control*, Volume 3, 2nd edn, London: Routledge & Kegan Paul.
Bland, Lucy, Trisha McCabe, and Frank Mort (1979), 'Sexuality and Reproduction: Three Official Instances,' in Michele Barrett *et al.* (eds), *Ideology and Cultural Production*, New York: St Martin's Press, 78-111.
Bourdieu, Pierre and Jean-Claude Passeron (1977), *Reproduction in Education, Society and Culture*, Beverly Hills: Sage Publications.
Bowles, Samuel and Herbert Gintis (1976), *Schooling in Capitalist America*, New York: Basic Books.
Bowles, Samuel and Herbert Gintis (1978), 'Reply to Sherry Gorelick,' *Monthly Review* XXX (November), 59-64.
Carnoy, Martin, (ed.) (1972), *Schooling in a Corporate Society*, New York: David McKay.
Carnoy, Martin (1974), *Education as Cultural Imperialism*, New York: David McKay.
Carnoy, Martin and Derek Shearer (1980), *Economic Democracy*, White Plains, New York: M. E. Sharpe.
Castells, Manuel (1980), *The Economic Crisis and American Society*, Princeton: Princeton University Press.
Clarke, John, Chas Critcher, and Richard Johnson (eds) (1979), *Working Class Culture*, London: Hutchinson.
Collins, Randall (1979), *The Credential Society*, New York: Academic Press.
Connell, R. W. (1979), 'A Critique of the Althusserian Approach to Class,' *Theory and Society* VIII (November), 303-45.
Dale, Roger, Geoff Esland, Ross Furgusson and Madeleine MacDonald (eds) (1981), *Education and the State*, Ringmer: Falmer Press.
Dale, Roger, *et al.* (1976), *Schooling and Capitalism*, London: Routledge & Kegan Paul.
Editorial Collective (1980), 'Introduction,' *Socialist Review* X (March-June), 5-17.
Eisenstein, Zillah, (ed.) (1979), *Capitalist Patriarchy and the Case for Socialist Feminism*, New York: Monthly Review Press.
Everhart, Robert (1979), *The In-Between Years: Student Life in a Junior High School*, Santa Barbara: University of California, Santa Barbara, Graduate School of Education, mimeo.

Gintis, Herbert (1980), 'Communication and Politics,' *Socialist Review* X (March-June), 189-232.

Golding, Peter and Graham Murdock (1979), 'Ideology and Mass Media: The Question of Determination.' in Michele Barrett *et al.* (eds), *Ideology and Cultural Production*, New York: St Martin's Press, 198-224.

Goldmann, Lucien (1976), *Cultural Creation in Modern Society*, Saint Louis: Telos Press.

Gorelick, Sherry (1977), 'Undermining Hierarchy: Problems of Schooling in Capitalist America,' *Monthly Review* XXIX (October), 20-37.

Hall, Stuart (1977), 'Rethinking the "Base and Superstructure" Metaphor,' in Jon Bloomfield (ed.), *Class, Hegemony and Party*, London: Lawrence & Wishart, 41-72.

Hibben, Sally (ed.) (1978), *Politics, Ideology and the State*, London: Lawrence & Wishart.

Hill, John (1979), 'Ideology, Economy and the British Cinema,' in Michele Barrett, *et al.* (eds), *Ideology and Cultural Production*, New York: St Martin's Press, 112-34.

Hindess, Barry (1977), 'The Concept of Class in Marxist Theory and Marxist Politics,' in Jon Bloomfield (ed.), *Class, Hegemony and Party*, London: Lawrence & Wishart, 95-107.

Hirst, Paul (1979), *On Law and Ideology*, New York: Macmillan.

Holloway, John and Sol Picciotto (eds) (1978), *State and Capital*, London: Edward Arnold.

Jencks, Christopher, *et al.* (1972), *Inequality*, New York: Basic Books.

Jencks, Christopher, *et al.* (1979), *Who Gets Ahead?* New York: Basic Books.

Jessop, Bob (1977), 'Recent Theories of the Capitalist State,' *Cambridge Journal of Economics* 1 (December), 353-73.

Johnson, Richard (1979), 'Histories of Culture/Theories of Ideology: Notes on an Impasse,' in Michele Barrett, *et al.* (eds), *Ideology and Cultural Production*, New York: St Martin's Press, 49-77.

Kaestle, Carl (1973), *The Evolution of an Urban School System*, Cambridge: Harvard University Press.

Kaestle, Carl and Maris Vinovskis (1980), *Education and Social Change in Nineteenth Century Massachusetts*, New York: Cambridge University Press.

Karabel, Jerome and A. H. Halsey (eds) (1977), *Power and Ideology in Education*, New York: Oxford University Press.

Kuhn, Annette and Anne Marie Wolpe (1978), *Feminism and Materialism*, London: Routledge & Kegan Paul.

Lazerson, Marvin (1971), *Origins of the Urban School*, Cambridge: Harvard University Press.

Levin, Henry (1978), 'The Dilemma of Comprehensive Secondary School Reforms in Western Europe,' *Comparative Education Review* XXII (October), 434-51.

Littlejohn, Gary, *et al.* (eds) (1978), *Power and the State*, New York: St Martin's Press.

MacDonald, Madeleine (1977), *The Curriculum and Cultural Reproduction*, Milton Keynes, England: The Open University Press.

MacDonald, Madeleine (1981), 'Schooling and the Reproduction of Class and Gender Relations,' in Roger Dale, Geoff Esland, Ross Furgusson and Madeleine MacDonald (eds), *Education and the State*, Ringmer: Falmer Press.

MacDonald, Madeleine (1980), 'Socio-cultural Reproduction and Women's Education,' in Rosemary Deem (ed.), *Schooling for Women's Work*, London: Routledge & Kegan Paul.

McRobbie, Angela (1978), 'Working Class Girls and the Culture of Femininity,' in Women's Studies Group, *Women Take Issue*, London: Hutchinson, 96-108.

Meyer, John (1977), 'The Effects of Education as an Institution,' *American Journal of Sociology* LXXXIII (July), 55-77.

Mouffe, Chantal (ed.) (1979), *Gramsci and Marxist Theory*, London: Routledge & Kegan Paul.

Ogbu, John U. (1978), *Minority Education and Caste*, New York: Academic Press.

Ollman, Bertell (1971), *Alienation*, New York: Cambridge University Press.

Olneck, Michael and David Bills (in press), 'What Makes Sammy Run: An Empirical Assessment of Bowles and Gintis,' *American Journal of Education*.

Persell, Caroline Hodges (1977), *Education and Inequality*, New York: The Free Press.

Sharp, Rachel and Anthony Green (1975), *Education and Social Control*, London: Routledge & Kegan Paul.

Spring, Joel (1972), *Education and the Rise of the Corporate State*, Boston: Beacon.

Spring, Joel (1976), *The Sorting Machine*, New York: David McKay.

Thompson, E. P. (1978), *The Poverty of Theory*, London: Merlin Press.

Whitty, Geoff and Michael Young (eds) (1976), *Explorations in the Politics of School Knowledge*, Driffield, England: Nafferton Books.

Williams, Raymond (1977), *Marxism and Literature*, New York: Oxford University Press.

Willis, Paul (1977), *Learning to Labour*, Lexington: D. C. Heath.

Women's Studies Group (1978), *Women Take Issue*, London: Hutchinson.

Wright, Erik Olin (1978a), *Class, Crisis and the State*, New York: New Left Books.

Wright, Erik Olin (1978b), 'Intellectuals and the Working Class,' *The Insurgent Sociologist* VIII (Winter), 5-18.

Wright, Erik Olin (1979), *Class Structure and Income Determination*, New York: Academic Press.

Young, Michael F. D. (ed.) (1971), *Knowledge and Control*, London: Macmillan.

Young, Michael and Geoff Whitty (eds) (1977), *Society State and Schooling*, Ringmer, England: The Falmer Press.

Chapter 2

Education and class formation:

the peculiarities of the Americans

David Hogan

I

In the last fifteen years debates about the public role of schooling in America have been dominated by a preoccupation with issues of inequality: educability, equality of educational opportunity, meritocratic ideology, élite control, desegregation, educational achievement, status attainment, and lately, economic and cultural reproduction. In this paper I wish to argue that although these issues are not without theoretical and political significance, this discourse has failed – and unavoidably so – to generate the fundamental questions necessary to understand the nature and role of schooling within a class society. This lacuna characterizes recent expositions of cultural reproduction as much as it does older explanations of status attainment, and suggests the need for a fundamental reorientation of educational research around issues of class and class formation.

To defend such a proposition is not a straightforward procedure; in fact it requires at least three kinds of arguments: an account first of all, of the meaning of class and class formation; second, an outline of the general characteristics of the process of class formation in America; and third, an account of the relationship between these historically specific processes of class formation and education.

II

The classic formulation of the process of class formation was made by Marx in the *Poverty of Philosophy*: through class struggle, a class-in-itself is transformed into a class-for-itself. As this formulation came to be understood by a later generation of Marxists – the generation of

Lenin, Trotsky, Kautsky, Luxemburg – a class-in-itself was merely a class in objective terms, a class without a revolutionary consciousness, whereas a class-for-itself was characterized by high levels of class organization and consciousness. The principle issue dividing this generation of Marxists was how the economic – the class-in-itself – was transformed into the political and ideological forms of a class-for-itself, but later generations of critics – from Gramsci and Lukács to E. P. Thompson and Althusser have developed additional criticisms.[1]

Among the current generation of Marxist theoreticians, Thompson and Althusser in particular both have undertaken major reformulations of the theory of class and class formation, and although they both strongly object to economistic and reductionist accounts of class formation, and although both lay claim to Gramsci as a theoretical mentor, their differences are as substantial as they are acrimonious. I do not intend, however, to pursue their theoretical and metatheoretical differences here – the nature of theory development, the importance of human subjectivity and agency, experience and consciousness, process, and contingency, causality and determination, history itself – since Thompson has already done so with brilliance and passion in his *The Poverty of Theory*,[2] but rather outline a theory of class formation that draws in part upon Thompson's own formulation.

For Thompson, in contradistinction to orthodox Marxist and Parsonian approaches, class is not a 'category' or a 'structure,' but an event, 'something which in fact happens (and can be shown to have happened) in human relationships.' 'Class happens,' he writes, 'when some men, as a result of common experience (inherited or shared) feel and articulate the identity of their interests as between themselves, and as against other men whose interests are different from (and usually opposed to) theirs.'[3]

Unlike the orthodox view of class formation, Thompson insists that 'class does not precede but arises out of struggle.' Classes are the continual effects of struggles, political, ideological, as well as economic.[4]

> Class formations . . . arise at the intersection of determination and self activity: the working class 'made itself as much as it was made.' We cannot put 'class' here and 'class consciousness' there, as two separate entities, the one sequential upon the other, since both must be taken together – the experience of determination, and the handling of this in conscious ways.
>
> Nor can we deduce class from a static 'section' (since it is a *becoming* over time), nor as a mode of production since class formations and class consciousness (while subject to determinate pressures)

> eventuate in an open-minded process of relationship – of struggle with other classes – over time.

Applying this conception of class to the history of the English working class, he wrote:[5]

> Nevertheless, when every caution has been made, the outstanding fact of the period between 1790 and 1830 is the formation of 'the working class'. This revealed first, in the growth of class concious-ness of an identity of interests as between all these diverse groups of working people and as against the interests of other classes. And, second, in the growth of corresponding forms of political and industrial organization. By 1832 there were strongly based and self-conscious working class institutions – trade unions, friendly societies, educational and religious movements, political organizations, periodicals – working class intellectual traditions, working class community patterns, and a working class structure of feeling.

Not the least of the advantages of this approach to class formation over traditional Marxist approaches is that it finesses the problem of identifying *the* working class that has preoccupied orthodox approaches to class formation.[6]

But even more importantly, Thompson's explanation of class formation in England provides many of the essential analytical categories necessary for a general theory of class formation that could be applied to other national or societal contexts.

The first requirement of such a theory of class formation is an account of proletarianization. Proletarianization refers to two processes intrinsic of capital accumulation. It refers, first, to the creation of markets in labor, that is, to the sale by workers of their labor power in exchange for wages. It is in this context that it is possible to analyze the development and reproduction over time of capitalist property relations or more simply, class relations. Class relations are social structures or social relationships of a certain kind, viz., those built upon the ownership and control of the means of production. Class relations are not simply interpersonal relations, or relations between individuals as such, but social relations between certain kinds of people defined by their relationship to the ownership and control of the means of production (for example, landlord and tenant, capitalist and proletarian).

It is entirely possible to describe these class relations without falling into nominalistic accounts of class of the kind feared by Thompson. Thompson's hostility to viewing class in nominalistic terms is an understandable and appropriate rejection of functionalist or stratification theories of class, theories in which class is reduced to discrete nominal level categories based on some index of inequality (usually, but not necessarily, occupation). But Thompson's hostility to 'categorical' approaches per se runs the risk of throwing the baby out with the bathwater. Historians after all do need concepts and theories to describe and explain the very real discrete differences between groups within social structure (for example, with respect to property relations and positions in the labor process), and to describe and explain the ways in which particular social structures and processes generate a specific form of social organization and the formation of social groupings. Thompson is right to emphasize the activity of people in creating social groupings – the process of class formation, and not merely their location in social space – but he neglects the structural processes intrinsic to a class society: the organization of the labor process and labor markets, the character of opportunity and ecological structures, the mechanisms – schools, families, labor markets – through which individuals are allocated into the social division of labor, and the various kinds of political, ideological, cultural and economic mechanisms involved in the reproduction of class relations.[7] To describe these ways in which class happens is to describe the dynamics of a particular class society, the forms, tendencies, and the 'historical logic' to use Thompson's term, of its mode of production.[8]

The second aspect of the process of proletarianization is the process of class recruitment: namely, the way groups of individuals are recruited into the wage labor force. This may occur through economic disenfranchisement, as in the enclosure movement and the destruction of the system of handicraft production; through immigration, for example from Europe to America in the nineteenth and early twentieth centuries or from the Mediterranean rim to the west European economies since World War II.[9]

The second requirement of a theory of class formation is a theory of class culture or cultural production. The crucial ingredient of such a theory is the notion of class experience. Class experiences are the particular kinds of social experiences individuals or groups in different classes experience in their daily lives. These experiences encompass all the specific and particular institutional settings that connect the individual to society: the workplace, the family, the community, the church, the party, the voluntary association. They involve, in other words, the whole texture of working-class life: not only relations at work but also relations with neighbors, ministers, grocers, policemen, wives, butchers, children, firemen and politicians. These experiences, however, are not all of equal importance, nor without an internal structure or logic; they are structured in distinctive ways, above all by the character of 'productive relations' – social relations – of the work-place.[10]

On the basis of these experiences, groups of people develop stable or coherent patterns of behavior, create distinctive institutions, and attempt, utilizing their available intellectual resources, to make sense of these experiences: that is, they create class cultures. The articulation of these class experiences into class cultures is a highly complex, contingent and variable process: much depends upon the character of class recruitment peculiar to a country, the form and strengths of class conflict, and the nature of the interaction between structural constraints and conditions – the nature of the labor process, the shape of labor markets and opportunity structures, the mechanisms of social allocation and legitimation – and the cultural resources and intellectual traditions of the nascent working class.

Politically the single most important outcome of these interactions is a distinctive form of what Thompson calls 'class development': the number and strength of typical working-class institutions – trade unions, political parties, voluntary associations – intellectual traditions, community patterns, and working-class 'structures of feeling.' A product of processes of class cultural production, class development is the key index to differences in class formation between different countries. Variations in the character of class development thus largely account for differences in the character of class formation and working-class politics.

A theory of class formation of this kind then focusses attention upon contingent and historically specific processes of class cultural production and class development. It does not assume that the process of class formation is ineluctable or automatic as the standard Marxist account presupposed; rather it assumes that it has to be approached relationally and historically. This is of particular importance in the conceptualization of social reproduction; it is because most analyses of social reproduction – including those focussed upon education and social reproduction – neglect the relational and historical character of class, that they are plagued by all manner of functionalist and reductionist difficulties.

Class reproduction has two referents: the reproduction of classes across generations (what stratification theorists term 'intergenerational inequality')[11] and the reproduction of class relations. The first refers to the processes that distribute people into positions in the social division of labor, or more generally, the class structure. Theoretically, this is the universe of educational achievement, opportunity structures, labor markets, social mobility, and occupational inheritance, that is, the universe of factors which influence the structural conditions of class formation.[12]

The second process of reproduction – the reproduction of class relations – relies heavily upon cultural and ideological processes. Its theoretical universe is quite different from that of the reproduction of classes: it is a universe of concepts developed principally by Gramsci and even Althusser in which ideology is conceptualized as a structure of social practices ('ideology has a material existence'), and hegemony is conceptualized as the reproduction of social practices – social practices that by their nature are structured by bourgeois ideology.[13] Hegemony is not simply ideological incorporation, but rather a problematic, contested, situational process.

Robert Gray, for instance, argues that hegemony is not so much achieved through the successful propagation of a certain world view but through immersion into structured forms of social practice:[14]

> Hegemony is correctly seen as a structured *practice*, in which diverse social practices and elements of consciousness are ordered in a fashion compatible with the perpetuation of the existing relations of production. . . . In this respect, it may be more appropriate to refer to a 'hegemonic structuring' of ideological consciousness; rather than to a single 'hegemonic ideology'.

Gray goes on to argue that from this perspective 'class hegemony is a dynamic and shifting relationship of social subordination.' On the one hand 'certain aspects of the behavior and consciousness of the subordinate class may reproduce a version of the values of the ruling class.' On the other these value systems become modified as they are adapted to different conditions of existence. In this manner, Gray suggests, subordinate classes follow a 'negotiated version' of ruling-class values.[15] Or as Raymond Williams observes, hegemony is a process that is 'continually resisted, limited, altered, challenged by pressures not all its own.'[16] Althusser not withstanding, human beings are not passive bearers or supports ('trager') of ideological structures, but as Paul Willis writes, 'active appropriators who reproduce existing structures only through struggle, contestation, and a partial penetration of those structures.'[17] In other words, it is in the nexus between cultural production and reproduction that we find the source of hegemony, not ideological incorporation per se; it is in the fact that 'oppositional initiatives and contributions' as Williams calls them, 'are in practice tied to the hegemonic. The dominant culture, so to say, at once produces and limits its own forms of counter culture.'[18]

In sum, the process of class formation is complex, contingent, conditional, and above all, inextricably historical in character. Social reproduction – the establishment of a hegemonic situation – is less a function of ideological incorporation than an unstable nexus between processes of cultural production and reproduction.

III

Any number of reasons might be proffered to explain the failure of a socialist movement to take root in America: the existence of the frontier and the relative scarcity of labor, the abundance of America's resources and the ambition of its inhabitants, the productivity of its industry and the affluence of its people, the size of its middle class and the opportunity for social mobility, widespread home ownership and the power of its individualist ideology, the bloody repression of strikes and radical political activity at key junctures in American history and the racial and ethnic stratification of the working class, the early achievement of liberal democracy and the conservative bent of its trade unions. All of these have undoubtedly influenced in one way or another the mobilization of the working class. It is not my intention to evaluate their relative significance, but to argue that a theory of class formation is the most useful framework with which to approach American 'exceptionalism.'

Proletarianization characterized the advent of capitalism in all capitalist societies, not just in America.[19] So too did the shift from what Marx called formal subordination to real subordination – that subsequent to the proletarianization of handicraft producers, the handicraft system was destroyed and the organization of the labor process was reconstituted upon a new social and technical basis which gave capital control of the labor process.[20] American 'exceptionalism' was not its freedom from these processes of class formation, but the peculiarities of its processes of class recruitment and class development.

Unlike the United Kingdom and continental Europe, where national wage labor forces were recruited chiefly from the pool of labor expelled from the land by enclosure movements or by the destruction of serfdom, in America the wage labor force was recruited internationally from an extraordinary variety of national, ethnic, and religious groups. It is just this fact that Herbert Gutman believes is primarily responsible for the relatively inhibited level of class development in America. Class formation in America, argued Gutman, was continually complicated by the repeated infusions of first generation industrial workers into the working class: '. . . the American working class was continually altered in its composition by infusions, from within and without the nation, of peasants, farmers, skilled artisans, and casual day laborers who brought into industrial society ways of work and other habits and values not associated with industrial necessities and the industrial ethos.'

As a consequence of the continuously changing composition of the American working class throughout the period 1815-1920, the major forms of oppositional collective behavior was 'pre-modern' usually only associated with the early phases of industrialization.[21] In effect, the process of class formation in America was shaped by the slowness of class development. Because the American working class acquired a new first generation working class every thirty years or so, the American working class did not develop institutions that linked the working class intergenerationally such as those described by Thompson. Class development in America was stymied by immigration.[22]

Although Gutman chronicles with great sensitivity the cultural clashes between artisans and immigrants on the one hand and the culture of modern industrial capitalism on the other, and narrates the manner in which these workers used their cultural traditions as resources with which to respond to their social experiences in America, his over-all explanation of the character of the relationship between the two cultures ('traditional,' 'modern') padlocks the character of the cultural changes taking place in the nineteenth century into a simple dichotomy of traditional-modern. It also seriously distorts the relationship between ethnicity and class formation.

Gutman is right to emphasize the enormous cultural clashes between first generation immigrant industrial workers and the cultural demands of industrial capitalism, but the outcome of this clash was not so much a 'modern' culture as a plethora of ethnically differentiated working-class cultures that developed as a series of accommodations to the character of the *class* experiences of immigrants at work, at home, in the community, in the church and in the political party. Alan Dawley put it well in describing the response of immigrants to their class experiences as wage earners in America: 'The experience of industrial employment – its privation, fatigue, risk of injury or death, ceaseless insecurity – compelled working people, in the absence of social supports to ease these hardships, to develop collective supports of their own. They created fraternal lodges, church burial funds and union benefit societies . . .'[23] The outcome was less cultural modernity, less melting pot assimilation or ethnic pluralism, than ethnically differentiated working-class cultures.[24] Whatever their ethnic affiliations, immigrants created parallel working-class institutions, developed similar aspirations, and behaved in parallel ways: if the content of the American working class varied by ethnicity, the cultural forms they created were remarkably similar.

South Chicago is a case in point. Here the steel mills dominate not only the skyline and work but the very texture and rhythms of neighborhood and community life. When William Kornblum went to live in the steel mill area in the late 1960s he found that 'from the first day in the steel mill it was clear that it would be impossible to understand the community or its people without working in the mills.' As he did so, he learnt much:

> Within a week all the comings and goings of humans, railway cars, and boats became intelligible; the open spaces and cramped neighborhoods fit patterns of land use determined by the steel industry; the temporal patterns of street life could be explained by the cycle of mill life; and the material life style of various neighborhoods fits patterns of seniority and skill inside the mills. In their leisure lives outside the mills, South Chicago families could attempt to segregate themselves within ethnic cultural worlds, or they might associate with diverse groups of neighborhood friends, but in every case ethnic segregation was limited by the more universalistic experiences of life on rolling mills, blast furnaces, coke ovens, ore docks, and the switchyards of the steel industry.

So, on the one hand, while Kornblum found that associational life – street corner primary groups, 'landsmannschaftern,' tavern friendships and patronage patterns, parish churches, fraternal benefit societies, precinct organizations and union caucases – was segmented into a 'structure of equivalent ethnic primary groups,' he also found that 'whatever their ethnic affiliations, South Chicago people share the common culture of working-class America,' and specifically the culture shaped by the steel industry: 'Steel-making brings South Chicago people together in the world of work. Steel presents all the ethnic groups with similar life chances and common aspirations for future generations.' In particular, the organization of the work process and the ethnic stratification of the labor force shaped both the process of working-class cultural formation and its internal differentiation along ethnic lines. Ethnic and occupational attachments depended upon the social and ecological organization of work and recruitment patterns; conflict or co-operation between mill work groups for example was 'one of the primary explanations of tavern association outside the plant.' In general,[25]

> In a typical mill neighborhood . . . bonds between people formed at work are carried into the outside neighborhood. Friendships and animosities formed in the steel mill interact with ethnic and residential attachments to create a neighborhood ecology of primary groups. These primary groups, in turn, create the institutions of the neighborhood, its church congregations, its tavern cliques, and its political associations. The membership of the groups reflects a range

> of individual solutions to the dilemma of ethnic isolation versus occupational integration. These primary groups, in which the members 'reconstruct' a history emphasizing commonality rather than differences, may then be enlisted into broader aggregations which are negotiated in the political organization of the workplace and the community.

In effect, 'immigrant' cultures were creations of the new world, not the old; immigrants did not import their 'ethnicity' with them in their suitcases or in their heads. Rather, in confronting the kinds of structural conditions of American society, they created ethnic class cultures. As Ericksen and Yancey point out, '. . . much of the substance of ethnic cultures may be the result of a selective process which consists of a constantly evolving interaction between the nature of the local community, the available economic opportunities and the national or religious heritage of a particular group . . . much of the behavior that is commonly associated with ethnicity is largely a function of the structural situations in which groups have found themselves.'[26] Ethnic cultures are products of the class structuration of social life, a mediation of class culture: it is the class content of ethnicity, not ethnic consciousness itself, that varies historically in the working-class community.

The peculiarities of America's class development derive in part then from the enormous impact of ethnicity upon class formation in America, in particular the ethnic differentiation of the working class that it fostered. But this fact alone does not exhaust the peculiarities of American class development. Also important were political developments rooted in America's unique chronological juxtaposition of the industrial revolution and the establishment of liberal democracy, the particular strength of pure and simple unionism in America, and the resilience of a bifurcation of working-class politics into a politics of the workplace and a politics of the community and party.

The early industrial politics of craftsmen centered upon their resistance to their formal subordination to capital; this was the politics of independent petty bourgeois producers pretesting their incorporation into the system of wage labor, a politics infused with the spirit of Paine, Jacobinism, democratic republicanism and the 'equal rights' philosophy.[27] Subsequent working-class reform movements – the Chartists in England, the co-operative movement and later the Knights of Labor in the United States, were still infused with republican ideology, but their politics were less a politics of rebellious craftsmen seeking a society of free and independent producers than of a working class seeking a co-operative commonwealth of associated producers.

It was the politics of a working-class subject to formal subordination but not yet to real subordination.[28]

The primary difference between the English experience and the American case – and it is a profoundly important one, accounting for much of the difference in the character and scope of class development in the two countries – was the appearance in America of democratic political institutions (at least for white males) *before* the entrenchment of industrial capitalism, and, particularly, prior to the shift to real subordination. The early development of political democracy in America profoundly influenced working-class views of the nature of state power: working-class people as a whole saw no need to develop a class theory of state power or to develop class-based political institutions. Indeed, to do so, they theorized, would be unAmerican and a betrayal of republicanism. Under the influence of Paine-ite republicanism and evangelical Protestantism (and often not insignificant doses of racism and nativism) working-class leaders did not perceive state power itself as a locus of class conflict but rather a means of preserving the democratic republic against the onslaughts of greedy monopolists, corrupt 'aristocratic' tendencies, or unschooled Catholic immigrants. Working-class people also saw government as an extension of the marketplace – a source of jobs, career opportunities and patronage.[29] (Later after the effective takeover of the economy by industrial capitalism, democratic processes, for example, elections, came to constitute a system of institutionalized class conflict through which the working class pursued its short term material interests.) Unlike the English working class, the native born, white male working class didn't have to develop class-wide political institutions and programs to achieve political democracy. Due to the peculiarities of America's non-feudal past, the revolution of 1776, and the nature of its politics in the early nineteenth century, much of the nineteenth century working-class politics was essentially *defensive*, protecting the earlier achievement of republican democracy against what they perceived to be its chief enemies: monopolists, aristocratic forces, Catholic foreigners, and later, socialists.

The defensive nature of working-class politics inhibited not only the formation of a powerful labor party, but also strongly influenced the politics of the shift from formal to real subordination in America. The shift in America produced as bloody, violent and threatening conflicts between labor and capital as occurred anywhere in Europe – perhaps even more so: think only of the great railroad strikes of 1887, the Eight Hour Movement of 1885 and 1886, Homestead in 1891, Pullman in 1894, the great wave of strikes in 1904-5, the steel strike of 1919, the general strikes in San Francisco and Minneapolis in 1934, the sit-down strikes of the mid-1930s and so on.[30] Indeed, for one brief moment in the mid-1880s middle-class America held its breath as the Knights of Labor seemed on the brink of shifting from a radical critique of capitalism and 'wage slavery' to a fully fledged socialist movement. Less the last gasp of 'reform unionism,' the Knights represented the first breath of a potentially revolutionary movement destroyed not, as in some Greek tragedy, by its own idealism, but by internal divisions, the forces of law and order, and by a massive onslaught by capital upon labor unleashed after the Haymarket Riot of 1886.

The subsequent growth of pure and simple unionism – a unionism committed to job control and wage issues – was not as Perlman, Commons and others would have us believe, the only 'realistic' or 'inevitable' response to the growth of corporate capitalism, but an outcome precipitated by the destruction of the Knights of Labor and the appearance of a labor aristocracy in American industry during the late nineteenth century. As craft control of the labor process was breached and the shift toward real subordination accelerated, the appearance of a labor aristocracy simultaneously represented the reorganization of the technical basis of the labor process and the development of a defensive political structure within the labor place. The labor aristocracy intended to protect itself from any further encroachments of capital upon the labor process and to strengthen its hand in the bargaining process with capital over job conditions and wages. But essentially the horse had bolted, since capital had already penetrated sufficiently far into the labor process to give it basic control of it. The appearance of the labor aristocracy was in fact a transitional phenomenon, and signalled a major success in capital's campaign to restructure the labor process on a new basis, and the further rationalization of the entire labor process through scientific management and Taylorism, the eventual displacement (with a few exceptions, notably in mining and printing) of the labor aristocrat by the modern skilled worker, and the stabilization of capitalist control of the labor process.[31]

Nevertheless, the legacy of the labor aristocracy was permanent and wide-ranging in its effects upon class development in America, for trade unionism – pure and simple unionsim – was largley the creation of the late nineteenth century labor aristocracy. Unlike the Knights, trade unionism – pure and simple unionism – was largely the creation labor-capital relation specifically, and it addressed it not to overthrow it, but to protect the skilled worker's interests – wages, and what control of the labor process they could – within the boundaries of industrial capitalism. This accommodation to capitalism represented less, however, an economistic capitulation to its culture, or the development of collaborationist politics, than a selective adaptation to the conditions that shaped the class experience of skilled workers.

The character of the accommodation varied with the character of the class experience: those workers, for example, shoemakers, who experienced a major dilution of their skills and job control, declining real income, and increasingly, employment in large manufactories and factories, prior to 1860, failed to develop organizational strength. After 1860, however, they dropped their artisan conception of society and developed militant trade-wide unions, first the Knights of St Crispin, and later the Knights of Labor, both of which accepted all workers in the trade, irrespective of skill, race, or sex, and both of which developed quite different conceptions of industrial society than that represented in artisan culture. Those workers whose class experiences were different exhibited a different political trajectory. Printers, for example, their skills less diluted, their opportunities less restricted, their labor process less segmented, their income more stable, were able after 1850 to gain considerable job control over the labor process with the introduction of power presses which required considerable experience to run. The political behavior of the printers was also different from that of the shoemakers: highly militant in pursuing job control at the workplace, they were also exclusionist and conservative in their attitude towards unskilled black and women workers in their trade. In effect, the character of class development varied considerably between industries depending largely upon the character of the work experiences of the nascent working class.[32]

Together, the early development of democratic political processes prior to the domination of industrial capitalism over the economy and the development of a cohesive working class, and the later development of pure and simple unionism, paved the way for another feature of class development in America: the bifurcation of working-class politics into a politics of work, centered upon informal shopfloor culture and trade unions, and a politics of the community, centered primarily upon the party. In one, industrial struggle often assumed explicit class conscious dimensions; in the other, party interest and status group conflicts – very often along ethnic and territorial lines – prevailed. To some extent the bifurcation of working-class politics is a feature of class development shared by other capitalist societies, a consequence of the gradual shift in the locus of working-class protest from the neighborhood to the workplace,[33] but in America the bifurcation seems to have become more firmly institutionalized.

Important exceptions exist, particularly in the antebellum period of the kind described by Dawley in Lynn, Massachusetts, and by Laurie in Philadelphia in the 1830s and for a brief period in the early 1850s. At this stage, however, we do not know how widespread the pattern described by Dawley and Laurie was, whether, for example it was sufficiently widespread to contest the model of working-class politics outlined in Montgomery's study of Kensington in the 1840s.[34] Dawley's emphasis upon the Civil War as the critical event that consolidated bourgeois power and fractured working-class politics into two modes might well be true of towns like Lynn with low percentages of foreign-born workers, but it seems unlikely that the Civil War can bear sole responsibility for the fractioning of working-class politics. After all, working-class politics had divided in Philadelphia by the mid-1840s. Other factors must also be counted: the separation of residence and work characteristic of urban areas during the ascendency of industrial capitalism;[35] the early achievement of liberal democracy; and the ethnocentric and economistic nature of the political culture of the American working class that developed as a consequence of the efforts of immigrant working-class groups to survive in a wage labor society characterized by severe and recurring cycles of unemployment and poverty. The Democratic and Republican machines provided jobs and services; if the numerous small socialist and labor parties of the late nineteenth and early twentieth centuries had been able to break the Democratic and Republican monopoly over local politics, their chances of surviving – even thriving – would have been considerably enhanced.[36]

In conclusion, two points about class development in America might be made. The first is the enormous irony, however poignant and tragic, in the fact that it was the way of life centered upon the union, the voluntary association, the school, the church, the saloon, the neighborhood, the machine and the party that the working class developed in the course of its struggle to survive and control the conditions of its own existence that in the long run locked it into the dominant structures, institutions and mentalities of bourgeois society. (This irony of course illustrates the nature of the 'hegemonic situation': the nexus between cultural production and social reproduction.) The second is that whatever the sources of the bifurcation of working-class politics in America, the significance of this bifurcation in shaping the character of class development was far from epiphenomenal. Party politics and community affairs were as much a part of the class experience of the working class as trade unions and informal shopfloor resistance to the imperatives of capitalist work organization. Politics, even bourgeois democratic politics, materially shaped the process of class development in America: no special *a priori* privilege for the importance of the economic can be claimed. Class formation in America was the outcome of the totality of all the struggles – economic, political, ideological; it had no preordained end, no telos built into it.

IV

Like work and community politics, schooling has been a central feature of the American working-class experience since the late nineteenth century. Schooling and class formation are related in two principal ways: through changes in the social structural conditions of working-class life, and through changes in the institutional matrix within which class formation takes place in America.

With the appearance of commercial capitalism in America in the early nineteenth century, the social structure of eighteenth-century America began to crumble. A small, decentralized, localistic, deferential, predominantly rural and relatively egalitarian society was replaced by a new society based on markets in labor, and characterized by transiency, a strident individualism, industrial production, and increasingly urban, unequal, heterogeneous and interconnected. Simultaneously, the social structural conditions of class formation began to take shape: the progressive extension of proletarianization, changes in the opportunity structure (particularly the increasing importance of educational credentials in determining occupational attainment) and ecological patterns of residential areas (particularly the separation of work and residence), and the development of stratified (ethnically, racially, sexually), dual (primary, secondary) and internal labor markets.[37]

During the nineteenth century the institutional matrix of American society also altered in fundamental ways. The breakdown of traditional networks of social organization and social welfare under the impact of capitalism spawned a rash of new institutions to deal with crime, poverty, disease, mental illness, delinquency, adolescents, and the ignorant. Not only common schools, but mental hospitals, penitentiaries, high schools, poorhouses, and reformatories, creating a wholly new institutional apparatus of social organization and social control.[38] In education, the development of capitalist property relations and its attendant social conflicts and disorganization generated a demand, in the name of Christian and republican citizenship, for compulsory schooling and a specific structure of schooling: age graded schools with an obligatory curriculum, teacher dominated pedagogies, full time compulsory attendance, and imbued with the official norms of bourgeois society: hierarchy, achievement, individualism, and mobility.[39] Subsequently, with the shift from formal to real subordination of the labour force – making the socialization of the labor force (its obedience, adaptability, industry, regularity) a technical as well as a social necessity – and the expansion of white-collar work, differentiated curriculum testing, junior high schools, and a 'learn by doing' pedagogy were introduced into the schools, and a philosophy of vocationalism grafted on to the philosophy of citizenship, and new corporate models of educational administration imposed.[40] By 1930, in both the public and parochial school systems, a peculiarly bourgeois structure of schooling was firmly established, and fully integrated into the institutional matrix of modern capitalism.

The significance of these structural and institutional developments for the process of class formation in America was considerable, the one altering the mediate structuration of class formation in America, the other the institutional matrix of class formation.[41] Together they both radically transformed the mechanisms of the reproduction of classes and class relations, inserting schooling into the heart of the reproduction process.

Nevertheless, these developments by themselves do not necessarily create a 'hegemonic situation,' for they tell us little about how much, to what extent, and in what manner they influenced working-class attitudes, behavior and aspirations. They tell us nothing about the nexus between cultural production and cultural reproduction. We do not know, in other words, from an examination of these developments alone, to what extent the American working class was 'made' by modern schooling. To know this, we also have to know the manner in which the working class made itself educationally.[42] To know the manner in which the American working class made itself educationally is to understand the role that class experiences play in the process of class cultural creation. To determine the influence of educational structures and practices is to understand something of the way in which hegemony is established and maintained through education. Hegemony may be born in the factory as Gramsci believed, but it is baptized in the political party, and bred in the school, although in complex and paradoxical ways. Unless accounts of social reproduction recognize this, and the inextricably historical character of these processes, it is difficult to see how any number of functionalist and reductionist mistakes can be avoided.

For example, unless attention is maintained upon concrete historical processes of production and reproduction, it is all too easy to assume that particular stages of capitalist development 'require' particular configurations of labor or workplace (when in fact the particular configuration is a contingent outcome of specific and particular class struggles), or assume that certain objective working-class factions will eventually, one way or the other, become a selfconscious working class. For similar reasons, although it is obvious that schooling plays certain roles or functions for capitalism, this emphatically is not to claim that schooling in capitalist societies can be explained in 'functionalist' terms. It is all too easy, as Katznelson suggests, 'to confuse the difference between the claim that capitalism and schooling have a functional relationship with the claim that schooling was the required institution to perform a given function for the reproduction of the system.'[43] The relationship between a particular structure of schooling and a particular structure of capitalism is irreducibly contingent, the outcome of complete conflicts and choices, not some 'functionalist imperative.' There can be few better reasons why the relationship between schooling and social reproduction needs to be approached historically.

To explore the implications of this argument for the relationship between education and class formation, I will examine three facets of working-class experiences related to schooling: school attendance, working-class educational politics, and the nature of working-class childrens' experience of schooling and the effect of this experience upon the reproduction of inequality and the reproduction of class relations. The first two issues illustrate the impact of changes in the social structural conditions of working-class life upon the character of class experiences and the process of class cultural production, while the third illustrates the nature of schooling as an institutional setting within which processes of class development occur, and as a site of processes of class cultural production and reproduction.

V

The transformation of the social and opportunity structure profoundly altered the structural conditions facing the working class. Each generated a complex set of adaptive responses that reflected both the relative cultural autonomy of the working class and its creative efforts – involving changes in the life cycle and the family economy – to accommodate to these altered structural contingencies. Unfortunately, however, little is known about the relationship between education and class formation. Some efforts have been made to describe, and occasionally measure, the impact of the structure of capitalist social relations, and the changing character of the opportunity structure upon working-class educational behavior and aspirations.

In research on the Chicago working class I found that despite extraordinary variations in educational aspirations of different ethnic groups, over time a common pattern of educationally related behavior, encompassing school attendance, child labor, and home ownership, gradually appeared. As immigrant groups initially sought to ensure their economic security against the vicissitudes of existence in a wage labor society – sickness, injury, death, unemployment, underemployment – they bought homes. Later, they sent their children to school, and for increasing periods of time in order to enhance the economic value of their children's labor power through educational certification.

Since this pattern of accommodation to wage labor occurred in all ethnic groups with very different initial educational aspirations and behavior, it seemed reasonable to conclude that it was the structure of class relations that the working class encountered that shaped working-class educational behavior.[44] The extent to which this accommodation was made to changes in the opportunity structure specifically and the structure of class relations generally, I did not attempt to determine. Joe Kett concluded that declining job opportunities were a critical factor in the changing educational aspirations of late nineteenth century Americans,[45] and Michael Katz and Ian Davey, in measuring the declining significance of ethnicity and the increasing importance of class background as a source of variation in school attendance, argue that job opportunities in industrializing Hamilton had a considerable impact upon the educational and work behavior of youth in that city.[46] Susan Hirsch suggests that in Newark changing job opportunities dramatically affected teenage employment patterns.[47] Likewise, Claudia Golden, using data developed by the Philadelphia Social History Project, found that variations in labor force participation rates – the work and school behavior of male children of immigrants, native whites, and blacks – were not rooted in different ethnic or cultural attitudes about work and school but in structural differences which distinguished the groups. When the economic, demographic, and educational characteristics of their households were controlled, the behavioral differences disappeared.[48] Again, Michael Katz and Mark Stern have described, in a study of Buffalo and Erie County between 1850 and 1915, clear and systematic relationships between class (conceptualized in terms of the relationship to the means of production) and changes in the labor process on the one hand, and fertility and school attendance on the other, relationships that cannot be explained by other factors (for example, explanations based on ethnic differences or embourgeoisement).[49]

These kinds of studies are immensely helpful in providing historians with an understanding of the relative significance of different determinants of educational behavior. But except for one or two exceptions, most studies of working-class educational behavior have failed to integrate into their analyses processes of class formation in which class and ethnicity are not alternative or competing discrete modes of behavior, but interactive – sometimes supporting, sometimes conflicting – pressures that are worked out on an individual basis.[50] When a Polish immigrant working in a steel mill in Pittsburgh or South

Chicago decides to buy a house or send his son to school or to vote for a Democratic Party candidate he doesn't say to himself 'shall I act as an ethnic or shall I act as a semi-skilled wage earner'; he acts because he *is* an ethnic working-class father working in a steel mill confronted by a certain set of constraints (low income, job insecurity, etc.). While it is analytically useful to examine the 'sources' of variations in educational behavior, the 'sources' or 'determinants' ought not to be viewed as proxies for concrete experience; the analysis of educational behavior needs to be rooted four-square in the analysis of class experiences and the process of class formation if the cultural content of these behaviors is not to be overlooked.

The same is true of the analysis of the effects of increasing school attendance upon the life cycle and the family economy. Working-class families in the late nineteenth and early twentieth centuries on average derived approximately a quarter of their family income from children between 10 and 19; in the case of families headed by unskilled fathers, children's income often represented a third of the family income. (Of particular importance were the years between 12 and 17, the very years pre-empted by secondary schooling.)[51] Increased schooling meant increased opportunity costs as well as direct costs to working-class families that often barely lived above the poverty line. In time this process would gradually undermine the older working-class pattern of sending children to work; increasingly wives rather than children entered the labor force to supplement the family income, a development that placed considerable strain upon working-class conceptions of the sexual division of labor.[52]

Working-class educational aspirations can be best understood then, not as imitations of middle-class behavior, but as a product of the structural contingencies that working-class families faced and the strategies of survival and the 'pursuit of dignity' pursued by working-class individuals.[53] Thus, on the one hand, they could exhibit, as they did in Muncie, Indiana, in the late 1920s, a faith in education that evoked 'the fervor of a religion, a means of salvation,' and an 'open sesame that will mysteriously admit their children to a world closed to them.'[54]

Yet, on the other hand, there is much evidence to suggest that working class-parental attitudes toward education were strikingly ambivalent. Immigrant working-class parents in Chicago in the early part of this century constantly complained of the fact that their children, particularly their sons, had lost all respect for parental authority and family loyalty – and they placed responsibility for this upon schools and peer groups. Undoubtedly, there was a great deal of truth in these complaints, as this poignant description by a Jewish boy of the cultural conflict experienced at school illustrates:[55]

> I didn't know any better when I came here, I was a regular *Zaddik* (extremely pious person). I had been brought up that way and didn't know any better. I even wore an *arba kanfoth*. I didn't think there was anything queer about it. I really didn't think about it at all, just as I don't think about eating or sleeping or breathing. But one day I got into a fight in the schoolyard and in the tussle my *arba kanfoth* was pulled out. The boys who watched us fight began to make fun of me. I found out that most of the American Jewish boys didn't wear them at all. The next day when I got to school a bunch of boys pulled my *arba kanfoth* out. I didn't feel so bad the first day, but the second day I felt ashamed of myself. The first day I was sore at them for making fun of it. I made up my mind that I wouldn't wear it any more and the next day I left it off. My mother found it and when I came home that night I got an awful bawling out. I told her that I wouldn't wear it any more, that other Jewish boys at school weren't wearing it and that I wasn't going to have them make a fool out of me again. It made her awful mad and she was afraid to tell my father at first. When he found out he gave me a beating, but I wouldn't wear it anyway. But that was just the beginning, I found out there were lots of things that I was doing that other Jewish boys weren't. It started me thinking about the Jewish religion and the more I thought about it, the less I believed in it. I thought that my father and mother were very old-fashioned, and I had many arguments with them. They don't think much of me any more and I don't think much of them.

It was not only the erosion of parental authority that worried immigrant parents, however; they also were deeply concerned about the threat that schools posed to their cultural identity. 'We all agree that the present time is ominous,' the Czech newspaper *Denni Hlastel* editorialized in 1919, 'and that unless energetic steps are taken at once, before long there will not be a trace of Czech nationality remaining in America.'[56] Immigrant groups opted for one of two solutions: teaching their native languages in the public schools, and the support of parochial education.

Yet the teaching of language and the establishment of parochial schools did not dispel for once and all the ambivalences of the American working class toward education. Some fifty years later on the west coast in a white, predominantly third or fourth generation native white suburb of San Francisco, Lilian Rubin found a deep ambivalence among working-class parents toward education: on the one hand believing it to be economically necessary for their children's welfare, yet deeply distrustful of the values, lax discipline and indulgent socialization processes their children were exposed to.[57] And across the continent in Boston, Sennett and Cobb portrayed the recognition by the Boston working class that education was the key to mobility, job choice, economic welfare and above all else self-respect, dignity and rational control over one's life. But at the same time, they were also scornful of the value and content of the work that educated people seemingly did: it wasn't quite 'real' work.[58]

All of the sketchy evidence available underscores the point then that working-class educational behavior and aspirations are formed in the crucible of class experiences and that the tensions within that experience are reflected in working-class educational aspirations. It is for this reason that there is no simple relationship between educational behavior and aspirations on the one hand, and social reproduction on the other. Working-class educational behavior and aspirations contribute to the process of social reproduction in an ironic and paradoxical rather than a determinist mode: working-class educational behavior and aspirations are less the outcome of a process of ideological incorporation or class determinism than of the very efforts of working-class people to take control of their lives. In so doing, in creating a working-class culture characterized by a view of education that was as much instrumentalist as it was ambivalent, they harnessed themselves to the dominant structures of liberal capitalist society. In short, it is in the nexus between cultural production and reproduction, and not in ideological incorporation or class determinism, that we find the heart of the relationship between education and social reproduction.[59]

Similar complexities characterize working-class educational politics. At first glance educational politics encompass all manner of issues: conflicts over compulsory education, textbooks, religious and language instruction, pedagogy, curricula structure, vocational education, the structure of governance, the purposes of schooling, testing, junior high schools – and so on. Moreover, these conflicts variously divided and joined Protestants and Catholics, native-born and immigrant, first and second generation immigrant, artisan workers and factory operators, traditionalists and revivalists, pietists and ritualists, unionists and non-unionists. Making theoretical sense out of all this is no easy task. For this reason, a number of preliminary observations about the nature of educational politics and the changing character of the political universe faced by working-class people need to be made.

The first set of observations concern the nature of educational politics. The first is that the bewildering variety of educational issues that have become political issues can be tentatively placed into one of four categories: structural politics centered upon the nature and strength of the alignment of the school with the economy (for example, conflicts over differentiated and vocational education) and conflicts over the structure of authority relations within schools (for example, conflicts over the centralization of administrative authority, unionization and professionalism); human capital politics generated by the efforts of parents or communities to enhance the rates of return to their children or school population relative to other children or school populations; cultural capital politics created by conflicts over competing definitions of legitimate knowledge, that is, conflicts over the distribution of symbolic authority in the society (for example, conflicts over curricula content or textbooks); and finally, displacement politics, in which educational issues (often, though not always, conflicts of a cultural capital kind) become proxies for other non-educational conflicts in the community.[60]

The second observation to be made about the nature of educational politics is that historians barely have begun the serious theoretical work of understanding the dynamics of educational politics: the conditions under which educational issues become political conflicts of various kinds, the relationship of these political conflicts to the form of the political process (interest group or ethnocultural pluralism, class determinism, class conflict) in which educational conflicts are fought out, and the relationship of these political conflicts and processes to the structure and control of schooling and to educational outcomes. And given the dearth – indeed, with one notable exception, the virtual absence – of theoretical attention to these issues, it is hardly surprising that our understanding of the relationship of these political processes to processes of capital accumulation and class conflict barely has reached first base.[61]

The second observation to be made about working-class educational politics concerns the character – the ecology – of the political universe within which working-class educational politics take place. Of particular importance in this regard is the change in the structure of urban – including educational – politics over the course of the nineteenth and twentieth centuries, particularly during the progressive era (1890-1920). American politics during the Jacksonian period were intensely decentralized and localized, and in some respects the legacy of that decentralization can still be seen in city-wide (as opposed to state- or nation-wide) educational systems. But during the common school reform era, and especially during the progressive era, two developments took place that centralized the structure of urban and educational politics: one was the appearance of powerful political machines in the major urban centers, and the other was the centralization of administrative authority (including the destruction of ward based control of local schools) in urban school systems.[62] The two developments are not unrelated in the context of educational politics, for while the second was intended in part to remove the schools from working-class political control, the growth of the machine allowed ethnic groups to exercise at least some indirect control over school governance, although nowhere as forcefully as previously.

Within this political universe, working-class educational politics both influenced and were influenced by general processes of class formation in America. Two issues are of particular importance. First is the legacy of the producer ideology and republicanism among native-born artisan workers; this legacy was of importance not only to the antebellum labor movement's conception of the purposes of public schooling, but also to the educational politics of the labor movement in the late nineteenth-early twentieth century. Indeed, in at least one city, Chicago, the influence of republicanism was still apparent in the late 1920s.[63] The second point is the interactive relationship between two principal aspects of the process of class development and schooling: (1) the bifurcation of working-class politics dating from the Jacksonian era, a consequence principally of the peculiar juxtaposition of the industrial revolution and the ascendency of liberal democracy in America, and (2) as a consequence of the peculiarities of processes of class recruitment into the system of wage labor in America, the depth of the ethnic differentiation of the American working class.

Schools – both public and parochial – have played significant roles in both processes, and in fact provided a major intersection between them, for local schools were an important focus and source of the establishment and maintenance of ethnic identities while reinforcing a localistic, community-based political culture. The development of an extensive Catholic parochial school system along ethnic or national lines, for example, provided Catholics with the opportunity to teach ethnic languages and the Catholic religion. More importantly, parochial schools were an instrument of intergenerational continuity, and as Thomas and Znaniecki pointed out, 'a necessary expression of the tendency of the immigrant community to self preservation and self determination.' For this reason it is perhaps difficult to exaggerate the significance of the parochial school in the formation of the American working class and its internal differentiation along ethnic lines[64]:

> Good or bad, the parochial school is a social product of the immigrant group and satisfied important needs of the latter. The most essential point is neither the religious character of the parochial school, nor even the fact that it preserves in the young the language and cultural traditions of the old country; it is the function of the parochial school as a factor of the social unity of the immigrant

colony and of its continuity through successive generations.

By and large, however, historians know precious little about the relative importance of different issues in working-class educational politics or the place of educational politics in working-class politics generally. They also know precious little about the relative importance of nativism, evangelical Protestantism, the desire for respectability, ethnic cultures, republicanism, mobility aspirations, or the Catholic church in working-class educational politics, and they have not yet begun to relate these issues to the development of cultural formations within the working class, despite the appearance in the last few years of several suggestive typologies of early nineteenth century working-class culture: the traditionalists, loyalists and radicals of Dawley and Faler, and Bruce Laurie's traditionalists, revivalists and radicals.[65] Traditionalists had little interest in and little use for education, and while revivalists, loyalists and radicals all supported compulsory education, they did so for remarkably different reasons. For revivalists and loyalists education was an instrument of moral uplift, social control and upward mobility, whereas for radicals it was a means of self-improvement, intellectual independence, and a guarantee of republican citizenship. Perhaps the 'labor-education' thesis has some life in it yet.[66]

VI

The second aspect of the relationship between education and class reproduction that needs to be examined is the relationship between work and schooling. Over time the school has increasingly occupied a strategic position within the institutional structure of liberal capitalist societies, shaping the destinies of generation after generation of children. How this happens, however, is no simple matter.

In attempting to narrow the gap between their ability to predict and their ability to explain occupational aspiration or job choice, researchers have developed different accounts ('models') of the relationship between family background, schooling and occupational attainment. The principle approaches are those that stress socialization processes, those that stress the distribution of knowledge, those that stress internal stratification and labelling processes, and those that stress processes of cultural production and reproduction within the school.

The most popular are socialization models. These specify some organizational feature of the school that is believed to be responsible for socializing children into the normative requirements, the values, behaviors and dispositions, of the world of work. In one such account, accent is placed on the formal bureaucratic features of schooling – the centralization of control and supervision, the standardization of procedures, the rationalization of the education process: class grading, uniform courses of study, standardized written exams, competition for grades, intense activity, strict behavioral rules.[67] Another approach, proposed by Robert Dreeben, links ecological features of the school with the normative requirements – universalism, specificity, achievement, and independence – 'required' of modern occupational life. Dreeben stressed that the age-graded, relatively autonomous classrooms of specific size, composition, degree of differentiation, scheduling and reward structure provide students with the social experience necessary for learning occupational norms. Schools teach students to work for the sake of grades rather than because of their personal emotional relationship with the teacher. They teach that performance and competence, what you do rather than who you are, are the basis of rewards and status. Because classrooms are large collectivities, children are treated impersonally. Yearly promotions, and the size and staff specialization of schools, systematically provide students with lessons in forming and breaking transitory relationships; this helps form the ability to distinguish between positions and persons. Schools reward merit and achievement with extrinsic rewards: grades and promotions. And schools also provide children with experiences that allow them to differentiate between the varying principles of superordination and subordination, that is, authority and obedience.[68]

In a slightly modified approach, Bowles and Gintis insist that schools systematically vary in what they call the social relations of education, and in the normative orientations toward work that schools generate. Bowles and Gintis claim that the major aspects of educational organization replicate the relationships of dominance and subordinancy in the economic sphere, specifically, that 'the social relations of education – the relationships between administrators and teachers, teachers and students, students and students, and students and their work – replicate the hierarchical division of labor.' As a consequence of their experiences of the social relations of education, students are socialized into the appropriate personality characteristics, habits, modes of self-presentation required by modern bureaucratic and hierarchically organized enterprises. Most schools, they argue, teach the kind of qualities and personality characteristics that are essential for the performance for low- and middle-level jobs: obedience, punctuality, respect, orderly work habits, the ability to follow instructions. Those schools, or level of schooling, that differ in the structure of social relations are for the most part engaged in 'soft socialization': the production of workers for upper-level jobs whose major work orientation is the 'internalization of norms.' Bowles and Gintis thus argue that systematic differences exist in the social relations of education and that these play an important role in the intergenerational reproduction of inequality.[69]

Whereas specialization approaches emphasize different organizational features of the school, 'cultural capital' approaches focus on the kind and distribution of knowledge within society that schools legitimate and distribute in systematic class based ways. Bourdieu and Passerson, for example, argue that schools trade in exclusive cultural capital – symbolic property or the knowledge of, and skill in the use of, the symbols, language forms and structure and meanings of bourgeois culture that are directly and indirectly defined by dominant groups as socially legitimate. Students with access to such cultural capital, primarily through their families, do well in school since educational achievement is determined by the ability to perform in meritocratic tests that measure those skills which the cultural capital provides.[70] Other sociologists – Young, Bernstein, Wexler, Apple – have also focused on the character and distribution of school or 'legitimate' knowledge, and have developed as Bourdieu and Passeron have, theories of social or 'cultural' reproduction rather than the 'economic' reproduction suggested by Bowles and Gintis; that is, they look to the nature of knowledge, its distribution and its legitimation, rather than the acquisition of specific values, behaviors and dispositions engendered by the social relations of education.[71]

A third approach, and one overlapping in part with the previous two, focusses on allocation and labelling processes within the school.[72] This approach posits that adult success is assigned to individuals on the basis of the type and duration of schooling received, whatever children may have learned in school. Schooling is viewed as a set of institutional rules which classify and allocate individuals to positions in society; it *symbolically* redefines graduates as possessing particular qualities and skills gained through attendance at school or college, and this occurs independently of whether or not any *actual* changes in competency, skill or values have occurred.

From this perspective the importance of school organization is that it legitimates the claim that students have had particular kinds of educational experiences. The major source of organizational diversity and change between and within schools are the symbolic conceptions or definitions of graduates that schools wish to project to their clients, for example, employers. The linkage between schooling and work is to be found in the legitimation of particular student characteristics rather than in actual socialization of specific behavior or attitudes.

The organization of schooling is approached less in terms of a structure of socialization processes than as a set of sorting and selecting processes that sort, classify and label students and allocate or distribute them into different curriculum tracks and/or positions of occupational structure. As Jencks pronounced, 'schools serve primarily as selections and certification agencies, whose job is to measure and label people, and only secondarily as socialization agencies, whose job is to change people.'[73]

Whatever the differences between these approaches in their views of the relationship between education and occupational choice, they do, however, have one overwhelming feature in common, namely, a tendency to treat the school as a black box, an institution devoid of an internal cultural politics of its own, an institution characterized by processes of conflict and contest, negotiation and exchange, resistance and accommodation, between different groups within the school. The fact that children are forced to attend school does not necessarily mean that they acquiesce to the normative structure of the school; it is important to view the school as an arena of tension between processes of cultural production and reproduction, as a locus of human activity, and occasionally as a locus of a form of class conflict between the official, bourgeois culture of the school and the informal cultural creations of its working-class constituency. It is simply too limited, too reductive – too embedded in a base-superstructure theory of a social formation – to assume that the bureaucratic or ecological features of school organization, or the social relations of education, bourgeois cultural capital, or labelling processes, determine, in any direct sense, as Paul Willis argues, 'the subjective and cultural formation of particular kinds of labor power.'[74]

A theoretically more convincing case can, I think, be made for the proposition that it is the tension between processes of cultural production and reproduction that constitutes the primary nexus between the home, work and schooling – the key to both the reproduction of classes and the reproduction of class relations. Although Willis's account of this nexus is developed within an English context, and is focussed on only one faction of English working-class youth (the 'lads'), his account can be modified and generalized, enabling it to be applied to an American context, other factions of the working class, and other classes.

Willis's account hinges on the claim that at school working-class children acquire a certain subjective sense of labor power, make an objective decision to apply it, and that both the development of a certain sense of labor power and the decision to apply it are processes associated with the creation of a working-class 'counter school culture.'

Out of their effort to resist official labels, meanings, impositions and demands, and to create a counter culture of masculine fraternity and self-worth, the 'lads' develop their own distinctive counter culture, encompassing clothes, cigarettes, alcohol, music, rituals, identities, symbols, argot and representations. Rejecting school work as mental labor, and associating mental labor with obedience, conformity, subordination and lack of manliness, they engage in an atavistic struggle to win symbolic and physical space from the institution, its rules, and its purpose: to make students work. Against the rules and meanings of the school they pursue strategies of resistance and survival: truancy, skipping classes, 'having a laff,' games, sleeping, smoking, drinking. Because of their belief that they are worldwise, their certainty that they can see through the educational exchange, that they understand and know the 'real' world, they refuse to participate and give up their mental labor; instead, they opt for the world of fraternity with friends, masculinity, autonomy from the school, and manual work. This process is the source of the paradoxical functionality of working-class oppositional culture, the heart of hegemony, for it is the creation of this cultural form that locks the 'lads' into manual working-class jobs, a process of 'self-induction' that is as powerful as it is poignant. It is a process nevertheless that accounts for both the reproduction of classes and the reproduction of class relations, and does so without recourse to notions of structural correspondence while insisting upon the relative cultural autonomy of working-class self activity and the process of cultural production.

Willis's account of the manner in which the 'lads' acquire a certain subjective sense of labor power and the process of 'self-induction' into manual labor relies upon two key arguments, one resting upon an 'exchange' model of pedagogical relations, the other upon a theory of intergenerational cultural continuity. It is these two key arguments that can be generalized and modified to provide a general account of the relationship between school and work for students other than those within the working class and for other national and historical contexts.

Willis argues that in England the lads evaluate and reject the pedagogical exchange offered by the school: knowledge for respect, guidance for control, success for obedience. They are not convinced of the worth of the exchange; they would give up too much: too much autonomy, too much masculinity, too much self-direction, for what they believe to be the empty and illusionary promises of conformity, mental work, and credentials. 'Ear'oles' on the other hand make a different evaluation of the costs and benefits involved, and opt for a strategy of conformity, accommodation and mental work. The theoretical significance of the different evaluations by the lads and the ear'oles is not in the difference of the evaluations but in the process of evaluation itself: the fact that all students eventually make evaluations of the costs and benefits involved, and 'negotiate' some form of exchange with teachers and the school authorities.

The second major feature of Willis's theory of cultural production and reproduction is his demonstration of the important continuities in the cultural forms of adult working-class life and the cultural creations of working-class children within schools. Although Willis fails to describe in detail the transmission of cultural forms between generations, he describes the profound similarities between school counter culture and shopfloor culture. This working-class culture is carried back into the home by the parents and comes to provide a set of unofficial criteria by which their children judge the world. As working-class children encounter the school and the outside society they gradually construct a picture of the world in which schooling steadily assumes the status of a working-class work environment; the school becomes a work place whose ostensible purpose is to make young people work – to extract labor from labor power – but without the protection of unions or the right to engage in collective bargaining. Authority is arbitrary, coercive, and backed up by the power of the State. Mental labor is effeminate and just 'theory,' divorced from understanding the real world. And so begins the process of cultural conflict, production and reproduction.

This explanation of the influence of cultural background in which the family mediates class cultural formations and schooling can, with appropriate changes in the character of the cultural background, be generalized to include other class cultural backgrounds, and modified to include other national class cultural formations. One possible key to generalizing the model to other class cultures lies in the use of Bourdieu's concept of 'cultural capital.' By virtue of their class cultural background, some children acquire the cultural capital – the sets of cultural outlooks, predispositions, skills and understandings – that, through making the appropriate exchanges, they can invest in schooling. By virtue of this investment in the meritocratic structures of the school, they are then able to enhance the value of their cultural capital.

Cross-nationally, the issue is one of differences in the process of class formation, and particularly class development. Compared to English working-class culture, American working-class culture is not as cohesive, thickly textured, or selfconscious; it is more diffuse, fractionated, internally divided along regional, racial and ethnic lines; its repudiation of bourgeois ideology less deep and incisive; its institutional infrastructure – trade unions, political organizations, voluntary associations – less extensive and weaker. In short, the character of class development in America has been very different from what it has been in Great Britain. The effects of this fact upon processes of cultural production within schools complicate the analysis of class cultural production in America. Certainly processes of class cultural production and reproduction take place in American schools, albeit within a different cultural matrix. Processes of cultural production in American schools produce an extraordinary variety of cultural forms that differ by region, race and ethnicity. These cultural forms are best understood as expressions of processes of class cultural production. But exactly how the nature of class development in America is responsible for these outcomes and the relative weakness of cultural bonds between generations – the continuity of motifs, themes, representations, identities, rituals – is far from clear.

Willis's theory of the relationship between the family, schooling and work, as provocative as it is, is still in need, however, of further theoretical development. The processes involved in cultural production and reproduction are clearly of a complex cognitive and cultural kind, requiring three kinds of supporting theories: an account first, of the process through which students construct a theory of the society, the school, and of the relationship between the two: not so much of the development of formal mental operations investigated by Piaget and Kohlberg, but the construction by children, as a consequence of the character of their class experiences, of a theory of the social world.[75] It requires, second, an account of the process through which children acquire the evaluative criteria with which they evaluate the character of the pedogogical and social exchanges offered by the school and society. And it requires, finally, an explanation of the acquisition of educational and social aspirations, and how for many working-class children, the tension between their understanding of the world and their aspirations results in the gradual transformation of their aspirations into lowered expectations – and lower educational achievement.[76]

Yet when all is said and done, the theory of cultural production and reproduction promises to dissolve the research paradox noted earlier: the ability of researchers to predict occupational choice reasonably well, but their inability to explain what determines it. What a theory of cultural production provides is an explanation of the looseness of the fit between family background and occupational attainment by emphasizing the critical importance of the interaction between institutional context and processes of class cultural production. On this account, occupational choice is the outcome of a structural process of cultural production and reproduction within a specific institutional context. This makes it possible to dissolve the research paradox; the point is not our ability to predict but not fully explain occupational choice; the point, rather, is that *we can explain but not fully predict occupational choice*.

Likewise, explanations of differences in educational achievement that look to differences in educability, or cognitive codes, or cultural capital, or socialization practices, or the social relations of education, all fall victim at some point to what Dennis Wrong almost thirty years ago diagnosed as the oversocialized conception of human nature. All of these approaches ignore the significance of human activity and agency – the process of cultural production – and class experiences in the reproduction of inequality. We urgently require, for example, a developmental theory of child development that takes human activity and class seriously – not class in a nominalistic sense of occupational background, income level, or even linguistic code or character of cultural capital – but class in its full experiential sense as a set of structured situations encountered, and conceptualized, by the child.

Richard deLone put the issue well recently calling for a 'situational' theory of child development rooted in the human – and therefore developmental – character of the class experiences of children. 'The essential character of social class as a developmental context,' he writes, 'is that it does provide messages that constitute a more or less congruent, continuous series of situations through family, school and the child's direct experience of the large social structure. Thus, development occurs in response to situations, and social class (or race or sex or other grouping) constitutes a master setting within which family and other institutions occupy subordinate and mediating status.'[77] Within this context, children act as active theory builders and relatively autonomous, certainly active, participants in their own development – and for many, entrapment.[78]

Undoubtedly, the mechanisms nominated by other approaches to the relationship between schooling and work – the bureaucratic and ecological organization of the school, the social relations of education, internal stratification procedures, pedagogical ethos – all contribute to the reproduction of classes and class relations. Exactly how all this happens is not certain, for against the concreteness and specificity of processes of cultural production and reproduction, processes of 'socialization' – whether they be the 'internationalization' of values, or 'identities' fostered by labelling, the 'acculturation' to certain behaviors, norms and dispositions, or 'incorporation' into the dominant ideology or structure of social practices – seem strangely elliptical and ultimately, unsatisfactory, and not just for the theoretical reasons considered, but also for methodological ones as well.

While for ethnographers none of these approaches poses insurmountable methodological problems, for historians they do, since there is no way for historians to ascertain whether, for example, children of past generations were in fact socialized into the specific sets of values, norms, dispositions specified by the school, or the extent to which they were, or which organizational features of the school were responsible for the socialization. We are thus faced with a hiatus between what is methodologically possible and what is theoretically sensible. This is not to suggest that the alternative mechanisms – socialization processes and particularly internal stratification processes – are not without affect.[79] But it is to suggest that they do not possess the theoretical comprehensiveness and depth of the cultural production-reproduction approach.

VII

At the opening of this essay I suggested that the dominant problematic within educational research and discussion for the past ten or fifteen years has been one focussed on issues of inequality: educability, equality of educational opportunity, status attainment, and so on.[80] I initially outlined a theory of class formation whose basic propositions are drawn largely from the work of E. P. Thompson: the foundation of history in human agency, experience and consciousness within determinate structural conditions, the overriding importance of class experiences in the 'making' of a class culture, the specific historicity of processes of class production, development and reproduction, and the complex, problematic character of hegemony (the nexus between cultural production and reproduction). I argued that a theory of class formation that was sensitive to the peculiarities of the American experience provides a theoretically compelling way of understanding the relationship between education and social reproduction.

Approaching education from this alternative problematic, another set of research questions come to the fore: the character of the class structuration of social life, particularly the manner in which markets in labor and changes in the opportunity structure shape the role of education in American society; the relationship between educational behavior and aspirations on the one hand and class experiences and class cultures on the other; the cultural relationship between inequality, class, and education; the increasing importance of schooling in the institutional matrix of the process of class formation in America; the impact of class development upon processes of cultural production and reproduction. In whatever there is left of the free marketplace of ideas, these are questions surely worthy of serious attention.

Acknowledgments

The writing of this essay was supported by funds from the National Institute of Education, Grant 9-0173.

For their helpful comments on earlier drafts of this essay, I wish to thank Fred Block, Herb Gintis, Bruce Laurie, Walter Licht, Dale Light, Michael Katz and Mark Stern.

Notes

1 A. Przeworski, 'Proletariat into a Class: The Process of Class Formation from Karl Kantsk'y *The Class Struggle* to Recent Controversies,' *Politics and Society* 7, 4, 1977. See also R. Williams, *Marxism and Literature* (Oxford: Oxford University Press, 1977), ch. 2, or his 'Base and Superstructure in Marxist Cultural Theory,' *New Left Review* 82, 1973, 3-16; C. Castoriadis, 'On the History of the Workers Movement,' *Telos* 30, Winter 1976-7, 25-7.

2 E. P. Thompson, *The Poverty of Theory* (London: Merlin Press, 1978). For a similar critique see R. W. Connell, 'A Critique of the Althusserian Approach to Class,' *Theory and Society* 8, 1979. For Althusser's position see G. McLennan, V. Molina and R. Peters, 'Althusser's Theory of Ideology' in Center for Contemporary Cultural Studies, *Ideology* (Birmingham University); L. Althusser, *For Marx* (London: Penguin Press, 1969), ch. 3; L. Althusser and E. Balibar, *Reading Capital* (London: New Left Books, 1970); G. McLennan, 'Ideology and Consciousness: Some Problems in Marxist Historiography,' Center for Contemporary Cultural Studies, (University of Birmingham (September 6), 6, 9, 1976); and R. Johnson, 'Critique: Edward Thompson, Eugene Genovese, and Socialist Humanist History,' *History Workshop* 84-6.

3 E. P. Thompson, *The Making of the English Working Class* (Harmondsworth, Middlesex: Penguin, 1968: 9-10). Elsewhere he wrote that 'When we speak of *a* class, we are thinking of a very loosely defined body of people who share the same congeries of interests, social experiences, tradition, and value system, who have a consciousness in relation to other groups of people in class ways,' E. P. Thompson, 'The Peculiarities of the English,' *Socialist Register* 1965: 357. See also *The Poverty of Theory* 334-54 for his most recent statement of his theory of class.

4 Thompson, *The Poverty of Theory*, 298. For very different reasons – and drawing very different conclusions – Althusser also argues that classes exist only in class struggles; see Connell, 313-21.

5 Thompson, *The Making of the English Working Class*, 211-13.

6 If class struggles have an autonomous effect upon class formation, then the identification of objective classes in the sense stipulated by the orthodox problematic loses its theoretical significance

in explanations of class formation. By avoiding the teleological suppositions of the orthodox class-in-itself problematic, this Thompsonian approach to class formation finesses a central issue of that problematic, the identification of the (objective) working class. In insisting that class is something which 'happens in human relationships,' that it happens when some men, as a result of common experiences develop a sense of class identity and perhaps class consciousness, Thompson is insisting that class formation should not be approached as a problem of how or when a group of proletarians, objectively defined by their relationship to the means of production, become a self-conscious class, but whether men and women come to think of themselves as a class and act as one. The process of class formation is not automatic or ineluctable, but contingent and existential. Although 'in the end' this is not its only definition, nevertheless Thompson's observation that 'class is defined by men as they live their own history' contains a profoundly important counterpoint to orthodox approaches to class formation. This is not to deny that the process of class formation is without a structure or a logic, it is rather to insist that in the final analysis class formation is a variable and contingent process of cultural creation, a human activity. Given this account of class formation, then the long preoccupation of Marxist theory with the identification of the working class seems much less pressing (of course in political practice the issue is more pressing, for as Poulantzas once observed, where class boundaries are placed determines whether class alliances are needed or not). The theoretical issue is less one of identifying proletarian groups – which groups to include, which to exclude, what criteria to use or not use – that come to constitute a working class, but rather one of analyzing the process of class formation itself, that is, of studying the process of class cultural production and reproduction *whatever* groups seem to be involved. The issue is not *a priori* or categorical, but empirical and historical. It is only possible, through retrospective historical analysis, to identify the particular conditions and contingencies – why this group, why not this group, why not this group, why that class experiences, not this one – that did *in fact* influence the process of class formation one way or the other. It might even be possible, with sufficient case studies, to construct predictive hypotheses, but it is not a question of *a priori* theorizing or categorical deductions about this or that group or this or that situation. For as Przeworski argues (p. 367),

> Class as historical actors are not given uniquely by any objective positions, not even those of workers and capitalists . . . the very relation between classes as historical actors (classes in struggle) and places within the relation of production must become problematic. Classes are not given uniquely by any objec-

> tive positions because they constitute effects of struggles, and these struggles are not determined uniquely by the relations of production. The traditional formulation does not allow us to think theoretically about class struggles, since it either reduces them to an epithenomenon or enjoines with freedom from objective determination. They are structured by the totality of economic, political, and ideological relations; and they have an autonomous effect upon the process of class formation.

See also Castoriadis, and Connell, 'A Critique,' 313-21.

7 For a further discussion, see R. Connell, *Ruling Class, Ruling Culture* (Cambridge: Cambridge University Press, 1977: 4-5). Connell also points out (p. 27) that the process of class formation in stratification theory is approached not as a question of how the major dimensions of social differentiation are formed, but of how the 'strata' defined them, became cohesive units; that is, they approach class as crystallization of networks, a coagulation of inequalities, within a social category, and not as a question of the dynamics of the social formation.

For the character of the class structuration of American society see E. O. Wright, 'Marxist Class Categories and Income Inequality,' *American Sociological Review* 42, February 1977: 33-53; N. Poulantzas, 'On Social Classes,' *New Left Review* 98, 1976: 3-41; M. Katz, M. Doucet, and M. Stern, *The Social Organization of Industrial Capitalism*, forthcoming; Dawley, *Class and Community* ch. 6; C. Griffen, 'Workers Divided: The Effect of Craft and Ethnic Differences in Poughkeepsie, New York, 1850-1880,' in S. Thernstron and R. Sennett (eds), *Nineteenth-Century Cities* (New Haven: Yale University Press, 1969); T. Hershberg *et al.*, 'A Tale of Three Cities: Black and Immigrants in Philadelphia, 1850-1880,' *Annals of American Academy of Political and Social Sciences* 441, January 1979; R. Edwards, *Contested Terrain* (New York: Basic Books, 1979); D. Hogan, 'Schooling and Capitalism: The Political Economy of Education in Chicago, 1880-1930,' unpublished PhD dissertation, University of Illinois, 1978.

8 Thompson, *Poverty of Theory*; M. Dobb, *Studies in the Development of Capitalism* (New York: International Publishers, 1947, esp. ch. 1); H. Braverman, *Labor and Monopoly Capital* (New York: Monthly Review Press, 1974); J. Foster, *Class Struggle and the Industrial Revolution* (London: Weidenfeld & Nicolson, 1974); G. S. Jones, *Outcast London* (Oxford: Oxford University Press, 1971); A. Sawley, *Class and Community* (Cambridge: Harvard University Press, 1970).

9 G. Kolko, *Main Currents in Modern American History* (New York: Harper & Row, 1976, ch. 3); K. Marx, *Capital* vol. 1 (New York: International Publishers, 1967), Part VIII; Dobb Studies.

10 Thompson, *The Making of the English Working Class*, 10; Foster,

Class Struggle and the Industrial Revolution, 224; Jones, *Outcast London* 'Working Class Culture and Working Class Politics in London, 1870-1900,' Notes on the 'Remaining of a Working Class,' *Journal of Social History* Summer 1974; W. Sewell, 'Social Change and Working Class Politics in Nineteenth Century Marseilles,' *Past and Present* 65, 1974: 75-109; P. Faler, 'Workingmen, Mechanics and Social Change: Lynn, Massachusetts, 1800-1860,' unpublished PhD dissertation, University of Wisconsin, 1971; A. Dawley, *Class and Community: The Industrial Revolution in Lynn* (Cambridge: Harvard University Press); B. Laurie, *Class and Culture: The Working People of Philadelphia, 1800-1850* (Philadelphia, Temple University Press, forthcoming); R. Gray, *The Labor Aristocracy in Victorian Edinburgh* (Oxford: Oxford University Press, 1976: 3).

11 Or in Weberian terms, of the institutional and other factors which intervene between the existence of market capacities and the formation of classes. See A. Giddens, *New Rules of Sociological Method* (New York: Basic Books, 1977: 123ff); *The Class Structure of Advanced Societies* (New York: Harper & Row, 1973: 107-8).

12 The assumption here is that the effect of closure for example of intergenerational mechanism of mobility provides opportunity for the reproduction of common life-class-experiences across generations.

13 For Gramsci's and Althusser's theory of ideology, see McLennan, Molina, Peters, 'Althusser's Theory of Ideology,' op. cit.; S. Hall, B. Lumley, G. McLennan, 'Politics and Ideology: Gramsci', in Center for Contemporary Cultural Studies, *Ideology* (Birmingham University); L. Althusser, 'Ideology and Ideological State Apparatuses' in *Lenin and Philosophy and Other Essays* (London: New Left Books,, 1971); A. Callinicos, *Althusser's Marxism* (London: Pluto, 1976). A more orthodox (but not Parsonism) sociological formulation of similar ideas can be found in Giddens, *New Rules of Sociological Method*, ch. 3, esp. 102-4, where he discusses the notion of the reproduction of structures of interaction.

14 Gray, *The Labor Aristocracy in Victorian Edinburgh*, 5.

15 Ibid.

16 Williams, *Marxism and Literature*, 108, 109, 110, 112.

17 P. Willis, *Learning to Labor* (London: Saxon House, 1977: 175).

18 Williams, *Marxism and Literature*, 114.

19 In 1780, prior to the era of industrial capitalism, approximately 80 per cent of the US labor force were self-employed, and chiefly in agriculture and handicraft production; one hundred years later that proportion had dropped to around 37 per cent, and 62 per cent (up from 20 per cent) of the labor force were wage and salaried employees. By 1930 the percentages were 23.5 per cent and 76.8 per cent respectively (with the balance accounted for by

salaried managers and administrators). A veritable revolution had occurred in the structure of American society: where at the beginning of the nineteenth century the majority of non-slave Americans were economically independent, by the decade of the Civil War a clear majority of the labor force sold its labor power in the labor market; where once the majority of Americans lived on farms as commercial farmers or worked in their craft shops selling their products for a price, by the end of the century most sold their labor power for a wage. See M. Reich, R. Edwards and T. Wisskoffe, *The Capitalist System* (New Jersey: Prentice Hall, 1972: 175).

20 The distinction between formal and real subordination was developed by Marx to differentiate between the development of capitalist property relations (the wage labor system) and the creation of a capitalist labor process in which the organization and control of the labor process is under the aegis of capital rather than labor. As with proletarianization, the shift from formal to real subordination has characterized all capitalist societies, but the level, pace, character and politics of the shift have varied from country to country.

Historically, formal subordination – capitalist and property relations – developed prior to the penetration and control of the labor process by capital. The outstanding analysis of the development of capitalist property relations in America has been undertaken by Alan Dawley in his study of the shoemaking industry in Lynn, Massachusetts, in the first half of the nineteenth century. Dawley traced the destruction, as a consequence of market forces and economic policies, of the system of petty commodity production by independent craftsmen (shoemakers), and the beginnings of wage labor in the production of shoes as artisan shoemakers were forced to leave their 'ten footers' for the 'central shops' (pre-factory, non-mechanized places of production) owned by merchant capitalists. Moreover, this process of class production, the transformation of the social relations of production around the system of wage labor, was completed *before* industrialization, that is, before mechanization of the production process was undertaken and institutionalized in the factory system.

The experience of the shoe industry was repeated in industry after industry. Formal subordination preceded the technical reorganization of the labor process, but contrary to the story recounted by Harry Braverman and Kathy Stone (and in the context of the English experience by Garreth Stedman Jones and John Foster) the technical reorganization of the labor process was not a one shot affair (the industrial revolution, Taylorism) but a gradual, recurrent, uneven process over time, both between industries and within industries. It was also a process that was not limited to the development of factories, whose distinctive characteristic was not so much the mechanization of the labor process, or the division of the labor process, but the use of external sources of power, which in most industries appear after the replacement of artisan work shops by sweatshops or manufactories (work settings without external power sources characterized by extensive division of labor). The appearance of manufactories ('central shops' in the shoemaking industry) was particularly significant for it enabled the capitalist to assemble under one roof workers from the same or different handicrafts to produce a commodity thereby enabling the capitalist to impose an extensive division of labor, to speed up the labor process, lengthen the working day, more fully control the production cycle, and pave the way for the eventual mechanization of the labor process in factories. Through mechanization capitalists assumed even greater control of the labor process by destroying the irregular work patterns of handicraftsmen, displacing the intelligence of the artisan with the rhythms of the machine, and reconstituting the division of labor and wage hierarchies upon an entirely new technical and social basis.

For an excellent discussion of the heuristic and theoretical value of periodizing work in capitalism through the use of Marx' distinction, see Bruce Bellingham's excellent unpublished essay 'Revised Literature Review on Artisans and Skilled Workers,' (Sociology Department, University of Pennsylvania, 1978) and G. S. Jones, 'England's First Proletariat,' *New Left Review* 90, 1975.

21 H. Gutman, *Work, Culture, and Society* (New York, Vintage, 1976: 15, 18).

22 Not the least of the difficulties of this argument is that it neglects a central feature of late nineteenth-century immigration, namely that a majority of the new immigrants did not intend to stay. During the 1880s emigration back to Europe is estimated to have reached thirty per cent of the total out migration; in the 1890s thirty-five per cent; between 1901 and 1914, thirty-nine per cent; and between 1915 and 1922, fifty-three per cent. Between 1907 and 1911, for every one hundred Italians who arrived in the US, seventy-three returned; for every one hundred southern Italians and Europeans as a whole, forty-four returned. Between 1908 and 1923, for every one hundred Hungarians and Rumanians, sixty-five returned; for every one hundred southern Italians, fifty-six; fifty-two per cent of the Russians and forty-six per cent of the Greeks; forty per cent of the Poles; twenty-one per cent of the English. The majority of new immigrants who came to America did so with the intent of only staying temporarily, accumulating sufficient savings through long hours and hard work, and then returning to the old country with the funds to buy a farm or set up a small shop. They did not intend to become trapped permanently into the American proletariat. Given their subjective orien-

tations toward their domicile in the United States, they were not particularly predisposed to engage in activities related to class development: the formation of strong class conscious labor unions, stable working-class communities and institutions, or a working-class political party. Since foreign born workers constituted the heart of the American working class – in 1909 fifty-eight per cent of the workers in the twenty principal mining and manufacturing plants were foreign born, and they constituted forty-five per cent of all unskilled labor and thirty-eight per cent of all the semi-skilled labour force – one perhaps ought not to be surprised at the low level of class development. See G. Kolko, *Main Currents in Modern American History* (New York: Harper & Row, 1976: 69-70, 74); G. Rosenblum, *Immigrant Workers: Their Impact on American Labor Radicalism* (New York: Basic Books, 1972: 45-53); T. Kessner, *The Golden Door: Italian and Jewish Immigrant Mobility in New York City, 1880-1915* (New York: Oxford University Press, 1977).

23 Dawley, 'E. P. Thompson and the Americans,' 40.

24 Much of the historiography of immigrants and ethnic culture has long been dominated by assimilationist and pluralist approaches. Assimilationists, deriving their theoretical models from the Chicago School of Sociology, view America as a melting pot that destroys ethnic differences; pluralists asset that the immigrant experiences are characterized less by assimilation than by the persistence – even strengthening – of ethnic loyalties. This position gained considerable support from Milton Gordon's argument that while it seemed to be true that the immigrants were 'acculturated' ('behaviorally assimilated'), they none the less were not 'structurally' assimilated in that they continued to maintain distinct subsocieties based on intra-ethnic marriage. The important theoretical issue, however, is not the extent of acculturation of structural assimilation, nor the saliency of ethnocultural identity in voting behavior, but how these processes are to be conceptualized as class experiences. In part this involves abandoning the ethnic-class dichotomy of much immigrant and ethnocultural historiography, in part it involves dropping class consciousness as a criteria of class, and in part it means viewing the urban immigrant experience not as one of assimilation but of the accommodation of immigrants – utilizing their cultural resources – to the structure of class relations, and to the opportunity structures confronting them. But above all, it involves understanding the character of this process and its consequences as the creation and recreation of ethnically-based working-class cultures.

25 W. Kornblum, *Blue Collar Community* (Chicago: Univ. of Chicago Press, 1974: 18, 32, 21, 17, 83, 69). Kornblum's study neatly dissolved what otherwise might appear as a paradox in so called 'ethnic studies'. For on the one hand researchers have noted

that for a whole range of social behaviors – school attendance, fertility, age of marriage, associational activities – ethnic differences disappear pretty quickly leaving class differences as the major determinant; yet, on the other hand, researchers have noted the simultaneous eruption of strong ethnic communities and institutions in American cities. The paradox can be partially dissolved in terms of Milton Gordon's distinction between behavioral acculturation and structural dissimilation, but it is much more convincing I think, to view it in a larger, more inclusive process of the development of ethnically differentiated working class cultures.

26 W. L. Yancey, E. P. Ericksen and R. N. Juliani, 'Emergent Ethnicity: A Review and Reformulation,' *American Sociological Review* 41, 3, June 1976: 399-400.

27 See Dawley, ch. 2; Laurie, ch. 4.

28 See Bellingham, 58-72.

29 By the 1840s the American working class had developed – alongside its faith in democratic republicanism – an instrumentalist and economistic view of political life: politics was a source of patronage and jobs and therefore a means to economic security, for some mobility. This view of politics was reinforced in subsequent years by the growing ethnic stratification of the labor market. Denied access to stable and respectable jobs, many immigrant groups – the Irish were the first to do it – turned to politics. For much of the working class, politics, quite literally, worked. And later, after the beginning of the twentieth century, this instrumentalist and economistic political culture was reinforced by the final destruction of artisanal work and cultures, the waning of the significance of the producer ideology and its version of democratic republicanism, and the appearance of consumerism. In this context, the Lynd's description of the formation of working-class culture in Muncie, Indiana, in the early decades of the twentieth century is as apocalyptic as it is poignant. That this culture failed to heal what Sennett and Cobb call the 'hidden injuries of class' – the psychological scars of low self-esteem, self-doubt, and the personalizing of failure, the sacrificial attempts to make power out of one's love, the ambivalences of the conflict between fraternity and achievement – has not diminished its capacity to prevent the development of a public political culture. See R. and H. Lynd, *Middletown* (New York: Harvest Books, 1929: 75-79, 80-81); S. Ewen, *Captains of Consciousness* (New York: McGraw Hill, 1976; W. E. Leuchtenburg, *The Perils of Prosperity* (Chicago: Univ. of Chicago Press, 1958 ch. 9); J. Tipple, *Crisis of the American Dream* (New York: Pegasus, 1968, chs 4, 6); R. Sennett and J. Cobb, *The Hidden Injuries of Class* (New York: Vintage, 1972); L. Rubin, *Worlds of Pain* (New York: Harper, 1976); M. Komarovsky, *Blue Collar Marriage* (New York: Vintage,

1967). For further discussion, see Przeworski, 374-5.

30 The best short story of these conflicts is J. Brecker, *Strike* (Greenwich, Conn: Fawcett Premier, 1974).

31 In general I am more convinced by the approach of Jones and Foster to the question of the labor aristocracy than I am by Hobsbawm's. For an excellent discussion, see Bellingham, and the review articles by H. F. Moorhouse, 'The Marxist Theory of the Labor Aristocracy,' *Social History* 3, 1, January 1978; and I. Field, 'British Historians and the Concept of the Labor Aristocracy,' *Radical History Review* 19, Winter 1978-9: 61-86.

32 My information on the shoemakers and printers is drawn from the published writings of Dawley and Laurie, and the unpublished work of Len Wallock who is currently completing a PhD in history at Columbia University. See also M. Burawoy, 'Toward a Marxist Theory of the Labor Process,' *Politics and Society* 8, 3-4, 1978: 267-374; S. Hirsch, *Roots of the American Working Class: The Industrialization of Crafts in Newark, 1800-1860* (Philadelphia: University of Pennsylvania Press, 1978); C. and S. Guffen, *Natures and Newcomers* (Cambridge: Harvard University Press, 1978, ch. 7, 8, 9 esp.); D. Nelson, *Managers and Workers* (Madison: Univ. of Wisconsin Press, 1975); Dawley, *Class and Community*, chs 1-3; R. Edwards, *Contested Terrain* (New York: Basic Books, 1979); D. Montgomery, *Workers Control in America: Studies in the History of Work, Technology and Labor Struggles* (Cambridge: Cambridge University Press).

33 See for example E. Shorter and C. Tilly, *Strikes in France, 1830-1968* (Cambridge Mass.: Harvard University Press, 1974); D. Montgomery, 'Strikes in Nineteenth Century America,' *Social Science History* 4, 1, Winter 1980: 81-104; E. Hobsbawm, *Laboring Men* (London: Weidenfeld & Nicolson, 1964).

34 Dawley, *Class and Community*; Laurie, *Class and Culture*; Dawley and Faler, 'Working Class Culture and Politics in the Industrial Revolution; Sources of Loyalism and Rebellion,' *Journal of Social History*, Summer 1976; D. Montgomery, 'The Shuttle and the Cross: Weavers and Artisans in the Kensington Riots of 1844,' *Journal of Social History*, 1974; Hirsch, *Roots of the American Working Class*, 1978.

35 To take Philadelphia as an example, the split between home and work did not, however, assume any real spatial significance until the end of the nineteenth century, some fifty years after the Kensington Riots which symbolizes as well as any other political event in antebellum America, the dominance of localistic, ethnic, republicanist politics over industrial class struggle as the major locus of political activity. In Detroit, on the other hand, as Olivier Zunz points out, a pattern in which work and residence were sharply spatially differentiated developed almost from the beginning of industrial expansion, a trend quite consistent with a work-

residence explanation of the bifurcation of working-class politics, although whether in fact they were causally connected he has not yet determined. It seems likely, consequently, that it will not be possible to make judgments about the general impact of the separation of work and residence upon working-class political culture until a large number of urban contexts are investigated and the impact that conflicts over home-ownership, zoning, public housing, bussing, freeways, rates have upon working-class political culture, is assessed. For Philadelphia, see Hershberg *et al.*, *A Tale of Three Cities*, 1979, and references cited therein; for Detroit, see O. Zunz, 'Work and Residence in Detroit,' paper presented to Social Science History Association, Cambridge, Mass., October 1979.

36 On machine politics and working-class politics see H. Gosnall, *Machine Politics Chicago Style*, 2nd edn. (Chicago: Univ. of Chicago Press, 1968); J. Allswang, *Bosses, Machines and Urban Votes: An American Symbiosis* (Port Washington, N.Y.: Kennikat Press, 1977); E. C. Banfield, *Urban Government* (New York: Free Press, 1961); M. Ebner and E. Tobin (eds), *The Age of Urban Reform: New Perspectives on the Progressive Era* (Port Washington, N.Y.: Kennikat Press, 1977); L. Wendt and H. Kogan, *Bosses in Lusty Chicago* (Bloomington: Indiana University Press, 1971); and D. Hogan, 'Schooling and Society in Chicago, 1880-1950', unpublished MS., University of Pennsylvania, Graduate School of Education, ch. 3.

37 For a review and analysis of the research literature on these and related topics, see my 'Making It in America: Work, Education and Social Structure,' forthcoming in D. Tyack (ed.), *Work and Education* (Stanford: Stanford University Press, 1981).

38 See M. Katz, 'On the Origins of the Institutional State,' *Marxist Perspectives* no. 4, 1978; D. Rothman, *The Discovery of the Asylum* (Boston: Little, Brown & Co., 1971); S. Schlossman, *Love and the American Delinquent* (Chicago: Univ. of Chicago Press, 1978); G. Grob, *Mental Institutions in America: Social Policy to 1875* (New York: Free Press, 1973); P. Boyer, *Urban Masses and Moral Order in America 1820-1920* (Cambridge: Harvard Univ. Press, 1978).

39 See M. Katz, *Class Bureaucracy and Schools* (New York: Praeger, 1975); D. Tyack, *The One Best System* (Cambridge: Harvard Univ. Press, 1974); R. Church, *Education in the United States* (New York: Free Press, 1976); S. Bowles and H. Gintis, *Schooling in Capitalist America* (New York: Basic Books, 1976); R. Dreeben, *On What Is Learned in School* (Reading, Mass.: Addison Wesley, 1968); E. Reimer, *School Is Dead* (Middlesex: Penguin, 1971); P. Aries, *Centuries of Childhood* (Middlesex: Penguin, 1973).

40 P. Violas, *Training the Urban Working Class* (Chicago: Rand McNally, 1978); Hogan, *Schooling and Capitalism*, chs 6, 7; Tyack, *One Best System*, Part II; Bowles and Gintis, *Schooling in Capital-*

ist America, chs 6, 7, 8, 9.

41 To date the only attempt to combine a structural and institutional history of American education is Bowles and Gintis' *Schooling in Capitalist America*. Bowles and Gintis describe the impact of the accumulation process upon the demand for labor and the character of the labor market structure, the growing role of educational certification in the opportunity structure, the effect of family background and educational achievement upon occupational attainment, the development of various mechanisms – particularly differentiated education and neighborhood schooling – that sort children and allocate them into the labor market, and the mechanisms of reproduction within the school, particularly socialization of children into acceptance of the capitalist social relations of production and the legitimation of meritocratic inequality. For Bowles and Gintis the 'logic' of educational development and organization is embedded in the logic of capitalism: the contradiction between accumulation and reproduction. This they demonstrate first by adducing evidence (1) of the structural correspondence between the social relations of work and education, and (2) the historical association between the development of capitalism and the development of education (Bowles and Gintis 1976: 224):

> We have been able to show more than a correspondence between the social relations of production and the social relations of education at a particular moment. We have shown that changes in the structure of education are associated historically with changes in the social organization of production. The fact that changes in the structure of production have parallel changes in schooling establishes a strong prima facie case for the causal importance of economic structure as a major determinant of educational structure.

Their next move is of a different kind: they claim these 'associations' and 'correspondences' exist *because* schooling contributes to the reproduction of capitalism: schools satisfy the labor demands of capital and inhibit the level of class struggle in society through the socialization of children into the social relations of production. Much of *Schooling* is taken up with establishing the historical associations, delineating the structural correspondences, and describing the mechanisms – chiefly political – linking the economy and schooling, but the heart of the book, theoretically speaking, is the analysis of the logic of capital accumulation and educational expansion and organization.

42 Gareth Stedman Jones' assessment of the impact of middle-class reforms upon working-class culture after 1850 in England is instructive, theoretically speaking, in this regard:

> . . . it is clear that by the beginning of the twentieth century

> a new working class culture had emerged in London. Many of its institutions dated back to the middle of the century. . . . This culture was clearly distinguished from the culture of the middle class and had remained largely impervious to middle class attempts to dictate its character or direction. Its dominant cultural institutions were not the school, the evening class, the library, the friendly society, the church or the chapel, but the pub, the sporting paper, the race course and the music hall.

Obviously, such conclusions can only be arrived at with a mode of analysis that is explicitly directed to the description and explication of concrete working-class experiences and behavior. See Jones, 'Remaking,' 478-9.

43 Katznelson, 'Class, Ethnicity and Urban School Politics, 1870-1930,' (NORC, University of Chicago, 1979: 64).

44 D. Hogan, 'Education and the Making of the Chicago Working Class, 1880-1930,' *History of Education Quarterly* 18, 3, Fall 1978: 227-70.

45 J. Kett, *Rites of Passage* (New York: Basic Books, 1977, ch. 6).

46 M. Katz and I. Davey, 'School Attendance and Early Industrialization in a Canadian City: A Multivariate Analysis,' *History of Education Quarterly* 18, 3, Fall 1978: 271-94.

47 S. Hirsch, *Roots of the American Working Class: The Industrialization of Crafts in Newark 1800-1860* (Philadelphia: Univ. of Pennsylvania Press, 1978).

48 C. Golden, 'Family Strategies and the Family Economy: The Role of Secondary Workers,' in T. Hershberg (ed.), *Toward an Interdisciplinary History of the City* (Oxford: Oxford University Press, forthcoming, 1980).

49 M. Katz and M. Stern, 'Fertility, Class and Industrial Capitalism: Erie County, New York, 1855-1915,' Graduate School of Education, Univ. of Pennsylvania, 1979.

50 Kett, *Rites of Passage*, chs 1, 6; M. Katz, *The People of Hamilton* (Cambridge: Harvard University Press, 1975, ch. 5); Katz and Davey, 'Youth and Early Industrialization.'

51 Kett, *Rites of Passage*, 169; Hogan, 'Education and the Making of the Chicago Working Class.'

52 Hogan, 'Schooling and Capitalism,' 407-14; Rubin, *Worlds of Pain*, chs 3, 7; M. Komarovsky, *Blue Collar Marriage* (New York: Vintage Books, 1967).

53 Hogan, 'Schooling and Capitalism,' ch. 9; Sennett and J. Cobb, *The Hidden Injuries of Class*, ch. 2.

54 R. and H. Lynd, *Middletown* (New York: Harvest, 1929) 187: 219-20.

55 Cited by C. Wirth, 'Cultural Conflicts in the Immigrant Family,' PhD dissertation, University of Chicago, 1925: 93.

56 *Denni Hlastel*, September 1919.

57 Rubin, *Worlds of Pain.*
58 Sennett and Cobb, 22-5.
59 There is still much obviously about this process that is not understood; for example, what are the relative significances of different aspects of a working-class experience: are parental experiences at work, position in the labor market, the nature of the opportunity structure, or the social relations of production more important? How significant are experiences in the church or in the community? Given that student educational aspirations have been found to be a critical determinant of educational performance at school, what are the determinants of student aspirations: family socialization methods, peer groups, prior success at school? How do working-class children reformulate their aspirations into lower 'Expectations' as a way of accommodating to the class realities of their world? How do we explain black educational aspirations which have remained consistently high for most of the twentieth century despite the low returns to education for blacks in the labor market? Are wages or family income or authority at work or cultural aspirations crucial to the determination of the educational aspirations and behavior of the labor aristocracy? See Rubin, ch. 2; Bowles and Gintis, ch. 5; M. Kohn, *Class and Conformity* (Homewood, Ill.: Dorsey Press, 1969); W. Sewell, R. Hauser, D. Featerman, *Schooling and Achievement in American Society* (New York: Academic Press, 1976); A. C. Kerchkoff, 'The Status Attainment Process: Socialization or Allocation?' *Social Forces* 55, 1976: 368-81; and Willis, *Learning to Labor.*
60 For further discussion, see D. Hogan, *Schooling and Capitalism: Chicago, 1880-1930* (forthcoming, 1982), chs 1, 9.
61 The one exception is Bowles and Gintis, *Schooling in Capitalist America.*
62 The best single study of progressive educational politics currently available is David Tyack, *The One Best System* (Cambridge: Harvard University Press, 1974).
63 Hogan, *Schooling and Capitalism*, ch. 7.
64 W. Thomas and F. Znaniecki, *The Polish Peasant in America* (New York: Alfred A. Knopf, 1927) 2: 1522-33.
65 Laurie, *Class and Culture*; Dawley and Faler.
66 For a review of the literature on the labor education thesis, see I. M. Paiva, 'Workingmen and Free Schools in the Nineteenth Century: A Comment on the Labor-Education Thesis,' *History of Education Quarterly* XI, 3, 1971: 287-302. See also R. T. Ely, *The Labor Movement in America* (New York: Thomas Y. Crowell and Company, 1886); A. Simons, *Class Struggles in America* (Chicago: H. Kerr and Company, 1906); F. T. Carlton, *History and Problems of Organized Labor* (Boston: D. C. Heath, 1911); P. R. V. Curoe, *Educational Attitudes and Policies of Organized Labor in the United States* (New York: Teacher College, Columbia Univer-

sity, 1926); M. Katz, *The Irony of Early School Reform: Educational Innovation in Mid-Nineteenth-Century Massachusetts* (Cambridge: Harvard University Press, 1968).

67 R. Merton, 'Bureaucratic Structure and Personality,' in *Social Theory and Social Structure* (Revised Edition) (New York: Free Press, 1957); R. Callahan, *Education and the Cult of Efficiency* (Chicago: Univ. of Chicago Press, 1962); Katz, *Class Bureaucracy and Schools*; J. M. Cronin, *The Control of Urban Schools* (New York: Free Press, 1973); Tyack, *The One Best System*, parts II and III.

68 Dreeben, *On What Is Learned in School.* See also T. Parsons, 'The School Class as a Social System,' *Harvard Educational Review* 29, 1959: 297-318; A. Inkeles, 'Social Structure and the Socialization of Competence,' *Harvard Educational Review* 36, 3, 1966: 265-83; A. Stinchcombe, 'Social Structure and Organizations,' in J. Y. March (ed.), *Handbook of Organizations* (Chicago: Rand McNally, 1965).

69 Bowles and Gintis, *Schooling*, ch. 5.

70 P. Bourdieu and J. C. Passeron, *Reproduction in Education, Society and Culture* (Beverly Hills, California: Sage, 1977).

71 M. Apple, *Ideology and Curriculum* (Boston: Routledge & Kegan Paul, 1979); M. Young (ed.), *Knowledge and Control* (London: Collier Macmillan, 1971); B. Bernstein, *Class, Codes and Control* vol. 3, (London: Routledge & Kegan Paul, 1977). For a useful short discussion, see M. Apple, 'The New Sociology of Education: Analyzing Cultural and Economic Reproduction,' *Harvard Educational Review* 48, 4, November, 1978: 495-503.

72 D. Kamens, 'Legitimating Myths and Educational Organization: The Relationship Between Organizational Ideology and Formal Structure,' *American Sociological Review* 41, April 1977: 208-19; J. W. Meyer, 'The Effects of Education as an Institution,' *American Journal of Sociology* 83, 1, 1977.

73 C. Jencks, *Inequality* (New York: Harper & Row, 1973), 135.

74 Willis, *Learning to Labor*, 171.

75 This is an area of research still in its embryonic stages. Willis provides no account of student's theory construction, the most promising research appears to lie in directions pioneered by Bob Connell, drawing upon cognitive development psychology. Sociolinguistics is also promising, but less in the manner undertaken by Bernstein, Bourdieu and Labov, than suggested by Noelle Bisseret. See Connell, *Ruling Class, Ruling Culture*, chs 7, 8, and his *The Childs Construction of Politics* (Melbourne: Melbourne University Press, 1974); for Bisseret, see *Education, Class Language and Ideology* (Boston: Routledge & Kegan Paul, 1979). For a useful discussion on the place of language in the production and reproduction of life, see Anthony Giddens, *New Rules*, 104-8. Toulmin's epistemological writings, drawing upon Wittgenstein

and contemporary philosophy of science, are important to understanding the epistemological problems in cognitive psychology and children's theory construction.

76 On aspirations and expectations, see Kerchkoff, 'The Status Attainment Process'; Hogan, 'Making It in America'; and Connell, *Ruling Class, Ruling Culture*, ch. 7.

77 R. H. deLone, *Small Futures* (New York: Harcourt, Brace, Jovanovich, 1979: 168).

78 Compared to the studies undertaken by the Centre for Contemporary Cultural Studies at the University of Birmingham, American ethnographers and sociologists have barely begun to develop a typology of the cultural form of the school. Currently the literature is composed of limited typologies of 'youth' culture (Coleman's *Adolescent Society*), a few remarkable personal reports by radical school critics of life in American schools (Herndon's *The Way It Spozed to Be*, and *How to Survive in Your Native Land*; Denison's *The Lives of Children*; Holt's *Why Children Fail*; Kozol's *Death at an Early Age*), a few general treatments of adolescent culture (Friedenberg's *The Vanishing Adolescent*, and *Coming of Age in America*), a few records (Richard Prior's 'Live in Concert'; Bruce Sprinsteen's 'Born to Run'), and an occasional movie ('Superfly,' 'Breaking Away').

79 For a discussion of the way in which these various mechanisms might work in different labor market structures, see my 'Making It in America.'

80 The reasons for the dominance of the inequality problematic are grounded in the legitimation and social policy needs of liberal capitalism, generating a research tradition that Habermas describes as 'rational-technical' or 'empirical-analytic.' See his *Knowledge and Human Interests* (Boston: Beacon Press, 1971); and *Theory and Practice* (Boston: Beacon Press, 1974). I thank Mark Stern for 'the Habermas connection.' For a fine general review of educational research, see J. Karabel and H. Halsey (eds), *Power and Ideology in Education* (New York: Oxford University Press, 1978), Introduction.

Chapter 3

Education, economy and the State

Martin Carnoy

Introduction

Traditional views of education and society emphasize the role that education plays in altering individual characteristics and the position of that individual in the economy, social structure, and polity. The focus of such views is on an institution (the school) and its relationship to individual youth. That does not mean that each pupil is treated as an individual case; to the contrary, individuals in their collectivity are immersed in a universal pool, and social and educational science attempts to find the universal norms and rules by which to understand the relation between institution and individual in that pool. We find that, at one and the same time, the individual is *universal* – is subject to behavior patterns that cut across culture, occupation, social position – and simultaneously is *separate*, each person responsible for himself or herself at this moment in history, separate from past history, past culture, and past interactions.

There *is* conflict in such analysis. Being separate, individuals struggle one against the other. But these struggles are resolved by universally accepted rules and regulations – universally accepted because they are fair and just: economic conflicts are resolved by the marketplace, particularly the price and wage system; social and political conflicts are resolved by the legal system, contained in the democratic State. And changes in these systems are arrived at by democratic consensus – the vote. Education, also part of the State, is therefore an expression of the consensual social mood, also subject to conflict, but a conflict which is acted out in the context of democratic decision-making and individual choice as to how much and what kind of education and training to take.

The Marxian view of education and society differs. It is class-based and historical. Individual behavior is the product of historical forces, rooted in material conditions. As material conditions change, through class conflict, so do relationships between individuals in different social positions, positions determined by the social organization of production and each person's relation to production (Karl Marx, preface to the *Critique of Political Economy* (1859)).

> In the social production of their life, men enter into definite relations that are indispensable and independent of their will, relations of production which correspond to a definite stage of development of their material production forces. The sum total of these relations of production constitutes the economic structure of a society, the real foundation, on which rises a legal and political superstructure and to which corresponds definite forms of social consciousness. The mode of production of material life conditions the social, political, and intellectual life process in general. *It is not the consciousness of men that determined their being, but, on the contrary, their social being that determined their consciousness.*

Thus, the organization of production – the social formation – and its historical development are central to the Marxian approach, for it is in this organization that we find the relations of human life, the meaning and value of individual characteristics, and the determinants of political power and social hierarchy. In capitalist production, capitalists (and more recently, managers) control and accumulate capital and are able, in the context of constant struggle with the working class, to shape society's development process, including its social mores and cultural formation. Both capitalist and worker consciousness are shaped by their relationship in production; it is this relationship itself which conditions individual social development and life styles. The individual and institutions are therefore the historical product of the development of the social formation and the relations of production.

Conflict in this approach is *not* resolvable by universal rules because such rules are class-based; they serve particular interests – the interests of the dominant class. So the market system and the State, far from being consensual, are the product of class domination and class struggle. The capitalist class – through its political power – is not only able to exploit the working class (those who only own their labor) but create a way of life which serves capitalist interests and leaves workers alienated and oppressed. The only resolution of the inherent conflict in this system of production is its replacement by another in which the working class has the political power to reorganize production and develop a different way of life.

This brings us to the problem of reproduction and its counterpart, social change. Since the Marxian approach considers capitalist society to be organized in the interest of capitalist and managers, how are the relations of production, the division of labor, and social classes reproduced from generation to generation? In the present version of the 'traditional' liberal view (pluralism), reproduction takes place through the selection of leaders who in some sense reflect the needs and wants of the electorate, at least that part of the electorate which is even interested in participating in politics and social change. According to this view, the present structure of capitalist society and its political counterpart, representative democracy, is acceptable to the mass of citizens. Change takes place through competition between élite groups who have different interpretations of how to achieve the greatest good within generally acceptable goals (Greenberg 1977: 36-42).

In the Marxian approach, this 'consensus' about the structure of society is absent; yet, capitalism continues to be the prevailing mode of production. Orthodox Marxist theories argue that reproduction is carried out largely by capitalists in the production sector itself – by a series of tactics which keep labor fearful of any attempts to organize against employers and maintain a division of labor along class lines. These theories also argue that the capitalist State is the repressive apparatus of the bourgeoisie, keeping workers in their place through the juridical system and the army/police.

More recent Marxian analyses, however, give greater weight in the reproduction process to superstructure. This is where schooling comes in. For it is in schooling that reproduction takes its most *organized* form: children go to school at an early age and are systematically inculcated with skills, values, and ideology which fit into the type of economic development suited to continued capitalist control. It is argued that through the schools and other superstructural institutions the capitalist class reproduces the forces of production (labor, the division of labor, and the division of knowledge) and the relations of production – the latter predominantly by the maintenance and development of a 'legitimate' ideology and set of behavior patterns (culture).

Reproduction in the interest of a particular social class automatically implies the existence of class antagonism and the potential for class struggle. It is this notion of class struggle inherent in all aspects of capitalist development and capitalist institutions, structure and superstructure, that forms the basis of a Marxian theory of social change. Capitalists' need to organize institutions for reproduction means that there is *resistance* to capitalists' concept of development and their necessary control of that development. Again, a Marxian analysis of schooling in the context of social change is couched in this over-all class struggle.

The role of the State and education

The general configurations of a Marxian approach to social change now have to be translated into a Marxian analysis of the educational system. This poses certain difficulties, since Marx himself dealt in a very limited way with public education. While it is worth going through what he and then Lenin said about schooling, to develop our analysis properly we have to turn to more recent Marxist writers. In particular, we will situate the analysis in the context of the discussion on theories of the State, a discussion which has been central to new developments in Marxian thought.

It is not only that the most interesting debate today among Marxists revolves around the role of the State: for practical reasons, any study of the educational system cannot be separated from some explicit or implicit analysis of the purpose and functioning of the government sector. Since power is expressed at least in part through a society's political system, any attempt to develop a model of educational change should have behind it a carefully thought out theory of the functioning of government – what we shall refer to as a 'theory of the State.' Yet, even if we didn't believe that an educational system has something to do with power in a society, we would still be compelled to discuss government in understanding formal education: in the nineteenth and twentieth centuries education has been increasingly and primarily a function of the State.

Marx, Lenin and the State

In keeping with Marx's view of superstructure discussed above, Marxian formulations of the capitalist State reject the idea of state power as ideally directed to the common good, the general interest, or to equal justice for all, even in western-style capitalist democracies. Marx argued that the State is an apparatus for the exercise of power not in the general interest but in the interest of a *particular group* – the 'ruling class'. And while he recognized that this State could be separated at moments in history from the *direct* control of the bourgeoisie (see for example *The 18th Brumaire of Louis Bonaparte*), the general Marxian concept of the State conforms to a historically determined society where the State acts as a committee of the dominant class, a committee whose particular function is to organize and concentrate repressive power in order to maintain that dominant class's control over production.

We can summarize the fundamentals of Marx's (and Engel's) theory of the State as follows:

First, as we have shown, Marx viewed the material conditions of a society as the basis of its social structure and of human consciousness. The form of the State, therefore, emerges from the relations of production, not from the general development of the human mind, nor from the collective of men's wills. The capitalist State is the political expression of the class structure inherent in production. Since the bourgeoisie – in capitalist production – has a particular control over labor in the production process, it also extends this power relation to the State and to other social institutions.

Second, Marx (unlike Hegel) argued that the State, emerging from the relations in production, does not represent the common good, but is the political expression of the dominant class. The capitalist State is a response to the necessity of mediating class conflict and maintaining 'order', an order which reproduces the bourgeoisie's economic dominance (*The 18th Brumaire*). Engels developed this concept further when he contended that the State has its origins in the need to control social struggles between different economic interests, and that this control is carried out by the economically most powerful class in the society (Engels 1968: 155-7).

> But in order that these antagonisms, classes with conflicting economic interests, shall not consume themselves and society in a fruitless struggle, a power, apparently standing above society, has become necessary to moderate the conflict and keep it within the bounds of 'order'; and this power, arisen out of society, but placing itself above it and increasing alienating itself from it, is the state . . . As the state arose from the need to keep class antagonisms in check, but also arose in the thick of the fight between the classes, it is normally the state of the most powerful, economically ruling class, which by its means becomes also the politically ruling class, and so acquires new means of holding down and exploiting the oppressed class.

Third, both Marx and Engels emphasized the State as a repressive apparatus of the bourgeoisie: an apparatus to legitimize power, to repress, to enforce the reproduction of the class structure and class relations. Even the juridical system is an instrument of repression and control since it sets the rules of behavior and enforces them in line with bourgeois values and norms.

It was on this basis that Lenin developed a much more detailed analysis of the bourgeois State (*State and Revolution*). His view – written in 1917 in the context of the Russian Revolution – was that the State is an organ of class rule and that while the State attempts to reconcile class conflict (in Engels' words, '. . . a power seemingly standing above society became necessary for the purpose of moderating the conflict. . .') that conflict is *irreconcilable*. Although bourgeois democracy *seems* to allow participation and even control of political (and economic) institutions by the working class if they choose to exercise that political power, and thus *seems* to produce a state apparatus which is the result of class reconciliation, Lenin argued that since the State is the repressive apparatus of a dominant class, the necessity for it does not exist unless there is class conflict (Lenin 1965: 8-9). Thus, the destruction of the bourgeois State is essential to any revolutionary change, and this destruction has to take place through armed confrontation, since the State *is* the armed force of the bourgeoisie. The key here is that the State in capitalist societies, for all its 'democratic' institutions, is controlled directly by the bourgeois class, and that its primary function is coercion. By meeting this coercive force head on, and defeating it by superior arms, the bourgeois State will be destroyed, the instrument of oppression will be removed, and the proletariat will take power, utilizing its own force of arms to protect that power.

Given this analysis of the State, it is not surprising that public schooling should not have had an important function in Marx's or Lenin's analysis of capitalism (Lenhardt 1979; Sarti 1979). Both certainly understood the class nature of capitalist schooling at all levels of the educational system. As Marx wrote in his *Critique of the Gotha Program* (1972: 30):

> What idea lies behind these words? Is it believed that in present day society (and it is only with this that one has to deal) education can be *equal* for all the classes? Or is it demanded that the upper classes also be compulsorily reduced to the modicum of education – the elementary school – that alone is compatible with the economic conditions not only of the wage workers but of the peasants as well? . . . . If in some states of the latter country (the United States) higher educational institutions are also 'free', that only means in fact defraying the cost of the education of the upper classes from the general tax receipts . . . it is the State that needs to receive a severe education from the people.

Furthermore, he argued (in that same *Critique*) that 'an early combination of productive labor with education (is) one of the most potent means for the transformation of present-day society' (Marx 1972: 32). Yet, in the first volume of *Capital*, written seven years earlier, he considers public education as a concession to the working class, opposed by capital owners on the grounds that education interfered with children's work. There are clear indications in *Capital* that Marx viewed public education as a working-class victory, inconsistent with capitalists' attempts to reduce manual labor to its lowest, least intelligent level (Marx 1906: 397-400, 436-7).

Lenin did not agree. He provided a much more complex analysis of bourgeois education and its implications for the transition to socialism. First, he recognized the relation between bourgeois education and the political apparatus, and in that sense, education's ideological function in a State which he considered as primarily 'society's organized and concentrated violence.' At one level, then, he did not put much *weight* on the role of schooling in maintaining capitalist relations of production (in contrast to repression), but at another, he saw that one of the greatest obstacles to socialist education was the strong connection between the inherited educational system and the former bourgeois political apparatus (Lenin 1978: 161). He also considered formal education as important in combatting bourgeois culture and enlightening the masses (Lenin 1978: 109).

> The bourgeoisie themselves . . . made their own bourgeois politics the cornerstone of the school system, and tried to reduce schooling to the training of docile and efficient servants of the bourgeoisie. . . . They never gave a thought to making the school a means of developing the human personality. And now it is clear to all that this can be done only by socialist schools, which have inseparable bonds with all the working and exploited people and wholeheartedly support Soviet policy.

While Lenin saw that capitalist knowledge and particularly the way that knowledge was presented in schools was also intimately tied to capitalist relations of production, he insisted that socialism had to be built through capitalist knowledge (1978: 142-4): 'Proletarian culture must be the logical development of the store of knowledge mankind has accumulated under the yoke of capitalist, landowner, and bureaucratic society' (1978: 142). In some sense, then, he accepted that some part of capitalist education is separate from capitalist relations of production; that knowledge (technology) is culturally objective and previous knowledge can be utilized unaltered in building socialism. His post-revolutionary speeches can therefore be interpreted as advocating a separation between 'political' education very different from its bourgeois counterpart, the replacement of the rote system of learning, the joining of book learning with practical work, but the preservation of the fundamental elements of knowledge presented in the bourgeois schools.

Martin Carnoy

Gramsci and the State

Given Lenin's and then Stalin's influence over Marxian theory in the nineteen twenties and thirties, it is remarkable that Gramsci was able to provide a powerful reinterpretation and expansion of Marx which differed so greatly from Leninist and Stalinist thought. Gramsci developed Marx's concept of superstructure and elevated it to an important position in understanding how societies function. That development, in turn, also gave the State and public education a new importance, both in describing the capitalist social system and in formulating strategies for alternatives to capitalism.

Gramsci took Marx and Engels's concept of 'hegemony' in civil society (as expressed in Marx, *The German Ideology* 1970: 64-5) and made it a *central* theme of his own version of the functioning of the capitalist system. Quite similar to Marx's and Engels's notion, this hegemony, in Gramscian terms, meant the ideological predominance of bourgeois values and norms over the subordinate classes. While for both Marx and Gramsci, the nature of civil society is the key to understanding capitalist development, in Marx's definition, civil society is structure (relations in production), and for Gramsci, civil society is also *superstructure*, which represents the active and positive factor in historical development; it is the complex of ideological and cultural relations, the spiritual and intellectual life, and the political expression of those relations. It is these rather than the structure which becomes the focus of the Gramscian analysis.

In elevating hegemony to a predominant place in the science of politics, he emphasized much more than earlier writers the role of superstructure in perpetuating classes and preventing the development of class consciousness. And he assigned to the State part of this function of promoting a single (bourgeois) concept of reality, and therefore, gave the State a more extensive (enlarged) role in perpetuating the class structure. Much more than Lenin, Gramsci saw the mass of workers as being able to develop class consciousness themselves, but he also saw the obstacles to consciousness as more formidable in western societies than Lenin had imagined. It was not merely lack of understanding of their position in the economic process that kept workers from comprehending their class role, nor was it only the 'private' institutions of society, such as religion, which were responsible for keeping the working class from self-realization, but it was the *State itself* that was involved in reproducing the relations of production. In other words, the State was much more than the coercive apparatus of the bourgeoisie; it included the superstructural hegemony of the bourgeoisie (see Anderson, 1977, for a further discussion of hegemony and the State).

The importance of the State as an apparatus of hegemony for Gramsci is therefore still *rooted in the class structure*, a class structure defined by and tied to the relations in production. This is key to understanding Gramsci: he provides an analysis of historical development which rejects the narrower Marxist version of civil society as incomplete and not relevant to the Western (Italian) situation. But at the same time, he does not deny that the superstructure – hegemony and its extension into and through the state apparatus – is intimately connected to relations in production: '. . . for though hegemony is ethical-political, it must also be economic, must necessarily be based on the decisive function exercised by the leading group in the decisive nucleus of economic activity' (Gramsci 1970: 161). It is not the *separation* of superstructure from structure which Gramsci stresses, but rather the dialectical relation between them (see the exchange between Norberto Bobbio and Jacques Texier in Mouffe (1979), for a further disccussion of this point). Hegemony and the hegemonic function of the State emanates from both the nature of the bourgeoisie as an ideologically all-encompassing class *and* its particular position of economic power in capitalist society. It is Gramsci's treatment of hegemony which explains the development (or lack of development) of working-class consciousness, so important to any Marxist political analysis.

Gramsci raises man's thought (consciousness) to a newly prominent place in the 'philosophy of praxis' (as he calls Marxism). *Control of consciousness is as much or more an area of political struggle as control of the forces of production*: 'Furthermore, another proposition of the philosophy of praxis is also forgotten: that "popular beliefs" and similar ideas are themselves material forces' (Gramsci 1971: 165). The State, therefore, as an instrument of bourgeois domination (as part of the civil society) *must be involved in the struggle over consciousness*, must be an intimate participant in that struggle. Bourgeois development is not only carried out through the development of the forces of production but through hegemony in the arena of consciousness. The State is involved in this *extension*, not only in the coercive *enforcement* of bourgeois economic power. Without the power (control) in the arena of struggle over consciousness (and only then), Gramsci argues, the bourgeoisie will try to fall back on the coercive power of the State as its *primary* instrument of domination. Otherwise, coercive forces remain in the background, acting as a system of enforcement and threat but not overt coercion.

If the arena of consciousness for Gramsci is the primary struggle between the dominant and subordinate classes, then how do things change? How do the subordinate classes overcome the hegemony of the dominant classes? There are three parts to the answer Gramsci gives to these questions: First, the concept of 'crisis of hegemony', derived in part from Marx's analysis of the *18th Brumaire*; second, the concept of the 'war of position'; and third, the role of the intellectuals.

Briefly, Gramsci contends (as did Engels and Marx before him) that there are periods of history in which social classes become detached from their political parties; that is, the class no longer recognizes the men who lead the parties as its expression. When this happens, the situation becomes dangerous, because violent solutions can occur, and the traditional means of using the State to maintain dominant class hegemony deteriorates. In this moment, those elements of the society – bureaucracy, Church, high finance, and other institutions which are less subject to the pressures of public opinion (according to Gramsci) increase their power and autonomy. How do these crises occur? They are the result of unpopular actions of the ruling classes (through the State), or the increased political activism by previously passive masses. In either case they add up to a 'crisis of authority.' This is what Gramsci calls the 'crisis of hegemony, or general crisis of the State' (1971: 210).

The 'war of position' is based on the idea of *surrounding* the State apparatus with a counter-hegemony, a hegemony created by mass organization of the working class and by developing working-class institutions and culture. 'A social group can, and indeed must, already exercise leadership (i.e., be hegemonic) before winning governmental power (this indeed is one of the principal conditions for the winning of such power' (1971: 207)). The basis of Gramsci's strategy, then, was not to organize workers and peasants in order to wage a frontal attack on the State, but to establish working-class organizations as the foundations of a new culture – the norms and values of a new, proletarian society. This proletarian hegemony would confront bourgeois hegemony in a war of position – of trenches moving back and forth in an ideological struggle over the consciousness of the working class – until the new superstructure had surrounded the old, including the State apparatus. Only at that time would it make sense to take over State power, since only then would the working class in fact control social values and norms to the point of being able to build a new society using the state apparatus.

Gramsci and education

This brings us to Gramsci's analysis of intellectuals, an analysis that has direct bearing on his conception of education and the role that education plays both in hegemony and counter-hegemony. Gramsci defined two types of intellectuals: 'traditional' professional intellectuals whose position in the 'interstices' of society has a certain trans-class aura about it; and 'organic' intellectuals – any person who is possessor of a particular technical capacity, and the thinking and organizing elements of every social class. Traditional intellectuals function to build the hegemony of the dominant class. Most of these are 'organic' to the dominant class; that is, they come from the dominant class and help in 'directing the ideas and aspirations of the class to which they organically belong' (Gramsci 1971: 3). The dominant classes also reach into the subordinate for additional traditional intellectuals to give homogeneity and legitimacy to the dominant group – to create an ideology which transcends classes. These working class traditional intellectuals cease to be organically linked to their class of origin: they, along with their dominant class organic counterparts, are for Gramsci agents of the bourgeoisie (Gramsci 1971: 12).

It is from this position on intellectuals in the context of hegemony, that we can understand Gramsci's position on public education. For Gramsci, the role of the traditional bourgeois educational system is to develop 'organic' intellectuals from the bourgeois classes and to reach into the subordinate classes for additional intellectuals to give homogeneity and self-awareness to the dominant group. As we noted above, the traditional intellectuals who come from the subordinate groups, while they are not distinguished professionally from their organic counterparts, are – for Gramsci – different: they cease to be organically linked to their class of origin. But Gramsci also recognized that for most of the subordinate class, the schooling they receive is different than that for the children of the bourgeoisie. The school system is class-divided despite the impression it gives of producing upward mobility – of being democratic.

What then is the role of formal schooling (if any) in Gramsci's strategy of the 'war of position'? Gramsci recognized that state schooling was class structured, part of the ideological apparatus of the bourgeois State and a contributor to bourgeois hegemony. He recognized that the educational system produces intellectuals which give the bourgeoisie 'homogeneity and an awareness of its own function not only in the economic but also in the social and political fields' (1971: 5). These intellectuals play an important role as 'the dominant group's deputies exercising the subaltern functions of social hegemony and political government' (1971: 12). Some of these intellectuals come from subordinate groups; for Gramsci, they cease to be organically linked to their class of origin.

Yet, there are those working-class intellectuals (like Gramsci) who *do* remain organically linked to the working class. It is up to the revolutionary party to weld together disaffected bourgeois professional (traditional) intellectuals, professional intellectuals from the proletariat, and organic proletarian intellectuals, the thinker-organizers with a conscious conception of the world which transcends their class interests. The first two categories of thinkers are definitely formed in the schools, even though their consciousness is raised *outside* the schools, in political activity directed by the revolutionary party. The third category, most crucial for Gramsci (since it is the organic non-professional intellectuals who give *permanence* and mass participation to the revolutionary party), would be formed outside the state school system. For Gramsci, as for Lenin, it would be the *Party* which is fundamental for developing proletarian consciousness.

But unlike Lenin, Gramsci could not accept state schools as having little relevance to bourgeois domination: he saw clearly – as we have discussed – that the type of knowledge taught and teacher/pupil relations in the school are crucial to intellectual formation and hence to the maintenance of bourgeois hegemony. Schools therefore not only favor the children of the bourgeoisie, they are *important* to the maintenance of class-based power relations. The schools, therefore, cannot be a source of developing proletarian hegemony; they can provide knowledge of a certain intellectual *motive*, but this knowledge can only be used for the proletariat by being *transformed* through a process of establishing proletarian hegemony. Gramsci also argued that once proletarian hegemony was established, the schools, as part of the bourgeois state apparatus, would have to be different, and he outlined the essentials of those differences – socialist education for Gramsci had to be part and parcel of a socialist culture, norms and values and relations that broke with the existing bourgeois values. Since bourgeois schools were essential to a domination of one class over others, proletarian schools would have to reflect a participative, mass-base society, where teachers who promoted these values and knowledge served the proletariat.

Nevertheless, this transformation takes place *after* the establishment of proletarian hegemony. Just as Gramsci sees the bourgeois State as surrounded, by proletarian hegemony, so he implicitly envisages the schools *surrounded* by an educational process directed through the revolutionary party. We will show below how two French sociologists, Baudelot and Establet, argue that, in addition to schooling ideology, French working-class pupils are subject to counter-ideological apparatuses (the working-class parties and union). These are the bases of proletarian hegemony – they *surround* the bourgeois ideological apparatus with a counter-ideology. At the same time, the existence of a counter-ideology emerges from and contributes to a *crisis of bourgeois hegemony*. The counter-ideology, in a Gramscian analysis, develops *resistance* to the ideology inculcated in state schools, and this interferes with the maintenance of the dominant hegemony – resistance becomes part of the crisis in domination.

The key to a Gramscian educational strategy, then, is the creation of counter-hegemony *outside* the state schools, and the use of this counter-hegemony to develop organic intellectuals, to mobilize disillusioned bourgeois intellectuals and those traditional working-class intellectuals who have become separated from their class origins, and to contribute to resistance by working-class youth to the use of schools as centers of maintaining and extending bourgeois dominance.

Althusser: ideology and the State

Louis Althusser has had an important influence on French philosophy and on Marxist educational analysis both in France (Baudelot and Establet) and the United States (Bowles and Gintis). In his major essay on the State and education (Althusser 1971), he carries forward the Gramscian idea of accenting the superstructural and cultural aspects of class domination more than its economic aspects. Relative to Marx and Levin, then, Althusser moves reproduction from the base to the superstructure. His essay, therefore, emphasizes the capitalist State as both the bourgeoisie's repressive and as its ideological apparatus, the latter intimately related to the educational system. His view can be summarized in four main points:

(1) Every social formation (such as capitalism) must reproduce the conditions of its production at the same time as it produces, and in order to be able to produce. That is, for feudalism or capitalism or socialism to function as such, it must reproduce the productive forces – the land, labor, capital, and knowledge that enter into production *and* the existing relations of production which are inherent in that production system – the hierarchy of power and control among landowners and serfs (feudalism), capitalists and labor (capitalism), directors or party officials and workers (socialism).

These productive forces, Althusser points out, are not reproduced at the level of firm but at the level of *class*: for example in capitalism, the capitalist class, as a class, reproduces labor power by paying workers wages with which they can feed themselves and raise the next generation of workers. The level of wages paid is determined by class struggle over the length of the working day and the hourly wage. But workers have to be reproduced as more than just homogeneous workers. They

have to be 'diversely skilled and therefore reproduced as such' (Althusser 1971: 131). This diversity is defined by the socio-technical division of labor – its different jobs and positions.
(2) How is the reproduction of the division of labor and skills carried out under capitalism? Here Althusser discusses a point left obscure by Marx and Engels, who treated labor as 'homogeneous' (undifferentiated) except in terms of Engels's conception of an 'aristocracy' of the working class, paid off by capitalists to divide workers against themselves. Althusser argues that unlike social formations characterized by slavery or serfdom, this reproduction of the skills of labor power tends (Althusser 1971: 132)

> decreasingly to be provided for 'on the spot' (apprenticeship within production itself), but is achieved more and more outside production: by the capitalist education system, and by other instances and institutions.

Reproduction here is not the same issue that Gramsci (and also Althusser, below) raises about the function of education (schooling) in reproducing the *relations* of production (the norms, values, and conception of society). In this instance Althusser brings education into another aspect of the picture – the development of particular production *skills* for *particular* people. As we shall discuss in more detail below, this 'know-how' is divided into different categories for different students-workers-to-be; furthermore, the schools also teach different children *different rules of behavior* depending on the type of job that they are likely to hold. Thus (Althusser 1971: 133),

> The reproduction of labor power reveals as its *sine qua non* not only the reproduction of its 'skills' but also the reproduction of its subjection to the ruling ideology or of the 'practice' of that ideology, with the provision that it is not enough to say 'not only but also' for it is clear that *it is in the forms of ideological subjection that provision is made for the reproduction of the skills of labor power*.

(3) Now, what about the reproduction of the relations in production? How is this reproduction secured? Althusser answers: 'I can say: for the most part, it is secured by the legal-political and ideological superstructure.' Furthermore, he argues that (again) '*for the most part*, it is secured by the exercise of state power in the state apparatuses, on the one hand the (repressive) state apparatus, on the other the ideological state apparatus' (Althusser 1971: 148). 'For the most part' because the existing relations of production are first reproduced by the reward and punishment system of production itself – by the materiality

of the processes of production. But repression and ideology are, of course, present in production.

Althusser's conception of reproducing the relations of production is almost identical to that of Gramsci's *hegemony*, except that for Althusser the State has a much more important role in reproduction than for Gramsci ('for the most part' v. the 'first line of trenches'). For Althusser, the State attains an overwhelming important position relative to the effects on reproduction of the production system itself and its related 'private' institutions, both in the reproduction of labor power (not discussed by Gramsci) and in reproducing the *relations* of production. And the most important single institution in the State used to carry out these two types of reproduction is the *school* (1971: 132, 152):

> (1) . . . this reproduction of the skills of labor power . . . is achieved more and more outside production: by the capitalist educational system . . . ; [and] (2) I believe that the ideological State apparatus which has been installed in the *dominant* position in mature capitalist formations *as a result of a violent political and ideological class struggle* against the old dominant ideological State apparatus, is the educational ideological apparatus.

Like Gramsci, Althusser roots superstructure in structure. The superstructure is determined 'in the last instance' by the base (1971: 135):

> the upper floors (the superstructure) could not 'stay up' (in the air) alone, if they did not rest precisely on their base.

He goes on to say that the determination of the superstructure by the base 'in the last instance' is thought of by the Marxist tradition in two ways: (1) that there is relative autonomy of the superstructure with respect to the base; (2) there is reciprocal action of the superstructure on the base – changes in the superstructure affect the base as well as the more traditional concept that changes in the base affect the superstructure.

(4) The State, then, is rooted in the base. It is – in Althusser's view – also the 'machine' of repression, which 'enables the ruling classes to ensure their domination over the working class, this enabling the former to subject the latter to the process of surplus-value extortion . . .' (1971: 137). He therefore returns me to the original Marxist conception of the State as the 'essential point' (1971: 137):

> The State apparatus, which defines the State as a force of repressive execution and intervention 'in the interests of the ruling classes' in

> the class struggle conducted by the bourgeoisie and its allies against the proletariat, is quite certainly the State, and quite certainly defines its basic 'function'.

Althusser thus considers the educational system as fundamental to *both* the reproduction of labor power and the reproduction of the relations of production in the capitalist social formation. It is the school, he argues, that reproduces the diversified skills required of the modern labor force. 'What do children learn at school?' he asks (Althusser 1971: 132). Two things, he answers: For one, they learn techniques – how to read, write, add, elements which may be rudimentary or thoroughgoing depending on the child's social class, but which are all useful in the different jobs in production. But besides these techniques and knowledges, children at school also learn the rules of good behavior (1971: 132):

> the attitude that should be observed by every agent in the division of labor, according to the job he is 'destined' for: rules of morality, civic and professional conscience, which actually means rules of respect for the socio-technical division of labor and ultimately the rules of the order established by class domination.

Thus, Althusser argues that the school provides for the capitalist social formation the two most important elements for the reproduction of its labor power: the reproduction of its skills, and the reproduction of its submission to the rules of the established order, i.e., 'a reproduction of submission to the ruling ideology for the workers, and a reproduction of the ability to manipulate the ruling ideology correctly for the agents of exploitation and repression, so that they, too, will provide for the domination of the ruling class "in words" ' (1971: 132-3).

In addition to the reproduction of labor power, however, the schools also contribute to the reproduction of the relations in production. It is the ideological state apparatus which 'certainly has the dominant role' in this reproduction (1971: 155-7):

> . . . it is by an apprenticeship in a variety of know-how wrapped up in the massive inculcation of the ideology of the ruling class that the *relations* of *production* in a capitalist social formation, i.e., the relations of exploited to exploiters and exploiters to exploited, are largely reproduced. The mechanisms which produce this vital result for the capitalist regime are naturally covered up and concealed by a universally reigning ideology of the School, universally reigning because it is one of the essential forms of the ruling bourgeois ideology: an ideology which represents the School as a neutral

> environment purged of ideology (because it is . . . lay), where teachers respectful of the 'conscience' and 'freedom' of the children who are entrusted to them (in complete confidence) by their 'parents' (who are free, too, i.e., the owners of their children) open up for them the path to freedom, morality and responsibility of adults by their own example, by knowledge, literature and their 'liberating' virtues.

Nicos Poulantzas: The organic relationship between State and base

Somewhat unique among the authors we have surveyed so far, Poulantzas makes his central focus the State rather than Marxist theory as a whole. Yet, since he comes from the Gramscian tradition of elevating the superstructure to a prominant place in understanding social structure and change, his studies of the State encompass most of the crucial elements in a theory of society (Poulantzas 1973, 1975, 1976, 1978).

He begins with two important formulations:

(1) The role of the state apparatuses, he argues is 'to maintain the unity and cohesion of a social formation by concentrating and sanctioning class domination, and in this way reproducing social relations, i.e., class relations' (1975: 24-5). Political and ideological relations are materialized and embodied, as material practices, in these apparatuses. Furthermore, social classes are *defined* by their relationship to the economic apparatuses – the place of production *and* the state apparatuses. So social classes and the class struggle are part of the economic and political relations in a society: 'The apparatuses are never anything other than the materialization and condensation of class relations' (1975: 25). He separates this concept from the institutionalist-functionalist analysis which has class relations arising from the situation of agents in institutional relationship. Weber, for example, had class relations emerging from relations of power in hierarchical institutions. But Poulantzas contends that state apparatuses do not have 'power' of their own – institutions have not 'power' as such, nor is power inherent in hierarchical relations. Rather, the State 'materializes and concentrates class relations, relations which are precisely what is embraced by the concept "power". The State is not an "entity" with an intrinsic instrumental essence, but is itself a relation, more precisely the condensation of a class relation' (1975: 26). It is therefore not hierarchy that creates classes, but social classes that produce the particular configuration of power in the state apparatus. At the same time, the state apparatus is inherently marked by the class struggle – class

struggle and the state apparatus cannot be separated.

(2) The second formulation defines the relationship of the State to the *dominant* class. Since the State apparatuses are the 'materialization and condensation of class relations', they attempt, in some form, to represent the interests of the dominant class. Poulantzas describes this representation in two stages of capitalism: one is the competitive stage, and the other, the more recent monopoly capitalism. In both stages, the State is 'separated' from the economic structure, giving it the appearance of having relative autonomy from the dominant class. This separation is carried out, according to Poulantzas, as part of the relative separation of the politic from the economic that is specific to capitalism. It derives from the 'separation and dispossession of the direct producers from their means of production that characterizes capitalism' (1975: 98). He argues that historically, capitalist ideology has promoted the concept of democracy in the political sphere as a sufficient condition for a mass democratic society. One person – one vote has shifted attention away from the class struggles inherent in capitalist production; political 'democracy' has *displaced* the struggle from the economic sphere to the voting booth. In the political arena – including the juridical apparatus – all members of society are equal. Rich and poor, old and young, (ultimately) women and men, all have the same power (one vote) to change or maintain the social situation. The inequality of economic relations is thus downgraded in capitalist society in favor of equality in political life. This diffuses conflict in economic matters, because it diverts such conflict into the political arena, into a contest over power in the state apparatus (Poulantzas 1973). In Poulantzas's view, the State, under these ideological conditions, has to 'appear' autonomous and neutral while at the same time keeping the dominated classes fractionalized and represent the interest of the dominant classes' power bloc. Relative autonomy is 'simply' the necessary condition for the role of the capitalist state in class representation and in the political organization of hegemony. But with the displacement of class struggle from the economic to the political arena, the State itself becomes subject to the struggle – it becomes, in Poulantzas' words, 'the condensation of a balance of forces' (1975: 98):

> The correspondence between the state on one hand, which ensures the social formation's cohesion by keeping the struggles that develop within the limits of the mode of production and by reproducing the social relations, and the interests of the hegemonic class or faction on the other hand, is not established by means of a simple identification or reduction of the state to this fraction. The state is

> not an instrumental entity existing for itself, it is not a thing, but the condensation of a balance of forces. The correspondence in question is established rather in terms of organization and representation: the hegemonic class or fraction, beyond its immediate economic interests which are of the moment or at least short-term, must undertake to defend the overall political interest of the classes and fractions that constitute the power bloc, and thus its own long-term political interest. It must unite itself and the power bloc under its leadership. In Gramsci's profound intuition, it is the capitalist state with all its apparatuses, and not just the bourgeois political parties, that assumes an analogous role, with respect to the power bloc, to that of the working class party with respect to the popular alliance, the 'people'.

In monopoly capitalism, the State takes on economic functions that it did not have in the competitive stage. Poulantzas argues that the State has a general economic function even in the competitive stage, but this consists of reproducing the general conditions of the production of surplus value: taxation, factory legislation, customs duties, and the construction of economic infrastructure such as railways, all constitute the liberal State's intervention in the economy within the context of the class struggle. In monopoly capitalism, however, the relation of separation between economic and political which we described above is modified: the difference between politics and ideology (the conditions of production) and the economic space (the relations of production) becomes much less clear. The State enters directly into the relations of production – into the valorization of capital (1974: 101). Thus, in the monopoly stage of capitalism, the functions of the State are extended directly into production as a result of the crises of capitalist production itself.

Poulantzas therefore extends Gramsci's concept of a State which is part of the (ideological) hegemony of the dominant class plus the repressive apparatus. Poulantzas sees both of these functions as carried out in the context of a class struggle (therefore the State is part of and the result of the class struggle), and sees the State as playing an economic role in reproducing power (1978: 49). Thus the apparatuses of the State are not simple appendices of power – the State is 'organically present in the production of class power' (1978: 50) – it is therefore fundamental to the conditions under which the bourgeoisie can accumulate and control capital, displacing struggle and conflict to the political from the economic sphere.

Briefly, Poulantzas sees the capitalist State differently from Gramsci in two fundamental ways: first, the State has economic functions (production) as well as ideological-repressive ones (reproduction). The State therefore enters directly into the economy as part of its attempt to resolve contradictions in production. Second, the State, in all its functions (ideological, repressive, and economic) is marked by contradiction because class struggle takes place *in the heart of the State* even as it tries to maintain an external dominant class hegemony. He insists that the State is neither an instrumentalist depository (object) of dominant class power, nor a subject which possesses an abstract power of its own outside the class structure. It is rather a place for the dominant class to strategically organize itself in its relation to the dominated classes. It is a place and center of the *exercise* of power but it does not possess its own power. Furthermore, according to Poulantzas, under monopoly capitalism the ideological and repressive functions of the State are less important than under commercial capitalism. 'The ensemble of State operations are presently organized in accord with its economic role' (1978: 186).

It is this last point which separates Poulantzas from Althusser. The State not only reproduces labor power and the relations of production through ideology and repression, it intervenes directly in the crises of production by investing in private production (defense industry in the United States, for example) and by producing itself, rescuing sectors of industry which have become unprofitable but are crucial employers and domestic suppliers of particular goods. This makes even the class struggle in production transcend the state apparatuses, since the State is a producer. (An analysis of labor-management conflicts in the State can be found in O'Connor, 1974).

Given this analysis, how does Poulantzas characterize the role of schooling in a capitalist society?

(1) Capitalist production, Poulantzas points out, is marked by a social division of labor which separates intellectual work from manual work, by a separation of technology from the process of work itself, by the use of science and technology to *rationalize* power, and by an organic relation between this separated intellectual work and political domination – a relation between knowledge and power. The State incorporates this division into all its apparatuses. 'It is in the capitalist State that the organic relations between intellectual work and political domination, between knowledge and power, are achieved in the highest form' (1978: 61). This State is the corollary and the product of this division, also playing its own role in the division's constitution and reproduction.

The State takes knowledge and participates in its transformation into language and rituals which serve to separate knowledge from mass consumption and from manual work – from the process of direct production. This legitimizes a particular ideology – the dominant bourgeois values and norms – by changing that juridic-political ideology into a set of technocratic 'facts' and decisions based on 'scientific' studies, on 'expertise', etc. But, Poulantzas argues, the knowledge-power relation is not only an ideological legitimization: the capitalist separation of intellectual from manual work also concerns science itself. The State incorporates science into its mechanisms of power – intellectual 'experts' as a body of specialists and professionals are controlled – through their financial dependence on the modern state apparatuses. They have largely become functionaries, in one form or another, of the State. For example, in the United States, a very high percentage of *all* professionals (about 25 to 30 per cent) are directly employed by Federal, state, or local government (many in education), while another important percentage depends indirectly on state expenditure for their livelihood (defense contracts, research contracts in private universities). Research is heavily influenced by such government contracts, and they also have an important effect on new technology.

(2) Education, for Poulantzas, is of course part of the state apparatuses; as we have seen, he analyzes these apparatuses in terms of their relation to the class structure – to the social formation in a particular place and period of time. Therefore, to understand the role of education in capitalist society, it is necessary to understand the social formation of such a society. . . . And since this formation changes from competitive to monopoly capitalism to the present stage of 'advanced' monopoly capitalism, the role of education must also change. Poulantzas is the first of the authors analyzed here who discusses education in the context, not only of class struggle, but of a class struggle whose nature changes as a result of previous struggle. The social formation changes in response to conflict, which changes the nature of conflict itself.

(3) Poulantzas insists – in contrast to the institutionalist-functionalists and in accord with Althusser – that the ideological apparatuses neither create ideology, nor are they even the sole or primary factors in reproducing relations of ideological domination and subordination. Ideological apparatuses, he argues, only serve to fashion and inculcate the dominant ideology. And, 'just as the ideological State apparatuses do not create the dominant ideology, so the revolutionary apparatuses of this working class (the party) do not create proletarian ideology; they rather elaborate and systematize it, by producing revolutionary theory' (Poulantzas 1975: 31).

(4) But he disagrees with Althusser about the 'division' of apparatuses into economic, ideological, and repressive. On the one hand, all social institutions are ideological (1978: 32):

> As the unit of production in its capitalist form, an enterprise is also

> an apparatus, in the sense that, by means of the social division of labor within it (the despotic organization of labor) the enterprise itself reproduces political and ideological relations affecting the phases of the social classes. In other words, the reproduction of the all-important ideological relations is not the concern of the ideological apparatuses alone: just as not everything that goes on in 'production' involves only the 'economic', so the ideological apparatuses have no monopoly over reproducing the relations of ideological domination.
>
> . . . this reproduction of the places of social classes does not just involve the ideological state apparatuses and the economic apparatus; it also involves the branches of the repressive state apparatus in the strict sense. . . . If the branches of the capitalist state's repressive apparatuses intervene in the reproduction of the places in social classes, this is because, while their principal vote is that of repression, which is what distinguishes them from the ideological apparatuses, they are not limited to this; they have also an ideological role, generally secondary, just as the ideological apparatuses themselves also have a repressive role, which is generally secondary.

So, all institutions are involved in the reproduction of the class structure and all have a multitude of functions. The separation of the ideological and repressive apparatuses, for Poulantzas, obscures the role that each plays. Schools, then, are not only an ideological apparatus but also a repressive one. And this is a key to understanding their functioning: it is not enough to say that the schools inculcate pupils with dominant ideology; the institution as such has repressive functions: by law, it can *force* students to behave in particular ways, to conform over to a predetermined behavior pattern, and it has the periodical power to keep pupils in school, in other words it can keep them physically bound to be exposed to the ideological training it chooses to give them and this in co-operation with the state's repressive apparatuses.

On the other hand, Poulantzas argues that the State (with its ideological and repressive apparatuses) plays – in the latest phases of capitalist development – an increasingly important *economic* role. It is impossible to understand this economic role with an analytical framework which strictly differentiates the state apparatuses. Poulantzas views the State's economic role as a direct intervention to raise the level of surplus value and therefore of capitalist level of exploitation (1978: 195). It is an effort to counteract the falling rate of profit. And while there are specific apparatuses of the State which have this as their *principal* function, representing different fractions of the dominant bourgeoisie (for example, many of the regulatory agencies directly controlled by the large corporations in that sector – the Commerce Department, the Small Business Administration, etc.), the ideological and repressive apparatuses themselves according to Poulantzas play crucial economic roles in the advanced monopoly stage of capitalist development. 'Defense' has become a key element in the economy, with public expenditures on weaponry forming the base of entire production sectors. Thus, the repressive apparatus is at the same time a means to subsidize capital.

Education plays a similar role. First, besides contributing to the reproduction of class structure through the distribution of youth into the various functions of the labor force based on their educational qualifications and the reproduction of the relations through its ideological inculcation of bourgeois values (see Althusser), the educational apparatus provides the technical skills and know-how necessary to the continued accumulation of capital. In other words, workers pay for the education of their children and part of the return to these expenditures goes to maintain the level of surplus value – to subsidize the rate of profit. So the schools not only distribute knowledge, they produce it (Poulantzas 1978: 195):

> This displacement (from the extensive exploitation of labor force and extracting absolute surplus to the intensive exploitation of labor and the extraction of relative surplus) henceforth assigns to the State an essential role in the enlarged reproduction of the labor force, a reproduction in which the space is extended well beyond the process of qualifying that labor force.

The production of knowledge is carried out not only in schools; it is produced by the State itself, through universities (public and private – the latter through government grants). The State plays an increasingly important role in guiding the direction of innovation by investing heavily in research and development – the space program, defense expenditures, grants to universities, all contribute to a particular direction of innovation, one that contributes to the extraction of surplus value by private capital and therefore reproduces the class structure.

Furthermore, the educational apparatus itself is an important source of employment for special groups in the society. Gramsci discusses the place of rural intellectuals (1971: 14) and the relationship of the state bureaucracy to the medium and small rural bourgeoisie (1971: 212). In advanced monopoly capitalism the teachers and administrators of the school system form part of the 'new petty bourgeoisie' (Poulantzas 1975: 191-332), drawn from sections of the working class. The US educational system has provided 'upward mobility' for women and minority males (more than half of all women and minority men professionals in the US are employed by the government, and most of those in local government, primarily in the education system (see Carnoy, Girling, and Rumberger 1975)). The schools are therefore also employers and contribute – through that employment – to the sustainment of bourgeois ideology about the justice of capitalism. (5) As we have seen, Poulantzas views state apparatuses as not only on an equal footing with the production sector in terms of the importance of reproduction versus production (the contributions of Gramsci and Althusser), but he considers both the State and the productive base to be part of and shaped by class struggle. Thus, the educational system is not simply an instrument of the bourgeoisie as a means to effect its domination over other groups but is the *result* of struggle between dominant and dominated groups. This struggle in other apparatuses, notably the production sector, affects the school system, just as that struggle shapes the state apparatuses in general. Furthermore, once the State, including the educational system, attempts to displace class conflict into the political arena, the educational process itself becomes part of the struggle. This struggle takes place between fractions of the dominant bourgeoisie, especially between those fractions who would like to see a greater expansion of the educational system for the training of more qualified labor, and those who see such an expansion as a threat to bourgeois hegemony, but also between the working class and the dominant groups. Thus, Poulantzas's model portrays education as the result of conflict and engaged in it – as the result of contradictions and the source of new contradictions (for a further development of these views, see Carnoy and Levin *et al.* 1982 forthcoming). This analysis suggests a dynamic in the development of the educational system and its relation to other apparatuses which is missing both in Gramsci and Althusser.

Recent empirical studies of education

Having reviewed Marxist theories of the State and what they imply for education, we can now turn to some specific recent analyses of education in two countries – France and the US – and assess their contribution to our understanding of schooling. The first of these, *Reproduction*, by Pierre Bourdieu and Jean-Claude Passeron, is *not* a Marxian analysis. We should be quick to point that out. The other two – Baudelot and Establet's *L'école capitaliste en France* and Bowles and Gintis's *Schooling in Capitalist America*, are works in the Marxian tradition and fit into the theories we have presented above. The principal common feature of all three is that they see a State and a public educational system which serve the interest of a particular social class – a dominant group which is able, in some way, to amass more political power than other social groups. The perspectives also share, therefore, the concept of a class-structured school system. But this is where the similarity ends: each of the views we present here has a different concept of the dynamic of change in the forces which dominate schooling and work; to a large extent, in fact, the analyses presented are either not dynamic at all, or deal only partially with the forces shaping changes in institutions. In this sense, they have important shortcomings which a more complete model would have to address. In the last section of the essay this is exactly what we attempt to do: we propose a model of education in advanced capitalist societies (which could, however, be adopted either to dependent capitalism or to socialist societies) more in Poulantzas's view of the State and its relation to the base.

The French institutional functionalists

For Bourdieu and Passeron (1977), the principal function of schooling is to reproduce the hierarchical relations between different groups or classes in the society and to legitimize those relations. The *raison d'être* of formal education is to reproduce the existing power relations, and it is these examinations which – in the French system parto generation, without having to use violence. The principal means to achieve this reproduction is through the system of teaching, and the language used as the basis of communication in the schools – the dominant group's 'cultural arbitrary': a system of values, norms and languages.

In addition, the schools impose a selection system based on examinations, and it is these examinations which – in the French system particularly – effectively separate dominant class children for promotion to higher grades while leaving children of the subordinate groups behind. In explaining the selection system (Why does the 'working class' get selected out, but the children of the 'higher class' continue on?), Bourdieu and Passeron stress the 'cultural capital' that different social classes bring to the school. According to them, academic changes for the French pupil are already fixed in primary school. The system places children from different social classes into different academic situations, so that workers' children are systematically put at a disadvantage relative to children from higher classes. Social class not only determines how far pupils will go in school, but, the kind of work they will do and the life they will lead, especially their attitudes and values. But, according to them, social class is important only because it is reproduced in the structures of the school system: it is the *basis* of division in the schools, but is *not* itself the source of adult values and attitudes.

In this model, then, it is apparatuses and institutions (particularly the educational system) which determine social groups (classes) with class relations arising from the situation of people (students) in institutional relations. Social classes themselves have no meaning except as they are certified and developed by some institution like the schools. As we shall see, this is a fundamentally different interpretation of the function of the schools from those models that see the apparatuses of the State (including schools) as *reflecting* a class struggle which *arises in the production system* and then becomes embodied in the institutions of the State themselves.

In delegating the power of selection to the school system, the privileged classes can appear to abdicate to a 'neutral' institution the 'power of transmitting power from one generation to the other and thus to be renouncing the arbitrary privilege of the hereditary transmission of privileges' (Bourdieu and Passeron 1977: 167). And, they argue, the school is in fact autonomous in some ways from the society as a whole (1977: 167), but this autonomy is a façade for the reproduction of the social hierarchy.

Although they never make clear why the working class is so *willing* to accept the false meritocracy of the schools, two arguments are implicit in their analysis: (1) as the allocator of social roles, the school holds out scholastic success, no matter how limited for working-class children, as the sole possibility of economic and social success (for example, 1977: 165); and (2) the operation of the school system is seen, in some broad sense, to serve the general welfare, largely through its stated goal of meeting manpower and cultural needs.

Bourdieu and Passeron's analysis provides us with a number of important insights into the education system and the process of teaching and selection, especially with regard to the 'class' nature of that process. They suggest a different kind of understanding of the relationship between an idealized, *meritocratic* school and the reality of who gets to higher levels of schooling and into higher-paying jobs. Yet, there are – from the standpoint of the development of an alternative perspective on education and work – a number of difficulties with their analysis.

First, it is mechanistic and deterministic: it is limited to showing how, through the school and *largely* through the school, each individual inherits the social class of his/her father. The school reproduces that which *exists*, and even though there may be school reforms, the reproductive function of the schools continues essentially unchanged. For example, before the French school reform of the 1960s, selection into higher levels of schooling took place with examinations at the end of primary school, with very few working-class children entering the academic track of the lycée, and even fewer reaching the university. With the reform, according to Bourdieu and Passeron, selection became somewhat more subtle, since all children allegedly had equal opportunity for high school academic training for four years and were only selected for academic training (leading to the grands écoles and universities) in the last three years of high school, but class and sex selection continued to be highly effective even after the reform (see also Levin 1978).

Second, there is no discussion of the *source* of power relations. We learn that the 'dominant group' is able to use the school system to reproduce its power. But where did the dominant group get its power in the first place? The implication of the analysis is that the source of power is power itself: being dominant allows you to reproduce your dominance through the institutions of society that you control because you are dominant. It gives you control over knowledge, learning, attitudes and values. Neither does resistance to power by the subordinate classes have any base but resistance itself. Resistance is implicit only, appearing solely in the fact that the schools are accepted by the working class against its own 'interest'. This theory of relations between groups has repercussions for Bourdieu and Passeron's characterization of education: school is seen as part of increased domination with a reduction of physical violence – the internalization of repression and the substitution of *symbolic* for real violence. Consent of the working class to domination is *assumed* and explained by the pedagogic authority and autonomy of the schools. Nowhere is evidence presented that the working class has indeed accepted a class-based schooling or dominant class domination. Nor are other forms of repression – openly violent forms which complement the more ideological nature of the schools – discussed.

The first and second difficulties lead to the third: their analysis has no dynamic: we are left without an analysis of how the system *changes*. Reform occurs, but the operation of the school system is fundamentally the same. Why did the reform occur in the first place? Why the necessity to mystify the real power relations in society and the function of the schools? Is this necessity simply a function of dominant group need to reduce physical violence? Bourdieu and Passeron do make one attempt to give their model dynamic character: they argue that it is possible to look at the school selection system over time, noting that although the level of schooling in a particular age group has been rising in France since the early sixties (as a result of the reform), the distribution of probability of reaching the highest levels of schooling for the different social classes remained the same. But neither the causes of reform, nor the internal dynamic of the schools is touched at all. By relying on the argument that the schools are relatively autonomous from other institutions of society, Bourdieu and Passeron lose the important interconnections of change and conflict which occur in the productive apparatus, in the political system, and in the schools.

A Marxian view of the French system

The assumption of power expressed through institutions – fundamental to the institutionalist-functionalist view – makes schooling itself a *definer* of the class structure. We have shown that the Marxian analysis rejects this assumption. Schools are not a 'subject' of power; institutions themselves are not considered the 'creator' of class or hierarchical relations. The power structure is defined by the system of production, outside the school system; what education does *reflects* class relations inherent in the way commodities are produced. A Gramscian-Althusserian view of *how* education reflects these class relations is derived from Althusser's emphasis on reproduction through the ideological function of the schools; this emphasis, in turn, is based on Gramsci's work. It leads to a strategy of working-class resistance to ideological domination in the schools while building a counter-ideology through other, non-school counter-hegemonic apparatuses, particularly the revolutionary party.

The Gramscian-Althusserian view of French education finds its clearest expression in the work of Charles Baudelot and Roger Establet (1975). While agreeing with much of what Bourdieu and Passeron say about education as a reproductive institution, Baudelot and Establet's interpretation differs on two essential points: (1) they describe French power relations in terms of their material base. Thus, they consider that one class dominates others and uses the school system to reproduce this relation of dominating-dominated, but the group or class which does this is not an abstraction in capitalist society, it is the bourgeoisie which dominates other groups and the bourgeoisie's power is rooted in their economic position as the owners of capital and controllers of investment. In this view, the school – which is outside the production system – is fundamental to the reproduction of capitalist's dominant position, primarily through the inculcation of dominant *ideology*; (2) they suggest, however, that working-class pupils do not fully accept this attempt by the dominant class to impose its ideology; i.e., the working class *does resist* in the schools. This provides the beginning of a dynamic which is absent from Bourdieu and Passeron's work.

Using the Althusserian typology, they argue that in France, primary school is the principal place where the division into class-based tracks is achieved, and this for two purposes: (1) the division of labor – individuals are distributed into materially different social and economic positions; and (2) the inculcation of bourgeois ideology. Both these functions are accomplished simultaneously and constitute the same purpose of the school system. However, they contend that the functions are not carried out harmoniously at all; ideological imposition creates contradictions and struggles, primarily through resistance by working-class youth to an ideology which rejects proletarian values developed in other institutions (in France, leftist unions and political parties provide the basis of a counter-ideology which is antithetical to school curriculum and teaching practices).

Contradictions occur because of the necessity of imposing the dominant ideology in two different and incompatible forms: one form is supposed to produce an uncomprehending proletariat which *accepts* bourgeois values and at the same time learns what is necessary for its participation in production; the other form creates the extenders and interpreters of the bourgeois ideology itself with a different body of knowledge for a different type of participation in production.

Unlike the institutional-functionalist view, this interpretation claims that the working class does *not* fully accept the school system in the face of apparent injustices. While the institutional-functionalists contend that the schools are able to gain acceptance because of their autonomy and pedagogical authority, Baudelot and Establet suggest that the schools may have autonomy, but physical coercion plays an important role in keeping pupils there (compulsory schooling, for example), and there is significant resistance to the dominant ideology. A certain amount of class consciousness exists in proletarian youth, they argue, but since the school is separated from production and the pupils are not subject to exploitation, the 'effects of proletarian class consciousness occur in school in forms very different from those that they take in production' (Baudelot and Establet 1975: 179). The resistance of working-class pupils in school is not an economic resistance, then, but an ideological one – working-class pupils perceive the imposition of the petit-bourgeois version of the dominant ideology as a 'veritable provocation'. These resistances are often violent, where the pupils attempt to deface and destroy the school, insult professors, etc. But more often, they simply display behavior which interrupts the process of socialization, which disturbs the culture of the school (1975: 186). According to Baudelot and Establet, the bourgeoisie must keep these individual and group resistances from burgeoning into a full-fledged transformation to a proletarian ideology – into a 'fusion of the scientific conception of history and of the concrete experience of the class struggle' (1975: 191).

Rather than speaking of institutional-functionalist *inequalities* in the school system, Gramscian-Althusserians like Baudelot and Establet argue that these are *contradictions* in the schools, '*inevitable contradictions* in the functioning of the school apparatus in which *the existence of two types of schooling*, camouflaged as the *single school*, is the evident proof. If the school apparatus had as its function to impose on the bourgeoisie the same *ideology, that couldn't take place, and is not in fact taking place, without struggles*' (1975: 312).

Yet, despite this dialectical element – the conflict between dominant and proletarian ideology in the schools – Baudelot and Establet do not establish any relationship between changes in the production system and changes in the education system, both of which should emanate from class conflict in their models. The lack of explanation leaves their treatment with distinct instrumentalist overtones: the education system is a direct instrument of the bourgeoisie, which uses schooling for its own ends, particularly imposing a dominant ideology and reproducing a division of labor which suits bourgeois needs. Baudelot and Establet's proposition that the schools are a means to control the formation of a proletarian ideology can be valid only when the government is tightly and directly controlled by the bourgeoisie.

Neither do they ever explain where contradiction in the schools leads; it is primarily a fixture of the system, produced by potential difficulties of attempting to impose the same ideology on all social classes. The best that could happen in such a model is that some portion of the proletariat resists the ideology imposed by the schools so that institutions producing a proletarian ideology can eventually establish what Gramsci called 'proletarian hegemony' – the dominance of proletarian values and culture.

A Marxian view of the US system

The best example to date of the Poulantzas version of structuralism is Bowles and Gintis's work on education in the United States (1976). They present a model which analyzes educational reform as a function of capitalist development – of changes in the production sector. Such changes in production – themselves a result of class conflict – determine the subsequent changes in the way schooling is called upon to reproduce the relations of production. Bowles and Gintis explicitly reject non-Marxist explanations of education's economic role in terms of 'the mental skills it supplies students and for which employers pay in the labor market' (1976: 9). Rather, they argue that the relation between the economy and education must be traced through schooling's effect on 'consciousness, interpersonal behavior, and [the] personality it fosters and reinforces in students' (1976: 9); therefore, any explanation of what schooling does depends on understanding the economy. Understanding the economy means – in the United States – understanding the essential elements of capitalism. And understanding capitalism means dealing with the social process of extracting surplus from workers, and the 'inherently antagonistic and always potentially explosive' process that requires.

Based on this view of the economic system, they outline five important implications of their analysis: (1) Economic inequality and personal development are 'defined primarily by the market, property, and power relationships which define the capitalist system'. Changes in inequality and development occur almost exclusively 'through the normal process of capital accumulation and economic growth and through shifts in the power among groups engaged in economic activity' (1976: 11). (2) The educational system is not an independent force in changing inequality or the nature of personal development. It is, in their terms, 'an institution which serves to perpetuate the social relations of economic life through which these patterns are set, by facilitating a smooth integration of youth into the labor force' (1976: 11). The system does this by legitimating inequality, allocating students to distinct positions in the economic hierarchy, reinforcing patterns of class, race and sex, fostering personal development which is compatible with the position of each student in the dominating/dominated subordinary relationships in production, and creating surpluses of skilled labor to put downward pressure on wages. (3) The educational system does not achieve these goals through the conscious intentions of teachers and administrators, but through the 'close correspondence between the social relations which govern close interaction in the work place and the social relations of the educational system' (1976: 12). (4) While the school system corresponds to the social relations in the workplace and serves 'the interests of profit and stability', it does not achieve this perfectly – it also develops some 'politicized egalitarian consciousness', and some misfits and rebels. This happens because the 'imperatives of profit often pull the school system in opposite directions', and because 'contrary forces external to the school system continually impinge on its operations' (1976: 12).

(5) The correspondence between school structure and job structure has 'taken distinct and characteristic forms in different periods of US history, and has evolved in response to political and economic struggles associated with the process of capital accumulation, the extension of the wage-labor system, and the transition from an entrepreneurial to a corporate economy' (1976: 13).

The model of education contained in these implications is thus very close to Poulantzas's view of capitalist state apparatuses: the education system reflects the relations in production (the inherent class relations) and acts to support (reproduce) them. This is an important function of the State and it is important in the over-all understanding of how capitalism works. As capitalism changes, the role of the schools changes as well. Moreover, the school does not act perfectly to achieve this reproduction – as a state apparatus, it is also marked by contradiction and conflict.

Bowles and Gintis' empirical work and subsequent analysis, however, accentuates certain of these relationships and not others. Despite their detailed and insightful explanations of the role of schooling in American society, they grant very little autonomy to the educational system in that over-all analysis, nor do they provide us with much understanding of the contradictions and the nature of the class struggle in the educational (superstructural) apparatus, nor of the eventual effect that struggle has on relations in production and the capital accumulation process, especially as education becomes an increasingly important mediator of contradictions in production. Rather, the accent is put on the role of education in *mediating class conflict in production*: US educational history is developed in terms of a dominant fraction of the ruling class using the educational system creatively to mediate class struggle in the economy.

There are three principal implications of their interpretation. First, the all important point that the dominant group in the ruling class turned and turns to superstructure to attenuate conflict in the base (supporting Althusser's view), but that the *class conflict* in the superstructure is *not* particularly successful in influencing the shape of the educational system – neither its organization nor its content (Bowles and Gintis 1976: 240):

> The evolution of U.S. education over the last century and a half was the result of a compromise – granted an unequal one – between the capitalist class and the very social classes it had unintentionally but nonetheless inexorably created. Though the business interests often struck their compromise under severe duress, and – as we have seen in numerous cases – did not always prevail, they were highly success-

> ful in maintaining ultimate control over the administration of educational reform. Working people got more schooling, but the form and content of the schooling was more often than not effectively out of their hands.

Second, Bowles and Gintis put primary emphasis on the *reproductive function* of the schools in all the different stages of US capitalist development. Reproduction is defined in the Althusserian sense: the reproduction of labor power – the allocation of skilled labor to different parts of the hierarchy based on pupil worker's social class background – and the reproduction of the relations of production. Thus, the reproduction of economic inequality and the legitimation of that inequality (as well as the legitimation of capitalist relations in production) receive top billing in the role that education plays. This does not mean that they ignore schools' function to enhance labor power in general and to produce innovation – to increase the skill level of workers and the productivity of capital as a means of maintaining capital accumulation, but they do accent the ideological repressive over the economic functions of schooling. To some extent, this changes in their analysis of university education and reform in the most recent stage of capitalist development (1976: 201-23), as we should expect, given the apparently higher level of skill content in higher levels of schooling and the role of universities in producing knowledge. Furthermore, the role of schools as employers, particularly as employers of minority and woman professionals with all the implications for the social mobility myth inherent in that role, is not discussed. Therefore, the economic-ideological function of the schools is generally less important than the ideological-repressive, even in the later stages of capitalist development.

Third, Bowles and Gintis do much better in analyzing the correspondence of the economic sector (structure) and the education system (superstructure) than in analyzing contradictions in the superstructure and its implications for the base. The principal purpose of their work, indeed, is to show the close connection between changes in the economy and changes in education, to focus on the close relation between changes in capitalist relations in production and educational reform. Their analysis of educational alternatives proposed in the 1960s as possible ways of humanizing education or making it less unequal therefore concentrates on showing that none of these alternatives can achieve more than marginal improvement in the face of an unchanged economic system (Bowles and Gintis 1976: 262-3).

> Many of the reforms discussed in this chapter are feasible within the context of present day U.S. society. . . . All would, with hard work,

> have the effect of improving, to some degree, the future lives and present comforts of our youth. As such, they are desirable indeed. However, we have argued that none, within its own framework, is capable of addressing the major problems facing U.S. society today. . . . Only revolutionary reforms have this potential. . . . The notion that the U.S. school system does – or ever can, under capitalism – effectively serve the interests of equality or human growth is going by the boards.

It is at this last point that their analysis departs most from the work of Poulantzas or even Gramsci. For if the contradictions in superstructure are essential to understanding capitalist crises; that is, if the State and its apparatuses are also subject to class struggle, then struggle in the schools can serve directly the process of change, and it is even possible to conceive that the schools in a capitalist society could become largely disfunctional to capitalist reproduction. The point is that Bowles and Gintis' analysis does not discuss this possibility, even though – in theory – their model allows for it. Because of their emphasis on the close ties between capitalist production relations and school reform (in its extreme form an instrumentalist view), they lose sight of the possibility that superstructure may gain in the process an autonomy which allows it to become a focus of revolutionary struggle. This could have implications for production itself, or at least for the struggle in the production sector. In a Gramscian analysis, this possibility would focus on the crisis of hegemony and the development of a counter-hegemony, particularly action in the schools which would tend to produce more working-class organic intellectuals (raise consciousness among working-class youth in the schools). In a Poulantzas view, increased control of the schools by working-class parents and youth within the context of a capitalist economy and petit-bourgeois consciousness, might allow for the increased development of alternatives which are contrary to capitalist interests, even though the State as a whole and the production structure would not be in a similar phase of conflict. Ultimately, then, Bowles and Gintis seem to reject the Poulantzas view that struggle within the state apparatuses can be a useful move in the over-all class struggle – at least they reject the possibility that the State or any of its apparatuses *can* be used for radical reform in the face of capitalist control of production. A broader interpretation of their work would argue that it is much less fruitful to struggle in the ideological apparatus than in the base itself. In either case, schools as a place of conflict seem to have much less importance in their analysis then schools as *mediators*, and this reduces the potential for them as points of raising consciousness and accentuating conflicts in the rest of the society.

A new interpretation

Baudelot/Establet and Bowles/Gintis have argued (correctly, we think) that the dominant bourgeoisie in capitalist societies *tries* to use schooling – along with other superstructural institutions (Gramsci's notion of bourgeois hegemony) – to *mediate* contradictions in production; i.e., to reproduce (in Althusser's terms) the social class-based division of labor and to reproduce the relations in production.

Both works are important analyses of education in advanced capitalist societies. However, in light of Poulantzas's past and most recent contributions – the concept of class struggle displaced from the base into the superstructure (1973) and the relationship between class conflict-created contradictions in the superstructure and the ever-present struggle in the base (1978) – we feel that the Baudelot/Establet and Bowles/Gintis analyses lack three important elements:

(1) Neither Baudelot/Establet nor Bowles/Gintis provides an adequate understanding of the process of contradiction and change in production and its relation to contradiction and change in education. As we have suggested, the French study emphasizes contradictions in the educational system without relating change in production to changes in the educational system (nor, by the way, the relation between contradictions in education and their effect on the base). Bowles and Gintis, on the other hand, develop an excellent analysis of educational change and its relation to production, but essentially provide no analysis of contradictions in the superstructure (State/education) and its relationship to class struggle in the base.

(2) The Gramscian and Althusserian influence has successfully separated the base (production) from social reproduction, and the ideological aspects of reproduction from its repressive aspects. Poulantzas argues (and we agree) that these divisions are artificial and incorrect. An important part of reproduction takes place in the base itself (Marx's analysis) – perhaps the most important part: the reserve army of unemployed, fear of unemployment, the reward structure, Taylorism and piece work, and the very success of capitalist accumulation in the advanced industrial countries to raise workers' living standard over a long period of history, all are *real* features of capitalist reproduction that are indeed ideological and repressive, but are not per se part of the ideological or repressive apparatuses of the State.

(3) Baudelot/Establet and Bowles/Gintis, in this Althusserian tradition, put primary emphasis on reproduction through the ideological apparatus of the State (hence the 'ideological' role of the educational system). The economic functions of the State in advanced capitalist economies, analyzed by Poulantzas in his most recent works (1975 and

1978) and by O'Connor in the US (1974) are disregarded, and therefore, so are the economic functions of the educational system. While these functions have fundamental ideological content, it is also critical to an analysis of the educational system to separate them out: as Lenin suggested, on the one hand elements of schooling may be important to the capital accumulation process (even in a post-capitalist society) and thus also important to reproduction; and, as Poulantzas argued on the other, economic functions of schooling are a source of contradictions which work their way back into the base.

Our model of education (Carnoy and Levin, forthcoming, 1982) begins with contradictions arising from class struggle in the base. These are *inherent* contradictions: under capitalism the return to capital must come from labor, and labor neither owns capital *nor controls its investment and deployment*. Bowles and Gintis have dealt with this point at length in their study, so there is no reason to review it again here. Struggle in the base leads to attempts by capitalists to 'mediate' that struggle, and one of the ways that mediation takes place is through the public educational system, as our previous review of education and theories of the State makes clear.

Before going on to spell out the specific manner in which education carries out this mediating function, and the contradictions which arise out of that process of mediation, there are two critical points to be made.

(1) Capitalists attempt to deal with contradictions in the base primarily in a *direct* manner. That is, contrary to the stress put by Althusser on the ideological reproduction of labor power and the relations of production through the state apparatuses, we cannot forget that capitalist relations in production are reproduced *in the base itself* by three principal means: (a) a reserve army of unemployed, created in various ways, which produces fear among workers of losing their jobs, and thus slows down or prevents organizing into unions, increasing productivity and keeps downward pressure on wages; (b) Taylorism, speed-up, and segmentation of labor markets, which attempt to increase productivity and control workers' use of time, and divides workers against each other; and (c) the favorable accumulation of capital and the resultant increase of average wages.

Reproduction, therefore is still handled largely within the base itself: workers continue to work in the alienating conditions of capitalist production not only because they are taught to 'believe' in the capitalist system and to accept their role in it ('socialization' or the creation of 'false consciousness') but because (a) they are afraid of the consequences of struggle against capitalists/managers; (b) the salary structure is such to punish those who don't conform and reward highly those who do, and (c) the capitalist system has been successful, at least in the industrialized west, in raising workers' standard of living over a long period of time (on this last point see Przeworski 1979a, 1979b).

Workers' choice is therefore not between an increasingly exploitative capitalism, steadily impoverishing workers or at best not letting them rise out of the chains of their poverty, and a nirvanic socialism. Rather, the more realistic choice, even in nineteenth-century US, was between a capitalism in which real wages were rising, and an unknown ideal. Today, the nature of socialist regimes (albeit in countries starting out at much lower levels of economic development and generally totally different political histories than those of the industrialized West) are not very attractive even for most industrial workers, not to speak of other types of employees.

(2) Crisis in production – economic crisis – should not be down played in the over-all dynamic of change. Gramsci's influence has been precisely to shift attention from economic crisis to crisis of hegemony, but in our view, this shift can be carried too far, despite the emphasis we will place here on contradictions in the superstructure. It is one thing to come to an understanding of the role of education in the process of reproduction and the contradictions in that process, and another to claim that education plays a *primary* role in reproduction (Althusser) or that contradictions in superstructure (including education) are much more fundamental to the process of change than contradictions in the base (interpretations of Gramsci, Althusser). One of the greatest victories of capitalism in the industrialized countries was to get workers to *accept* economic crisis as part of the development process. But this acceptance was *not* necessarily the result of ideological dominance, but rather of the consistently successful resolution of such crises with a subsequent period of economic growth and rising wages. Workers came to believe that crises would be followed by boom – by resolution – that things would get better, and that over the long run, things would get steadily better. If they stop getting better for a significant period of time, belief in the system will erode.

The most important change we observe in industrial capitalist societies over the last fifty years is the increasing role of the State in ensuring that crises will be less deep and will be resolved. As Poulantzas's analysis explains, this is the result of class struggle: workers compelled the State to reduce the injustices of capitalist development, just as capitalists attempted to turn these interventions to their advantage, themselves pushing for direct State support for capitalist expansion. Again, state intervention in a *reproductive* role through the capital accumulation process (as well as its productive role) is important and cannot be ignored. In contributing directly to smoother capital accumulation through economic intervention, the State contributes to increased faith in the system to deliver the goods. The better capitalism actually works, the less likely workers are to overthrow it in favor of some other system. This is not a direct ideological intervention, but an economic intervention with ideological roots.

A model of education that does not account for the importance of reproduction in the base itself misses an important function of the role of education as it relates to both means of reproduction within the base – the reserve army and the favorable accumulation of capital. In this context, we can describe the functions of education as not only *ideological* (in Althusser's terms, the reproduction of labor – the division of labor along class lines – and the reproduction of the relations of production through the ideological relations in the schools) but *economic-reproductive*: the contribution of education to developing a reserve army of skilled unemployed and its contribution to increased productivity, both directly and through the production of technocratic cadres willing and able to control other fractions of the labor force. In addition, education operates as part of the *repressive* apparatus of the State: children are *required* to attend school until age sixteen and if they 'misbehave' in school, they are sanctioned, if not physically, then with continuous harassment of other kinds.

Education therefore functions as part of the productive and reproductive mechanisms of society at various levels: (1) it produces skills which contribute, particularly in advanced capitalist societies, to the accumulation of capital. Skill production not only contributes to production largely at the expense of the working class itself (workers pay taxes which pay for the schools, and often less well-off workers subsidize the children of higher income employees to attend university – see Hansen and Weisbrod 1971) but, as we have argued, contributes to important reproductive mechanisms within the base by providing a reserve army of highly skilled cadres, creating fear of unemployment on lower status jobs among those cadres already working, and by increasing the possibilities of generating surplus and hence maintaining faith in the growth capacity of the system. The educational system is also an important employer of highly educated professionals, particularly the highly educated who have difficulty finding professional level employment in the private sector – minority men and women, women in general, and lower social class men in general. Thus, the educational system helps reproduce the relations in production by providing (along with the rest of the state bureaucracy) social mobility for those groups least likely to achieve it through the private sector; (2) as Althusser, Baudelot and Establet, and Bowles and Gintis have shown persuasively, education reproduces the distribution of skills along class lines – reproduces inequality – and reproduces the relations in production by socializing youth into a class-structured, unequal and inequitable production system, and inculcates them with an ideology which displaces class conflict into certain channels – voting and consumerism – defines knowledge in particular ways, convinces youth that failure and success is each individual's responsibility, and generally separates each individual from every other individual. The ideology promulgated in the schools does include a reverence for bourgeois democracy, individual rights, and human rights which, in one sense, serves the capitalist class, but, as we shall see, also contains important contradications for continued capitalist development; (3) education is also repressive, as we have mentioned. Children *must* attend school – it is not voluntary. Those children who do not behave while in school are usually not punished physically, but are subject to some kind of repressive action, even calling the police to school. Furthermore, employers require school certificates for employment.

Public education is thus part of the state effort to support the mediation of contradictions within the base. Education attempts to support *direct* mediation (the formation of skills to increase the supply of skilled workers (reserve army of unemployed), particularly professional cadres. Such mediation contributes to the accumulation of capital, helping capitalist development to be more successful than it might otherwise be. Education is also part of the state attempt to reproduce the class division of labor (inequality) and to reproduce the relations of production (capitalist/managers as controllers of the investment and its deployment, workers as powerless wage labor) by socializing youth into wage labor and into accepting their lot as dictated by the schooling meritocracy (some succeeding in the struggle for social mobility, most not), a lot which the school claims is fairly and equitably determined, and by inculcating youth with a profound belief in the perfection and justice of bourgeois democracy. Finally, education is repressive and part of the repressive state apparatus, although this is not its main function.

It is impossible to separate these functions into clear and distinct categories, since they operate together. The characteristics of each function are colored by the existence of the others. For example, the formation of skills cannot be distinguished from the socialization of different social class youth into different kinds of jobs. The role of the school system as an employer (a form of *direct* mediation) cannot be separated from its role as reproducer of the class division of labor or as reproducer of the class relations of production: government employment serves, among other things, to incorporate minority and women professionals into positions not available in the private sector, thus helping to support the myth that social mobility exists and that capitalist development (and the bourgeoisie) are *universal* incorporators.

But this process of mediation is rife with contradictions. Before discussing them, we should say something about contradictions themselves. Contradictions, in our model, do *not* occur *between* the superstructure (education) and the base (as mentioned in Poulantzas 1975 and Bowles and Gintis 1976). Contradictions develop in the base out of the inherent necessity of capitalist production to extract surplus from labor and of the capitalist class to control investment (capital), leaving workers out of the control process, separating them from their produce, taking away their *right* to work, and forcing them into a consumer fetishism. Attempts are made by capitalists/managers, both directly through their 'private' hegemonic apparatus and through the State, to mediate these contradictions. The mediation process itself, however, generates contradictions. These are not contradictions *between* the mediation process and the base. How, indeed, could a process which emerges as an attempt to mediate contradictions in the base be contradictory to the base? This is an incorrect formulation of the dialectic. The contradictions generated by the attempt to mediate are contradictions *in* the superstructure, since the superstructure is in and of itself the mediation process. And contradictions in the superstructure influence reproduction of capitalist relations, since the mediation process is important to that reproduction. Of course, contradictions in the base continue to occur even while contradictions in the superstructure also exist. Crisis in production and crisis of hegemony are intertwined, and as Poulantzas shows, part and parcel of the same over-all class struggle.

Furthermore, before discussing contradictions in the superstructure we should say something about the capability of the base *and* the superstructure to deliver a *reality* acceptable to the mass of workers. While Marxian literature concentrates on the inherent contradictions of capitalism, we also have to acknowledge that advanced capitalist societies, to one degree or another, are capable of compromising with worker demands: the standard of living of the mass of workers in the US, for example, has risen by 50 per cent since World War II, economic crises have been short, and unemployment, while pervasive, has been restricted (over long periods) to youth and minorities. The political systems of advanced capitalist countries have also allowed considerable democracy: while bourgeois hegemony in these countries has certainly held down the percentage of the vote received by working-class parties, the fact is that in many capitalist countries, working-class parties have done well politically, and in some cases, like Sweden, this success has led to considerable advancement of workers' *economic* rights. We are not suggesting that capitalism is slowly evolving into socialism. To the contrary, the point is that capitalists in certain countries have only been able to maintain their control over the means of production (avoiding a revolutionary situation) by yielding considerable ground in the class struggle: workers have won higher wages, a high degree of political participation and 'potential' access to power.

Keeping all this in mind, what are the contradictions particular to the mediation function of the schools? In our model, we identify two principal contradictions. [Much of the following has been developed in close collaboration with Henry Levin. See particularly Levin's 'Economic Democracy, Education and Social Change,' presented at the Fifth Vermont Conference on the Primary Prevention of Psychopathology, University of Vermont, June 19-23, 1979.]

(1) The schools are called upon to increase the number of skilled cadres and managers available to employers. At the same time employers tend to displace less highly schooled older workers with highly schooled newer ones. In conjunction with these types of mediations and the direct effect they have on the productivity-earnings spread, schools also promote youth to take more schooling in conjunction with the social mobility ideology: the only way to succeed in a 'meritocracy' is to get as much schooling as you can. Workers also demand more schooling for their children *because* they believe (correctly, to some extent) that more schooling means more economic opportunity for their children. All of this has served to increase rapidly the average level of schooling in the labor force of advanced industrial (and also low-income) countries. The contradiction emerging from this rapid growth is the 'over-education' of workers for the kinds of jobs available to the large majority. In the US, for example, average schooling relative to job requirements increased rapidly between 1965 and 1975 (Rumberger 1978). The greatest increase occurred in the most menial jobs.

As long as the economic system expanded in the aggregate and moved from agriculture to production to the services, there was an expansion of the occupational structure at the levels that could absorb a more and more educated labor force. At each level of education it was possible for workers to view a set of occupational prospects and earnings that was better than the prospects for less-educated persons. And, in general, those with college educations were able to achieve technical, managerial, and professional positions while those with less education had to settle for lower earnings and less-prestigious careers. Thus, the training and socialization provided by the schools at each level also seemed to dovetail relatively well with the eventual demands of the workplace at the appropriate occupational level.

In recent years, though, the rate of economic growth has diminished at a time when there is an unusually large number of persons of college age and when a very high proportion of those entering the labor force have obtained at least some college-level training. The reduction in the rate of economic expansion and the maturation of the structure of the economy have resulted in an inability of the economy to absorb the increase in the number of persons with college training (Freeman 1976; Rumberger 1978). Instead, it appears that young persons with college training will have to accept increasingly those jobs which were filled traditionally by persons with much lower educational attainments.

What is evident is that the same incentives that stimulated the expansion of enrolments in the schools for socializing a growing labor force for capitalist and government production will continue to operate even when the opportunities to employ more educated persons do not expand at a commensurate rate. The so-called private returns on educational investment depend not only on the earnings for the additional education, but also on the earnings that would be received without further education. Even if the earnings for college graduates grow slowly over time or decline when adjusted for rises in the price level, a college education may still represent a very good investment if the opportunities for high school graduates decline at an even greater rate (Grasso 1977).

Further, education represents one of the few hopes for social mobility from generation-to-generation for most families and individuals, so as the ideology of educational attainment continues to persist, the quest for more education as an instrument of status attainment will also persist. Both the existence of an ideology of education as a path of social mobility as well as the fact that even with declining opportunities for college graduates there is an even greater deterioriation for high school graduates lead to the following conclusion. The educational system will continue to turn out more and more educated persons regardless of the inability of the economy to absorb them.

On the economic side, there is little on the horizon that suggests that the long run prospects for economic growth will improve much. First, problems of high energy costs and rising costs of other natural resources run counter to technologies that have been predicated on cheap and unlimited energy and other natural resources. Second, to a large degree the government can not use either fiscal or monetary policy to increase the economic growth rate without triggering various shortages, bottlenecks in production and price increases in markets that are dominated by the monopolistic elements that characterize the economic system. Third, the costs of labor and the stability of production in many of the third world countries promises much greater profits than further investment in the US.

To further aggravate the situation, many existing jobs are being transformed by technology and capital investment into ones that are becoming more and more routinized and devoid of the need for human judgments and talents. Studies of automation have suggested that the critical skills and judgments that are associated with particular jobs are eliminated by greater use of technology and capital (Braverman 1974). Even many traditional professions have become increasingly proletarianized in this way as the expansion of professional opportunities has shifted from self-employment to corporate and government employment. Under the latter forms of organization, the professional is given a much more specialized and routing function, rather than choosing for himself or herself the types of clients, practices, hours, and work methods that will be employed.

Thus, not only do the alternatives for the educated person seem to be deteriorating in both quality and quantity, but an analysis for the longer run suggests that the forces that are creating this deterioration will continue to prevail. Thus, young and educated persons are likely to find themselves in situations where their expectation and skills exceed those which are associated with available jobs. Since most jobs will not have the intrinsic characteristics that would keep such persons engaged, the inadequate nature of the extrinsic rewards will operate to make it more and more difficult to integrate such persons into the labor force. That is, the lack of opportunities for promotion, and the limited wage gains in conjunction with the relatively rountinized nature of most jobs, will tend to create a relatively unstable workforce. It is also important to note that the availability of public assistance in the form of food stamps, medical care, and other services as well as unemployment insurance tends to cushion the impact of losing employment, so the negative impact of losing or quitting one's job is no longer as powerful a sanction for job conformance.

(2) The schools, as an important part of the state's ideological apparatus, must inculcate youth with the sense that they live in a political democracy, and that the economic system is fair and just. On the one hand, we could argue that the schools, in themselves inherently and obviously not democratic, make clear to youth that the democracy discussed in history and civics classes is an abstraction, so much so that they come to accept the abstract nature of democracy in their post-school, everyday lives (by neither voting nor otherwise participating in the political system). This *symbolism* of democracy is precisely what the bourgeoisie strives to promote. On the other hand, even symbolism creates danger for bourgeois hegemony, both for reproduction of the relations of production and for the State. Inculcating

students with democratic ideals, even if discussing the historic role of the working class in forcing those ideals into a practicing universal suffrage is avoided *does* promote an ideology of individual and human rights. This mass ideology can be and is directed against big business as well as big government, can be and is directed against a state which is overly repressive or attempts to make foreign wars in the name of protecting a country's imperial 'options,' can be and is directed against oppressive hierarchies in enterprises.

In addition to these two principal contradictions, inherent in the role schools *must* play in the mediation process is the need to legitimize schools as reproducers of labor (this is the point raised by Bourdieu and Passeron). This necessity of legitimacy gives the schools a formal autonomy from the base and the private hegemonic apparatuses, and autonomy (in theory) allows teachers, administrators, and students to follow independent educational strategies which are not consistent with the mediation functions required for softening contradictions in the base. Furthermore, the very bringing together of large numbers of youth in the same institution promotes the development of youth culture which may be inconsistent with social reproduction.

The importance of these contradictions in interfering with the reproductive process is not altogether clear. We do know that workers with schooling greater than that required to perform their jobs are less likely to be satisfied in those jobs, and would therefore tend to be less productive (HEW 1973). Workers who are anti-authoritarian in hierarchical organizations are also likely to be less productive. Productivity is an increasing problem for capitalist expansion in the advanced economies. The dissatisfactions that result from frustrated expectations with respect to the quality of work and its extrinsic rewards can create threats to productivity in a variety of ways. Most notable among these are rising absenteeism, worker turnover, wildcat strikes, alcoholism and drug usage, and deterioration of product quality. Even rising incidences of sabotage are possible responses by young workers who feel that they are overeducated for the opportunities that have been made available to them and who do not see the possibilities of major improvements in their situations. But employers have other ways to deal with these problems, particularly by disciplining the labor force directly (recessions, increasing immigration, bringing increased numbers of women into the labor force, runaway shops, repression on the job, or even allowing a limited amount of worker control in the work process). Whether these ways can work, over the long run, to increase productivity or decrease wages relative to productivity remains to be seen.

The overproduction of educated persons relative to available opportunities is not only creating disruptive potential for the workplace, it is also suggesting difficulties for the educational system as well. As the exchange value of a college degree and high school diploma have fallen, there is a number of indications of a relaxation of educational standards. For example, there is considerable evidence that average grades have risen at the same time that standardized test scores in basic skill areas have fallen (Wirtz *et al.* 1977).

While there are many possible causes for these phenomena, one of the most intriguing is that these are natural responses to the falling commodity value of education. Thus, the educational system seems to be providing higher grades for relatively poorer quality work, and students no longer seem willing to put in the effort to acquire the various cognitive skills. This explanation fits our over-all framework in that to a large degree existing educational activities will be undertaken for their extrinsic values rather than for their intrinsic worthwhileness. As the extrinsic value of education falls in the marketplace, the grades given for any level of effort must rise to ensure a given performance. Moreover, the effort that a student will put in to acquiring an education will also decline as the financial and prestige rewards decline.

A further example of this type of disruptive potential of the schools is reflected in the increasing problem of discipline. To a large degree, the discipline of workers is maintained through the promise of good pay, steady work, and possible promotion for those who conform. Since the work is intrinsically without value to the worker, it is these incentives that must be used to ensure appropriate working behavior. A similar situation has existed in the school, where the fear of failure and of low grades and the attractions of promotion and high grades has helped to maintain discipline among students. These systems of extrinsic rewards have served to ensure that students see it in their best interests to 'follow the rules.' But, as the job situation and possibilities of social success from education have deteriorated, even the grading system is no longer adequate to hold students in check. In fact, recent Gallup Polls of problems in the schools are consistent in implicating discipline as the most important difficulty (Gallup 1977).

Contradictions in the educational system do decrease the mediating potential of schools. Schools are mediators because of the class struggle in production, but in being mediators, themselves become part of the class struggle. As long as the capitalist system is functioning smoothly, increasing the masses' standard of living at an acceptable and steady rate and providing charismatic and effective leaders who are able to give the masses a participatory feeling – a sense of 'progress,' these contradictions may be 'latent.' But in economic crisis and crisis of hegemony, they manifest themselves in the directions we have suggested. They contribute to these crises, particularly in the sense that the schools turn out to be much less effective mediators of contradictions in the base than supposed.

In such cases, the power bloc attempts – through schools reforms – to bring schools 'back into line' as more effective mediators of contradictions in the base. The bloc will also take measures to mediate contradictions directly, as we have already mentioned, in the base itself, through action against labor. Yet, how much action it can take may be constrained by the contradictions emerging from the superstructure – from the crisis of hegemony – of which the schools are a part.

Our analysis therefore differs from previous Marxian approaches: we suggest that action in the superstructure – in the schools – which exacerbates contradictions inherent in the educational system's mediating function can serve to exacerbate contradictions in the base, or at least constrain the types of direct action available to the power bloc to take against labor in the base itself. In our model, actions in the schools have the potential to contribute positively to labor's position in the class struggle by dint of the organic relation between struggle in superstructure and struggle in the base.

Thus, there exists a constellation of relations between the schools, and the workplace that can provide either reinforcement or disruptive potential. While historically the operations of schools cannot be understood without an examination of their correspondence with the requirements of the capitalist workplace, the independence dynamic of schools and their internal contradictions also represent forces for challenging the institutions of the workplace. The result of these forces is that it is becoming more and more difficult to integrate students into either school life or working life than it has in the past. And the disruptive aspects of this situation are stimulating various responses in both the educational and work setting.

Acknowledgments

The research forming the basis of this work came from two sources: a National Institute of Education grant to the Center for Economic Studies on 'Education and Industrial Democracy,' and a grant from NIE to the Institute for Finance and Governance at Stanford University which helped finance a study of 'Education and Theories of the State.' The ideas in the paper are more fully developed in a soon-to-be finished book with Henry Levin called *The Dialectics of Education*.

I owe a particular debt to Hank and to Gero Lenhardt for reading and commenting on this paper and generally contributing to my understanding of the issues discussed.

Bibliography

Althusser, Louis (1971), *Lenin and Philosophy and Other Essays*, New York: Monthly Review Press.

Anderson, Perry (1977), 'The Antimonies of Antonio Gramsci,' *New Left Review* 100 (June), 5-78.

Baudelot, Christian and Roger Establet (1975), *La Escuela Capitalista*, Mexico: Siglo XXI.

Bobbio, Norberto (1979), 'Gramsci and the Conception of Civil Society,' in Chantal Mouffe (ed.), *Gramsci and Marxist Theory*, London: Routledge & Kegan Paul.

Bourdieu, Pierre and Jean-Claude Passeron (1977), *Reproduction*, Beverly Hills: Sage.

Bowles, Samuel and Herbert Gintis (1976), *Schooling in Capitalist America*, New York: Harper & Row.

Braverman, Harry (1974), *Labor and Monopoly Capital*, New York: Monthly Review Press.

Carnoy, Martin, Robert Girling, and Russell Rumberger (1975), *Education and Public Employment*, Palo Alto, California: Center for Economic Studies.

Carnoy, Martin, and Henry M. Levin (forthcoming 1982), *The Dialectics of Education and Work*, Stanford: Stanford University Press.

Engels, Frederick (1968), *The Origin of the Family, Private Property, and the State*, New York: International Publishers.

Freeman, Richard (1976), *The Overeducated American*, New York: Academic Press.

Gallup, George (1977), 'Ninth Annual Gallup Poll of the Public Schools,' *Phi Delta Kappa* (September), 33-48.

Gramsci, Antonio (1971), *Selections from Prison Notebooks*, New York: International Publishers.

Grasso, J. (1977), 'On the Declining Labor Market Value of Schooling,' paper prepared for the 1977 Annual Meeting of the AERA, New York (April).

Greenberg, Edward (1977), *The American Political System*, New York: Winthrop.

Hansen, W. Lee and Burton Weisbrod (1971), 'Distribution of the Costs and Benefits of Higher Education Subsidies in California,' *Journal of Human Resources*, (Summer), 363-74.

HEW (Department of Health, Education, and Welfare) (1973), *Work in America*, Cambridge, Mass: MIT Press.

Lenhardt, Gero (1979), 'Educational Politics and Capitalist Society:

Marxist Perspectives on Educational Reform in the Federal Republic of Germany,' Berlin: Max Planck Inst., mimeo.

Lenin, V. I. (1965), *The State and Revolution* (1917), Peking: Foreign Language Press.

Lenin, V. I. (1978), *On Socialist Ideology and Culture*, Moscow: Progress Publishers.

Levin, Henry (1978), 'The Dilemma of Comprehensive Secondary School Reforms in Western Europe,' *Comparative Education Review*, 22 (October) 434-51.

Marx, K. (1970), *Critique of Political Economy* (1859), New York: International Publishers.

Marx, K. (1972), *Critique of the Gotha Programme* (1875), Peking: Foreign Language Press.

Marx, K. (1970), *The German Ideology* (1846), New York: International Publishers.

Marx, K. (1906), *Capital, Vol. I* (1867), New York: Modern Library.

Mouffe, Chantal (ed.) (1979), *Gramsci and Marxist Theory*, London: Routledge & Kegan Paul.

O'Connor, James (1974), *The Corporations and the State*, New York: Harper & Row.

Poulantzas, Nicos (1973), *Political Power and Social Classes*, London: New Left Books.

Poulantzas, Nicos (1975), *Classes in Contemporary Capitalism*, London: New Left Books.

Poulantzas, Nicos (ed.) (1976), *La Crise de l'Etat*, Paris: PUF.

Poulantzas, Nicos (1978), *L'état, le pouvoir, le socialism*, Paris: PUF.

Przeworski, Adam (1979a), 'Social Democracy as an Historical Phenomenon,' University of Chicago, mimeo.

Przeworski, Adam (1979b), 'Economic Conditions of Class Compromise,' University of Chicago, mimeo.

Rumberger, Russell (1978), 'Overeducation in the U.S. Labor Market,' Unpublished PhD thesis, Stanford University.

Sarti, Ingrid (1979), 'A Critique of the Ideology of Capitalist Education: its vision and impasses,' Rio de Janeiro, mimeo.

Wirtz, W. *et al.* (1977), *On Further Examination: Report of the Advisory Panel on Scholastic Aptitude Test Score Decline*, New York: College Examination Board.

Chapter 4

Education and the capitalist State:

contributions and contradictions

Roger Dale

The State in the sociology of education

Given all that sociologists, economists and political scientists have had to say about the meanings and assumptions, the processes and practices, the functions and outcomes, of education systems in recent years, it is really very surprising to find almost no analysis of the implications of state provision, irrespective of the particular approach adopted. This relative neglect is even reflected in the title, if not in the introduction, to this book. It seems that both for sociologists and economists of education who effectively ignore, and for those political scientists who study, the inner workings of the 'education sub government', the State is regarded as an effectively neutral means of delivery of intended outcomes decided elsewhere; the sociologists and economists have concentrated on revealing the intended outcomes, while the political scientists have looked for organizational obstructions to the achievements of those outcomes. The State is, then, put in the position that teachers were put in in much early curriculum reform work – it is assumed to be unable to contribute anything of its own (and it is undesirable that it should do so) to the achievement of desired outcomes, but it may unwittingly interfere with it; the best that can be hoped for of the State (or of the teacher) is that it will remain as neutral a conduit as possible for the achievement of outcomes decided elsewhere.

Consider, briefly, the three major approaches to the sociology of education over the last decade or so, broadly the structural-functionalist approach, the 'new' sociology of education, and the political economy of education. In none of them is the fact of state provision taken as anything more than marginal and in most work they have generated it is ignored. The first, with its assumptions of consensus and integration and its focus (post Sputnik) on the technological contributions of education to the economy, implicitly relegated everything that happened between input to and output from the education system to 'black box' status. This omission was partly repaired by the 'new' sociology of education, with its concentration on the content of schooling and on how particular conceptions of reality were constructed and sustained in schools and classrooms. The State, though, still remained in the black box, and so it did, more surprisingly, in the political economy critique of the new sociology. This stressed the neglect of conceptions of power and structure in the 'new' sociology of education, but leap-frogged the fact of state provision and went directly to the needs of the capitalist system, again implicitly marginalizing and neutralizing the importance of state provision; even though it is never clear quite how the needs of the capitalist system are conveyed to and met in each school and classroom.

On the other hand, writers who do make the State the focus of their interest have normally paid little attention to education. This applies as much to the contributors to the recent resurgence of interest in Marxist theories of the State (though I shall be attempting to extract implications for education from some of them below) as it does to mainstream political science. There are, though, exceptions in both approaches which it will be instructive to consider. One Marxist exception is Althusser's ISA (Ideological State Apparatuses) essay (Althusser 1971). In this education is seen as the key ideological state apparatus in the reproduction of the capitalist mode of production. The particular conception of a state apparatus which Althusser holds, however, is not one which permits increased understanding of the implications of state provision of education. For, as Laclau (1977: 68-9) has pointed out, 'implicit in the conception of ideological state apparatuses there lies a conception of the State which entirely ceases to consider it as an institution. . .' (for Althusser) '*everything* which serves to maintain the cohesion of a social formation forms part of the State. In that case . . . the State must simply be a *quality* which pervades all the levels of a social formation' (emphasis in original). Trying to explain education systems through analysing them as Althusserian ISAs, then, is not much different from explaining education solely or pre-eminently as a form of social control, in both its question-begging and its negativity.

Those political scientists who have focussed on education have confined their studies very much to education politics rather than the politics of education.[1] By this I mean that they have concentrated much more on studying the effectiveness of education systems and forms of education government in achieving goals presented to them, rather than on the relationship between the production of goals and the form of their achievement. To put it another way, political questions are bracketed out and replaced by questions about processes of decision-making; politics are reduced to administration. The focus is on the machinery, rather than on what powers it, or how and where it is directed.

The approach I intend to adopt to the analysis of the relationship of the State and education may perhaps be inferred broadly from the two preceding paragraphs. What is not clear is why such an analysis is worthwhile. After all, may it not be the case that there are very good reasons for the relative neglect of the State in analyses of education? Could it be that it really doesn't make any difference?

There are two broad justifications. First, I hope to demonstrate below that the approach I am advocating can *explain* patterns, policies and processes of education in capitalist societies more adequately than existing approaches. As has been suggested many times before, macro and micro approaches are mutually blind. The one attempts to explain all education systems on the basis of a single principle – system integration, or the capitalist mode of production, or whatever. The other seeks to achieve understanding through the continuing assembly of detailed studies of schools or classrooms. The one can explain everything in general, but nothing in particular, the other can explain everything in particular, but nothing in general. Just as importantly, their explanations are neither complementary nor overlapping. There are areas of problems to which neither speaks effectively. Among these areas is one of the most important tasks for the sociology of education, that of understanding the source and nature of educational stability and change.

The second justification for an approach concentrated on the role of the state, then, is that it permits questioning in this area. The political economy approach of Bowles and Gintis (1976), for instance, is able to produce few strategies for bringing about change, short of (working towards) a revolutionary overthrow of capitalism, largely because it has little place for politics. Crudely, the schools are regarded, implicitly, as being directly controlled by the needs of capitalist accumulation and hence it is only by changing that that we can change what goes on in schools. Why the needs of capitalist accumulation are expressed in such different forms in different social formations, and the implications of this for a politics of education that could reveal some levers of educational change, are never made clear. On the other side, micro studies which insulate schools from society are equally unable to indicate the source and nature of the control over even the schools they study, and which it would be crucial to establish before bringing about any change in them. Focussing on the source and nature of control over education and schools entails focussing on the immediate provider of education, the State, and it is in the analysis of the State that we may begin to understand the assumptions, intentions and outcomes of various strategies of educational change.

In the next section of this paper I will isolate three core problem areas confronting state education systems and argue that the means of their solution are mutually contradictory; this mutual contradiction provides a dynamic for education systems. In the following section, I will examine some basic characteristics of education systems as state apparatuses, and their implications for educational policy and practice. Following this is an appraisal of the way that education acts to legitimate the broader social/political/economic system of which it is part; particular stress is laid on its positive contributions to this process. Finally, the implications of state provision for the kind of opposition and alternatives found within education systems are briefly examined.

The nature of the capitalist State

It will be my argument in this section of the paper that the most important consequence of focussing on state provision of education is that it enables us to see that the basic problems facing education systems in capitalist countries derive from the problems of the capitalist State. Before attempting to indicate what those problems might be and how they might contribute to an agenda for education, however, I should make clear two limitations on this discussion. First, in arguing that the problems of the capitalist State derive from its relationship to the maintenance and reproduction of the capitalist mode of production, I do not make the assumption that all state activity derives from this relationship. Rather, I take here Gramsci's point that 'The democratic-bureaucratic system has given rise to a great mass of functions which are not at all necessitated by the social necessities of production, though they are justified by the political necessities of the dominant fundamental group' (Gramsci 1971: 13). Second, I do not intend to suggest that everything that goes on in schools is explained by, or related to, the problems of the capitalist State. The questions raised by both of these areas are very important and they are discussed as refinements to the central thesis in later sections.

It is probably true to say that the dominant conception of the State in political sociology sees it as a neutral means of distributing social goods among competing groups or élites on the basis of their relative strength and effectiveness. This approach has been subjected to increasing criticism in recent years from resurgent Marxist work on the theory of the State.[2] The first line of criticism came through the instrumentalist approach chiefly associated with the name of Ralph Miliband. As he puts it (Miliband 1968: 31),

> What is wrong with pluralist-democratic theory is not its insistence on the fact of competition but its claim (very often its implicit assumption) that the major organized 'interests' in (advanced capitalist) societies, and notably capital and labour, compete on more or less equal terms, and that none of them is therefore able to achieve a decisive and permanent advantage in the process of competition. This is where ideology enters and turns observation into myth . . . business, particularly large scale business (enjoys) such an advantage *inside* the state system, by virtue of the composition and ideological inclinations of the state elite . . . (and) enjoys a massive superiority outside the state system as well, in terms of the immensely stronger pressures which, as compared with labour and any other interest, it is able to exercise in the pursuit of its purposes.

State activity then, is not neutral, but is the result of the state apparatus being taken over by, and used, as the instrument of the ruling class. However, Miliband does not move beyond the democratic élite theorists except by showing that they make the wrong assumptions about who controls the State and how. The State is still conceived as a neutral instrument, with the nature of the policies it follows decided by the desires of those who control it. Moreover, as David Hogan (1979) has recently pointed out, the functions of institutions cannot be 'read off' from an analysis of who controls them. This is basic to the critique which suggests that the functions of the State in capitalist societies are given not by the direct control of capitalists or capitalist sympathisers within the state apparatus, but are in fact objectively given by the imperatives of the maintenance and reproduction of the conditions of existence of the capitalist mode of production.

It is important to examine this approach in a little greater depth since its implications for an analysis of education which starts from the view that the dominant problematic for education systems derives from their states' problematic, are of clear and central importance. It is necessary initially to try to settle difficulties associated with the term 'function'. It is not clear, for instance, when the functions of the education system are referred to, whether 'function' is being used teleologically, in the sense of the *purposes* of the education system, or descriptively, in setting out what the education system does. The approach I wish to adopt excludes both those uses of the term, the former use because that way of asking questions about education systems prespecifies one set of answers and precludes others *a priori*, the latter because understanding and explaining education systems (or anything else) entails more than merely cataloguing what they do. The procedure I intend to adopt is to identify what I will call 'core problems' of the capitalist State as a whole and of education systems in capitalist States. This does not involve any pre-judgment about their relative prominence on the agenda of any particular state apparatus, nor of how, or how effectively, they will be dealt with. It does involve a conception of the capitalist mode of production, and the positing of a particular kind of relationship between the State and the capitalist mode of production in those social formations where the capitalist mode of production is dominant, such that those core problems are permanently insoluble and permanently on the agenda of the state apparatus, (without, again, specifying their relative importance, or claiming that they exhaust the activity of state apparatus). The point of this approach is to lay down non-arbitrary priorities and guidelines for the analysis of education systems.

Briefly then, all modes of production have a number of basic conditions of existence, but in the capitalist mode of production, capital cannot by its own efforts provide or secure the conditions of its existence or reproduction. At one level, the nature of the necessary 'rules of the game', the whole legal framework of contract and property, the guarantee of money, can be neither provided nor guaranteed by capital, since those rules have to be specified by a disinterested party with the power to enforce them. At another level, the existence and reproduction of the mode of production which generates both competitors and antagonists has to be protected from attacks both internal and external to the social formation in which it is (assumedly) dominant. And third, individual capitals are not only highly mutually competitive, but also largely confined within particular economic sectors whose separate conditions of optimum existence may conflict with those of others. As Offe puts it, drawing on Rosa Luxemburg, 'Simply stated, the irrational limitation of individual capitals concerning their particularized and short-term realization interests prevents "long-term planning of the conditions for the survival and expansion of the capitalist mode of production" '. Hence there has become established within the framework of the state apparatus 'the logic of the compensatory plugging of functional holes which, in the capitalist accumulation process, are the result of the irrational limitation of individual capitals and the pressure to compete. Individual capitals thus endanger the unbroken continuity of this process, whose "anarchic" character precludes correction by genuinely capitalist mechanisms (accumulation and competition). It is inevitable, therefore, that eventually a "high authority" has to step in (i.e. through the use of public power)' (Offe 1975a: 103, 104).

It is possible, then, to derive from this analysis a list of 'core problems for the capitalist State' which it can then be assumed will be on the agenda of all state apparatus and institutions including the education system. However, (a) drawing up a list of the core problems of the capitalist State does not exhaust the contribution of the kind of political sociological analysis of the State I am suggesting, as I hope to demonstrate in the following three sections of this paper, and (b) there are a number of qualifications to be made before the value of isolating 'core problems for education systems' can be realized and, indeed, to prevent such an approach becoming sterile, mechanical and counter productive.

It will be useful to outline what seem to be the core problems for the capitalist State and then to go into the ways that these raw concepts have to be refined for effective use to be made of them. I would suggest that three broad core problems can be isolated, (i) support of the capital accumulation process, (ii) guaranteeing a context for its continued expansion, (iii) the legitimation of the capitalist mode of production, including the State's own part in it. The isolation of these three problems is relatively arbitrary, and relatively unimportant in that the analytic approach being put forward is not dependent on their close and unambiguous definition.

What qualifications and refinements have to be made? First, *specifications* of the problems facing the State in any particular social formation cannot be laid down theoretically in advance; they do not always appear in the same form. They have to be extracted through an analysis of each separate social formation. Therborn outlines a useful approach to this when he notes (1978: 163):

> The ability of a particular bourgeoisie (or fraction thereof) to hold state power is . . . structurally determined by: (1) the stage reached by capitalism in the society in which it functions; (2) the central or peripheral position, and the advanced or retarded stage of the capital it represents, as well as the expansion, crisis or contraction of international capitalism as a whole; (3) the manner in which its relations to feudalism and petty commodity production, as well as its own internal cleavages, have historically evolved and currently manifest themselves in the given constellation of forces; and (4) the international conjuncture facing the social formation – the peculiar strengths and weaknesses of the latter within the international configuration of harmonious or conflicting forces.

Thus, for instance, the common problem of supporting the process of capital accumulation will present itself in very different forms, not only between social formations but within them as well. The range of assumptions made about whether, how and why education should contribute to 'economic growth' illustrates this in one narrow area.

Second, identifying the core problems of the capitalist State does not entail identifying the particular means by which they will be tackled. Neither does such identification imply that the state apparatus as a whole is well attuned to overcoming the problems, nor that the machinery available in any given social formation is especially relevant to tackling them in the form they manifest in a particular conjuncture. We should note, too, that the State is not a monolith; there are differences within and between its various apparatuses in their prioritizing of demands made on them and in their ability to meet those demands.

Third, state policy makers do not possess perfect knowledge of the State's needs or of how to meet them, through education or any other means at their disposal. Even if the need to 'plug' a particular 'functional hole' were rather obvious, the implications for any particular state apparatus are by no means necessarily equally obvious, nor is it necessarily obvious that any particular state apparatus can contribute to their 'plugging'. This again will be dependent in part on the historical evolution of particular state apparatuses, and what it is supposed they can achieve.

Fourth, even where a particular programme may be designed to meet a particular demand, there is no guarantee that it will be possible to implement it. Offe (1973, 1975b) points to two reasons for this. First, he argues, there is no adequate model of internal structure of the organizational form for meeting the demands made of the capitalist state. The three possible models he discusses each contain a specific contradiction: the bureaucratic is 'wasteful at best and ineffective at worst and thus *insufficient* as a model for productive state activity; the purposive-rational may be both efficient and effective in itself, but its application requires interference with the prerogatives of the private accumulation process, the resistance to which on the part of the accumulating units makes its application impossible,' while participating models 'tend to crystallize conflict and protest and can thus easily become *subversive* of the balance between the state and the accumulation process' (Offe 1975b: 143). More generally, there is a 'structural discrepancy' between abstract, surplus-value related functions of state support of the capitalist order and the concrete use-value related forms such support takes; the introduction of this alien, parasitic, yet crucial element potentially threatens the whole accumulation process at the same time as it preserves and defends it. For, as Offe puts it 'No "higher insight" can *a priori* guarantee that recourse to the state as a steering mechanism will not simultaneously reinforce the state's capacity of acting as a relatively self-autonomous "alien element". The question that remains unanswered, left solely open to contingencies, is whether the intervention of any "separate" sector of the State to counteract the functional gaps arising in the market-controlled capital accumulation process will, in the long term, serve to stabilize or jeopardize this process' (Offe 1973: 111).

Fifth, as has been repeatedly stated, the core problems do not account for everything either the State or the education system does. This may in part be linked to the difficulties of specification and execution just mentioned. In this situation, Offe argues, 'there is a very real possibility that in order to retain their capacity of control (derived from political power and legitimacy) the state agencies will feel compelled to block the purpose of use value production strictly complementary to capital accumulation by giving in to the claims which emerge merely from party competition and political conflict, but in no way directly result from the actual requirements of capital accumulation itself' (Offe 1973: 115).

Those views bring us back a little closer to earth and introduce a sixth and perhaps the most important qualification about a core problems approach. This is that there is no place in it for any opposition or resistance. It implies not only a smooth identification of problems based on omniscience of state functionaries but also a conflict free implementation of solutions through the thorough confidence in them of everyone involved. Just as we have seen that identification is exceptionally difficult, so we should recall that the State we are discussing is a class State, that the problems identified for it are to be settled in pursuance of the maintenance of class rule and that in a class society this has necessary repercussions for the subject class, which it is likely to resist. Indeed the continuing subjection of that class is one of the problems of the capitalist State. Opposition, then, not support, must be expected and a major part of state policy is concerned with dealing with that opposition in one way or another.

Finally, and equally importantly, is the assumption that because all the problems are related to the same over-all purpose, their solutions must be complementary with each other; they are, in fact, mutually contradictory. The central contradiction is, of course, that while the capitalist mode of production is driven by the creation (through the universalization of the commodity form) and realization of surplus value, the conditions for its success and reproduction can only be guaranteed through the extraction of some part of that surplus value by the State and its diversion into non-commodity forms. This creates a central tension between State and capital. Beyond this, we have seen that the provision of the conditions of capital accumulation are not monolithic, but varied. However, the most important point is that they are not merely varied but mutually contradictory. The contradictions involved in tackling the core problems of the State are seen as intrinsic and incapable of permanent solution. Developments in one area inevitably require changes in the other areas, but cannot provide or sustain the means of such changes. At one level this leads to a 'fiscal crisis of the State' (O'Connor 1973) where the ever increasing level of state expenditure in absolute terms becomes ever less tolerable to capital, but also where the proportion of occupational activity involved in surplus value creation (from which state spending is financed) is failing to a point where it will be impossible to maintain existing levels of state expenditure. So, while capital is increasingly dependent on the State for maintaining and improving the conditions for capital accumulation – Keynesian remedies are the obvious example – those very remedies themselves set up not only fiscal, but also wider political and legitimatory requirements. For instance, such state intervention has the effect of making unemployment not a 'natural' phenomenon, but one which is infinitely adjustable by state intervention and hence a crucial political matter, whereby levels of employment are decided as much on political as economic criteria. Such strains are not avoidable but are intrinsic to the system; and this creates obvious legitimation problems.

Rather similar is the whole welfare state apparatus, which gave capitalism a much more human face, and by demonstrating that it (capitalism) could care for all its dependents, enabled the State to preserve a context amenable to capital accumulation. However, the maintenance and increase of the benefits of the welfare state became major political matters, throwing immense strain on the process of surplus value creation to provide the means for it to continue delivering the goods, and on the legitimation mechanisms to make up for any shortfall of such delivery. The point is that the State does not have at its disposal the means of quickly and cleanly cauterizing these contradictions. They can only be solved in ways that lay the seeds of further contradictions. Thus 'buying loyalty' in various ways is fine but the price keeps going up as privileges become rights; creating mechanisms to disguise the nature of the state activity is fine, but there is the danger that they will come to be taken at their word. ('Education for personal development' is one of the best examples of this.)

The problems faced by the State overall are writ small in the education system. It may be required to find solutions in all three core problem areas simultaneously and it is unable to do so. In education as elsewhere, these solutions are often mutually contradictory.

For instance, the basic question of whether the *process* or the *context* of accumulation is to receive priority treatment, reverberates through education policy. The process argument calls for an élitist system of education, devoted to the early recognition and fostering of 'ability' and its processing through a largely 'instrumental' curriculum. Such a policy clearly has enormous implications for several of the 'basic myths' which comprise the legitimating function of the State and of the education system in particular. But legitimation is achieved not only through the rhetoric, but through the practice of the education system, and the fundamental changes which such an élitist policy would entail would represent a major threat to education's continuing successfully to legitimate the system.

It is hardly necessary in order to make the point about contradiction to spell out the consequences of a policy which took an opposite line, i.e. one which sought to strengthen the *context* of accumulation by, for instance, adding more substance to the rhetoric of, say, educational equality, by applying itself to achieving equality of educational outcomes rather than equality of educational opportunity.

Such contradictions are to be found at all levels of the education system, not just at the policy making level. Controversies over such issues as streaming represent in part a reflection of the existence and mutual contradictoriness of the various demands made on education. So too, do arguments over the optimum content of education. In so far as they define the shifting parameters of the structural context within which schools operate, their mutual contradictoriness even becomes evident, and important, at the level of the classroom (Dale 1977). It is particularly at times of major crisis of accumulation, which set up reverberations throughout the whole state apparatus, that the intrinsic mutual contradictoriness of the various demands of education becomes clear; at other times it may remain muted, seem non-existent. However, all the time, the existence of these contradictions, reflecting contradictions in the capitalist State, provides a major dynamic in education systems. Moves to meet one demand inhibit moves to meet another, not just because of limited budgets, but because the three core problems identified above, are intrinsically mutually contradictory (as well as being, as Offe argues, jointly contradictory with surplus value production and realization).

This recognition of the contradictory nature of the demands on education is quite crucial to any adequate explanation of it. Isolating a single dominant requirement not only impoverishes the study of education systems by failing to provide a comprehensive account of their work, but the account it does provide of the particular highlighted feature cannot be adequate even of that feature in isolation if we recognize that the various demands on the education system take their character at least in part from their relationships to other demands on it. But not only are 'single dominant function' explanations of education systems separately inadequate, it is not sufficient either merely to aggregate them, to establish that education does have a number of, albeit overlapping different functions. In order to understand why education systems are as they are, we have to understand the *relationship* between the ways they tackle the various problems confronting them, and that I have argued, is a relationship of contradiction.

Education as a state apparatus

A major emphasis in the foregoing section was on the relative autonomy of the education state apparatus. While it was suggested that certain core problems were permanent features of its agenda, it was also stressed that this did not either guarantee their prominence on the agenda or stipulate the means by which they would be tackled. Though recognizing the existence of the core problems and their mutual contradictions is a necessary condition of an adequate understanding of educational policy and practice, it is by no means sufficient. As a further step in that direction, we have to consider the effect of the form of the state apparatus on educational policy and practice.

Examining education as a state apparatus enables us to raise a number of questions that usually go unasked and to clarify some of the ambiguities and confusion that frequently seem to attend discussions of the State. For instance, the distinction between the State and the Government often goes unremarked either because no such distinction is recognized or because it is considered irrelevant. One consequence of this confusion is the assumption that the study of the effect of state provision on education systems is exhausted by, or identical with, the study of educational policy making; this is another defect of the tendency to reduce the politics of education to education politics, which I mentioned above.

Government is clearly a most important part of the State. It is the most active and the most visible part of it, but it is not the whole of it. This is demonstrated, for instance, in the ability of states to carry on functioning in the absence of governments. So, while government action constitutes a key part of the work of any state apparatus, it does not account for all of it. It is essential, therefore, to try to identify the limits of governmental and other aspects of state apparatus bearing in mind that these limits are not common to all social formations (compare, for instance, centralized and decentralized education systems), and that they are not fixed; they are fluctuating counters in the political game.

Very broadly, then, we might say that governments attempt to represent the short-term interests of the temporarily dominant coalition within a social formation; these coalitions are located largely in political parties, and party policy reflects on the one hand the shifts of interest and influence between those represented in the coalition, and on the other, its concepts of what is required to secure majority electoral support. In one sense, then, the government acts to mediate the State and its subjects to each other. It is the activity generated by such intra-governmental problems which creates what Gramsci referred to as the 'great mass of functions which are not all necessitated by the social necessities of production' or what Offe called 'the claims which emerge merely from party competition and political conflict, but in no way directly result from the actual requirements of capital accumulation itself'. One consequence of this is that it helps to confirm Parliamentarism as the key mode of state rule and thus both disguises the nature of the basic functions of the State and deflects attempts to change the type and direction of state activities into channels which, while they are far from negligible, are intrinsically incapacitated as sole means of bringing about such changes.

There are two kinds of limit to government control over state apparatuses. The first is directly practical. It is quite impossible for the whole range of activities of a state apparatus to be regarded permanently as politically problematic, for everything that is at any one time *administered* to become a subject for government. What aspects are the focus of government activities at any time is a valuable and interesting topic of study, but it does not exhaust the possibilities for a political sociology of education.

The second kind of limit, is what I will call the organic; I will concentrate on it in the remainder of this section. 'Organic' in this case refers to the relative autonomy of state apparatus from government control which derives from their own particular history. Partly because of the inability of governments to effectively institute day to day control over every aspect of an apparatus's activities, they (the apparatuses) develop in directions, and take on a broad over-all character, within the constraints of the basic demands made of them, which does not merely *not* follow the design of any one government, but can render them ineffective or inadequate vehicles for the execution and implementation of particular kinds of policy. State apparatuses are not directable at will. As Therborn (1976: 35) puts it:

> In the historical course of the class struggle, the state apparatuses came to crystallize determinate social relations and thus assume a material existence, efficiency and inertia which are to a certain extent independent of current state policies and class relations. It

> follows that, although the variance between state power and the state apparatus is limited by the fact that they express the class relations of the same society, at any given moment significant disjunctures appear between the two. The possibilities of variance are substantially increased by the co-existence within a particular state system of several apparatuses, in which different sets of class relations may have crystallized.[3]

What can be achieved through education then, is constrained not only by the basic problems confronting it, but also by the nature of the apparatus for tackling them – and everything else it does. If we want to understand the similarities as well as the differences between education systems in capitalist countries, and their implications, one crucial area of investigation is the similarities as well as the differences in their state apparatuses (Archer's (1979) very detailed analysis of the origins and consequences of centralized and decentralized systems contributes usefully here). Let us then examine the education state apparatus in more detail. This is clearly much more difficult than establishing the core problems, for while capitalism as a mode of production dominates many social formations, the capitalist mode of production alone does not determine the form that education state apparatuses will take.

We are dealing here with two levels of the selectiveness of state institutions. At the one level, their selectiveness in terms of policy options, may be seen to be broadly guided by the 'needs' of the capitalist mode of production; it is at this level that the arguments in the previous section were cast. The other level at which they operate selectively concerns how their particular form of operation facilitates the putting of certain kinds of relevant questions, and inhibits others. What is at issue here is much more a matter of the histories of the individual state apparatuses; within particular social formations, education systems as different as the American and the French are possible.

One generalization we can make is that state apparatuses everywhere tend to be organized in the form of bureaucracy. The immense scope of the questions opened up by a consideration of bureaucracy makes it necessary to limit the discussion here rather brutally. Thus we shall not be considering the purpose for which the bureaucratic mode was introduced (whether, for instance, rationality or repression was dominant – though they are not necessarily exclusive alternatives) or the extent of its penetration into all kinds of institutions. Rather, the focus will be very narrowly on one area of the consequences of its dominance, that of what kinds of questions and answers it facilitates in respect of the problems confronting it.

As is very well known, Weber's ideal type bureaucracy was characterized by the maximization of rationality, specialization, impersonality, hierarchy and accountability, all in the interest of efficiency. (A further characteristic of fundamental importance to education systems is that bureaucracies recruit on the basis of objective educational qualifications and credentials; the almost universal spread of the bureaucratic form of organization has placed a major requirement of credentialling on education systems.) This ideal type of organization has been supplemented (or supplanted) by what Therborn calls managerial technology. We may leave aside the question of whether this development represents a quantitative or a qualitative change, but we need to address its consequences. This change results from the changing role of the capitalist State. In Offe's (1975b) terms this has involved a change from 'allocative' state policies, where resources and powers that intrinsically belong to, and are at the disposal of the State, are allocated, to 'productive' state policies, where the State acts to remedy actual or anticipated disturbances in the accumulation process or to avoid or eliminate perceived threats to accumulation. In Offe's view, the ideal type bureaucracy is appropriate to the former type of state activity, while the 'application of predetermined rules through a hierarchical structure of "neutral" officials is simply insufficient to absorb the decision load that is implied by productive state activities'. What is involved is a different set of evaluation criteria. Under bureaucracy the most successful action is that which conforms most closely to established rules and procedures; under managerial technology the effectiveness of the product is the criterion of success.

Naturally, in any particular state apparatus, these two forms of organization will co-exist in various, and shifting, combinations. While there is an apparent effort to subsume an ever wider range of activities under technological criteria, i.e. to cast an ever wider range of problems in a form susceptible to technical solutions, what technological processes are incorporated where and how, are not decided solely on the basis of technological rationality. As we shall see below there is a great deal of what often presents itself as inertia within organizations, that prevents this coming about. It is clear, though, that the nature of the problems confronting the contemporary capitalist State is such as to push it in the direction of increasing 'productive' intervention, and thus away from the purely Weberian model of bureaucratic organization.

What, then, does this very basic knowledge of the organization of state apparatuses tell us about their 'selectiveness'. I want to consider just two contributions. First, it helps us recognize more clearly how the way the apparatus is organized constrains what it does. Policy options are selected on the basis of solutions available, and often it seems, questions are framed with available answers in mind. What appear as the available answers will result from the particular combination of bureaucracy/technology dominant in a state apparatus at a given time, which is obviously a matter for empirical investigation in any particular case. What we have here is something similar to the celebrated notion of 'the politics of non-decision making', except that the agenda is not assumed to be directly manipulated in favour of a particular individual or group; rather the process of agenda formation itself affects the agenda.

The second point concerns the direction in which this selection process operates. We cannot infer from the absence of direct manipulation involved, that the effects of the organization of the apparatus are in the end neutral, with one balancing out the other, as it were. Both forms, the purely bureaucratic and the technological, contain built-in biases, and both tend in the same direction. Both for instance, emphasize the importance of expertise and specialization; only the areas favoured differ. Both then are not only predisposed towards expert-devised and administered solutions, rather than 'popular' ones, but both have an inbuilt tendency to undervalue 'popular' reactions to and appraisals of, policies. Further as Erik Wright (1977: 218) puts it: 'Effectiveness and responsibility are not "neutral" dimensions of technical, formal rationality; they intrinsically embody certain broad political orientations.' At the same time, as has been frequently pointed out, attempts to reduce complex political problems to technical problems tend to have conservative implications. Thus the problem of rationality or repression as the purpose of bureaucracy may be an illusory one. Rationality entails social control; repression is a necessary concomitant of an organization based on impersonality and conformity. It hardly needs saying that it cannot be inferred from the foregoing sketch of the changing form of state apparatuses that they are effective in discharging the tasks laid upon them. This is far from the case, and this topic is the centre of one of the most important 'sub debates' about the nature of the capitalist State, namely whether state apparatuses can ever have the capacity to do what is required of them.

We must turn now from considering the form of the state apparatus in general, to an examination of the substance of education state apparatuses. This examination will focus chiefly on the nature of the teaching profession. Just as it is difficult to generalize about the nature of state apparatuses, so it is about teachers. They are not all paid, or everywhere licensed, by the State; in any particular case the character of the teaching profession will be the product of the relationship between the conditions available at different levels of the education system, and between the public and private sectors. However, in this area, there is a good deal more consistency and we would be justified in assuming that most teachers in all capitalist States are publicly trained, certified and paid. It is also important to note the different intra-societal positions of teachers at different levels of the education system. While it seems that in all societies greater prestige and autonomy attaches to tertiary than to secondary teachers and to secondary than to primary teachers, there is no similar consistency with respect to the absolute and relative extent of such differences.

The key point to be made, however, is that while teachers are typically state employees, they are not typically state officials. That is to say, their role performance does not conform to that of the ideal type bureaucratic official. They are not mere rule followers; they do not have access to a set of correct answers on procedures, or to a means of ensuring that problems will be posed in ways appropriate to such correct answers and procedures. Teaching in a mass education system is intrinsically inimical (though not necessarily impervious, or successfully resistant) to attempts at bureaucratic routinization and it is this that is the basic source of whatever classroom autonomy teachers have.

It is similarly difficult to make technicians of teachers. If bureaucracy is essentially characterized by rule following, technology is essentially characterized by the achievement of successful outcomes.

Here, the problem has to do with defining successful educational outcomes. We have already laid considerable emphasis on the mutually contradictory nature of the demands of education, and their closer specification in terms of immediate, technically-realizable, objectives seems likely to do little more than make such contradictions more salient. None of this is to say that attempts have not been made to counter this intrinsic resistance to routinization.

Teachers, then, enjoy a certain autonomy from direct control – the very nature of the circumstances which inhibit routinization also makes it difficult for any but 'insiders' to evaluate teachers' work. The extension and defence of this intrinsic autonomy by organized teachers' organizations is basic to our understanding of what is typically regarded as the 'inertia' of education systems, their lack of responsiveness to new requirements. Very broadly, the autonomy has been extended through (not always successful) attempts to adapt new demands to existing structures and practices, rather than vice versa, to an extent where education systems might almost be said to be self-reproducing. This applies both to curriculum and pedagogy, both of which currently display similarities to the practice of fifty years ago which are truly remarkable given the nature and pace of technological and social change in that period, and the supposed close relationship of education systems to such changes. What is typically characterized as the 'inertia' of education systems, then, as if it were somehow inherent in their nature, is better seen as an extension and defence by teachers of the autonomy intrinsic to their practice, which has as its target the protection of what they see as their own interests (and such perceptions will obviously differ across time and space) rather than the fulfilment of any broader or narrower appeal, especially one which might substantially damage those perceived interests.

Credence in the 'inertia' thesis is strengthened by the fact that the kind of resistance just mentioned has traditionally been, and been able to be, passive. This was possible due to the comparatively restricted, allocative, role played by the State; and also, associatedly, to a period of apparently permanently and regularly increasing economic prosperity. In such circumstances where the need for the State (and education system) to meet all the demands on it was not so pressing, and where, hence, their mutually contradictory nature not so apparent, the kind of control over the education system ceded by the State to the teachers under what I have called elsewhere (Dale 1979) 'licensed autonomy' was not inappropriate or ineffective. Economic slump, however, totally wipes out such preconditions. It effects all state apparatuses, both directly and indirectly, in two ways.

The direct effects appear in the form of cutbacks in financing and resources of all kinds. These are, in fact, comparatively easily dealt with without major changes in the relative autonomy of the education system or of the teaching profession within it. Booms, like slumps, do not develop at an even pace, and even within the era of continuing expansion there were hiccups which caused temporary cutbacks, with the result that the education system and the teaching profession had become used to administering them in ways which did not affect the basic balance of forces. Cuts, up to a certain point, and never willingly, can, like other external pressures on education systems, be interpreted within, and made to fit, the existing pattern of control over the education system.

What is proving much less easy to incorporate, and is, indeed, in England certainly, threatening to bring about a qualitative change in the nature of control over the education system, is the form of the indirect effects of economic decline. This has major effects on the nature, as well as the extent of state activity. Not only is the State compelled to take on new activities, which necessarily has implications for its existing activities of all kinds, but it is compelled to review and redirect those existing activities. That is to say, there is a change in the core problems of the State, bringing about a tighter – and quite possibly different – specification of the requirements of each of the state apparatuses, and the necessity, following this respecification, of attempting to curtail all state activity which now appears to be irrelevant or non-effective. What this entails for education systems, then, (and we should note that it is not just education systems which are affected – the widespread militancy among state employees in many countries can be seen as evidence of this) is not just cutbacks in resources, or intensified external pressure for redirection of the system, but a partial restructuring of the whole state apparatus.

It is at this point that the two halves of the state apparatus identified in this section, come together. As has been implied, there is a permanent tension between the bureaucratic form of the state apparatus and the substance of its practice. The outcome of this tension at any given time frames the kinds of questions that can be answered, and the kind of answers that can be given, through education as a state apparatus. Currently, we are witnessing strenuous efforts to impose greater central control on the education system, to impose some kind of bureaucratic/technology form(s) on teachers as state employees. Exactly what form(s) are put forward will be dependent on the outcome of the struggles between 'the bureaucrats' and 'the technocrats' within the state apparatus which we briefly discussed above, and of the nature and effectiveness of the teaching profession's resistance to them.

Three points need to be made in brief conclusion to this section. First, the existence of a degree of autonomy does not, of course, determine how it will be exploited, or in what ways it will be expanded, or what parts of it will be most strenuously defended, or how they will be defended. Such uses will be affected by the nature of the relationship between the levels of education, the relationship of education to other state apparatuses, the relationship between the organized teaching profession and major political groupings, power blocs and trade unions, and the nature and extent of state penetration of educational provision, all these in the historical context of a particular social formation.

Second, and associated with the previous point, it is essential to recognize the limited nature of this autonomy. It is a relative autonomy in respect only of the *execution* of the work of education systems. Teachers' autonomy does not extend to deciding the goals of education systems, nor their level of funding; though it has undoubted (but fluctuating) influence in such matters, the teaching profession has no control over them. This is clearly exemplified in the case of spending cuts. These are always resisted by the teaching profession, but scarcely ever successfully. So, while he who pays the piper always in the end calls the tune, he can specify more or less broadly what kind of tune he wants, but only with far greater difficulty exactly how it should be played. Under 'licensed autonomy' the teaching profession was given what amounted to a negative programme by the paymaster – 'play anything you like but Russian music and folk songs'. Under regulated autonomy the requirement is much more positive – 'play only modern German music, as far as possible just like the Germans do it – and we'll be listening to make sure you do'.

This argument is directly relevant to the problem of prominence and priority. While applying itself to the core problems may not be an objective necessity for an education system, there are significant pressures keeping them out of the 'any other business' place on the agenda, and ensuring that typically the core problems are amongst the most prominent targets of its activity. This does not mean that they are all equally prominent all the time, or at all levels of education. But while the State is dependent for its revenue on successful capital accumulation, guaranteeing the conditions for its continuation must come high on the list of priorities of all state apparatuses.

Third, a major intention behind this brief consideration of the nature of education as a state apparatus has been to point to ways of locating key points of tension within it, and to try to identify the ways in which different patterns of control over the education system create different spaces and opportunities for initiating or resisting change in education. Only by understanding not only the tasks confronting education systems, but the ways they are set up to carry out such tasks and the problems they have in arriving at and implementing programmes of action, can we effectively determine how programmes might be made to serve the needs of those for whom they are the only source of enlightenment and understanding of the world.

Education and hegemony

Three core problems have been identified for education systems in capitalist societies, furthering the process of capital accumulation, contributing to the provision of a societal context amenable to capital accumulation, and somehow legitimating the dominant mode of production. How education systems have tackled and do tackle the first two problems is relatively clear. The first problem has been translated into that of providing new members of the workforce possessing appropriate levels of knowledge and skill. The second, equally clearly, becomes translated into a question of social control; schools keep children off the streets, and ensure that for a large part of most days in the year they cannot engage in activities which might disrupt a social context amenable to capital accumulation but are exposed to attempts to socialize them into ways compatible with the maintenance of that context. It is, though, much more difficult to specify even broadly what is entailed in legitimation. A large part of the difficulty seems to me to inhere in the essentially compensatory connotation of the concept of legitimation; it has tended to be restricted to identifying ways in which the education system can make excuses for shortcomings of capitalism, or at least make life tolerable in spite of them. My view is that education systems make a much more basic contribution to the legitimation of capitalism through the way that they make so many of its key features seem absolutely normal. I propose, therefore, to label this core problem that of hegemony rather than one of legitimation (or ideology). Given the forgivable confusion existing around the concept of hegemony, it will be useful if I indicate in what sense I am using it. To begin with, it is necessary to distinguish it from both ideology and legitimation. The advantage of hegemony over ideology is that whether or not ideology is taken as intentionally distorting, it tends to have about it some notion of contrivance, of deliberate manipulation, and at the same time of having an identifiable source, of being devised to forward or protect a particular interest. Legitimation has rather more of a negative connotation. Its role typically seems to be of a post hoc compensatory or remedial character; it fills in for shortcomings in the desired course of events. Now there is no question at all that the range of both what are seen as ideological and legitimatory problems of the State increases as the State takes on an increasingly 'productive' character – this has been constantly argued above – but there is equally no doubt that such cosmetic or apologetic activities do not exhaust the state's, or the education system's, activity in this area. For it is not the case that the only way that the State legitimates the capitalist mode of production is by apologizing for it or disguising it. It frequently glorifies it, though not necessarily explicitly; the assumptions associated with the capitalist mode of production penetrate whole areas of state activity and form the basis of much of 'everyday life'. These assumptions, which taken together form the basis of bourgeois hegemony, exist in respect of societal, institutional and personal levels. At a societal level, what the nation is is defined in terms of qualities associated with the dominant mode of production – all that's best in its past is interpreted as leading inexorably to its present and its potential. At an institutional level its forms of government, its conceptions of property, and of public and private spheres further define the 'specialness' of the nation, though still in accordance with the preconditions of the dominant mode of production. At a personal level we find 'Protestant ethic' assumptions about both 'public personal' – citizen – and 'private personal' – individual – behaviour. The former is law-abiding, self-denying; the latter is motivated by 'possessive individualism' and the need to achieve. Education has always been a key means of encapsulating and perpetuating this hegemony, most neatly defined by Raymond Williams (1973) as 'a whole body of practices and expectations: our assignments of energy, our ordinary understanding of man and his world. It is a set of meanings and values which as they are experienced as practices appear as reciprocally confirming. It thus constitutes a reality for most people in society, a sense of absolute because experienced reality beyond which it is very difficult for most members of society to move in most areas of their lives'.

Further, as Femia puts it 'Hegemony is . . . the predominance obtained by consent rather than force of one class or group over other classes; and it is attained through the myriad ways in which the institutions of civil society operate to shape, directly or indirectly, the cognitive and affective structures whereby men perceive and evaluate social reality' (1975: 31).

In stressing the pervasiveness of hegemony it is possible to imply that it arises somehow spontaneously from the workings of the capitalist system. This would be a mistaken assumption. Hegemony has to be consciously and actively worked for and maintained; consent must be maintained among possibly recalcitrant groups. In this way it is to be distinguished from two theories which claim that capitalism provides its own justification and support. The first, the 'end of ideology' thesis, saw the material abundance provided by technological society, together with the possibility of technical solutions to all problems, as signalling the end of the need for ideological justification, the rolling up of the terrain of ideology. This theory reached its peak in the 1950s and 1960s; subsequent events have done little to justify its optimism/pessimism. The second theory is particularly associated with the work of Herbert Marcuse (see Trent Schroyer's (1973) very useful summary of it in *Critique of Domination*) where developing technology served to crush, control, or incorporate all individual aspirations or possible social conflict. Once again, these fears have not been realized, again in part because of the failure of technology to justify the faith, hopes and fears it engendered. It is interesting to compare these fears and hopes of 20 to 30 years ago with those engendered currently by the micro-chip revolution, which focus much more on the effects it may have on the structure of society than on how it will effect individual lives.

While neither of these theories is entirely valid, both of them reveal important truths about the 'self-reproduction' of the capitalist mode of production. They demonstrate that while it is not entirely able to reproduce itself, it contains elements which at certain conjunctures contribute substantially to that process. The danger with acknowledging this, however, – and it seems to me that it is widely if tacitly recognized – is that it can nudge the analysis back towards a search for the compensatory/remedial mechanisms which make up the shortfall of self-reproduction. I want to challenge this assumption that mass loyalty is made up of consumer gratification + legitimation, with the former the independent variable and the need for the latter increasing or declining with the fluctuations of the world economy. This approach amounts, in an era of economic contraction, to a paralleling of the 'end of ideology' thesis by what we might call a 'shortfall of legitimacy' thesis. The consent of the ruled in this view, has to be sought, and when the price is too high it has to be achieved through manipulation.

This kind of approach is based on the assumption, then, that 'in normal times', the status quo is self-reproducing. The strength of the concept of hegemony is that it not only enables us to see that it is not self-reproducing, but also points to how one might analyze the mechanism of reproduction. That mechanism has to be constructed and maintained, always under severe and conflicting pressures. As Richard Johnson (1979: 233) puts it 'Hegemony . . . concerns the extent and the modes by which common sense is made to conform to "the necessities of production" ' and to the construction of 'consent' and a political order. Common sense, lived experience, are articulated to and through ideas which express and encapsulate the requirements of the dominant class.'

This is a major task and one in which the mass media and the education system are of key significance. The studies by Bourdieu and Passeron (1977) and Apple (1979) have begun to explore how the education system contributes to hegemony, though in neither is the role of the State made explicit. I want very briefly to extend that work by attempting to reveal something of the complexity of the notion of hegemony, and how it is 'practised' as well as 'preached' – materialized in, as well as propagated through – education systems. The starting point of this approach is that hegemony refers both to the ultimate goals and values pursued by groups or individuals and to processes of attaining them; to use slightly different terminology, it is both expressive and instrumental.[4] However, these two aspects of hegemony are not necessarily in harmony with each other; it is not the case that goals determine processes, or even vice versa. The relationship between the two is variable and so too is their relative salience. Thus at a broad national level, it might be argued that in Germany a particular conception of process is dominant, while in Britain broad goals have been much more prominent. So we have on the one hand 'Teutonic efficiency' and on the other 'the gifted amateur' – and it is possible to trace if not the source then at least the support for these types in the respective education systems. Bourdieu and Passeron (1977) have done so brilliantly in their analysis of the means and modes by which 'polytechnical ease' has maintained its perceived superiority over 'technical mastery' in France and the consequences of this for the reinforcement of the existing class system.

Much recent writing, especially that around the theories of the end of ideology and the dominance of technological consciousness, has tended to concentrate exclusively on hegemony as it operates at the level of process, to see it as wholly instrumental, through focussing on the extent and effects of the penetration of technological consciousness. This has three shortcomings. First, it tends to imply, as I argued above, that such consciousness is self-generating and self-reproducing. Second, technological consciousness is rarely specified; it tends to be based on the extension of an ideal-type Taylorism, which is plainly inadequate. Third, it leads to a neglect of the problem of goals; Marcuse's fears are indeed born out at this level.

It may be useful at this point to suggest some of the specific ways in which schools serve to maintain hegemony. At the process (instrumental) level schools reinforce and consolidate hegemony largely through their own internal assumptions and procedures. They emphasize things like rule following, punctuality and hierarchy. They divide the mass of children into groups on a more or less arbitrary basis – the fact of division into groups seems to me almost as important as the basis of it. The importance of that basis – an inconsistent recipe whose chief ingredients are 'ability', 'personal characteristics', 'background' and 'achievement' – in legitimating inequality through an ostensible demonstration of the 'fairness' of social stratification has, of course, been appropriately documented and emphasized by Bowles and Gintis. Another set of the routine procedures of schools which has recently been receiving attention is that drawing on particular assumptions about gender differences (Macdonald 1980). Schools typically reflect in their own reward system – both in what kind of thing is rewarded and how it is rewarded – the reward system of capitalism – individual 'payment' for individual work. Through these processes schools reinforce the values of possessive individualism and achievement motivation. And it is important to note that such values are of critical importance not just to 'attitudinally attune' students to the demands of the workplace (which is where Bowles and Gintis place much the greatest emphasis), but also to socialize good consumers and good citizens. As Femia (1975: 34) puts it, 'political and social preferences . . .

reflect a man's assumptions about how society is and should be run, and in capitalist societies these assumptions are largely set by the ruling class through its highly developed agencies of political socialization.'

Interestingly, 'Taylorist technology' and a direct emphasis on the prime importance of efficiency are not common in schools. Their assumptions do, though, penetrate the wider education system. This has been particularly clearly demonstrated by Michael Apple (1979), in his identification of the influence of common sense categories in making decisions about curriculum content, of the assumptions and consequences of the dominant modes of evaluation (both programme and individual) in education, and of the pervasiveness of a particular conception of accountability.

There is an apparently permanent tendency – which is equally frequently repelled – for the instrumental to appear to overwhelm the expressive in discussions of the functions of schooling. The chief way this occurs is for economic growth to be put forward as an end in itself, as if contributing to the achievement of a lasting economic prosperity exhausted what education could do for maintaining the conditions of existence of a mode of production. This is not so. As Peter Berger is fond of pointing out, Man does not live by bread alone. He is not only a possessive individualist. And in any case, relying on continuing economic growth is a pretty shaky basis for legitimation.

It is a central function of hegemony, then, to encapsulate what a nation is; it must reflect back to the citizens an image of themselves, their individual and collective hopes and fears, possibilities and limitations, which does not conflict with the requirements of the dominant mode of production. Thus we live in a Christian, or an Islamic, or a scientific socialist country, whose history tells us that there are preferred ways of behaving for an Englishman, an Arab, or an Albanian. What the country is about is reflected and reinforced in what is taught (and much more in what is *not* taught) in schools, and in their rituals. English school children must experience a daily act of (implicitly Christian) worship, and have holidays for Royal Weddings, while American school children begin their day by saluting the flag, and celebrate their country's independence; the American, or English, way of life is celebrated in myriad minor ways every day.

It is clear that continuity and compatibility between the instrumental and expressive aspects of hegemony will not automatically be present. Business ethics and religious ethics are not always in tune – national interests cannot always be secured through national values. And so there is a crucial tension at the heart of hegemony, generating the permanent possibility of a crisis in hegemony and especially in the school's effectively tacking its hegemony problem; the crisis in English education which produced the Ruskin College speech, the Great Debate and the 1977 Green Paper may be seen as at least partly a result of this.

It is at least as important as recognizing the tension between the two aspects of hegemony to recognize that the assumptions and values encapsulated in the procedures and practices of schools are not necessarily shared by the pupils or students in those schools or reflected in their experiences. Any of them may be opposed at any time; some of them may be opposed all the time; to many of them most pupils are quite indifferent. Schools, then, as important sources of the consolidation of hegemony are at the same time key sites of what are usually referred to as 'struggles' over hegemony. We should note though that the terrains of the struggles, what is to be resisted, and the channels of resistance, are demarcated by the State through its control of the education system and the schools. The implications of this will be considered in the next section.

Modes of control and modes of resistance

While many analyses of state apparatuses emphasize their control tasks, often making such tasks central to the functioning of the apparatus, and while, on the other hand, there are analyses of resistance to such control, the mutual influence of forms of control and forms of resistance has been much less frequently remarked. I want in this section to argue that particular forms of control generate particular forms of resistance which themselves act back upon and modify the forms of control; the two elements cannot be separated from each other.

I suspect that part of the reason for the common separation of modes of control and resistance is to be found in the unsatisfactory nature of the concept of 'class struggle'! While many other basic Marxist concepts have been subjected to rethinking and refinement in recent years – the base/superstructure metaphor, for instance, or the 'October' concept of the revolution, – class struggle has remained in a rather bald, unreconstructed form. Worse than this, it has been introduced, unexplicated, to sidestep difficulties thrown up by attempts to refine other basic Marxist concepts – its existence is, for instance, given as the reason why apparently functionalist Marxist accounts are not subject to the same criticisms as the dreaded Parsonian functionalist accounts. So, while this is not the place to begin a wholesale reassessment of class struggle, I do want to indicate some ways in which it is unsatisfactory as an explanation, and certainly as the sole or even dominant explanation, of resistance within schooling, and to point to some possibly profitable extensions of, or modifications to, it.

In fact, 'class' is one of the Marxist concepts that has recently undergone some useful revision. Laclau, for instance, has convincingly argued for it to be at least accompanied, if not wholely replaced, by a conception of 'popular democratic' struggle. But even here, 'popular democratic' is used to qualify 'struggle'. The problem is that while it is frequently emphasized that 'the struggle goes on on many levels' etc., it is hard to escape the feeling that while that may be so, all these separate struggles are part of, and contributions to, one final cataclysmic struggle, which is almost certainly bound to be played out at the economic level, and the implicit model for which might be taken to be the general strike. Whatever the precise details, what seems often to be implied is a two-sided, if multi-layered, conflict with the sides and their commitments drawn up in advance, and the eventual outcome inevitably pre-ordained. The notion of *struggle* tends to be reduced to and equated with the notion of two-sided *contest.*

The major problem with class struggle as it has typically been used, then, is that it restricts our vision to certain forms and facets of resistance and this, combined with the tendency to try to fit every form of resistance to the contest format (and to dismiss as worthless any forms that cannot be so fitted) has the effect of obstructing or even denying access to the full complexity of forms of resistance and hence of their influence on forms of control.

Let us very briefly look at some of the ways that education systems are controlled. First of all, they are legally constituted. What can and should be done through them, and how, is broadly defined in legal terms. Apparent breaches of this legal framework can only be challenged through the courts, always a costly and lengthy process, which is thereby limited in its availability as a form of bringing about change. The courts though, have been successfully used to bring about educational change; it is very interesting to note that in the United States legal action has been successfully employed to bring about broadly 'progressive' changes (in the desegregation of schools etc.) while in England the opposite has been the case. Here, the courts have most notably been used to thwart attempts by Labour governments to introduce comprehensive secondary schooling (e.g. the Enfield and Tameside cases).

Education systems are also run as bureaucracies, emphasizing rule following, objectivity, and, of particular importance in this discussion, universalism, the view that all the rules and provisions apply equally to everyone. These characteristics imply that to change any particular situation it is necessary to change the rules pertaining to all similar situations. This is, of course, to accept the 'ideal type'. In the 'real world' no system of rules is sufficiently comprehensive or unambiguous to ensure that interpretation and negotiation are not only not possible but unnecessary. This produces grounds for contestation between the various affected parties at three separate levels – that of the rules themselves, that of the area(s) it is appropriate to apply rules to, and that of their implementation and interpretation. In all state education systems contestation over the implementation and interpretation of rules goes on throughout the system, including individual schools; its intensity in any particular sector will be partly a function of the established mode of educational administration, with the centralized/decentralized distinction of particular importance. Disputes over the nature and appropriateness of rules are typically fought out in the 'higher echelons' of the system, though not in total isolation from the practitioners and clients. A good example is the current discussion over the introduction of a 'core curriculum' in English schools. Any decisions on its desirability or content will be made by government: it becomes therefore a party political contest, though not exclusively so, for it is obvious that no government or opposition can afford wilfully to neglect or reject out of hand the views of practitioners. Those views, though, have to be put in a form in which they can be assumed to have an impact on party political deliberation. (On this latter point see Nigel Wright's (1976) discussion of the different strategies and policies of the National Union of Teachers and the Rank and File group within the NUT.)

The other characteristic of state apparatuses highlighted above was their tendency towards technocratic management, their increasing eagerness to replace politics with technical solutions. Examples of this tendency can be seen in the introduction of corporate management techniques to local government in England (see Cockburn 1977) and in the seemingly permanent attempts to 'technicize teaching' (of which teaching machines are only the most visible form). Part of the intention behind these attempts appears to be increasing 'teacher accountability' (though more rarely the accountability of other functionaries within the system or indeed of the system as a whole).

Major moves in this direction have been recently, and are still being, made, especially in the United States, but with considerable British interest and imitation. Two broad forms of opposition suggest themselves here, the demonstration of the ineffectiveness of the techniques/instruments in achieving their ends, and the demonstration that the ends themselves are seriously flawed. Both these strategies were, of course, employed in the eventually successful campaign against selection at 11+ in England. In considering forms of control and resistance at the level of the school it is necessary to specify the chief relevant implications of state provision. What difference, if any, does state provision make? First we should remember that state schools are part of a bureaucratic state apparatus. Headteachers or principals are bureaucratically accountable to their superiors for what goes on in their schools. This may be contrasted with the recent experiments with voucher systems to education which involve almost commercial notions of accountability with the introduction of market principles and consumer sovereignty to education. State schools have very little, if any, control over the amount of funds and resources they receive, and frequently this applies to the disbursement of those funds too. They have no way of getting emergency or immediate increases in funds – Parent Teacher Association jumble sales and social events may provide some schools with a few extras but they cannot ordinarily pay the salary of an extra teacher. On the other hand, its clients have no financial sanctions they can use directly against a state school – in fact they have very few sanctions of any kind.

The State has an obligation to educate all children between certain ages and the power to enforce compulsory attendance. Disaffected pupils may under certain circumstances be expelled from particular schools but they cannot be expelled from the system as a whole; the State retains the responsibility of providing them with education until the minimum school-leaving age. State schools have little control over whom they will educate: most of their pupils are allocated to them on the basis, usually, of age and residence, sometimes together with gender and/or measured ability. Such formulae effectively restrict parental choice of school very closely, even where there are possible alternatives. Parents can have very little official influence over what goes on in schools generally; schools are formally controlled by boards or authorities made up of representatives elected by the whole community and not only by those with a demonstrable interest in the schools.

State schools cannot, then, choose whom they will teach or, except within certain broad limits, what they will teach (the English Headteacher's much vaunted seignorial authority over his/her domain had its real limits rather sharply exposed in the William Tyndale case: see Dale 1980). They are only indirectly accountable to their clients; what they offer is not determined by their clients' perceived needs. They do not exist, in other words, primarily to serve the needs of any particular cohort of clients but of the community as a whole. State schools are, then, an imposition on all their clients; just how much of an imposition they are varies with the degree of coincidence between what they want from schools and how what the community wants from them is interpreted. It varies, that is to say, with the continuity between the values and aims of the school – as expressed in its rituals for instance – and those of the home.

What this kind of legal bureaucratic framework of schools produces is what Corrigan and Frith (1975) call 'institutional incorporation'. It ensures the attendance of all children between certain ages and their exposure to certain forms of educational experiences. This institutional incorporation is policed at the school level through the medium of school rules, a quasi legal framework of operation with sanctions to ensure compliance (at least theoretically). However, as Corrigan and Frith argue 'institutional incorporation' is not *necessarily* ideological incorporation '. . . to take account of an institution is not necessarily to accept it'. They go on,

> (Working-class children) *do* go to bourgeois schools: their ideas about what education is and what it is for and how it should be organised are the ideas embodied in their schools; there are no alternative, working class, 'educational' institutions; no notion of resisting education *as* education. And yet the evidence is that working class kids do, to a greater or lesser extent, resist something in the school system – how else explain the overwhelming evidence (that any teacher would confirm) that a school is a battleground, the pupils' weapons ranging from apathy through indiscipline to straight absence. And in this battle the school always is (precisely in terms of ideology) the loser. Every use of formal, repressive power reinforces working class experience of education as *imposition* (and not as a good-thing-that-will-extend-my-horizons-and-make-me-a-good-person); every (regular) experience of failure confirms the reality that 'this place has *nuthin*' for me'.
>
> The irony of this situation is that the kid's ideological resistance to bourgeois education (ie. their rejection of a set of norms and values) takes place in the context of and as *a result of* their incorporation in bourgeois institutions. The point is actually an obvious one: working class *experience*, even of bourgeois institutions, is not bourgeois experience; the working class situation, even within bourgeois institutions, is not a bourgeois situation.

This line of argument has been extended most notably by Paul Willis (1977), and by Corrigan himself (Corrigan 1979), while the essential continuity between the values of the school and the bourgeoisie's requirements of the school have been described by Bourdieu and Passeron (1977). In an important sense, it is a key theme of this whole collection of articles and I do not wish to extend this already superficial account to areas which are dealt with in greater depth in accompanying pieces. It is important to note, however, that if we are correct in stating that the central problem facing state education systems is the maintenance of an hegemony not inimical to the capital accumulation – presenting and having accepted as valid and appropriate a version of the world and the way it works which is in conformity with continuing capital accumulation – this does not mean that hegemony is static or unchanging. On the contrary, it is constantly changing under pressure of events, constantly forced to assimilate potential alternatives to its forms. So, and this is very important, incorporation does not entail subjugation; it can involve the hegemonic form being changed as well as, or even rather than, the alternative form. Neither is hegemony monolithic. Its various components (whose own boundaries and classifications are permanently shifting) develop and incorporate unevenly, so that alternative forms incompatible within one sector of hegemony are not so within others; again the various forms of hegemonic gender relations are the best example. It also seems to follow from this that hegemony is not so much about winning approval for the status quo, winning consent for it or even acceptance of it. Rather, what seems to be involved is the prevention of rejection, opposition or alternatives to the status quo through denying the use of the school for such purposes. It seems to me that if we seek a positive and active role for the school in the maintenance of hegemony, we rapidly find ourselves in deep theoretical and empirical waters (how is it laid down and by whom? how do the teachers react? etc.). On the other hand if we see the status quo being maintained by the 'normal process' of a relatively autonomous state apparatus with the occasional checking of excesses we may be nearer terra firma.

Finally, it is important to recognize that the economic and political reproduction that goes on in school goes on in a particular political context, the main parameters of which have been outlined above. Different kinds of resistance, with both different targets and different forms are called forth from different groups. The state apparatus is by no means monolithic in either its aims or its modes of operation; the forms of control implemented through educational institutions will not themselves be entirely consistent or free of contradictions. Thus, not only do the basic forms of control – bureaucracy and technocratic management – in their 'pure' forms themselves call forth particular kinds of resistance, but so do the various common combinations of them.

And, furthermore, the nature of their combination will itself be affected by the forms of resistance experienced. What we are faced with then is not either preparations for, or the early (or late) stages of a set piece battle, but a continuing series of rarely conclusive skirmishes on shifting terrain, between shifting alliances, in an over-all context of a system attempting to carry out contradictory functions, through means that may conflict with its objectives. It is in the spaces and interstices created by these and other contradictions that we must look for resistance to coalesce.

Acknowledgments

I would like to thank Kevin Brehony, John Fitz, Ann Wickham and especially Gordon West for their valuable comments on an earlier draft of this paper.

Notes

1 I have in mind here the work of, for instance, Robert Manzer and Maurice Kogan. See Boyle and Crosland (1970), Kogan (1971, 1975), Kogan and Packwood (1974), Kogan and Van der Eyken (1973), and Manzer (1970). Interesting and partial exceptions to this tendency are Kogan's own latest book, Kogan (1978) and Tapper and Salter (1978).

2 I cannot go into an adequate discussion of that work, but will rather put forward a particular position which owes most to the work of Claus Offe. Valuable summaries of, and contributions to, that debate on the nature of the capitalist state are to be found in Frankel (1979), Gold *et al.* (1975), Holloway and Picciotto (1978), Jessop (1977), and Esping-Anderson *et al.* (1976).

3 The effects of this heterogeneity of state apparatuses are particularly visible in the different definitions of women and children they separately use. For an analysis of definitions of childhood used in different legal discourses, see John Fitz, 'The Construction of the Child as a Legal Subject', in Dale, Esland, and MacDonald (1980), vol. II.

4 This usage follows that of Bernstein, Elvin and Peters. They speak of the expressive and instrumental cultures of the school, if not in a sense identical to that intended here, at least not incompatible with it. Their description of the function of the rituals is similarly compatible. 'The symbolic function of ritual is to relate the individual through ritualistic acts to a social order, to heighten respect for that order, to revivify the order within the individual and, in particular, to deepen acceptance of the procedures used to maintain continuity, order and boundary and which control ambivalence towards the social order. . . The rituals control questioning of the basis of expressive culture and so are conditions for its effective transmission and reception. They buttress the formal authority relations and evoke respect through the ritualization of difference and similarly of function; they create continuity in individual and social time and relate the value system and its derived norms to

an approved external order' (Bernstein, Elvin and Peters 1971 version: 160-1).

Bibliography

Althusser, Louis (1971), 'Ideology and Ideological State Apparatuses', in *Lenin and Philosophy and other Essays*, London: New Left Books.

Apple, Michael (1979), *Ideology and the Curriculum*, London: Routledge & Kegan Paul.

Archer, Margaret (1979), *Social Origins of Education Systems*, London: Sage.

Bernstein, Basil, Elvin, H. L., and Peters R. S. (1971), 'Ritual in Education,' in Cosin, B. R., Dale, I. R., Esland, G. M. and Swift, D. F. (eds), *Schools and Society*, London: Routledge & Kegan Paul (first published in *Philosophical Transactions of the Royal Society of London* B (1966), 251 (772), 429-36).

Bourdieu, Pierre and Passeron, Jean-Claude (1977), *Reproduction*, London: Sage.

Bowles, Samuel and Gintis, Herbert (1976), *Schooling in Capitalist America*, New York: Basic Books.

Boyle, Edward and Crosland, Anthony (1971), *The Politics of Education*, Harmondsworth: Penguin.

Cockburn, Cynthia (1977), *The Local State*, London: Pluto.

Corrigan, Paul (1979), *Smash Street Kids*, London: Macmillan.

Corrigan, Paul and Frith, Simon (1975), 'The Politics of Youth Culture', *Working Papers in Cultural Studies*, 7/8 (Summer), 231-9.

Dale, Roger (1977), 'Implications of the Rediscovery of the Hidden Curriculum for the Sociology of Teaching', in Dennis Gleeson (ed.), *Identity and Structure*, Driffield: Nafferton, pp. 44-54.

Dale, Roger (1979), 'The Politicization of Deviance: Responses to William Tyndale', in L. Barton and R. Meighan (eds), *Schools, Pupils and Deviance*, Driffield: Nafferton, pp. 95-112.

Dale, Roger (1980), 'Control, Accountability and William Tyndale', in Dale, Esland and Macdonald, vol. I.

Dale, Roger, Esland, Geoff and Macdonald, Madeleine (eds) (1980), *Education and the State* vol. I, *Schooling and the National Interest* vol. II, *Politics, Patriarchy and Practice*, London: Routledge & Kegan Paul.

Esping-Anderson, Gosta, Friedland, Roger, and Wright, Erik Olin (1976), 'Modes of Class Struggle and the Capitalist State', *Kapitalistate*, 4-5 (Summer), 186-220.

Femia, Joseph (1975), 'Hegemony and Consciousness in the Thought of Antonio Gramsci', *Political Studies* 23, 1, 29-48.

Fitz, John (1980), 'The Construction of the Child as a Legal Subject', in Dale, Esland and Macdonald, vol. II.

Frankel, Boris (1979), 'On the State of the State', *Theory and Society*, 7, 199-242.

Gold, David, Lo Clarence, and Wright, Erik Olin (1975), 'Recent Developments in Marxist Theories of the Capitalist State', *Monthly Review* Part I, October, Part II, November.

Gramsci, Antonio (1971), *Selections from the Prison Notebooks*, Quintin Hoare and Geoffrey Nowell-Smith (eds), London: Lawrence & Wishart.

Hogan, David (1979), 'Capitalism, Liberalism and Schooling', *Theory and Society*, 83, 387-413.

Holloway, John and Picciotto, Sol (1978), *State and Capital*, London: Edward Arnold.

Jessop, Bob (1977), 'Recent Theories of the Capitalist State', *Cambridge Journal of Economics*, 1, 4, 353-73.

Jessop, Bob (1978), 'Capitalism and Democracy: The Best Possible Shell?' in Gary Littlejohn *et al.* (eds), *State and Power*, London: Croom Helm, pp. 10-51.

Johnson, Richard (1979), 'Three Problematics: Elements of a Theory of Working Class Culture', in Charles Critcher, John Clarke and Richard Johnson, *Working Class Culture*, London: Hutchinson, 201-37.

Kogan, Maurice (1971), *The Government of Education*, London: Macmillan.

Kogan, Maurice (1975), *Educational Policy Making*, London: Allen & Unwin.

Kogan, Maurice (1978), *The Politics of Educational Change*, Manchester: Manchester University Press.

Kogan, Maurice and Packwood, Tim (1974), *Advisory Councils and Committees in Education*, London: Routledge & Kegan Paul.

Kogan, Maurice and van der Eyken, Willem (1973), *County Hall*, Harmondsworth: Penguin.

Laclau, Ernesto (1977), *Politics and Ideology in Marxist Theory*, London: New Left Books.

Macdonald, Madeleine (1980), 'Schooling and the Reproduction of Class and Gender Relations', in Dale, Esland and Macdonald, vol. II.

Manzer, Robert (1970), *Teachers and Politics*, Manchester: Manchester University Press.

Miliband, Ralph (1968), *The State in Capitalist Society*, London: Quartet.

O'Connor, James (1973), *The Fiscal Crisis of the State*, New York: St Martin's Press.

Offe, Claus (1973), 'The Abolition of Market Control and the Problem of Legitimacy (1)', *Kapitalistate* 1, 109-16.

Offe, Claus (1975a), 'Further Comments on Muller and Neususs' *Telos*, 25, Fall, 100-11.

Offe, Claus (1975b), 'The Capitalist State and the Problem of Policy Formation', in Leon J. Lindberg, Robert Alford, Colin Crouch and

Claus Offe (eds), *Stress and Contradiction in Modern Capitalism*, Lexington, Mass: Lexington Books, 125-44.

Schroyer, Trent (1973), *Critique of Domination*, New York: Braziller.

Tapper, Ted and Salter, Brian (1978), *Education and the Political Order*, London: Macmillan.

Therborn, Goran (1978), *What Does the Ruling Class Do When It Rules?* London: New Left Books.

Williams, Raymond (1973), 'Base and Superstructure in Marxist Cultural Theory', *New Left Review*, 82, December, 3-16.

Willis, Paul (1977), *Learning to Labour*, Farnborough: Saxon House.

Wright, Erik Olin (1977), *Class, Crisis and the State*, London: New Left Books.

Wright, Nigel (1976), 'Teacher Politics and Educational Change', in Geoff Whitty and Michael Young (eds), *Explorations in the Politics of School Knowledge*, Driffield: Nafferton, pp. 244-56.

Chapter 5

Schooling and the reproduction of patriarchy: unequal workloads, unequal rewards

Gail P. Kelly and Ann S. Nihlen

Reproduction theorists assert that the schools reinforce the division of labor in the society by maintaining class, race and gender inequalities. The argument states that schools do not mediate or seek to change the structures of society or the characteristics of individuals who occupy positions of wealth, status and power. The schools are static because they are a microcosm of the society, rather than an agent for change as some theorists maintain.

While there is a large literature documenting the schools' roles in the reproduction of inequality, for the most part, it has not dealt systematically with the issue of gender (Frazier and Sadker 1973; Sexton 1976; Stacy *et al*. 1974). Research on women's schooling sees a direct relation between women's education and the status of women, and seeks to reform school practices in the hope that the schools could be made a force for equality. Yet that literature has been extremely vague concerning several issues. First and foremost it has glossed over the nature of sex inequality and tended to see it unidimensionally in terms of the paid labor force (MacDonald 1980b). It has neglected issues of 'private (or 'domestic') life' – notably marriage and child-bearing and raising – and how it affects sexual inequality. Much of our evaluation of the school's role in reproduction of the division of labor within the society is framed in terms of wage and workforce status of women versus men. By so doing we deny the impact of the family in patriarchical society where women, regardless of class, ethnicity and race, and their wage and status, retain major responsibility for household chores and for bearing and raising children, which men do not.[1] Given this, an evaluation of the school's role in reproduction of the sex division of labor cannot proceed on the basis of whether the schools prepare women for the same 'public' or workforce roles as men. Rather, it must also deal with forms of inequality in terms of responsibility for domestic life. Thus, inequality can be seen not only in terms of public life, but in terms of the burdens of women versus men in private life. Women could conceivably have wage and status equity with men within the workforce, but inequality remains if women still work their job in the household.

A second problem which the literature has yet to address, which we believe crucial, relates to what students are taught as opposed to what students learn or choose to learn. Research on women's education, as we will show in this essay, has always presumed that (1), the schools impart a unitary message regarding appropriate division of labor between the sexes and (2), that whatever the schools teach, students learn. Many studies have taken curriculum or an analysis of staffing patterns of the school as the sum total of school knowledge. They have not asked whether contradictory messages exist within the school environment to be considered separately as formal and informal (or 'hidden') curriculum. In addition, the presumption of student as passive agent persists without any understanding that students may not learn what schools teach by choice, or may filter knowledge and use it to their own advantage.[2] The circumstances under which 'resistance' occurs and when it becomes significant in countering attempts of the schools is an area relatively untouched by the literature on women's schooling. It is one which needs to be developed, for there have been major changes in women's public and private lives historically which cannot be explained if we presumed female students did not renegotiate the messages of the schools.

This essay reviews the evidence linking the schools to the reproduction of the sex role division of labor within US society. The essay begins with a discussion of the nature of the sex role division of labor in the United States in public and private life. It then turns to an analysis of the schools and evidence linking them to this division of labor. Finally, we point to new ways of thinking about women's education and its significance for future research.

The nature of sex inequality

Inequality between the sexes at its simplest level consists of separate spheres of work which result in differences in status, wealth and power. Much of it derives from the distinction between the value of work in private (or domestic) and public domains. The origins of this distinction are unknown, scholars have documented its intensification with the development of capitalism and industrialization, but have also shown that in many socialist nations, notably the Soviet Union and

China, the same distinctions and the inequalities implicit in them are maintained (Croll 1978; DuBois *et al.*, in press; Lapidus 1979; Rosaldo 1974; Sacks 1974; Weinbaum 1976).

What we know to be true is that industrialization means that the workplace is separated from the household and that production for surplus becomes differentiated from production for use value, although one does not extinguish the other. Put more simply, income generation is placed outside the family, yet the family remains as a social and economic unit dependent on the work performed both inside and outside the home. As industrialization increases, the separation of household from income generation becomes more intense as does the necessity for wage labor. The family as a unit is charged predominantly with reproduction (or procreation), and child-rearing and the division of labor becomes such that women, by and large, become responsible for the household and child-rearing dependent on income earned outside the home by men. In most societies this is structurally imposed; it is not a 'natural' phenomenon, and it is directly related to the wage structure for males. Employers can pay men less if unpaid females labor in the household to prepare food, clean, clothe, and rear the children.[3]

Sex role divisions of labor within the society are not necessarily contingent on women versus men confined to domestic versus public spheres, but rather on primary responsibility within one sphere versus another. Women's work is to maintain the home and the family, bear and rear the child, buy, clean, and prepare the food, 'make life beautiful', and to nurture man and child (DuBois *et al.*: chapter 3). Men's primary responsibility is work outside the home in wage labor. These definitions of sex role divisions are all but idealized; women's work has rarely been confined to the domestic sphere even if it is the female's prime responsibility.

The sex role division of labor relates not only to the division of labor between public and private, but also to the division of labor within public life. Women have always, and increasingly, worked outside the home at wage labor while retaining their 'jobs' in the domestic sphere. Inequality between the sexes, then, can be seen as the double job wherein women work two full-time loads, while men do not.[4]

The division of labor between the sexes is also a division of labor that manifests itself in inequalities in wage labor. While approximately 45 per cent of women in the US are active in the American workforce – and this figure increases yearly, and varies as to whether women are working-class, minority, or white middle-class – women are in inferior positions to men in income-generation and status. Women earn less than 56 per cent of male income, regardless of job categories; they are concentrated in the lowest paying jobs in both service and industrial sectors of the economy; they are segregated into occupations which permit very little upward mobility; and they are concentrated in the 'marginal' areas of the workforce (Chafe 1972; Smuts 1971). Women are, in short, not stratified in the workforce as are men. A few statistics will make this clearer.

In 1972 less then 7 per cent of all clerical workers were male while 25 per cent of minority and 36 per cent of white women worked at such jobs. 15 per cent of white men (and 9 per cent of minority males) were managers and administrators versus 2 per cent of minority and 5 per cent of white women. In blue-collar jobs, 16 per cent of minority and 21 per cent of white men were employed as skilled workers versus 1 per cent of women, both white and minority. Thirty-seven per cent of minority and 19 per cent of white women were employed as service workers while but 15 per cent of minority and 7 per cent of white men held similar jobs (Allen 1979: 676-7).

The pattern of employment reflects a hierarchy wherein women are subordinate to men in income and status, compounded by race. Black men are in a subordinate position to white men; white women to men and black and minority women subordinate to white women and all men.

Workforce status inequality for women is a function both of discriminatory practices imposed by employers and the sex role division of labor that places prime responsibility of the family and child-rearing on women. Marriage and children tend to drive women out of the workforce or to reduce their wage labor to less than full time (Standing 1976). Working-class and minority women stand as an exception, poverty drives women into the workforce regardless of marriage, age and number of children. As of 1974, of the 35.8 million women in the US workforce, 14.8 million were single, either having never married, or having been divorced or widowed and 21 million were married. The workforce participation rates of women with children show the effects of child-rearing. About 10.5 million women in the workforce have children; of these 6.5 million have children between the age of 6 and 17; only 4 million have children under the age of 6 (US Department of Labor 1975). Because of the structure of work and the family within the society, women's 'double burden', coupled with discrimination, tends to produce both workforce status and wage inequalities between men and women (Seccombe, in press).

When one looks at education and the reproduction of inequality within the society there are several questions that need to be asked. First, to what extent does education normalize the separation of prime responsibility in public and private domains that we have discussed here? Does the school, through formal and informal instruction, seek consistently to portray domestic life as the female domain, with work outside the household as secondary, and the public domain as the male preserve? Second, does the school system provide ideological rationales for women's lesser status and income-producing role within the workforce? And, does it do so for all women, regardless of class, race and ethnicity? Third, how does the school prepare women for the workforce? Is the pattern of women's income and occupations a function of the double burden which the schools either normalize or mitigate, or is it a function of the schools channeling women away from occupational preparation that would qualify women for jobs within the workforce of higher status and income? These sets of questions will allow us to see if the schools reinforce the private/public division of labor within the society or seek to equalize male/female domestic roles which account in large part for the pattern of sex inequality. They will also allow us to see whether the schools seek to provide women with qualifications equal to those of men which might conceivably, at least for single women, women heads of households, or women with grown children, produce a stratification pattern equal to that of men if workforce discrimination were broken? Finally, and related to this last question, do schools, outside of occupational preparation, encourage or discourage women's resistance to the sex role division of labor? This latter question is particularly important, given the fact that historically women have sought, and sometimes have succeeded in breaking the pattern which we have described here. The current sex role division of labor, at least in the workforce, is not what it has always been. In the 1920s, the 1940s and since the 1960s women have resisted and to some extent renegotiated their roles both within domestic and public life (Chafe 1972). Has this been a school-produced phenomenon or a phenomenon that functions independent of, or despite, education?

Schooling and sexual inequality

School knowledge consists of both formal and informal curriculum. The formal curriculum is the knowledge transmitted through textbooks and curriculum guides, certified by school examinations. The informal curriculum, sometimes referred to as the 'hidden' curriculum, is not always sanctioned by examination or congruent with the knowledge prescribed by the formal curriculum. Rather, it is the 'noise' of the school – the messages implicit in the authority structure of the school, its staffing patterns, and the ways in which the curriculum is transmitted, and the systems of rewards and 'correct' behavior. In the discussion which follows, we will focus on both the 'hidden' and formal curricula of the schools, beginning first with the formal sex role division of labor in the schools in authority and staffing patterns and then the formal curriculum and the ways it is transmitted. Finally, we will turn to the issue of whether the messages transmitted in the school, however consistent or inconsistent they may be, are internalized by female students.

Authority patterns and staffing

The schools in the US are staffed predominantly by women. Superficially, one could argue that the high visibility of women in the school system stands as encouragement for girls to enter the workforce. While this may well be the case, and explains why so many girls see teaching as a desirable occupation, entry into paid labor is not necessarily key to ending sex inequalities. As we pointed out earlier, the nature of sex inequality has to do with not only women's roles in public life, but also the responsibility for domestic life and its relation to inequality.

School authority patterns represent a microcosm of the relative status of women in the workforce, despite the large number of women on school staffs. The school system places males in positions of authority and women in subordinate roles, and it does this regardless of qualification. A few statistics will illustrate this. In the early 1970s, out of 14,379 district superintendents, 90 were female; 55 out of 731 associate superintendents were women; and women accounted for 126 out of 4,402 assistant superintendents. Women fared better as administrative assistants to superintendents where they numbered 356 out of a total 2,345 persons. This is the case despite the fact that women hold over 20 per cent of doctoral degrees of individuals employed at this level (Estler 1975: 364-5).

The pattern of male authority over females holds in each school in the United States where 67.2 per cent of all teachers are women, yet women are less than 16 per cent of all principals or assistant principals. These figures mask the status and wage hierarchies of education institutions. Female principals are elementary school principals. Twenty per cent of all elementary school principals are women; less than 7 per cent of middle school and secondary school principals are female (Estler 1975).

The underrepresentation of women in positions of authority in public school is relatively new, for in 1928 women were 55 per cent of elementary school principals (Estler 1975). The pattern does mirror women's place in the contemporary workforce. In the school system women are segregated into the lowest status jobs. The higher the level of education the fewer the number of women in administrative and teaching positions. Women, when in positions of authority, supervise, for the most part, women rather than men. This reflects the vertical segregation of the American workforce where the few women in management positions are found in predominantly female occupations.

Women, as classroom teachers, dominate the elementary school where they constitute close to 90 per cent of the teaching force (Frazier and Sadker 1973; Simpson 1974). In the junior and senior high schools the percentage of women teachers declines. The more adult the student becomes and the closer he or she is to entering the workforce, the less visible women workers become. This pattern is often a product of conscious hiring practices of school districts (Estler 1975: 364).

In higher education the dominance of male over female intensifies. Less than 3 per cent of all top-level college and university administrators in 1972 were women (versus 11 per cent in 1969/70). Most women college presidents are presidents of all or predominantly female institutions. Women form but 22 per cent of the faculties of institutions of higher education. They are concentrated in the lower ranks of instructional staffs and underrepresented in the higher ranks. The lower the status of the institution (e.g., two-year colleges versus four-year colleges versus universities), the greater the number of women administrators, women faculty, and women full professors (Kilson 1976; Sexton 1976: 124). These statistics tell a simple tale: schools mirror gender inequalities in status and income of the workforce at large.

The schools perhaps may also reflect inequality which has less to do with status wage differentials and positions of authority in the workforce. Adult work in the school may also promote the separation of public and private domains and the concept that while women may work, work for a wage is secondary to them if they are married or have children. They may also imply that in order to work women cannot be married and have families. There are, to our knowledge, almost no studies which deal with the characteristics of women school staffs beyond those depicting educational backgrounds, income and positions within the hierarchy. We do not know whether, for example, the few women who are in positions of authority are women who are single or are married with small children. If they are single, this may serve to remind all that women can choose to work for a wage, but that choice involves forsaking marriage and children, which it does not for men. If women in positions of authority are single and childless and women in subordinate positions are not, then the school's messages may be even stronger.

Another dimension that has yet to be examined is the extent to which school authority patterns and personnel policies preclude 'motherhood.' School systems have traditionally enforced leaves for pregnant women, in some districts from the moment a woman begins to 'show.' This normalizes the concept that maternity and work are incompatible.

Systematic research on female teachers and staff and the extent to which messages normalizing inequality either in terms of the primacy of the domestic domain for women versus men or the choice between family and women's work is sorely needed.

Subject matter staff segregation

One dimension of school staffing patterns that relates to inequality within public life is the segregation of teaching staffs by subject matter, which occurs predominantly in post-primary education and which both normalizes occupational segregation and transmits messages about 'appropriate' knowledge for women versus men.

In the US school system women are teachers of some subjects and not others (Simpson 1974). They are, by and large, concentrated in language arts, foreign languages, and to a lesser extent social studies. They become rare in mathematics and the sciences (except for biology). In higher education women constitute less than 1.9 per cent of the Business faculties; 0.4 per cent of Engineering teachers, 4.3 per cent of teachers of Physical Sciences, Mathematics and Computer Science faculties. They are, however, 20.6 per cent of teaching faculties in Education and 10.2 per cent in Health Sciences (concentrated in nursing and health-related professions) (Sexton 1976: 124).

The concentration of female teaching staffs in these fields parallels women's workforce participation patterns. The subjects taught predominantly by female teachers correspond to preparation for occupations in which women are represented. Conversely, the absence of women in business administration, the sciences and mathematics-related fields corresponds with the low number of female teachers in them. The gender of a teacher, when sex-segregated by subject area, may well tell students that particular subject matter is legitimate knowledge for one sex, rather than both sexes.

The authority and staffing patterns of the school, in sum, represent the type of inequality between the sexes that exist in the workforce in terms of status and income distribution. Women are segregated into lower, less prestigious positions and into specific institutions (the primary school) and specific subject areas mirroring the vertical and horizontal segregation in the workforce. This is well documented. What we do not know is the extent to which the school staffing patterns transmit messages about the division of labor between the sexes in domestic and public spheres. Does the staffing pattern promote domestic life as primary to women who work and not primary to men who work? Does it normalize the concept of women's double job? By virtue of which women are placed in positions of authority does the school 'teach' all that women who wish to succeed in work must not marry or have children – a choice which men, given the structure of work and the family, do not have to make?

Formal curriculum

A formal curriculum does not represent all 'school knowledge,' but it does represent what schools purport to teach. Who the knowledge is distributed to is yet another question; here we will treat solely sex differentiation within curricular materials, taking textbooks as our example. We will ask whether the messages transmitted in the formal curriculum of the school are similar to those reflected in the authority structure and staffing patterns. Does the formal curriculum reinforce the primacy of the domestic sphere for women? Does it legitimate occupational segregation and the position of women in the workforce? Does it present women's role in public life as opposed to the ability to marry and have children?

There have been numerous analyses of school textbooks, predominantly beginning reading primers and children's literature.[5] They show that, for the most part, women are ignored in the curricular materials. Women either do not exist or, if they exist, they are confined to domestic life, although this varies by grade level. Primary school texts more often than secondary and college level books, depict women. In some, 25 per cent of textual space and illustrations contain females (Weitzman *et al.* 1972). Women, however, are background figures and not central to the numerous readings. Adult women are almost never depicted outside the house; they also engage predominantly in domestic chores – cleaning, cooking, sewing, nurturing. In some illustrations women are shown cooking dinner while the male (father) sits in an easy chair smoking his pipe and reading the newspaper. In the primary texts few women work outside the home for a wage. The few who do are in nursing, teaching, or secretarial jobs. Interestingly enough, those who work are not portrayed either as married or having children.

While women are present in elementary primers, albeit in a minority, they are scarcer in secondary and college level books. Treckler, who studied secondary school history texts found that in the rare instances they mentioned women, they deliberately distorted women despite the advancements in knowledge about women's history since the mid 1960s (Treckler 1973). Women were side-lined to roles of pioneer wife, sewer of flags, social worker, nurse, presidential helpmates, and the like. The women's suffrage movement, women's trade unionism, etc. were either ignored or relegated to one-line. Women simply did not shape history; rather, Treckler points out, they simply were present and their contributions were ancillary to men's and domestic in nature.

The rigid stereotyping in the texts is well documented as is their language, which invariably uses the generic 'he' (which also appears on school report cards which read 'The information contained in this report card will show you how well your child is succeeding with *his* school work') (Buffalo, New York, Public Schools 1980). The use of male pronouns and nouns conveys the message that only males act or are important; 'she' is not. This point is made cogently by the studies of mathematics texts where 'he' always solves the problem (Kepner and Koehn 1977; Jay and Schminke 1975).

The studies of school texts underscore the presence of curricular messages that deny women major roles in public life and emphasize the primacy of women in the domestic domain. Current research has suggested that these messages change by level of education, but it has not documented how thoroughly. Nor has attention been paid to whether they are consistent across all subject matter. In addition, we do not know whether the same images are conveyed in the multitude of workbooks and dittoed handouts used in the classroom.

While current school texts reinforce inequality between the sexes, their messages differ from those transmitted by school staffing patterns and authority structures in which women are actively involved in work outside the home. The texts deny such roles, but that denial is one which legitimates women's secondary status in public life and within the school system. Women are subordinate to men in society because, according to the texts, public life is 'unnatural' for women. The texts also contain implicit rationalization of occupational segregation within the labor force. They depict 'traits' of women appropriate to certain occupational roles. For example, women are portrayed as nurturing, passive and dependent. Nurses, elementary school teachers and secretaries are considered good workers then they embody these characteristics. Finally, the texts normalize the double job for women. Women may work for a wage (which the texts rarely mention), but they must take primary responsibility for rearing children, cooking, and maintaining the home.

Channeling and counseling

Formal instruction and hiring practices are not the only elements in the schools that correspond with inequality between male and female in society. Counseling procedures also do. There is an extensive literature which points to vocational testing and guidance procedures as active agents in sex role reproduction.[6] Until recently, the Strang Vocational Inventory had pink and blue forms, proposing different ranges of occupations for males and females. Females, for example, could choose to be stewardesses and nowhere could indicate preferences to become pilots, engineers or mechanics. They could opt to be 'businessmen' though. On the basis of these tests high school counselors have been accused of actively channeling girls into educational programs that prepare girls only for such occupational roles.

The recently developed Vocational Awareness programs for elementary schools similarly channel men and women. These programs do not counsel or test students; rather, they expose students to the world of work through visits to local factories and businesses. This 'reality of work' is an object lesson of male/female roles. No longer does the school feel it need mediate, it merely exposes students to patriarchical relations in work without comment. The texts normalize separate and unequal relations between the sexes by omission and commission regardless of reality; counseling programs, in the attempt to be realistic, normalize these relations by bringing students to witness them.

Formalized curriculum and programs, school staffing patterns and authority structures as well as counseling are easily identifiable elements in the school. More subtle and perhaps more critical are the ways in which knowledge is transmitted in the classroom where it is distributed through regularities in classroom interactions. These interactions may or may not be consonant with the formalized aspects of the school.

Knowledge distribution in the classroom

Reproduction theorists and scholars of women's education have focussed their efforts on analysing the formal curriculum and school authority patterns. There is a relative paucity of research that deals with differential knowledge distribution within the classroom between the sexes except as it relates to access. We know, for example, that women are systematically denied certain knowledge because they are channeled in the high school away from it; in higher education they are often simply denied admission into certain programs. Women are thus schooled in subject matter which carries gender weight. Mathematics and science are 'male' provinces, education, nursing, social work, literature, and English are 'female' domains. While Title IX of the 1965 Civil Rights Act has attempted to remove access barriers, albeit somewhat unsuccessfully in higher education, those who have assessed its impact have not tackled the issue of differential distribution of knowledge within the classroom in which both males and females are present.

Are there regularities in the classroom which reinforce sex role divisions of labor? There are a few studies which suggest that through schooling, teachers, regardless of their gender, tend to interact less with girls than with boys and that this pattern intensifies at secondary and college levels.[7] This may well mean that the female student is taught that education is not as important for her as it is for her male peers. Research has shown us that teachers do not interact with girls as frequently as with boys. When they do, they tend to respond to them either neutrally or negatively, although this varies by a girls' class and race. Students in a SUNY/Buffalo Sociology of Education course found that teachers in all black secondary school classes tended to interact more and more positively with female than with male students; the reverse was the case in a predominantly white working-class school. In classes in hetereogeneous integrated schools teachers followed the regularities of the white working-class school with some exceptions; they responded more positively to white middle-class girls than to black males or females or white working-class girls or boys.

While teachers tend to reinforce girls less frequently than boys, with variations by class and race, what they reinforce girls for is in, and of, itself important. Reinforcement tends to be for passivity and neatness, not for 'getting the right answer.' Nihlen (1976) found in her study of a working-class primary class that teachers did not attempt to change girls' emphasis on 'sociability' which meant that the girls began de-emphasizing academic performance and achieved below their capabilities. These working-class girls literally began doing different kinds of work in the school room from their working-class male peers and a similar group of middle-class children, and were systematically positively reinforced for not learning academic tasks by their teachers.

The few studies that we have on classroom knowledge distribution by gender suggest that teachers do not take female students seriously and that within the classroom girls' academic performance is systematically devaluated. This implies that the school is not 'for keeps' for the female. While fragmentary data suggest such conclusions, we have far too little hard data. We do not know, for example, whether these patterns vary by school subjects. Do female students receive greater reinforcement for academic performance in 'female' subjects like English and foreign languages than in 'male' subjects like mathematics and physical sciences? Are there differences in these regularities among black women, white working-class women and middle-class females by subject matter and are they dependent on the class or racial mix of the schools? Are there differences in these patterns between co-educational and sex-segregated schools, between traditional classrooms and open classrooms, in various tracks within the schools? These questions are yet to be answered and are essential to a deeper understanding of the school's roles in reproducing sex inequality.

Reproduction and resistance

There is much evidence to suggest that the schools do not mitigate and may indeed actively reinforce inequality by gender and that the dimensions of this inequality extend beyond occupational channeling and stratification to inequalities in workload. Thus far, we, as have most who investigate education in the framework of the reproduction of inequality, have been guilty of presuming that students internalize the schools' messages or that student rejection of school knowledge, if it exists, makes very little difference. Such assumptions may not be warranted.

We wish, for the remainder of this essay to turn our attention to the issue of whether girls in fact do become what the messages of the school would have them become. This question may be crucial to understanding the ways in which schools operate to reinforce sexual inequality and the ways in which other questions about women's schooling may be posed.

So much research has gone into examining how school staffing and curriculum differentiate male from female, that we have very little real knowledge about whether girls accept what the schools teach. Instead we find a confusing literature examing whether girls internalize school messages which is inconclusive and rests on an assortment of evidential bases. Some of it suggests that girls either ignore the sex role messages of the schools, or renegotiate them.

For example, if, as the regularities in the classroom suggest, school achievement is 'not for girls', we would expect to find that girls systematically underachieve. And, achievement studies that base themselves on standardized tests indicate that girls out achieve boys across the board until tenth grade; thereafter boys score higher (Finn 1980; Finn, Dulberg and Reis 1979). This would seem to indicate that it takes the schools ten years to teach girls to learn to live down to expectations. However, if one takes actual school grades as a basis for assessing achievement, a different result emerges (Ellis and Peterson 1971). Girls get higher marks than boys throughout the primary and secondary schools regardless of subject area. This contradiction is not resolved in the research literature.

If girls are not interested in success, we would expect that they would not enter higher education at the same rate as males, and this is somewhat the case. Since 1973 women form 44 per cent of the full-time student population in higher education. This is an aggregate increase both numerically and proportionally since the 1960s. But while women enter institutions of higher education, not all institutions have the same status, nor do they provide credentials of equal currency in the society. Women make up 52 per cent of the population in public two-year post-secondary institutions and only 41 per cent of the population in major public universities and 37 per cent of students in private research universities (Fitzpatrick 1976: 8-9). This pattern is certainly quite different from that of white males. It replicates, although not on as gross a level, the pattern of minority groups in education. White middle-class women get a 'better shake' in access to the status hierarchy than minorities, both male and female, but are still inferior to the educational patterns of white males. This concentration of women in lower status institutions is a function of scholarship distribution and parental unwillingness to invest much in their daughter's education as much, if not more than it is a function of school channelling (Fitzpatrick 1976: chapter 2).

In addition, it has been amply documented that women do seek entry into fields that are supposedly 'all male,' such as engineering, business, mathematics, law, and medicine, and have been prevented from so doing only by discriminatory admissions policies. As soon as the force of law has been brought, women have enrolled in such fields. Obviously the 'messages' did not get through, suggesting that the pattern of enrollments that persist may be due to discrimination rather than women internalizing the messages of the school. Likewise, the workforce patterns too may be employer imposed rather than school induced, and family induced rather than school imposed.

While the above suggests that women may not necessarily incorporate all 'school knowledge,' it should not be taken by any means to deny what school knowledge in fact is or its attempted transmission in the classroom. Rather, it is to point out that within the classroom sets of knowledge renegotiation and/or active filtering occurs that may counter what the schools consider legitimate. How this renegotiation occurs we do not know, yet there is ample evidence to suggest its existence.

Matina Horner's (1972) controversial 'fear of success' study shows us that women don't fully internalize school teachings. The women she studied were in higher education preparing for professions. Horner attributes their exit at the point when they are about to succeed as ambivalence to becoming 'unfeminine' as schools and society have defined successful professional women. Scholars like Levine and Tressemer acknowledge that women exit from the professions but they dispute Horner's conclusion with evidence that demonstrates that women are pushed out of professions by discrimination and by the structure of work and the family, not by their own internalized fear (Levine and Crumrine 1975; Tressemer 1976).

Many autobiographical sketches of women also point to a 'filtering' of the school's messages and women using knowledge not intended for them. Several, like Naomi Weisstein, said they did not expect the discrimination they experienced once in the workforce or the impact that marriage and the family had on their work. Said Weisstein after all those years in school, 'I didn't know I wasn't supposed to succeed' (Ruddick and Daniels 1977). Weisstein's case is interesting in that she went through the US school system at the time when there were the fewest women administrators, the most rigid sex differentiated curriculum and the heyday of the Strang pink and blue vocational interest inventories.

Clearly some women escape the messages of the schools in sex roles as they do the messages of race and class. Do groups of women slip through the cracks of socialization? How many actually do? And, at what cost? We have not yet studied these questions systematically, despite the fact that emerging feminist scholarship has shown women's resistance to very real oppression. Both the power *and* the contradictions of these forms of resistance need much greater attention. As McRobbie's (1978) study of working class girls so clearly documents, these resistances do have real costs as well as benefits.

The difficulty with the reproduction framework as it has been used thus far is that it fails both to deal with 'deviations' and chart how and when they occur or become significant. Part of the difficulty lies with the a-historic nature of the literature and its assumption that social protest movements have little impact on those who attend school. Most of our data on the schools and the reproduction of gender inequality states simply that because the school's authority and staffing pattern and curriculum are what they are women are not of equal status with men. Yet, this denies the structure of work and the family and it ignores history. We know that women have entered and exited the workforce in waves through American history, just as their educational attainments have had their ups and downs. But we do not know to what extent the schools have been responsible for this, or whether the schools have been affected by the development, strength and ebbing of the women's movement. The current upswing in women's workforce participation rates and status as well as educational levels (since the 1950s) has accelerated, with the onset of the women's movement (as did the wave of the 1920s) and its organization in the schools and development of women's studies programs on the secondary and college levels. It well may be – and more research is needed – that the presence of a women's movement provides a means of making resistance 'count' and sets a tenor for the renegotiation of knowledge within the classroom.

Notes

1 See especially the special issue, 'The Labor of Women: Work and the Family,' *Signs* IV (Summer 1979), Boulding (1976) and Safilios-Rothschild (1976).
2 This is suggested by, for example, Wax (1970) in the case of Native Americans.
3 An excellent review essay on women's housework and male wage structures can be found in Glazer-Mablin (1976). See also Seccombe (in press).
4 This is clearest in male/female time budget studies. See, for example, Boulding (1976) and Lapidus (1979).
5 Examples of this growing literature include Children's Rights Workshop (1976), Frasher and Walker (1972), Jay and Schminke (1975), Kepner and Koehn (1977), National Organization of Women (1972), Pottker (1977), Treckler (1973), and Weitzman *et al*. (1972). For further theoretical work on this, see MacDonald (1980a).
6 A number of studies might be mentioned here, including Boring (1973), Frazier and Sadker (1973) especially chapters 4 and 5, Piotrofesa and Schlossbert (1977), Saario, Jacklin and Tittle (1973), Thomas and Steward (1971), Tittle (1974), and Verheyden-Hilliard (1977).
7 Among these investigations are Gaite (1977), Levy (1972), Levitin and Chananie (1972), Meyer and Thompson (1956), Palardy (1969), Saario, Jacklin and Tittle (1973), and Seewald, Leinhard and Engel (1977).

Bibliography

Allen, Walter R. (1979), 'Family Roles, Occupational Statuses and Achievement Orientations Among Black Women in the United States,' *Signs* 4 (Summer), 676-7.

Boring, P. Z. (1973), 'Sex Stereotyping in Educational Guidance,' in National Education Association (ed.), *Sex Role Stereotyping in the*

Schools, Washington, D.C.: NEA, pp. 14-22.

Boulding, Elsie (1976), 'Familial Constraints on Women's Work Roles,' *Signs* 1 (Spring), 95-118.

Chafe, William H. (1972), *The American Woman: Her Changing Social, Economic and Political Roles, 1920-1970*, New York: Oxford University Press.

Children's Rights Workshop (1976), *Sexism in Children's Books: Facts, Figures and Guidelines*, New York: McGraw-Hill.

Croll, Elisabeth (1978), *Feminism and Socialism in China*, London: Routledge & Kegan Paul.

DuBois, Ellen, Gail P. Kelly, Elizabeth Kennedy, Carolyn Korsmeyer and Lillian Robinson (in press), *The Impact of Feminism on the Disciplines*, Urbana: University of Illinois Press.

Elementary School Report Card (1980), Buffalo, New York Public Schools.

Ellis, Joseph R. and Joan L. Peterson (1971), 'Effects of Same Sex Class Organization on Junior High School Students' Academic Achievement, Self-Discipline, Self Concept, Sex Role Identification and Attitude Toward School,' *Journal of Educational Research* 64 (July-August), 455-64.

Estler, Suzanne E. (1975), 'Women as Leaders in Public Education,' *Signs* 1 (Winter) 364-5.

Finn, Jeremy D. (1980), 'Sex Differences in Educational Outcomes: A Cross National Study,' *Sex Roles* 6 (February), 9-26.

Finn, Jeremy, Loretta Dulberg and Janet Reis (1979), 'Sex Differences in Educational Attainment: A Cross National Perspective,' *Harvard Educational Review* 49 (November), 477-503.

Fitzpatrick, Blanche (1976), *Women's Inferior Education: An Economic Analysis*, New York: Praeger.

Frasher, Ramona and Annabelle Walker (1972), 'Sex Roles in Early Reading Textbooks,' *The Reading Teacher* 25 (May), 741-9.

Frazier, Nancy and Myra Sadker (1973), *Sexism in School and Society*, New York: Harper & Row.

Gaite, A. J. H. (1977), 'Teachers' Perceptions of Ideal Male and Female Students: Male Chauvinism in the School,' in J. Pottker and A. Fishel (eds), *Sex Bias in the Schools*, Teaneck, New Jersey: Farleigh Dickinson University Press.

Glazer-Mablin, Nona (1976), 'Housework,' *Signs* 1 (Summer), 905-22.

Horner, Matina (1972), 'Toward an Understanding of Achievement-Related Conflicts in Women,' *Journal of Social Issues* 25, 157-75.

Jay, W. T. and Clarence W. Schminke (1975), 'Sex Stereotyping in Elementary School Mathematics Texts,' *The Arithmetic Teacher* 22 (March), 242-6.

Kepner, Henry S. and Lilane R. Koehn (1977), 'Sex Roles in Mathematics: A Study of Sex Stereotypes in Elementary Mathematics Texts,' *The Arithmetic Teacher* 24 (May), 379-85.

Kilson, Marion (1976), 'The Status of Women in Higher Education,'

Signs 1 (Summer), 935-42.

Lapidus, Gail Warshofsky (1979), *Women in Soviet Society*, Berkeley: University of California Press.

Levine, A. and J. Crumrine (1975), 'Women and the Fear of Success: A Problem in Replication,' *American Journal of Sociology* 80, 964-74.

Levitin, Teresa A. and J. D. Chananie (1972), 'Response of Female Primary School Teachers to Sex Typed Behaviors in Male and Female Children,' *Child Development* 43 (December), 1309-16.

Levy, Betty (1972), 'The School's Role in the Sex Role Stereotyping of Girls: A Feminist Review of the Literature,' *Feminist Studies* 1 (Summer).

MacDonald, Madeleine (1980a), 'Schooling and the Reproduction of Class and Gender Relations,' in Roger Dale, Geoff Esland and Madeleine MacDonald (eds), *Education and the State*, London: Routledge & Kegan Paul.

MacDonald, Madeleine (1980b), 'Socio-Cultural Reproduction and Women's Education,' in Rosemary Deem (ed.), *Schooling for Women's Work*, London: Routledge & Kegan Paul.

Meyer, William J. and George G. Thompson (1956), 'Sex Differences in the Distribution of Teacher Approval and Disapproval Among Sixth Grade Children,' *Journal of Educational Psychology* 47 (November), 385-96.

National Organization of Women (1972), *Dick and Jane as Victims*, Princeton, New Jersey: Central New Jersey National Organization of Women.

Nihlen, Ann (1976), 'The White Working Class in School: A Study of First Grade Girls and Their Parents,' unpublished PhD. dissertation, University of New Mexico.

Palardy, J. Michael (1969), 'What Teachers Believe – What Children Achieve,' *Elementary School Journal* 69 (April), 370-4.

Pietrofesa, J. J. and N. K. Schlossbert (1977), 'Counselor Bias and the Female Occupational Role,' in J. Pottker and A. Fishel (eds), *Sex Bias in the Schools*, Teaneck, New Jersey: Farleigh Dickinson University Press, pp. 221-9.

Pottker, J. (1977), 'Psychological and Occupational Sex Stereotypes in Elementary School Readers,' in J. Pottker and A. Fishel (eds), *Sex Bias in the Schools*, Teaneck, New Jersey: Farleigh Dickinson University Press, pp. 111-25.

Rosaldo, Michelle Zimbalist (1974), 'Women, Culture and Society: A Theoretical Overview,' in Michelle Rosaldo and Louise Lamphere (eds), *Women, Culture and Society*, Stanford: Stanford University Press, pp. 17-42.

Ruddick, Sara and Pamela Daniels (eds) (1977), *Working It Out: 23 Women Writers, Artists, Scientists and Scholars Talk About Their Lives and Work*, New York: Pantheon.

Saario, Terry N., Carolyn N. Jacklin and Carol Tittle (1973), 'Sex Role Stereotyping in the Public Schools,' *Harvard Educational Review*

43 (August), 386-416.

Sacks, Karen (1974), 'Engels Revisited: Women, the Organization of Production and Private Property,' in Michelle Rosaldo and Louise Lamphere (eds), *Women, Culture and Society*, Stanford: Stanford University Press, pp. 207-22.

Safilios-Rothschild, Constantina (1976), 'Dual Linkages Between Occupational and Family Systems: A Macrosociological Analysis,' *Signs* 1 (Spring), 51-60.

Seccombe, Wally (in press), *Domestic Labour and the Working Class Household*, Toronto: Canadian Women's Press.

Seewald, Andrea M., Gaea Leinhard and Mary Engel (1977), *Learning What's Taught: Sex Differences in Instruction*, Pittsburgh: University of Pittsburgh, Learning Research and Development Center, report no. 15.

Sexton, Patricia (1976), *Women in Education*, Bloomington, Indiana: Phi Delta Kappa.

Simpson, Richard L. (1974), 'Sex Stereotypes of Secondary School Teaching Subjects,' *Sociology of Education* 47 (Summer), 388-98.

Smuts, Robert W. (1971), *Women and Work in America*, New York: Schocken.

Stacey, Judith, *et al.* (eds) (1974), *And Jill Came Tumbling After: Sexism in American Education*, New York: Dell.

Standing, Guy (1976), 'Education and Female Participation in the Labor Force,' *International Labor Review* 114 (November-December), 281-97.

Thomas, Arthur and Norman Steward (1971), 'Counselors' Response to Female Clients with Deviate and Conforming Career Goals,' *Journal of Counseling Psychology* 18 (July), 352-7.

Tittle, Carol (1974), 'The Use and Abuse of Vocational Tests,' in Judith Stacey *et al.* (eds), *And Jill Came Tumbling After: Sexism in American Education*, New York: Dell, pp. 241-8.

Treckler, Janice L. (1973), 'Women in U.S. History High School Textbooks,' *International Review of Education* 19, 133-9.

Tressemer, David (1976), 'Do Women Fear Success?' *Signs* 1 (Summer), 963-74.

US Department of Labor (1975), *U.S. Working Women: A Chartbook*, Washington: Bureau of Labor Statistics, Bulletin 1880.

Verheyden-Hilliard, Mary E. (1977), 'Counseling Potential Superbomb Against Sexism,' *American Education*, 13 (April), 12-15.

Wax, Rosalie (1970), 'The Warrior Dropouts,' in H. Lindquist (ed.), *Education: Readings in the Processes of Cultural Transmission*, Boston: Houghton Mifflin, pp. 207-17.

Weinbaum, Batya (1976), 'Chinese Women in the Transition to Socialism,' *Review of Radical Political Economists* 8 (Spring), 34-58.

Weitzman, Lenore J., Deborah Eifler, Elizabeth Hodaka and Catherine Ross (1972), 'Sex Role Socialization in Picture Books for Pre-School Children,' *American Journal of Sociology* 77 (May), 1125-50.

Chapter 6

The arts in class reproduction

Paul DiMaggio and Michael Useem

The arts in class reproduction

The purpose of this paper is to provide a brief overview of the role of high culture in the reproduction of the class structure from generation to generation. The paper's first section summarizes work on the distribution of involvement in the high arts at the individual level and on the role of familiarity with high culture in interactional exchanges. The paper's second section takes a more macrosociological approach, concentrating on organizational, historical, and political factors that set the parameters for the preceding micro-analysis. Our emphasis on the role of art in maintaining the existing structure of domination by no means implies that the arts have no other social functions; nor that the arts, under certain circumstances, cannot play a destabilizing or revolutionary role. Rather our concern in this paper is limited to exploring just one aspect of art's social role, that of facilitating class reproduction. In providing an overview, we will at times draw from our own and others' research; and, at times, engage in speculation that, while grounded in evidence, requires a great deal more empirical attention.

Part I: The role of culture in class reproduction

The high concentration of wealth has remained relatively unchanged in recent decades; rates of inter-class mobility, never high, have changed little in recent years, and, compared with other advanced capitalist democracies, American politics is still remarkably free of class-oriented rhetoric. This stability of the class structure is, in the first instance, undoubtedly a product of special economic and historical circumstances (Karabel 1979); but other institutions are not without a contributing role. The organizations that produce and sustain the dominant culture constitute one such institution. Relatively little is known, however, about the specific ways in which culture and its organizational foundation bolster class continuity and social immobility.

Culture, taken here to include social values, aesthetic interests, and behavioral styles, plays a dual role in preserving the class structure. Social class stability depends on, first, general acceptance of the propriety, if not the necessity, of the class hierarchy and, second, on the effective placement and socialization of youth into the system. By reinforcing the symbolic justification for the class hierarchy, the dominant culture can assist in system legitimation. And by offering a convenient yardstick for assessing the merit and cultivation of persons, culture can help in sustaining class continuity. To the extent that the familiarity and ease with high culture that Bourdieu refers to as 'cultural capital' has become a prerequisite for ascent into the top of the class hierarchy, and to the extent that its possession is limited to those who are the offspring of high-status parents, then intergenerational continuity is bolstered.

The institution most centrally concerned with cultural propagation in both of these ways is, of course, education. The dominant value system is instilled by schools, and virtually all occupational opportunities are tied to the schools' assessment of their graduates' cultural capital. Though obviously of less pervasive significance, the high arts none the less play an analogous role, particularly in the reproduction of the upper tier of the class structure. We shall suggest several ways in which the high arts – reproduced and consumed in schools, museums, and live performing arts settings – facilitate class reproduction through their legitimation and screening value for the upper and upper-middle classes. (The upper class comprises those who own or manage large business firms, as well as families of substantial inherited wealth, while the upper-middle-class consists, in large part of 'agents of symbolic control' (Bernstein 1975) – teachers, attorneys, physicians, journalists, scientists – who are highly educated and whose work involves the manipulation of symbols and knowledge.)

The *legitimation* value of the high arts is now most evident in corporations' use of the high arts to foster favorable élite attitudes towards large companies and private enterprise. Close identification of big business with high culture through patronage and service on governing boards can yield an image of respectability and civic-mindedness for large capital at a time when corporations are under increasing public suspicion.

The *screening values* of the high arts is apparent in the use of familiarity with high culture as an interactional token of class acceptability.

Possession of cultural capital, of which familiarity with the arts is a central component, is of considerable salience for ascent into the top positions of large companies and for participation in élite status groups.

These two roles, the screening role and the legitimation role, have rather different implications for the behavior of élites in the patronage and governance of arts organizations. For the screening role, the content of high culture is less important than the fact that it can be monopolized by upper and upper-middle-class status groups. For the legitimation role, the content of high culture is crucial, since business legitimacy is furthered only through support of artistic works consonant with the values of individualism and hierarchy.

In this paper's following section, we shall discuss the role of cultural capital in reinforcing class solidarity and in screening the admission of persons to élite positions. We shall also describe, and attempt to explain, patterns of attendance at cultural events that are consistent with this view of high culture's status-defining role.

In the subsequent sections, we shall describe the organizational bases of the traditional system of class domination of the arts, which we refer to as *élite control*; such control is oriented towards the *screening role* of cultural capital, the monopolization of cultural resources, and the maintenance of exclusive cultural tastes within the upper-class status group. We shall then suggest that this traditional mode of control is being challenged by the rise of public subsidy for the arts, the increasing adoption by arts organizations of business administrative procedures, and the evolution of cadres of professional arts managers. As a consequence of these trends, it will be argued, the mode of class domination of the arts is shifting from *élite control* to *corporate control*. Corporate control is oriented towards the *legitimating role* of the arts and involves changes in the goals and, to a lesser extent, composition of boards of directors of arts organizations. In conclusion, we will discuss briefly some of the possible implications of these shifts.

The distribution and functions of cultural capital

Weber (1968) contended that status groups vie with one another to monopolize scarce cultural resources, and use these resources as bases of group solidarity to identify members and to exclude outsiders. In addition to maintaining solidarity, adherence to a shared status culture, defined as merit or cultivation, is used as a basis for the allocation of scarce social goods, like educational credentials, jobs, or wealthy spouses. By using cultural criteria in this way, dominant status groups both ensure the overselection of their offspring and the appropriate socialization of new members. Following Weber, Bourdieu has restated and extended the theory of class fractions and class domination, asserting that in modern societies classes adopt the characteristics of status groups and class struggle becomes transported, in part, to the cultural and educational fields (Bourdieu 1973; Bourdieu and Boltanski 1978; Bourdieu and Passeron 1977, 1979). Valued cultural goods, styles, and competencies, which Bourdieu refers to as 'cultural capital,' include, as a major component, familiarity with the high arts (Bourdieu 1968). To the extent that this view, which Bourdieu has elaborated in his work on France, is descriptive of the United States class structure, we would expect to find involvements with high culture spread very unequally among the adult population. This, in fact, is what the data show.

A wide variety of surveys of cross-sections of the population of the United States and of several states and urban areas all indicate that the high arts, including visual arts, opera, ballet, modern dance, theater, and classical music, are consumed most frequently by professionals, next in frequency by other white-collar employees and managers, and less frequently as one descends the class hierarchy. This pattern is not unique to the United States, but has been found as well in Canada, France, England, and the Netherlands (Book and Globerman 1975; Bourdieu 1973; Mann 1967; Zweers and Weltens 1977). One study of respondents in twelve metropolitan areas in the United States found professionals almost three times as likely to report attending the theater, more than four times as likely to have attended symphony or ballet, and five times as likely to have attended opera presentations as blue-collar respondents. By contrast, the differences in attendance at popular-music concerts and motion pictures were considerably smaller (Ford Foundation 1974). Similar differences are found when one compares groups by educational attainment. A Harris survey of a national cross-section of Americans reported that college graduates were about four times as likely to visit art museums and attend theater performances, and about three and a half times as likely to attend classical-music concerts as persons who had not graduated high school (National Research Center of the Arts 1976: 77-86, 118). Once again, attendance differentials for popular-culture events were far smaller (DiMaggio and Useem 1978a).

Multivariate analysis of attendance data indicates that educational attainment is the best predictor of arts attendance, that occupation is also a powerful predictor, and that income has only minimal impact on attendance when education and occupation are controlled (Ford Foundation 1974, pp. 14-16; Gruenberg 1975: 62-9).

Similar conclusions can be drawn from inspection of surveys of persons in the audiences for specific cultural events (see DiMaggio and Useem 1978b). In a summary of the findings of 268 audience studies, college graduates were found to be represented among attenders to museums and performing-arts events in a proportion four times their share of the population as a whole. Non-high-school graduates were underrepresented, in comparison to their population share, by 70 per cent. Similarly professionals composed over half of the average high-arts audience, as compared to 15 per cent of the employed labor force; blue-collar workers, who constituted over a third of the labor force, averaged only a scant 3.7 per cent of the typical arts audience. These figures varied somewhat by art form, with classical music and ballet and dance attracting the most upscale audiences, and theaters attracting the least.

These distributions may stem from several specific factors. First, members of different classes and class fractions pass down distinctive cultural preferences to their young. These family differences are reinforced by peer groups. Individuals from homes where high culture is valued develop early in life a familiarity with artistic forms; they learn the codes implicit in artistic products (Wolf 1977), internalize transposable dispositions to value high-arts works (Bourdieu 1968), and remain more open to high-cultural experience than their less prosperous peers.

Second, the social contexts in which high cultural works are presented are more familiar to members of the upper and upper-middle-class than to those of less prestigious backgrounds. The norms of appropriation of the work of art, the posture with which one listens to a symphony or regards a painting, the very physical structure of the museum or concert hall, are more easily assumed or negotiated by members of élite families. (Consider, for example, the difference in demeanor and behavior of audiences at chamber-music and country-western concerts.) As several working-class informants told Robert Coles about their city's art museum: 'It's not for me – for us . . . this place, it's for people with money, or people who are going to get money later on . . .' (Coles 1975: 26).

Third, members of the upper and upper-middle classes have unequal access to the networks through which information about high-culture events flows. Information about arts events remains primarily word-of-mouth; to the extent that marketing is undertaken, it is usually aimed at the prosperous and well educated. Network effects and marketing policies reinforce the existing class composition of the high-arts public.

Such factors work to reproduce the screening role of cultural capital. In a society sufficiently complex and mobile that status groups are not solidly demarcated, status cultures overlap, and individuals frequently interact with and are evaluated by strangers, involvement in high culture provides a means for high-status individuals to affirm their claims to class position and for upwardly mobile persons to establish the legitimacy of their aspirations in face-to-face 'cultural markets' (Collins 1979). Cultural tastes and styles thus become insignia of class status (Goffman 1951).

The school in cultural reproduction

To the extent that high-status students persist longer in school, class differentials in involvement with high culture are supported by the educational process (DiMaggio and Useem 1980). Students are more likely to receive arts instruction the longer they remain in school, and such instruction is associated with adult arts attendance (National Research Center of the Arts 1975: 137, 1976: 101).

Jencks and Riesman (1968) suggested that increases in average educational attainment accompanying the extension of mass higher education might encourage massive cultural mobility. While this proposition deserves careful study, there are several reasons for skepticism. First, formal schooling cannot be counted on to erase initial differences in cultural preference based in family socialization. Many schools do not offer instruction in the arts and, of those that do, in many such instruction is optional (Rindskopf 1979). Indeed, variation in high-cultural involvements among high-school students in the same grade is substantial. In one cross-section of American eleventh-graders, it is found that a high proportion of the variation in their cultural involvement can be attributed directly to their parents' influence (DiMaggio 1980a).

Second, to the extent that inequality of educational attainment declines, parents may strive with increasing ardor to ensure their children's cultural differentiation. Culturally oriented strategies of reproduction (Bourdieu and Boltanski 1978) are likely to be embraced particularly by families with heads employed in labor markets characterized by informal information networks and jobs for which no clear technical criteria of evaluation exist (Collins 1974; Granovetter 1974; Pfeffer 1977). Thus cultural differentiation might be particularly important for children of professionals, workers in people-processing organizations, business consultants, and staff, as opposed to line, managers.

Third, the differing tendencies of different families to reconvert educational advantages into distinctive cultural styles may be reinforced by the increasing differentiation of higher education (Karabel

1979). Junior colleges and state universities with narrowly technical curricula, catering to nonresidential working-class student populations, cannot be expected to inculcate high cultural involvements to anywhere near the extent as have traditional liberal-arts institutions.

Even within the school, differences in the possession of cultural capital appear to have significant impact on students' success. The one study which included measures of student artistic interests and activities found that high-cultural involvements (but not middlebrow creative pursuits) had small but significant and robustly consistent positive impacts on the grades of a cross-section of American eleventh-graders, even after controlling for test-taking ability. For girls, but not for boys, differences in high-cultural involvements reinforced the positive impact of family background on academic achievement (DiMaggio, 1980a).

Part II: The organizational bases of class domination of the arts

It has been argued that involvement in the arts is useful as a ritual for ratifying élite solidarity and for screening prospective members of élite status groups for acceptability and trustworthiness. Data on attendance at a range of arts events have been presented that are consistent with this view; and cultural capital has been shown to have an independent impact on one measure of life success, high-school grades. The maintenance of high-cultural involvement as a source of solidarity and screening over a long period of time has depended on the development and maintenance of characteristic means of control of organizations that produce, exhibit, and perform the high arts. The principal mechanism, we will argue, has been the control of organizations by boards of directors whose members belong to solidary, localized, and tightly integrated upper-class status groups. The development of such organizations was itself essential in establishing the nature of cultural capital in an American context in the second half of the nineteenth century.

The rise of élite control

Élite control of the arts emerged with the creation of non-profit organizations – art museums, symphony orchestras, and opera companies – for the exhibition and performance of high-cultural materials in the late nineteenth century. Such organizations played an important role in clarifying what had been rather hazy boundaries between high and popular culture.

In Boston, for example, in the first half of the century, European fine-arts music was commonly presented on the same bill as popular and devotional songs and even stand-up comedic recitations. Performers were either amateur or free-lance (often European) musicians, combining in unincorporated and irregular ensembles.

By the end of the nineteenth century, these informal groupings had been largely replaced by the Boston Symphony Orchestra, operating under the strict control of its founder, patrician businessman Henry Lee Higginson. With control by élite boards came standardization of repertoire and exclusive attention to European fine-arts music. Where the creation of fine-arts performing ensembles preceded élite patronage, by 1900 orchestras were no longer musician-run co-operatives, but had become hierarchical organizations controlled by wealthy boards (Couch 1976).

Similar clarifications of the high and popular culture categories, accompanied by the increasing monopolization of control over arts organizations by élites, occurred in the visual arts during this period. The major museums of mid-century America were boisterous carnival-like commercial ventures that combined art with scientific and historical curiosities (Harris 1973). By contrast, the non-profit Boston Museum of Fine Arts, founded in the early 1870s, was devoted solely to visual art, as were many similar museums founded during this period. While the new museum was inaugurated with widespread public support and largely educational purposes, within thirty years it had abandoned many of its educational goals in favor of building and presenting a collection justified on aesthetic and scholarly criteria (Harris 1962; Whitehill 1975). This process was accompanied by a decline in public enthusiasm.

Élite institution builders of the nineteenth century not only defined and monopolized high-status art; they also developed, through a process of trial and error, conventions of deportment and self-presentation in artistic settings. Only under continued attack from middle-class German opera lovers and *New York Times* editorial writers did the Metropolitan Opera's wealthy first families curtail noisy visiting during performances, and adopt norms of silence, assume respectful attitudes, and applaud and bravo in the correct places (Brenneise n.d.).

The exact composition of non-profit arts boards and patron groups differed from city to city. In Boston and Chicago such activities were carried forth in relative unity by integrated élites, while in New York institution-building was sometimes marked by keen status competition between rival upper-class fractions (Brenneise n.d.; DiMaggio 1980b;

Horowitz 1976). In some smaller cities, institution-building may have provided a basis for integration of local élites with middle-class commercial families, as, in Europe, orchestra patronage played a key role in integrating feudal remnants and the rising bourgeoisie (Weber 1976). Despite variations, however, by 1900 urban élites had not only appropriated but defined the nature of American high culture. In so doing, they created a form and legacy of élite control that has proven highly resistant to change.

Élite arts boards: composition and behavior

Analyses of boards of trustees of major arts organizations bear witness to the extent to which such institutions are controlled by members of the upper class, often local, closely linked, and socially exclusive. A study published in 1972, for example, found that of sixteen trustees of the Cleveland Museum, thirteen were either descended from or employed by firms founded by past trustees or benefactors (Glueck 1972). Similar studies of the Boston Museum of Fine Arts and the Chicago Art Institute (Glueck 1972; Zolberg 1974) yielded similar findings. An analysis of biographies of 156 art-museum trustees noted that 60 per cent were graduates of Ivy League universities, about a third were in finance and banking, a fifth were lawyers, and almost two-fifths were Episcopalian (Meyer 1979: 224). As one observer noted, (museum) 'boards do not elect new members; they clone them' (Meyer 1979: 224).

Boards of major performing-arts organizations, particularly symphonies and operas, are no less distinguished (Thompson 1958). Over 70 per cent of thirty-three Philadelphia Orchestra trustees in the mid-1960s were listed in the *Social Register*, and all but four were businessmen or corporate lawyers (Arian 1971). An analysis of the trustees of the Seattle Opera found that group composed primarily of businessmen, lawyers, and residents of a small set of exclusive neighborhoods. What is more, the Opera was directly interlocked with every major arts organization in Seattle (Salem 1976). Not all arts organizations are dominated by such high-status boards; but most major ones are and, it has been argued, a new arts organization's success may depend upon its ability to recruit élite trustees (Estes and Stock 1978).

When one moves from the composition to the behavior of boards, generalization becomes substantially more difficult. We shall argue that boards consisting of prestigious trustees may be either *élite* or *corporate* depending on the strength of trustees' social, kinship, and communal ties. Thus the available demographic data does not permit us to distinguish between the two types in concrete instances. We are forced to rely on suggestive evidence describing behavior consistent with our ideal-typical distinction between *élite* and *corporate* domination. The key difference is that *élite* boards, as class-based status groups, are most concerned with the screening function of high culture, and thus with exclusivity, while *corporate* boards are most concerned with the *legitimating* functions of the arts and arts patronage.

Élite boards are composed of individuals who, whatever their formal occupational affiliations, represent a solidary upper-class social community. They are committed, after the ensuring of the survival of the organization itself, to preserve the exclusivity of artistic presentations, maintain the community's monopolization of cultural capital, and ensure that the organization remains a fitting site for rituals of class solidarity. Such boards are likely to resist any extension of decision making control, or extension of services any further into the upper-middle class than necessary to maintain financial solvency. This is because democratizing policies would, in the long run, dilute the value of their group's cultural capital and threaten the role of the arts organization in the social life of their group.

There is some evidence that many boards have, in fact, operated in this way. Status concerns were undoubtedly behind the opposition of symphony trustees to public subsidy for the arts in the early 1960s. And élite boards have often greeted with a certain dismay evidence of rising popular interest in the arts. In the words of one experienced museum director (Shestack 1978):

> It is possible that the greater democratization of our museums has something to do with the waning enthusiasm of a number of former donors. In the past, some wealthy people have, consciously or not, thought of the museum as a kind of aesthetic country club.

While the American faith in democracy has historically shaped the rhetoric of those who controlled high-arts institutions, the extent to which it has affected their programs deserves more careful study than it has received (Leavitt 1979: 94).

Writing of the Philadelphia Orchestra Board of the 1960s, Arian contends that 'the outspoken antipathy which some Board members display towards those whom they characterize as "pushy" individuals with "brash new money" ' (p. 64) led them to forego the patronage of parvenus. Arian also reports that concerns for exclusiveness led the trustees to refuse to financially support or formally endorse that orchestra's only major series of public concerts; and to turn down major funding from a labor union in exchange for a seat on the board. Salem (1976) reports similar antipathy on the part of many board members towards the manager of the Seattle Opera, who used unconventional but highly successful marketing techniques to bring in new audiences and to counteract opera's 'snobbish' public image. The willingness to behave with *economic* irrationality, in the interest of *collective social* and *cultural* interests, is the hallmark – more than demographic traits – of élite as opposed to corporate board control.

The traditional élite mode of class domination, with its emphasis on maintaining culture's screening role and exclusiveness, may be succumbing to the corporate mode of class domination for a variety of reasons, including the increase in support from large corporations; the rise of public subsidy; the adoption of conventional commercial management practices; and the evolution of a cadre of professional arts managers.

Corporate support for the arts

'The top executives of American Can, Atlantic Richfield, AT&T, Exxon, GE, GM, IBM, Mobil, Prudential and US Steel invite you to perform with them at Kennedy Center.' Such executives have committed their companies to financially support the center and have encouraged others to do the same. According to a widely circulated advertisement, 'of all the stars who've ever performed at Kennedy Center, these executives are certainly among the brightest' (Corporate Fund for the Performing Arts at Kennedy Center 1977). In the last decade, corporate contributions have risen as fast as government subsidy. One survey of business support to the arts estimated business grants at $211 million, more than twice the amount provided by the business community a decade before. Leading businessmen formed the Business Committee for the Arts in the 1960s to further mobilize and articulate the growing corporate interest in the high arts.

Though support for the arts still probably constitutes less than 10 per cent of businesses' total philanthropic outlay, the practice of arts giving has become so widespread that 95 per cent of large companies report providing at least some support. Museums were the favored recipients, followed by public broadcasting, and classical music (Conference Board 1978).

Such contributions are often cloaked in the rhetoric of corporate 'social responsibility;' but a more plausible reason is the increased concern of large companies with their loss of public legitimacy; polls consistently find that public esteem for large corporations in general, and for certain companies (like those in oil) in particular, is at a nadir (Ladd 1978; Lipset and Schneider 1978). As public confidence in large corporations has eroded, numerous anti-corporate groups have challenged company practices in areas ranging from environmental pollution to investments in South Africa (Lydenberg 1977; Vogel 1978). One response to these image problems is for corporations to affiliate themselves with prestigious cultural institutions, both through direct corporate subvention and through the participation of corporate executives in the governance of arts organizations.

Selection of recipients for corporate largesse is generally based on the prestige of the arts organization, the visibility of its programs, and their consistency with business interests. Mobil Oil, for instance, which has a 'public affairs' budget of well over $20 million a year, denies support to public television programs that 'knock business' (Gerrard 1978: 64). A recent survey of corporate support for private universities revealed that the vast majority of the nearly three hundred top executives contacted attributed some importance to the economic and political views of the faculty in deciding which university to support (the Committee for Corporate Support of Private Universities 1979).

But reputation is an equally salient criterion in choosing beneficiaries of corporate support. This same survey also revealed that reputation was the foremost criterion in the selection of universities to be assisted. Another study of company support for the arts in a large midwestern city found that financial support and the provision of board members are both disproportionately directed to the city's most prestigious arts organizations (Galaskiewicz and Rauschenbach 1979). The appearance of a company's name on a benefactor roster in the program for a prestigious performing arts event, or its listing as the chief donor for a public television show, have considerable value for both a company's reputation and for the standing of business as a whole, at least among opinion leaders. The Exxon corporation, which, like Mobil, aggressively supports the arts, has reported evidence from its own surveys that such high-status respondents, at least, now view Exxon as a 'public-spirited company' (Brooks 1976). Moreover, companies in politically sensitive industries like oil are among the most active in supporting the arts on public television (Ermann 1979).

Corporate support, potentially, changes the interests of boards of trustees in several ways. First of all, organizations that receive support from business firms may be particularly reluctant to perform or display materials with critical or political messages. To the extent that corporations seek legitimation in supporting the arts, their purposes are not consistent with backing programs that fail to reflect business values. Thus theater companies have received less company backing than organizations like orchestras or dance companies, whose presentations have less literal content. Second, when individuals are placed on boards of directors to represent patron corporations, they are less likely to participate in the life of the urban upper-class status group than individuals chosen for their personal characteristics. Such business representatives, we hypothesize, are less likely to be integrated with their peers by ties of kinship, social interaction, or perhaps educational background, and thus less likely to share the group's status concerns. Persons who sit on boards as *representatives* of business may be more willing to trade off exclusivity for efficiency, more concerned about the content of artistic programs and less concerned about monopolizing them, than businessmen and others who sit on boards because they belong to a common élite status culture.

Public subsidy for the arts

Before 1960 public support for the arts was limited to subventions to arts organizations by a few states and municipalities. Now every state has an arts council, most cities have arts councils as well, the National Endowment for the Arts' 1965 maiden budget of $2.5 million has increased seventy-fold, and such federal agencies as the National Endowment for the Humanities, C.E.T.A., the Institute for Museum Services, the Smithsonian Institution, the Commerce Department, and the Department of Education support arts organizations and artists as well (DiMaggio and Useem 1978c).

The lion's share of public funding continues to flow to traditional high-culture organizations. But because federal and state arts budgets are subject to legislative approval, such funding introduces pressures for accountability, responsiveness, and breadth of distribution; these subtle pressures may, in the long run, have substantial effects on the governance and control of arts organizations. First, public agencies require that fund recipients maintain careful records on the disposal of those funds and on the number of individuals who receive publically supported services. While counting heads is nothing new, the legitimacy of those funds and on the number of individuals who receive publicly organizational goal, has increased. What is more, the heightened importance of public legitimacy for arts organizations seeking funds has boosted the authority of managers who can claim expertise in such fields as marketing, public relations, and intergovernmental affairs. To the extent that managerial authority comes to rest on business expertise rather than either artistic or art-historical credentials or social ties to trustees, the power of élite boards is challenged.

Finally, public subsidy also challenges traditional definitions of art and class control by mobilizing new constituencies and by legitimating, through the bestowal of grants, new kinds of art. Support to non-élite-controlled organizations, among other things, enables such organizations, which have little stake in maintaining the exclusiveness of cultural consumption, to organize to demand more aid. In the case of public subsidies for non-traditional art forms like jazz or folk arts, support alters the social definition of art itself (DiMaggio 1978).

Administrative reform

Yet another threat to élite control comes from the increased reliance of arts organizations on expanding the market for their services and from their adoption of management practices generally associated with profit-seeking firms (DiMaggio 1978; Martorella 1977; Peterson 1978). A major case in point is the use of modern mass marketing techniques, primarily direct-mail. Direct-mail campaigns oriented towards building strong subscription audiences were pioneered in theater companies (where, because of the relative newness of most theater organizations, élite domination of boards has perhaps been weakest) at the behest of the Ford Foundation (Newman 1977). They have since spread throughout the performing arts. Such marketing strategies reinforce the exclusion of working-class audiences from arts events as they aggressively strengthen and increase arts organizations' middle-class constituencies. None the less, in shifting the balance of power from upper-class patrons to middle-class consumers, they challenge the former's ability to maintain exclusivity. What is more, the adoption of businesslike management practices, while it may be initiated by dramatic board intervention in an organization's daily affairs, eventually leads to the hiring of professional managers, with claims to administrative expertise, who demand autonomy from board 'meddling.'

Professional arts management

A final threat to élite domination is the development of cadres of professional managers in the artistic disciplines. Earlier managers tended to be genteel souls who shared educational and often social backgrounds with board members themselves – refined art-historical specialists with few administrative skills, unpaid trustees, or flamboyant (often European) artistic directors reliant on trustee support.

Anecdotal evidence now suggests that, in all the disciplines, top managers are now drawn from a broader range of social backgrounds, have more diverse career trajectories which may include stops in the public sector, maintain broad horizontal ties and professional identification with their colleagues, and, as a consequence, may have interests that diverge substantially from those of traditional élite boards. If élite boards wish to maintain exclusiveness and control, professional managers wish to expand budgets, operations, and audiences, and to cultivate a plurality of funding sources in order to maximize their own autonomy.

The development of a managerial cadre has been stimulated by financial deficits and real skills required to negotiate with and meet the accountability requirements of public funding sources, to map campaigns to boost earned income, and to negotiate with trade unions. It has been further developed by the professional projects (Larson 1977) of arts managers themselves, often carried out through their trade associations, to justify their claims to expertise and to legitimate and defend managerial prerogatives against board incursions. (Note for example, the accreditation program of the American Association of Museums and the America Symphony Orchestra League's program to train a cadre of managers for the orchestras of the 1980s.) Finally, these professionalization projects have been aided directly by public agencies, which have treated trade associations as legitimate bargaining agents for their fields, supported their activities with grants and contracts, and funded training programs, workshops, and consultancies for managers in several fields.

From élite to corporate domination of the arts

Such tendencies as those sketched above may be eroding the traditional *form* of class domination of arts organizations without seriously challenging that domination itself. The change from *élite* to *corporate* control, at the organizational level, involves six components: a shift in board composition; a change in board interests and priorities; increasing importance of professional managers; increased reliance on marketing and public subsidy; expansion, and consequent de-emphasis of exclusiveness and the screening role; heightened concern with content and emphasis on the legitimating role.

First, unlike the élite board, the corporate arts board consists of individuals appointed by virtue of their positions in formal organizations rather than their membership in local upper-class status groups. Where élite boards maintain clubby, high-consensus atmospheres by recruiting *persons* with a wide range of social and kinship ties, corporate boards attempt to achieve organizational ends by recruiting *repre-*

sentatives or large organizations that can provide useful connections and access to resources.

Since corporate board members are less likely to be part of a tightly organized élite status culture, their interest in social and cultural exclusivity is secondary to their interest in the economic survival and, often, the expansion of the organization itself. Their relative lack of status concerns and their concerns with efficiency form the basis for a community of interest with the new managerial cadre, who, while of less distinguished social backgrounds, command specialized administrative skills their predecessors lacked. These managers, with the support of corporate boards, are likely to seek increased levels of corporate and government subsidy, and higher levels of earned income; corporate trustees, it can be hypothesized, are less likely than élite patrons to reach into their own pockets, preferring to facilitate other kinds of fund-raising. Corporate boards are also likely to support managerial efforts at organizational expansion, because such growth reflects credit on board members and their corporations as well as upon managers, and because they have less to fear from a dilution of cultural capital. Because of the importance of the legitimating function, corporate boards, it may also be hypothesized, will be more concerned than élite boards with the content of exhibits and performances, less ready to support risky artistic ventures, and quicker to censor offensive programs. If the *élite* mode of class domination set firm *social* limits on the diffusion of high art to the public at large, the *corporate* mode of class domination may instead set *ideological* limits on the content of the art that is presented.

Conclusion

If, indeed, control of the arts is undergoing the kind of shift that we have described, what are the implications of this transition for the role of the arts in class reproduction? If the structure of the distribution of cultural capital described in the first part of this paper was founded on the élite mode of class domination, will a shift to a new mode of class domination lead to a new pattern of distribution of cultural capital?

The most likely impact of the changes described above – reduced interest in exclusiveness and the screening role; organizational expansion and increased public subsidy; the widespread use of marketing – will be to diffuse high-cultural tastes and pastimes throughout a broader sector of the upper-middle and middle classes. To the extent that this occurs, traditional forms of cultural capital will be slightly devalued, and those class fractions, principally professionals, richest in cultural capital are likely to develop new arenas of cultural differentiation. Indeed the inflation of traditional forms of cultural capital may be responsible for the apparent boom in interest in chamber music and dance.

Heightened competition for the most prestigious kinds of cultural capital at the top of the class hierarchy and the wider availability of high-cultural resources may be reflected in increased demand for formal instruction, often in less élite cultural forms like jazz piano or tap dancing, among the middle and lower-middle classes. It may also encourage sharper competition for (socially) debased forms of cultural capital among lower-middle-class groups. Thus the fusion of modern and popular dance forms creates lower-middle-class arenas of cultural competition like disco and roller disco, mastery of which requires far more skill and training than did success in earlier popular dance crazes.

Changes in the mode of domination of high culture need not, however, directly affect the cultural patterns of the working class or the poor. For one thing, involvement in the arts is not a salient factor for screening into the jobs and careers open to all but a handful of the children of the poor and working people. For another, the attractiveness of high culture to the middle classes is partly contingent upon the continued exclusion of the poor and the working classes; large-scale marketing to the latter is neither appealing nor necessary to either arts managers or boards. Finally, marketing the high arts to these groups would be difficult in light of the tenaciousness of existing barriers – educational, social, psychological, and informational – to blue-collar participation. The extension of the arts to these groups, if it is to occur at all, will depend upon substantial quantities of public subsidy to programs explicitly aimed at audience development among the poor and working classes and, perhaps more important, to the development of non-traditional art forms in which working people and the poor are already involved.

Note: The authors' names are in alphabetical order in title. This paper is a completely collaborative product.

Bibliography

Arian, Edward (1971), *Bach, Beethoven, and Bureaucracy: The Case of the Philadelphia Orchestra*, University of Alabama: University of Alabama Press.

Bernstein, Basil (1975), *Class, Codes, and Control*, vol. 3, London: Routledge & Kegan Paul.

Book, S. H. and S. Globerman (1975), *The Audience for the Performing Arts: A Study of Attendance Patterns in Ontario*, Toronto: Ontario Arts Council.

Bourdieu, Pierre (1968), 'Outline of a Sociological Theory of Art Perception,' *International Social Science Journal* 20(4): 589-612.

Bourdieu, Pierre (1973), 'Cultural Reproduction and Social Reproduction,' pp. 71-112 in *Knowledge, Education, and Cultural Change*, Richard Brown (ed.), London: Tavistock.

Bourdieu, Pierre and Jean-Claude Passeron (1977), *Reproduction in Education, Society and Culture*, Beverly Hills, Calif.: Sage Publications.

Bourdieu, Pierre and Jean-Claude Passeron (1979), *The Inheritors: French Students and their Relation to Culture*, Chicago: Univ. of Chicago Press.

Bourdieu, Pierre and Luc Boltanski (1978), 'Changes in Social Structure and Changes in the Demand for Education,' pp. 196-227 in *Contemporary Europe: Social Structures and Cultural Patterns*, Salvador Giner and Margaret Scotford Archer (eds), London: Routledge & Kegan Paul.

Brenneise, Harvey (n.d.), 'Art of Entertainment? The Development of the Metropolitan Opera, 1883-1900,' MA thesis, Andrews University.

Brooks, John (1976), 'Fueling the Arts, Or, Exxon as a Medici,' *New York Times* January 25, 1976, pp. D1ff.

Coles, Robert (1975), 'The Art Museum and the Pressures of Society,' *ARTnews* 74: 24-33.

Collins, Randall (1974), 'Where are Educational Qualifications for Employment Highest?' *Sociology of Education* 47: 419-42.

Collins, Randall (1979), *The Credential Society: An Historical Sociology of Education and Stratification*, New York: Academic Press.

Committee for Corporate Support of Private Universities (1979), *Corporate Support of Private Universities: An Attitudinal Survey of Top Executives*, Boston: Committee for Corporate Support of Private Universities.

Conference Board (1978), *Annual Survey of Corporate Contributions, 1976*, New York: The Conference Board.

Corporate Fund for the Performing Arts at Kennedy Center (1977), Advertisement.

Couch, Stephen R. (1976), 'Class, Politics, and Symphony Orchestras,' *Society* 14 (November/December): 24-9.

DiMaggio, Paul (1978), 'Elitists and Populists: Politics for Art's Sake,' *Working Papers for a New Society* 6 (September/October): 23-31.

DiMaggio, Paul (1980a), 'Cultural Capital and School Success: The Impact of Status-Culture Participation on the Grades of U.S. High-School Students,' manuscript, Institution for Social and Policy Studies, Yale University.

DiMaggio, Paul (1980b), 'The Classification and Framing of Artistic Experience: Notes Towards an Organizational Theory of Art's Social Role,' manuscript, Institution for Social and Policy Studies, Yale University.

DiMaggio, Paul and Michael Useem (1978a), 'Social Class and Arts Consumption: The Origins and Consequences of Class Differences in Exposure to the Arts in America,' *Theory and Society* 5: 141-61.

DiMaggio, Paul and Michael Useem (1978b), 'Cultural Democracy in a Period of Cultural Expansion: The Social Composition of Arts Audiences in the United States,' *Social Problems* 26: 180-97.

DiMaggio, Paul and Michael Useem (1978c), 'Cultural Property and Public Policy: Emerging Tensions in Government Support for the Arts,' *Social Research* 45: 356-89.

DiMaggio, Paul and Michael Useem (1980), 'Arts-in-Education and Cultural Participation: The Social Role of Aesthetic Education and the Arts,' *Journal of Aesthetic Education*, 14, 4: 55-72.

Ermann, David (1979), 'Corporate Contributions to Public Television,' *Social Problems* 25: 504-14.

Estes, David and Robert Stock (1978), 'The San Diego Symphony: Problems of Institution Building,' San Diego, Calif.: School of Public Administration and Urban Studies, Institute of Public and Urban Affairs.

Ford Foundation (1974), *The Finances of the Performing Arts* 2 vols, New York: Ford Foundation.

Galaskiewicz, Joseph and Barbara Rauschenbach (1979), 'Patterns of Inter-Institutional Change: An Examination of Linkages Between Cultural and Business Organizations in a Metropolitan Community,' paper presented at the Annual Meetings of the American Sociological Association, Boston.

Gerrard, Michael (1978), 'This Man Was Made Possible by A Grant from Mobil Oil,' *Esquire* (January): 62ff.

Glueck, Grace (1972), 'Power and Esthetics: The Trustee,' pp. 117-30 in *Museums in Crisis*, Brian O'Doherty (ed.), New York: George Braziller.

Goffman, Erving (1951), 'Symbols of Class Status,' *British Journal of Sociology* 2: 298-312.

Granovetter, Mark (1974), *Getting a Job*, Cambridge, Mass.: Harvard University Press.

Gruenberg, Barry (1975), 'How Free is Free Time? Analysis of Some Determinants of Leisure Activity Patterns,' manuscript, Department of Sociology, Wesleyan University.

Harris, Neil (1962), 'The Gilded Age Revisited: Boston and the Museum Movement,' *American Quarterly* 14: 545-66.

Harris, Neil (1973), *Humbug: The Art of P. T. Barnum*, Boston: Little Brown.

Horowitz, Helen Lefkowitz (1976), *Culture and the City*, Lexington, Kentucky: University Press of Kentucky.

Jencks, Christopher and David Riesman (1968), *The Academic Revolution*, New York: Doubleday.

Karabel, Jerome (1979), 'The failure of American socialism reconsidered,' pp. 204-27 in *Socialist Register 1979*, Ralph Miliband and John Saville (eds), London: Merlin Press.

Ladd, Everett Carll (1978), 'What the Voters Really Want,' *Fortune* 98 (December 18): 40-6.

Larson, Magali Sarfatti (1977), *The Rise of Professionalism*, Berkeley, Calif.: University of California Press.

Leavitt, Thomas W. (1979), 'The Beleaguered Director,' pp. 91-102 in *Museums in Crisis*, Brian O'Doherty (ed.), New York: Braziller.

Lipset, Seymour Martin, and William Schneider (1978), 'How's Business? What the Public Thinks,' *Public Opinion* 1 (July/August): 41-7.

Lyndenberg, Steven D. (1977), *Minding the Corporate Conscience, 1978: Public Interest Groups and Corporate Social Accountability*, New York: Council on Economic Priorities.

Mann, P. H. (1967), 'Surveying a Theater Audience: Finding,' *British Journal of Sociology* 18: 75-90.

Martorella, Rosanne (1977), 'Art Administration in the Performing Arts,' paper presented at the annual meeting of the American Sociological Association, Chicago.

Meyer, Karl (1979), *The Art Museum: Power, Money, Ethics*, New York: Morrow.

National Research Center of the Arts (1975), *Americans and the Arts: A Survey of Public Opinion*, New York: Associated Councils of the Arts.

National Research Center of the Arts (1976), *Americans and the Arts: A Survey of the Attitudes toward Participation in the Arts and Culture of the United States Public*, New York: National Committee for Cultural Resources.

Newman, Danny (1977), *Subscribe Now!* New York: Theater Communications Group.

Peterson, Richard A. (1978), 'Rational Administration in the Arts,' manuscript, Department of Sociology, Vanderbilt University.

Pfeffer, Jeffrey (1977), 'Toward an Examination of Stratification in Organizations,' *Administrative Science Quarterly* 22: 553-67.

Rindskopf, David (1979), 'Arts Education in Public Secondary Schools: Offerings, Enrollments, and Their Determinants,' St Louis: CEMREL, Inc.

Salem, Mohamed (1976), *Organizational Survival in the Performing Arts: A Study of the Seattle Opera*, Lexington, Mass.: Lexington Books.

Shestack, Alan (1978), 'The Director: Scholar and Businessman, Educator and Lobbyist,' *Museum News* 57 (2): 27ff.

Thompson, Helen M. (1958), *Governing Boards of Symphony Orchestras*, Vienna, Virginia: American Symphony Orchestra League.

Vogel, David (1978), *Lobbying the Corporation: Citizen Challenges*

to Business Authority, New York: Basic Books.
Weber, Max (1968), *Economy and Society*, New York: Bedminster Press.
Weber, William (1976), *Music and the Middle Class in Nineteenth Century Europe*, New York: Holmes and Meier.
Whitehill, Walter Muir (1975), *The Boston Museum of Fine Arts: A Centennial History*, 2 vols, Boston: Houghton Mifflin.
Wolf, Thomas (1977), 'Reading Reconsidered,' *Harvard Educational Review* 48: 411-29.
Zweers, W. and L. A. Weltens (1977), 'Theatre and Public in the Netherlands,' English summary in *Summary Report 1970-1977: Selected Summaries of Boekmanstichting Research in the Field of Art and Culture*, Amsterdam: Boekmanstichting.
Zolberg, Vera (1974), 'The Art Institute of Chicago: The Sociology of a Cultural Organization,' PhD Dissertation, University of Chicago.

Chapter 7

Television's screens: hegemony in transition

Todd Gitlin

Popular culture and hegemony

No society lacks popular culture. Everywhere, at all times, there seem to be more or less regular forms and occasions of symbolic expression through which creators articulate meanings which are widely valued. Neolithic society produced the peerless art of the European, Indian, and Australian caves, which, whatever their 'magical' or 'religious' functions (these are pale, ethnocentric terms for a society we do not understand), were more than imitations or training exercises: they stood forth, and stand forth today, *as art* (Giedion 1962). During the Middle Ages European balladists and troubadours carried representations of longings, witticisms, political statements and private passions from village to village, nation to nation, social estate to social estate (Burke 1978). Street shows and festivals were occasions for indulging the spirit of celebration, of public display, even of revolt (Altick 1978; Burke 1978; Huizinga 1955; Ladurie 1979). Popular sentiment empowered artistry, and artistry was granted its cultural occasions, its institutions. Popular culture carried meanings which were aesthetic and, at the same time, religious, political, or, simply, incarnations of everyday sentiment. It exhorted, celebrated, cautioned, and denounced; it embodied morality and provided release from it; it gave pleasure and attached that pleasure to particular symbolic constructions. Because its artifacts were concrete, the forms of popular culture could crystallize values out of their state of potential: popular culture could make values stand forth to be recognized, appreciated, refined, and if need be, rejected. Social identity, whether of class, region, nation, community, religion, 'people,' or political ideal, could become publicly manifest when it was embedded in the stone and glass of cathedrals, in the rituals of dance and passion play, in song and in story.

Popular culture is, then, a fixture of social life; and its artifacts are culture incarnate. But its forms, its modes of production, consumption, and distribution, and its meanings, are not eternal. Corporate capitalist society presses popular culture into distinctive molds, and shapes it to particular uses. Four aspects of contemporary popular culture seem novel in history. First, the mass production and distribution of films, television, and radio records, magazines, newspapers, and books, billboards and their advertising slogans, sports, games, and toys, and the attendant apparatus of design, architecture, fashion and images – all has been condensed into rather centralized, co-ordinated corporate enterprises of national and international sweep. John Brenkman (1979) makes the point that 'late capitalism overcomes the sheer separation of the symbolic from the economic, but does so by bringing the symbolic under the dominance of the economic.' Second, these enterprises churn out a vast volume of cultural commodities. The turnover is ferocious; obsolescence is structured into popular taste, and the rise and fall of celebrity and style becomes routine, like the rhythms of the mass production of goods. Third, this co-ordinated popular culture, bureaucratically organized in its production and private in its consumption, has become pervasive in an unprecedented way. Television is the culminating institution of the culture of corporate capitalism, invading and reshaping the private space of the home, filling it with an unending procession of mass-produced images. No cultural system since medieval Christianity has the pervading and unifying potential of mass culture in the age of television. Television suffuses the private domain with a new order of experience; the watching of television takes up more of the average American's time than any other waking activity besides work. And fourth, although popular culture often borrows from religion's ritual forms, and much religiosity attends some of its rituals, from the hush of the museum to the hysteria of the rock concert, the doctrinal context of much earlier popular culture is now undermined: popular culture is secular. These modern traits make it all the easier for popular culture to infuse everyday life, and to embody and reproduce the dominant complex of ideology: in the West, the legitimacy of private control of production, and of the national security state; the necessity of individualism, of status hierarchy, of consumption as the core measure of achievement; and overall, as in every society, the naturalness of the social order.

And yet, at the same time, popular culture helps to transform the momentary incarnations of that ideology, and the terms of its dominion over alternatives. For alternatives do exist, however partially: they are lived in fragments of everyday existence, as well as in shards of traditional and centrifugal ideology that exist in tension with the hegemonic. Mass culture produces artifacts and practices which register transformations in ideology – transformations that are incompletely wrought by those more or less coherent, often inchoate, often self-contradictory resistances and departures. The dialectical rhythm of incorporation and resistance helps account for the enormous energy of capitalism's popular culture, the excitements it generates: for the commercial producers borrow energy from lived social experience and fantasy, transforming it into salable objects. They juggle old mythologies and new ones manufactured for the occasion, traditional images and fashionable ones, searching for conscious and unconscious resonances that will translate into economic success. In form and content, popular culture ordinarily affords its consumers the pleasure of desires both expressed and contained; it intimates some kind of happiness that workaday social conditions will not permit.[1] That promise of happiness is what binds the audience to the commodities themselves, and to one corner or another of the glittering pop world.

In advanced capitalist societies, popular culture is the meeting ground for two linked (though not identical) social processes. (1) The cultural industry produces its goods, tailoring them to particular markets, and organizing their content so that they are packaged to be compatible with the dominant values and mode of discourse, and (2), by consuming clumps of these cultural goods, distinct social groups help position themselves in the society, and work toward defining their status, their social identity.[2] By enjoying a certain genre of music, film, television program, they take a large step toward recognizing themselves as social entities. To study popular culture fully is to study the ensemble of this complex social process. The artifacts are produced by professionals under the supervision of cultural élites themselves interlocked with corporate and, at times, state interests; meanings become encased in the artifacts, consciously and not; then the artifacts are consumed. The act of consuming appropriates and completes the work: it activates from among the work's range of possible meanings – those that are actually present in the work – those that will embody what the work means, here and now, to a given social group and to individuals within it. What requires study is the totality of this process of production, signification, and consumption. But before decomposing popular culture into its component parts, I want to insist on the density of their complex interrelation. For each of these 'moments' presupposes the others, and is partly determined by them. The totality of popular culture is a tense one, at once institutionalized and changing. It contains the possibility of its own transformation and even the transformation of the society, and it contains these possibilities in two senses: it includes them, and it limits them.

The key to grasping the popular culture process of corporate capitalism, in all its dynamism and ornery self-contradiction, lies with Gramsci's concept of hegemony, and the particular version of it which I have distilled (Gitlin 1980) from the British neo-Gramscian work of Raymond Williams (1973, 1977), Stuart Hall (1973, 1977) and Paul Willis (n.d. 1978). By hegemony I mean the process in which a ruling class – or, more likely, an alliance of class fractions – dominates subordinate classes and groups through the elaboration and penetration of ideology into their common sense and everyday practice. Through training and reward, the dominant social groups secure the services of cultural practitioners – producers, writers, journalists, actors, and so on. To articulate ideals and understandings, to integrate the enormous variety of social interests among élites, and between élites and less powerful groups, in a modern capitalist society, the corporate and political élites must depend on the work of skilled groups of symbolic adepts, what Gramsci called 'organic intellectuals.' In order to make their livings, these practitioners organize their production to be consonant with the values and projects of the élites; yet in crucial respects they may depart from the direct programs of the élites who hire, regulate, and finance them. (Indeed, the competitive corporate élite may not be able to formulate 'its' common interests without the work of the symbolic adepts.) The content of the resulting cultural system is rarely cut and dried, partly because the cultural practitioners have their own values, traditions, and practices which may differ from those of the élites, and partly because there are market constraints which keep the hegemonic ideology flexible. (The bald, uncontested affirmation of the value of corporate greed, for example, would probably fail to attract organic intellectuals, and would probably, moreover, fail to entertain the mass audience.) Ideological domination, in other words, requires an *alliance* between powerful economic and political groups, on the one hand, and cultural élites, on the other – alliances whose terms must, in effect, be negotiated and, as social conditions and élite dispositions shift, renegotiated.

Hegemony encompasses the terms through which the alliances of domination are cemented; it also extends to the systematic (but not necessarily or even usually deliberate) engineering of mass consent to the established order.[3] It is best understood as a collaborative process rather than an imposed, definitively structured order; in general, hegemony is a condition of the social system as a whole, rather than a cunning project of the ruling group. As Michael Burawoy so lucidly writes (1979: 17-18, citing Poulantzas 1975: 31),

Ideology is . . . not something manipulated at will by agencies of

> socialization – schools, family, church, and so on [one could easily add mass media – T.G.] – in the interests of a dominant class. On the contrary, these institutions elaborate and systematize lived experience and only in this way become centers of ideological dissemination. Moreover, dominant classes are shaped by ideology more than they shape it. To the extent that they engage in active deception, they disseminate propaganda, not ideology. As a first approximation, it is lived experience that produces ideology, not the other way around. Ideology is rooted in and expresses the activities out of which it emerges.

Ideology is generally expressed as common sense – those assumptions, procedures, rules of discourse which are taken for granted. Hegemony is the suffusing of the society by ideology which sustains the powerful groups' claims to their power by rendering their pre-eminence natural, justifiable, and beneficent.

The decisive point is that hegemony is a collaboration. It is an unequal collaboration, in which the large-scale processes of concentrated production set limits to, and manage, the cultural expressions of dominated (and dominating) groups. Yet it is a collaboration nevertheless. Absolute power coerces; hegemony persuades, coaxes, rewards, chastizes. Absolute power forbids alternatives; hegemony organizes consent and allocates a certain limited social space to tailored alternatives. Both parts of this formulation are important. Hegemony is a process of organization in which cultural élites occupy top positions and supervise the work of subordinates in such a way as to draw their activity into a discourse which supports the dominant position of the élites; at the same time, hegemony cannot operate without the consent of those subordinates. Hegemony takes place behind the backs of its operatives; it is a silent domination that is not experienced as domination at all. Hegemony is the orchestration of the wills of the subordinates into harmony with the established order of power.

The system of popular culture is one important domain through which the terms of hegemony are affirmed and negotiated. The process of renegotiation is mandatory because the hegemonic ideology in liberal capitalist society is inherently contradictory and changeable. The hegemonic ideology in the United States attempts to bridge the rival claims of freedom and equality: it propounds equality of opportunity rather than equality of results. It affirms patriarchal authority – currently embodied most successfully in the national security state – while at the same time embracing individual worth and self-determination: it accomplishes this compromise by propounding the ideal of meritocracy, promotion of the most competent, as a principle of technocratic rule within all institutions.[4] The dominant ideology of corporate capitalist society cannot for long be unbridled individualism, but must also render homage to the legitimate claims of a wider community – familial, religious, ethnic, or national or even supra-national (as in the sometime internationalism of scientists). Nationalist sentiment is the most readily adaptable.

These tensions within hegemonic ideology render it vulnerable to the demands of insurgent groups and to cultural change in general. Insurgencies press upon the hegemonic whole in the name of one of its components – against the demands of others. *And popular culture is one crucial institution where the rival claims of ideology are sometimes pressed forward, sometimes reconciled in imaginative form*. Popular culture absorbs oppositional ideology, adapts it to the contours of the core hegemonic principles, and domesticates it; at the same time, popular culture is a realm for the expression of forms of resistance and oppositional ideology. Popular culture is the expressive domain where pleasure is promised and contained, articulated and packaged. The mass culture industry of advanced capitalist society packages the representations; it organizes entertainment into terms that are, as much as possible, compatible with the hegemonic discourse.

But this does not necessarily mean that popular culture suppresses alternative or even oppositional ideology.[5] Indeed, in a *liberal* capitalist order, suppression proceeds alongside accommodation: sometimes one predominates, sometimes the other. The blandness of television entertainment in the 1950s (perhaps partly an assurance to purchasers of the new, expensive receivers) was displaced in the 1970s by a style of entertainment which takes account of social conflict and works to domesticate it – to individualize its solutions if not its causes. Likewise, the light, innocent romance of popular music of the early 1950s ('Tennessee Waltz,' 'Memories Are Made of This,') as recorded by singers like Patti Page, Perry Como, Dean Martin, and Frank Sinatra, and mass-distributed through radio, was supplanted by black-based rock and roll, which embodied in lyrics but more, in beat and instrument, a certain pre-political youth revolt, and carried a certain stylized anger and collective passion. The visible hand of the market rewards those corporate cultural ventures that succeed in attracting public attention: mass market imperatives dictate that the culture industry respond, however partially, sluggishly, and reductively, to public moods and tastes.[6] Diverse cultural enterprises respond differently to their markets. They all take account of hegemonic ideology in the ways they package their contents. But the degree to which they are incorporated into hegemonic ideology depends on several features of their industrial organization, as well as the particular historical situation: it depends on the degree of economic concentration in the industry, the amount of capital required to enter the field, and the ideology of cultural producers. In popular music, for example, the ideological range is relatively inclusive, since the capital required to manufacture a record is relatively small (a few hundred dollars suffice to press a record in a garage), and market segmentation sets the tune. (Of course distribution to stores and through radio is much more highly controlled by oligopolistic companies.) By way of contrast, network and syndicated television, with their vast markets dictated by a combination of oligopoly and high capitalization, are less open to genuinely independent entries. Yet television too, as I shall argue below, must strive for audiences which cut across class, race, and ideological lines. Thus the commercial core of the culture industry aims for middle-of-the-road (MOR) productions, the stylistic center of gravity shifting in response to certain (not all) cultural changes. Mass-cultural élites and gatekeepers do not simply manipulate popular taste; they do not write on tabulae rasae. Rather, they shape and channel sentiment and taste that churn and simmer in the larger society, and express popular desires in one form or another.

The genius of Marx's critique of capitalism, as opposed to the romantic protest against it, began with his insistence that the capitalist's exploitation of labor was the exploitation of something socially desirable and full of potential for enlarging the scope of human existence. Let the analysis of popular culture proceed in a similar spirit. The production and promotion of cultural meanings is also a necessity: in a diverse society, it is in popular culture that groups can declare themselves, converse with each other, consolidate their identities, and enact – on the symbolic level – their deepest aspirations, fears, and conflicts. The genius of the cultural industry, if that is the right word, lies in its ability to take account of popular aspirations, fears, and conflicts, and to address them in ways that assimilate popular values into terms compatible with the hegemonic ideology. The cultural industry packages values and beliefs, relays and reproduces and focusses them, distorting and adjusting elements of ideology that are constantly arising both from social élites and from social groups throughout the society, including not least, media practices and their social worlds. The culture industry does not invent ideology from scratch. To paraphrase the old saying about hypocrisy, the forms of commercial culture amount to the tribute that hegemony pays to popular feeling. The executives who sit uneasily at the commanding heights of the cultural industry, desperately holding on to their tenuous positions, are not so much managers of the mind as orchestrators of its projects and desires.[7]

Likewise, their products are commodities but not commodities only. They are always containers of works that appeal to popular aesthetics and beliefs, containers which work to smooth out the rough edges, to tame the intractible feelings, and to reconcile emotions and images which may well be irreconcilable, at least in the established society.

One further note of prologue: My discussion of popular culture centers on entertainment, not news. Yet the workings and functions of the hegemonic news-selecting and -distributing industry are not essentially different from those of entertainment. (On news, see Gans 1979; Gitlin 1980; Tuchman 1978.) In news as in entertainment, hegemony is the product of a chain of assumptions, concretely embedded in work procedures, which rarely require directorial intervention from executives or political élites in order to produce a view of the world that at key points confirms the core hegemonic principles: individualism, technocracy, private control of the economy, the national security state. Hegemony in news as in entertainment takes notice of alternatives to the dominant values, descriptions and ideals, and frames them so that some alternative features get assimilated into the dominant ideological system, while most of that which is potentially subversive of the dominant value system is driven to the ideological margins.

Indeed, in important respects, news and entertainment are converging. News borrows from entertainment important conventions of structure and content. In *structure*, television news stories are ordinarily organized as little narratives (Epstein 1973; Gitlin 1977a). A problem is set forth, and the action proceeds in a standard curve. Conflict takes place between rival actors. At least one solution is set forth (generally by duly sanctioned authority, the main protagonist of the tale). The disinterested narrator stands for the viewer, certifying either that the problem is being taken care of, or else that the problem is beyond human agency altogether. The narrative curve now descends to earth with a certain closure: an action will be taken; or, if not, the narrator supplies an artificial rhetorical closure, in the easily-mocked empty formula of 'It remains to be seen . . .' And in content, as already mentioned, television news stories are built around images of particular personages and dramatic conflict (Gitlin 1977a, 1980). Stories are personified; they issue forth from sanctioned politicians and certified authorities. Stories include visual images that will secure the flickering attention of the mass audience. Other things being equal, the dramatic image – a burning flag, a raging fire, a battle – gets priority, especially the image that lies on the surface, immediately available to the camera. These devices are borrowed from the theatre, and from ancient and modern myths, trickster myths, homecoming myths, and all manner of others, refurbished to encompass the concerns of the hour. The story about the Vietnam veteran returning home draws on, and plays against, the Odyssey; a story about the war, or about devastation in the South Bronx, draws on imagery from the Indian wars.[8]

As for entertainment, it borrows liberally from the conventions of news – that is, from realism. As Ian Watt (1957) has argued, the English novel from its emergence in the eighteenth century has always insisted that it represents reality. The recent trend toward the 'non-fiction novel' (Mailer) or the fictional appropriation of actual historical personages (Capote, Doctorow) only continues a longer tradition: the novel indulges in the artifice that it describes something that actually happened, and readers suspend disbelief. Photography obviously traded on its claim to transparency (see Benjamin 1978; Sontag 1977) and so did the fiction film, capitalizing on its appearance of permitting direct representation of some sort of actual life, even as the viewer is at another level aware that 'it's only a movie.' The recent vogue of the television 'docudrama,' in which actors 'recreate' the lives of great individuals at great moments in history (the Cuban missile crisis, Truman firing MacArthur, the travails of Eleanor and Franklin Roosevelt), simply continues the grand tradition; as defenders of the non-fiction novel enjoy pointing out, Tolstoy put lines into Napoleon's mouth in *War and Peace*. One need not endorse Georg Lukács', (1964) dismissal of modernist heresies to acknowledge the truth of his larger claim: that realism is the distinctly bourgeois literary mode.

In short, only a misguided formalism would draw a hard and fast line between news and entertainment; their mythic and realistic conventions touch, and influence each other. And just as the news organizations process reports of reality into packages of information and imagery which help reconfirm the legitimacy and completeness of the hegemonic worldview, so do the organizations of entertainment production selectively absorb elements of discrepant ideology, ensuring that the hegemonic ideology remains up to date, encompassing, sufficiently pluralistic in accent to attract different audiences, while transposing social conflicts into a key where the hegemonic ideology is re-legitimated. Both news and entertainment thus reinforce each other to reproduce the dominant ideology – *in all its contradiction and sometime instability*. It is one paradox of the culture of liberal capitalism that its reproduction takes place through partial and limited transformations. It stands still, in a sense, by moving.

The making of television entertainment

The dialectic of cultural assertion and hegemonic incorporation is well illustrated by the production of American network television entertainment, which shall be the principal subject of the rest of this essay. In one way, TV entertainment imprints its content with hegemonic ideology, aiming to organize the largest possible consuming audience and to work a hegemonic effect on it. The result is generally what the industry calls LOP: Least Objectionable Programing (Barnouw 1978). Yet in another way, TV entertainment enfolds and amplifies centrifugal tendencies in the culture.

Television critics have been heard to complain that television shows are insipid and slovenly. True enough; assembly-line production schedules are not kind to quality. But much of TV's insipidity may be understood as a patterned ambiguity. If, from an aesthetic point of view, simplistic ambiguities amount to equivocations, from a sociological point of view they are perfectly tailored to appeal to the components of a complex society. The aesthetic and political blandness of most TV entertainment results not from the technology of television as such – not from the size of the screen, not from the texture of the image – nor from the shortage of money for production, nor from the audience's presumed lack of intelligence, but from television's dominating social purpose.[9] Networks in the United States, and state-controlled TV organizations in Europe, set out to communicate to mass audiences. But mass audiences contain a myriad of subcultures, each inclined (though not unambiguously) toward a distinct (though not autonomous) system for decoding, inflecting, stretching the culture's central symbols. Contrary to any vulgar Marxism or ethnographic relativism that might read the culture as nothing but a field of essential conflict over premises, feelings, and values, corporate capitalist societies have certain collective representations: this is the truth in Durkheimian and Tocquevillian assessments of modern culture. The function of mythic images is to deny social cleavage and to formulate a collective identity for a fragmented society. (What the conservative tradition cannot explain, though, is the nature and source of the unifying myth. Why *capitalist* hegemony, and who gets to articulate its symbolic forms?) Not least amidst the universal grounding of contemporary culture is the high value placed on images themselves; the realm of spectacle emerges, conditioning experience and penetrating it (Debord 1977). Still, the society as a whole *is* no homogeneous whole: despite tendencies in that direction, it is also culturally polyglot. Fragments of folk culture remain, regionally and ethnically distinct. And distinct groups selectively appropriate and construe what they find in the larger cultural domain; new formations arise and position themselves *vis-à-vis* others; subcultures conflict, transform themselves, and sometimes decay.

Amidst this flux, the culture industry cannot take it for granted that its audiences will read its products unambiguously.[10] One consequence is that production is dominated by the LOP formula. And the shows' susceptibility to multiple interpretation becomes the fulcrum of production strategy in a second way as well: television, far from fleeing ambiguity, *makes possible* a certain range of counterposed, discrepant, and even oppositional interpretations. How people will read a program is not fully predictable. Entertainment taken as a whole, and even, at its most sophisticated, show by show, can thus please several audiences at once: its messages may run with more than one grain. How can this happen? The denotations of visual signs are relatively unambiguous: the image of a man wearing a white hat and riding a horse stands for a real man riding a real horse. But connotations vary: the image may stand for a heroic man-to-the-rescue, a countercultural rebel, or a reprehensible imperialist, depending on who is watching. The first reading is dominant and conventional; the second might be alternative; the third, oppositional. Connotations will depend on group identity and ideology, as well as individual cognition and circumstance. The point is that multiple connotations coexist in the artifact; they are layered into it, although rarely in a premeditated way, from the start. Bundled together, they permit different segments of the audience to partake of the same artifact yet not quite the same experience; they permit the audience to decompose the show differently, to take more or less account of different parts and characters, and to draw different conclusions – while tending to take the show's hegemonic definition of the situation as a fixed point of departure, an imposing symbolic universe. Varying 'effects' amidst hegemony result from the fact that the people who watch television are simultaneously (1) members of a mass audience, rendering the show popular, binding themselves in webs of contemporaneous though invisible relations to others as serialized consumers; (2) members of families and subcultural groups who take the show in and digest it through their respective interpretive filters; and (3) individuals imposing their personal interpretations on the shows, and perhaps insisting on their individuality by thinking or saying, 'I don't know what anybody else thinks of it, but I think . . .' The mass audience is not only the arithmetic sum of disconnected individuals,[11] but a skein of social clumps.

Against this background, the packaging process is no simple matter of élites fastening on their purposes and generating material to suit, as if the media of communication were simply spigots. Amidst a welter of social forces, many choices are overdetermined. Other emerge from a conflict among forces, and the outcomes are contingent: they might have turned out differently, even given the organizational structure of the culture industry. To account for the emergence and shape of any given program, a comprehensive analysis needs to take account of a range of factors:

(1) *The organizational structures of the production process*: specifically, among networks, advertisers and advertising agencies, and producers. Networks retain determining power because they control access to the major markets; beneath them, the major producers have oligopolistic power. One filter controls access to the one beneath it. The networks commission pilots, and then choose from among them. Given the dominion of professional standards, the costs of production are so great as to give the networks and major production studios (which occasionally produce 'independently' for syndication as well) enormous power over what is finally broadcast. In the words of Bob Daly, President of CBS's entertainment division, 'We get 2000 ideas for series every year. Out of that 2000, we commission 200 scripts. Out of those 200 scripts, we make 40 "pilots" so that we can look at them to decide if they should go out on the air. Of those 40 pilots, only eight actually become series and get shown. And of those eight – only three actually survive one season' (quoted in Lewin 1980). To explain the three survivors, of course, we must have recourse to audience mentalities.

(2) *The networks' market strategies*: the networks aim to garner the maximum attention from that part of the total possible audience which spends the most money. Thus, other things being equal, a show attracting a given share of the 18-to-49-year-old audience, as measured by the A. C. Nielsen Company, will succeed more than a show attracting the identical share of an older audience. Increasingly sophisticated 'demographic' measurements enable the networks to make increasingly specific market judgments. The demise of Westerns may be traced partly to the fact that their major audience is disproportionately older and disproportionately rural: not the audience most capable of high-volume consuming.

(3) *The values, beliefs, and strategies of popular-cultural élites*: network executives and producers, and then, secondarily, writers and even actors. Class identifications, shifting aesthetic and political ideals and ideological tolerances, the producers' and packagers' and writers' sense of 'what's in the air,' 'what might fly,' all play a part in generating ideas for pilots. But story ideas are neither born free nor promoted equally; they must appeal to the élite of the production process or they cannot proceed to the stage of production. They do not get a chance to

find their audience unless they filter through all the layers of the corporate choice system. Moreover, despite the obligatory references to individual talent in the industry, individuals succeed only in so far as they match the corporation's expectations.

(4) *Specific corporate habits and practices*: I refer here to contingencies: factors in corporate choice which stand relatively free of the deeper structural constraints and strategies. The positioning of a show has a great deal to do with its ratings, since people tend to watch television continuously and would rather not change channels unless impelled to do so. Thus, other things being equal, a show that appears just after a high-rated show will do better than the same show appearing just after a lower-rated one. A show that appears opposite a high-rated show on another network will do less well than if it appeared opposite lower-rated shows. The networks' maneuvering their shows in relation to others can get ferocious. Another corporate habit is a particular adaptation to the networks' competitiveness: when a particular show succeeds, the networks tend to reproduce what they deem to be its salient features. The success of a cop show generates other cop shows: *Charlie's Angels* generates 'T & A' clones (to use one industry term; 'jiggle shows' is another). The pendulum generally swings too far: interest audience in a given formula does not extend to cheap imitations, and the market for the formula is oversaturated within a season or two.

(5) *Audience mentalities*: audiences do not express their preferences directly; what audience ratings measure is not what people might abstractly prefer in a world they might imagine, but what they will at least tolerate, at most like, given what television offers and what else they might do with their time. Producers have only shadowy images of what audiences want. They reconnoiter. They rely on their immediate social circles, and the ideas that gravitate their way (partly affected, of course, by new entries' ideas of what is commercial), and on the versions of popular belief that filter into their life-worlds – through mass media, ironically enough. Audience mentalities do affect programing, but indirectly; the culture industry does not passively *reflect* audience desires, but *refracts* them, actively and darkly, through its organizational and ideological glasses.

So much for the abstract, *a priori* categories of explanation. How particular shows emerge, having percolated through this set of filters, must be studied empirically. Mindful of the appalling fact that there is not a single book-length sociologically-informed study of American television's ideological content, I am about to launch into such an investigation. I will be looking to analyze an entire season's array of entertainment series, interpreting their contents, looking to explain which pilots and which scripts do and don't get produced, and which series do and don't last. By interviewing producers and studying television archives, I hope to understand the relative weights of the above-mentioned shaping forces. Before I go at interpreting the material with the care it deserves, and plumbing specific audience responses to the shows (see the Note on Methods of Study below), it makes no sense to claim too much for an assessment of the meanings that TV entertainment carries. But at this early stage I do want to set out a sketch, a rough prospectus, enumerating a number of elements of the television discourse, conventions in which ideological hegemony is embedded: format, plot formula; genre; setting; character type; images of social and psychological conflict and its solution; images of authority, the State, family, work, and social movements; images of emotion, its texture and legitimacy. Consider the following discussion a sort of prospectus for the more detailed, more systematic, more historically grounded and socially situated study to come.[12]

Format

Until recently at least, the TV schedule has been dominated by standard lengths and cadences, standardized packages of TV entertainment appearing, as the announcers used to say, 'same time, same station.' This week-to-weekness – or, in the case of soap operas, day-to-dayness – obstructed the development of characters; the primary characters had to be preserved intact for next week's show. Perry Mason was Perry Mason, once and for all; watching the reruns, only devotees could know from character or set whether they were watching the first or the last in the series. For commercial and production reasons which are in practice inseparable – and this is why ideological hegemony is not directly reducible to the economic interests of élites – the regular schedule prefers the repeatable formula: it is far easier for production companies to hire writers to write for standardized, static characters than for characters who develop. Assembly-line production works through regularity of time slot, of duration, and of character to convey images of social steadiness: come what may, *Gunsmoke* or *Kojak* will occupy a certain time on a certain evening. Should they lose ratings (at least at the 'upscale' reaches of the demographics, where ratings translate into disposable dollars),[13] their replacements would be – for a time, at least! – equally reliable. Moreover, the standard curve of narrative action – stock characters show their standard stuff; the plot resolves – over twenty-two or fifty minutes is itself a source of rigidity and forced regularity.

In these ways, the usual programs are performances that rehearse social fixity: they express and cement the obduracy of a social world impervious to substantial change. Yet at the same time there are signs of routine obsolescence, as hunks of last year's regular schedule drop from sight only to be supplanted by this season's attractions. (The very concept of 'season,' in TV as a fashion and in the opera, ballet, and theatre of high culture, claims the authority and normality of nature's cycles for man-made products.) Standardization and the likelihood of evenescence are curiously linked: they match the intertwined processes of commodity production, predictability, and obsolescence in a high-consumption capitalist society. I speculate that they help confirm audiences in their sense of the rightness and naturalness of a world that, in only apparent paradox, regularly requires an irregularity, an unreliability which it calls progress. In this way, the regular model changes in TV programs, like the regular changes in auto design and the regular elections of public officials, seem to affirm the sovereignty of the audience while keeping deep alternatives off the agenda. Élite authority and the illusion of consumer choice are affirmed at once – this is one of the central operations of the hegemonic liberal capitalist ideology.

Then too, by organizing the 'free time' of persons into end-to-end interchangeable units, broadcasting extends, and harmonizes with, the industrialization of time. Media time and school time, with their equivalent units and curves of action, mirror the time of clocked labor and reinforce the seeming naturalness of clock time. Anyone who reads Harry Braverman's *Labor and Monopoly Capital* can trace the steady degradation of the work process, both white- and blue-collar, through the twentieth century, even if Braverman has exaggerated the extent of the process by focussing on managerial *strategies* more than on actual work *processes*. Something similar has happened in other life-sectors. Leisure is industrialized, duration is homogenized, even excitement is routinized, and the standard repeated TV format is an important component of the process. And typically, too, capitalism provides relief from these confines for its more favored citizens, those who can afford to buy their way out of the standardized social reality which capitalism produces. Beginning in the late 1970s, the home videocassette recorder enables upscale consumers to tape programs they'd otherwise miss. (By 1980 there were 1.2 million in American homes.) The widely felt need to overcome assembly-line 'leisure' time becomes the source of a new market – to sell the means for private, commoditized solutions to the time-jam.

Commercials, of course, are also major features of the regular TV format. There can be no question but that commercials have a good deal to do with shaping and maintaining markets – no advertiser dreams of cutting advertising costs as long as the competition is still on the air. But commercials also have important *indirect* consequences on the contours of consciousness overall: they get us accustomed to thinking of ourselves and behaving as a market rather than a public, as consumers rather than producers or citizens. Public problems (like air pollution) are to be understood as susceptible to private commodity solutions (like eyedrops). In the process, whether or not we are offended or annoyed by commercials, they acculturate us to interruption through the rest of our lives. Time and attention are not one's own; the corporations in effect advertise their own dominion along with their products. By watching, the audience one by one acquiesces. Regardless of the commercial's effect on our behavior, we consent to its domination of the public space. Yet we should note that this colonizing process does not actually require commercials, a long as it can form discrete packages of ideological content that call forth discontinuous responses in the audience. Even public broadcasting's children's shows take over the commercial forms to their own educational ends – and supplant narrative forms by herky-jerky bustle. The producers of *Sesame Street*, in likening knowledge to commercial products ('and now a message from the letter B'), may well be legitimizing the commercial form in its discontinuity and in its invasiveness. Again, regularity and discontinuity, superficially discrepant, may be linked at a deep level of meaning. And perhaps the deepest privatizing function of television, its most powerful impact on public life, may lie in the most obvious thing about it: we receive the images in the privacy of our living rooms, making public discourse and response difficult. At the same time, the paradox is that at any given time many viewers are receiving images discrepant with many of their beliefs, challenging their received opinions.

TV routines have been built into the broadcast schedule since its inception. But arguably their regularity has been waning since Norman Lear's first comedy, *All in the Family*, made its network debut in 1971. Lear's contribution to TV content was obvious: where previous shows might have made passing reference to social conflicts, Lear brought wrenching social issues into the center of his plots. Lear also let his characters develop. (Previously, only the children in family series had been permitted to change – a forced maturation.) Edith Bunker grew less sappy and more feminist and commonsensical; Gloria and Mike moved next door, and finally to California. On the threshold of this generational rupture, Mike broke through his stereotype by expressing affection for Archie, and Archie, oh-so-reluctantly but definitely for all that, hugged back and broke through his own. Other Lear characters, the Jeffersons and Maude, had earlier been spun off into their own shows. (Since Lear's success with spin-offs, popular actors on other shows have been able to bargain themselves into their own series – *Rhoda* from *The Mary Tyler Moore Show*, *Flo* from *Alice*, ad infinitum.) Lear's precedents have flourished; they were built on intelligent business perceptions that an audience existed for situation comedies directly addressing racism, sexism, and the instability of conventional families. But there is no such thing as a strictly economic explanation for production choice, since the success of a show – despite market research – is not foreordained. In the context of my argument, the importance of such developments lies in their partial break with the established, static formulae of prime-time television.

Daytime soap operas and their prime-time variants have also been sliding into character development and a direct exploitation of divisive social issues, rather than going on constructing a race-free, class-free, feminism-free world. And more conspicuously, the 'mini-series' has now occasionally disrupted the taken-for-granted repetitiveness of the prime-time format. Both content and form mattered to the commercial success of *Roots*; certainly the industry, speaking through trade journals, was convinced that the phenomenon was rooted in the series' break with the week-to-week format. When the programming wizards at ABC decided to put the show on for eight straight nights, they were also, inadvertently, making it possible for characters to develop within the bounds of a single show. And of course they were rendering the whole sequence immensely more powerful than if it had been diffused over eight weeks. The very format was testimony to the fact that history takes place as a continuing process in which people grow up, have children, die; that people experience their lives within the domain of social institutions. This is no small achievement in a country that routinely denies the continuity and directionality of history.

Plot formula and genre[14]

The conventions of television entertainment are flexible precisely because they operate under limited but real market constraints: they enable popular forms to express and manage shifts in the available stock of ideology. In the 1950s, the networks tended to reproduce the image of a society at one with itself, without significant social tensions – though even then, the shows sometimes did register a muted sense of the routine frustrations caused women by male supremacy (*I Love Lucy*) and the routine psychic injuries done to workers (*The Honeymooners*). For the most part, the world of television was what

Herbert Gold called a world of 'happy people with happy problems.' Then, after social conflict grew explosive in the 1960s, television began, gingerly and selectively, to incorporate certain symbols of dissonance and changing 'lifestyles' – racial and ethnic consciousness, hip professionalism, new living arrangements, ecological awareness, and sanitized middle-class versions of feminism. Where the family dramas and sitcoms of the 1950s usually denied the existence of deep social problems in the world outside the set, or sublimated them into obscurity, programs of the 1970s much more often acknowledged that the world is troubled and problematic, and then proceeded to show how the troubles could be domesticated. From *Ozzie and Harriet* and *Father Knows Best* to *All in the Family* and *The Jeffersons* marks a distinct shift in formula, character, and slant: a shift, among other things, in the image of what the larger social world amounts to, how stable it is, and how a family copes with it.

Some shows become popular by speaking directly to a compact, socially homogeneous public. But more likely – or so it seems on the near side of systematic research – the most popular shows are those that succeed in speaking simultaneously to audiences that diverge in social class, race, gender, region, and ideology: and this because of the mass market imperative of network television. To package the largest possible audience, the networks must offer entertainment which is literally broadcast: which appeals to a multiplicity of social types at once. It may embody its values directly or indirectly, overtly or covertly, but it will do best if it embodies them ambiguously enough to attract a variety of audiences at once. The 'socially relevant' situation comedies produced by Norman Lear, beginning with *All in the Family* in 1971, may well have broken through to ratings success precisely because they directly and ingeniously broached the divisive social issues of race and political culture. Some studies of audience response have suggested that *All in the Family* permitted audiences on both sides of the generational and political chasms to feel confirmed in their attitudes: older conservatives rooted for Archie, younger liberals rooted for Mike (Vidmar and Rokeach 1974). (One aspect of the series' hegemonic framing was that most of the divisive issues were represented as matters of generation, not class or power.)

Why the great success of Lear's new genre? A brief excursus may suggest more general explanations for shifts in program formula. For one thing, the historical timing of a show bears heavily on its commercial prospects. ABC rejected *All in the Family* in the years before CBS bought it. In contrast, consider an earlier attempt to bring problems of class, race, and poverty into the heart of television: CBS's 1963-4 *East Side, West Side*, in which George C. Scott played a caring social worker who was consistently unable to accomplish much for his clients however hard he tried. As time went on, the Scott character came to the conclusion that politics might accomplish what social work could not, and went to work as the assistant to a liberal Congressman. It was rumored about that the hero was going to discover there, too, the limits of reformism – but the show was then cancelled, presumably for low ratings. In the middle and late 1960s social conflict had been too inflammatory, too divisive, to permit network television to indulge in Lear's formula for accommodation through ambiguity. And Lear's shows, by contrast to *East Side, West Side*, have lasted partly *because they are comedies*. Audiences will partake of comedy's ready-made defenses to cope with threatening impulses, especially when the characters are, like Archie Bunker, ambiguous normative symbols. The comedy form allowed white racists to indulge themselves in Archie's rationalizations without seeing that the joke was on them. And finally, as Michael J. Arlen once pointed out, Lear was further inspired to unite his characters in a harshly funny *ressentiment* that was peculiarly appealing to audiences of the Nixon era and its cynical, disabused sequel. One alluring subtext of the show was that a family could hold together despite everything pressing on it from outside; the family could encompass the social conflicts that had seemed to be tearing the country apart.

So here we see the range of textual features that an interpretation can take into account. But how was the show possible in the first place? Structural and organizational explanations for the show's origins and success begin on the shoulders of the interpretive reading. Lear was in a position to shatter conventions, first of all, because producers had gained in the power to initiate. In the 1950s sponsors directly developed their shows, and were thus better able to control and sanitize content. When the networks took much of that power away in 1960, in the wake of the quiz show scandal, they began to make decisions in the interest, as it were, of advertisers in the aggregate. By the late 1960s television had become so important an advertising medium that advertisers were standing in line to buy scarce commercial time. Thus networks were somewhat more willing to take chances with risky shows, knowing that if a few advertisers were offended there would likely be others eager to replace them, unless the content were in flagrant violation of hegemonic norms (the adventures of a union organizer, say, or a fundamentalist preacher).

Changes in content also flow from changes in social values and sensibilities – changes among producers, writers, and other practitioners, but also changes they are aware of in the audiences that are most salient to them. Lear's own political position – he is a major contributor to liberal causes – was mostly beside the point: it mattered only in so far as it attuned him to a new marketing strategy. Lear was aware that there was, in the 1970s, a large audience nurtured ideologically in the opposition movements and counter-culture of the 1960s, and now preferring to acknowledge and domesticate social problems, hoping to reconcile contraries in imagination, rather than to ignore or deflect them. The whole texture of social life had changed: where the official mythology of the 1950s had stressed cultural consensus, the consensus had cracked in the 1960s and ideological divisions had surged into the open. And crucially, there were now writers available who had ideological roots in the opposition movements of the 1960s, though by themselves they could not account for content or success; there was also, after all, such a supply in the 1950s, but it was cut off by the blacklist, which exercised a chilling effect on subject matter and plot formula.

That chill had been produced by the networks, which accorded veto power to police agencies and professional associations (notably the American Medical Association), thus acting instrumentally in behalf of a hegemonic interest originating outside it. ABC, for example, gave routine veto power to the FBI over its long-running series of the same name. On one occasion the TV writer David W. Rintels was asked to write an episode of *The FBI* on a subject of his choosing. Rintels proposed a fictionalized version of the 1963 bombing of a Birmingham church, in which four black girls were killed. Rintels wrote later 1974a: 389-90):

> The producer checked with the sponsor, the Ford Motor Company, and with the FBI – every proposed show is cleared sequentially through the producing company, QM, the Federal Bureau of Investigation; the network, ABC; and the sponsor, Ford, and any of the four can veto any show for any reason, which it need not disclose – and reported back that they would be delighted to have me write about a church bombing subject only to these stipulations: the church must be in the North, there could be no Negroes involved, and the bombing could have nothing at all to do with civil rights.
>
> After I said I wouldn't write that program, I asked if I could do a show on police brutality, also in the news at that time. Certainly, the answer came back, as long as the charge was trumped up, the policeman vindicated, and the man who brought the specious charge prosecuted.

On another occasion, a network acted as direct guardian of the hegemonic limits: NBC refused to permit *Dr Kildare* to run a show about venereal disease, this time despite clearance from the AMA, the National

Educational Association and the Surgeon General of the United States (Rintels 1974b: 391).

But times have changed. Medical shows on venereal disease have been aired. *The FBI* is no longer exalted. Beginning in 1977 *Lou Grant* began to take account of contemporary issues from a muckraking point of view. The networks now arrogate to themselves the right and the power to legitimize the respectable framing of social problems, and yield less authority than before to agencies of the State. Now, when a specific show slants to the Right (see my discussion of *The Six Million Dollar Man*, below), it is most likely because the producers anticipate an audience in that direction; direct state intervention is not necessary. By the 1970s, in short, the cocky, commercially booming networks had eclipsed specific advertisers and government agencies; they had made themselves the direct shapers of hegemonic content. And they had devised a new formula to coexist with some older ones and to displace others. Observing shifts in the tolerances and potential enthusiasms of the market – especially the younger, more liberal, more 'permissive' upscale market – they had downplayed crude censorship, and preferred to take account of shifts in social ideology by domesticating them, by offering hegemonic solutions (as we shall see below) to real problems.

This active processing of deviance and lifestyle novelty seems automatic, the sum of innumerable production decisions played out as if by reflex and commercial instinct. Yet this hegemonic strategy at times surfaces into the thinking of culture industry élites: it may be quite sophisticated, quite precise in its implications for television content. In a March 1980 speech (*Broadcasting* 1980a) to the Southeast and Southwest councils of the American Association of Advertising Agencies, held at St Thomas, Virgin Islands, the senior vice president of the research firm of Yankelovich, Skelly & White, Jane Fitzgibbon, told advertising executives that television's role has been 'to legitimize new life styles after they have emerged,' rather than to inaugurate them. 'I think we can also honestly say,' she went on, 'that the television medium has speeded up what you might call the filtration of new values and new life styles throughout the population. Television does this simply by *documenting* new life styles, particularly through its news service.' She took account of cultural conflict:

> We now have at least two audiences to appeal to if we talk in *grosso modo* terms: traditional values – and they are still around – and new values. But within the new values segment there are two groups. There's the self-fulfilment, quality-of-life, self-improvement segment; and there's the experience and the escapist-oriented new

> values segment. What I see this leading to is more and more audience fragmentation, probably smaller market shares, smaller rating shares and probably few blockbuster shows.

And finally, she nicely articulated the hegemonic managerial task for program developers:

> Television must be consistently attuned and alert to life-style changes (this goes for the advertisers as well as the writers), so that it can accurately and responsibly portray them at a point in time when the public will neither be bored because they are too outdated, nor outraged because they are too far out on the fringes. Instead, television's portrayal of societal change can insure that the public be stimulated, informed, sensitized, reassured about what is happening in their own personal lives and the lives of other people in the world at large.

The 'accurate and responsible portrayal' that foreswears both the outdated and the far-out; the combination of stimulation, information, sensitization, *and reassurance* – these are the terms with which the strategy of domestication is accomplished.

Another example suggests both the subtlety and the possible intentionality of this process. The popularity of *Charlie's Angels*, beginning in 1976, suggests that television producers have learned how to appeal to elements of the new feminism and to its opposition at the same time. The Angels are highly skilled, motivated, working women; they show a certain amount of initiative. How else would they appeal to a certain female audience, toward whom many of the show's ads are beamed? (They represent, paradoxically, the subordinated side of Mary Tyler Moore, the progenitor of the single-woman show, who signals that some sort of feminism is here to stay as a 'new life style' for the single career woman.)[15] At the same time, plainly the Angels are sex objects for men, as the cults of Farrah Fawcett-Majors and Cheryl Ladd attest. And they are subordinated: they usually rely on Charlie's aid to bail them out of the dangers to which their spunk has exposed them. It is no small element of the show's appeal to men that Charlie, the detective boss, is never seen. Male authority is invisible, and the 'girls' are kept free of romance. Thus, in the male viewer's fantasies, the Angels remain available – to him and him alone. He, in unconscious fantasy, *is* Charlie, ever supervising, ever needed, ever jovial, ever returned to. The show thus caters simultaneously to feminism and to backlash against it; it permits men to indulge prurience while psychologically admitting women's importance to the workforce. (I must add that I had thought this for months, marveling at the impersonal ingenuity of television production process, when I came upon a quotation from an anonymous 'top television executive of one of America's big three networks [who] said quite seriously, "A series like *Charlie's Angels* performs a very important and valuable public service. Not only does it show women how to look beautiful and lead very exciting lives, but they still take their orders from a man" ' (quoted in Lewin 1980). Which is not to say, before further investigation, that such thinking preceded the show and its popularity. A post hoc theory of function is not a program for strategy. But it is interesting that savvy network executives may become conscious theorists of hegemony, may recognize it when they see it, and may become quite skilled in layering complex images into a single artifact.)

In general, then, genre is necessarily sensitive; in its rough outlines, if not in detail, it brews a blend of popular sentiments.[16] Sometimes genre runs in advance of hegemonic ideology; more often it lags; a fine analysis of its themes will probably reveal elements of both in any given case. New genres coexist for a time with old ones, which may themselves be rooted in traditional forms: the Western, the detective story, the variety show. New genres sometimes transpose old ones: the ever-popular *Star Trek*, for example, was essentially a Western whose team of professional lawkeepers operated in space.

Without attempting here a thorough account of the metamorphoses of TV genre, I can suggest by way of hypothesis a few other signs of network sensitivity to actually *and potentially* shifting moods and group identities in the audience. One decisive clump of questions to be asked of television entertainment is: What is its attitude toward authority? Where does it locate legitimate and illegitimate sources of authority? How does authority cope with transgression? To take one example, the adult Western of the middle and late 1950s, with its drama of solitary righteousness and suppressed libidinousness, can be seen in retrospect to have played on a subterranean casualness about authority that was at odds with the dominant hierarchical motif of the Eisenhower years: TV drama here was vaguely preminitory of a counter-culture that had not yet crystallized into social action. Richard Boone's Paladin in *Have Gun, Will Travel*, and James Garner's Bart Maverick in the series of the same name, were lone heroes standing solidly within the tradition of frontier insouciance. Like classical good-guy Western moralists, they took official law-and-order wryly.[17] And yet, unlike the Lone Ranger and his puritanical ilk, they mixed their pursuit of outlaws with a pursuit of pleasure; they were hedonists. In the meantime, *Gunsmoke*'s Matt Dillon was a decent Eisenhower-like public official, affirming the necessity of paternalistic law and order against the temptations of worldly pleasure (Kitty, the saloon-keeper? madam?) and the depredations of unaccountably wicked outlaws. In the early 1960s the Western declined, and with the rise of Camelot counterinsurgency and the vigorous 'long twilight struggle' of John F. Kennedy, its values were taken over into spy-adventure drama. Series like *Mission: Impossible* and *The Man From Uncle* capitalized on the CIA's mystique, and reined individualism into teamwork; such shows were more or less synchronized with official government policy. *Star Trek*, launched in 1966, continued the teamwork and processed the cast's internationalism (intergalacticism, rather, if we allow for Spock) into a benign interstellar imperialism: the disordered universe, full of misguided Utopians and deceitful aliens, needed a continuing United Nations police action operating under the cool white American head of Captain Kirk.

Police shows also display a metamorphosis which matches the decomposition of the dominant view of crime and punishment. In Jack Webb's *Dragnet*, beginning in 1952, the police are in harmony with society's values; they detect according to the book; they are pure technicians ('Just the facts, ma'am'), representing the coincidence of technical and political capacities in the state. Organization is strictly hierarchical: Sgt Friday's authority is undisputed. Crime never pays: each installment ended by telling the audience that the criminal was convicted and sentenced to a definite term in prison (see Knutson 1974). But by the late 1960s the social consensus about the decency and the effectiveness of the State has unraveled, and the next generation of police shows display uncertainty about the legitimacy and consequence of the law and of the police within it, and about the organization of authority within the police. There is a range of new possibilities, all sharing, though, an unsettled plot: dedicated cops try to surmount humanist illusions (and hamstrung or meddling superiors) to draw thin blue lines against anarcho-criminal barbarians who stalk the cities. One continuing message is the practical futility of liberalism, a sense imported from the larger political culture. Police style now varies from *Mod Squad*'s reformed hip criminals, with the values of social workers, to *Barney Miller*'s ethnic pluralism, from *Starsky and Hutch*'s muted homo-eroticism to *Kojak*'s tough-tender no-nonsense efficacy.[18]

In cop and detective shows, there are a variety of hybrid mixtures of authority and outlawry, elaborating, in turn, a range of popular ambivalences toward bureaucracy, law, and the State. Hierarchy is no longer taken for granted, and is no longer harmonized with effective law-enforcement. Insider official authority and outsider cowboy integrity and restlessness have been combined and condensed into the character of the private detective, halfway between the police force (which continually gets in his way and must be outfoxed) and the criminal (who shares his resistance to corporate norms, yet testifies to the permanence of evil). The ex-cop private detective, from fiction's Lew Archer to TV's *Harry O*, is the anarchist as refugee from the organization. He shares the police's goals, but disdains the standard rules. He is the classic American frontier individualist, but in the service of a law and order whose primary institutional embodiment, the police force, he scorns. He is half anarchist, half vigilante. He represents the individualist's partial resistance, partial accommodation to a bureaucratic order that conditions his own ideals and yet cannot contain his spirit. Through his persona, scriptwriters who are confined to the organized strictures, however remunerative, of series formulae, pay tribute to the glimmering image of the autonomous writer they want to be. This imago, straining at the social leash, speaks to the frustrated aspirations of employees in living rooms. So, in a different way, does Kojak, the anti-bureaucratic cop trapped in red tape, scornful of criminal-coddling officials who are pushed around by the courts and let legal niceties stand in the way of rough justice (see Alley 1979: 138-9; Sage 1979).

The transformations in other genres also register shifts and variations in the condition of hegemonic ideology. The technologically-enhanced super-hero, for example, has metamorphosed over the course of four decades. In work not yet published, Tom Andrae of the Political Science Department at the University of California, Berkeley, shows how the Superman archetype began in 1933 as a vaguely Nietzschean menace to society; then he grew into a New Dealing, anti-Establishmentarian individualist casting his lot with the oppressed and, at times, against the State. Only in the 1940s was he altered to the current incarnation, prosecuting supercriminals in the name of 'the American way.' In the 1960s, the straight-arrow Superman was supplemented by the whimsical, self-parodying Batman and the Marvel Comics series, symbols of power gone slightly silly, no longer prepossessing. In playing against the conventions, their producers were doubtless affected by the modernist selfconsciousness so popular in high culture at the time. Thus do shifts in genre presuppose the changing mentality of critical masses of writers and cultural entrepreneurs; yet these changes would not take root commercially without corresponding changes in the disposition (even the self-consciousness) of large audiences. Changes in cultural ideals and in audience sensibilities must be harmonized to make for shifts in genre or formula.

If I have left the impression that television entertainment ordinarily tilts toward liberal variants of the hegemonic worldview, this is an apt moment to correct the picture. Recent turns in the career of the technological super-hero correspond to militarist tendencies in the

American polity. *The Six Million Dollar Man* and *The Bionic Woman* are not only obediently patriotic, they are organizational products through and through. These team players have no private lives from which they are recruited task by task, as in *Mission: Impossible*; they are not fortuitous arrivals from another planet, nurtured by sturdy farm folk, like *Superman*; but they have been rescued by the State and equipped by it. They owe their very existence to the State's fusion of moral right and technological know-how. Not only are they strong right arms of the State, but they and their strong arms, legs, eyes exist at the State's behest. And occasional topical slants anchor these shows' general support of military solutions to international problems. One 1977 episode of *The Six Million Dollar Man*, for example, told the story of a Russian-East German plot to stop the testing of the Air Force's new B-1 bomber; by implication, it linked the domestic movement against the B-1 to the foreign Red menace. A topical slant is by no means the whole of hegemonic framing; but the slant takes on special meaning in the context of the series' routine hegemonic setting.

Setting and character types

Just as prevailing television genres shift in historical time, so do the settings and character types associated with them. Shifting market tolerances and producer interests make for noticeable changes, some of which we have already discussed. Even in the formulaic 1950s, a few comedies were able to represent discrepant settings, permitting viewers both to identify and to indulge their sense of superiority through comic distance. Jackie Gleason's *The Honeymooners* and *The Phil Silvers Show* (Sergeant Bilko) capitalized on their stars' enormous personal popularity and theatrical experience, and were able to confer dignity on working-class and deviant characters in situations the opposite of glamorous (see Czitrom 1977).

Indeed, these examples point to the general importance of stars *as such* in binding the audience to the show. Stars who exude sexual auras are, of course, especially alluring, although talent scouts are notoriously unable to predict which auras are going to work. Part of the audience then is psychologically involved with the actor, who is perceived beneath the momentary mask of the character (Holland 1975: 97). But all television (like film) rests on libidinal identifications with characters, whether explicitly sexual or not (Metz 1976). Audiences invest stars with powers that descend from residues of infantile experience, experience that comes back into play during the provisional regressions of viewing. It is a nice fancy that particular stars embody particular aspects of hegemonic ideology, particular dimensions of the audience's structures of feeling, most likely in transposed forms; but how this embodiment takes place concretely, in particular stars at particular times, requires a full-blown analysis of its own.

Suffice to say, for the moment, that two uniformities of setting and character underlie almost all the variation. For one, the set itself almost always propounds a vision of consumer happiness. Living rooms and kitchens usually display what David Riesman has called the standard package of consumer goods. Even where the set is ratty, as in *Sanford and Son*, or working-class, as in *All in the Family*, the bright color of the TV tube almost always glamorizes the surroundings so that there will be no sharp break between the glorious color of the program and the glorious color of the commercial. In the more primitive 1950s, by contrast, it was still possible for a series like *The Honeymooners* or *The Phil Silvers Show* to get by with one or two simple sets per show: the life of a good skit was in its accomplished acting. But that series, in its sympathetic treatment of working-class mores, was exceptional. Color broadcasting accomplishes the glamorous ideal willy-nilly.

For a second thing, the major characters are winners. Most of the time, networks and sponsors want to convey images of glamor and fun; the settings and characters must be showcases not only for commercials but for an entire fantasy world that will entice the mass audience. Although program control has shifted from sponsors to networks – with certain implications for settings and character types, as we shall see below – what has not changed is television's preference for winners. In 1954, for example, one advertising agency wrote to the playwright Elmer Rice explaining why his *Street Scene*, with its 'lower class social level,' would be unsuitable for telecasting (quoted in Barnouw 1970: 33):

> We know of no advertiser or advertising agency of any importance in this country who would knowingly allow the products which he is trying to advertise to the public to become associated with the squalor . . . and general 'down' character . . . of *Street Scene*. . . .
>
> On the contrary it is the general policy of advertisers to glamorize their products, the people who buy them, and the whole American social and economic scene. . . . The American consuming public as presented by the advertising industry today is middle class, not lower class; happy in general, not miserable and frustrated . . .

Twenty-five years later, it is the networks that are directly enforcing this cheer. Television's professionals must get results; they must return each week, like fixed stars, to embody the upbeat.[19] Bob Shanks, an ABC vice-president who has written a revealing insider's book about TV, explains bluntly why he would advise against a series about a black ex-convict: 'Perry Mason must win every week. So must Dr. Welby.' Shanks's (1977: 149) rationale reveals the mentality of television executives, if not necessarily the whole audience:

> Comedians and social critics may scoff; we ourselves know life is not like that. So what? People, masses of people, do not watch television to learn what life is like, but rather to escape it. Defeat and dreariness are what happen to you during the day. At night, in front of the box, most people want to share in victories, associate with winners, be transferred from reality.

For dramatic purposes, victory should be hard-won. There is nothing more boring than the inevitable. Therefore, week after week, the hero should confront forces which are convincingly wicked, whether social (the cops' 'bad elements') or natural (the doctor's diseases). In either case, wickedness usually erupts outside social contexts; it has no deep cause. It happens, it needs to be fixed, period. The melodramatic need for the service justifies the hero's power in the situation. Clients, fools that they are, often start out recalcitrant, then turn out co-operative as they discover what is good for them. The patient is part of that intractible material world that makes the professional's job so difficult – yet, in the end, so rewarding, so necessary, so worthy of the prestige that attends it.

And yet knowledge is not the decisive attribute of the hero's status; he (or, rarely, she) deserves respect by virtue of his personality. Dr Marcus Welby was not just any doctor; he was the persona created by the paternal Robert Young we already knew best for his crinkly smile and moral excellence. This professional was no know-it-all, certainly no intellectual. Even if gruff, he was warm-hearted, dedicated to keeping families together. *Father Knows Best* . . . Welby Knows Best. Many of the most successful shows were adept at fusing skill and character in the same hero. In the highest form of this fusion the actor succeeds in investing himself with the character's prowess, carries his aura from character to character, and also exploits it commercially. Karl Malden (playing his character in *The Streets of San Francisco*) advertises American Express Travelers' Checks to foil crooks; Robert Young heaps praise upon decaffeinated coffee to ease tension. As I have pointed out above, it is in the nature of the viewing process that some portion of the audience-clientele will respond to this blurring of fact and fiction: during *Marcus Welby*'s years of popularity, Robert Young got 5,000 letters a week seeking medical advice (Real 1977: 118).

The senior professional hero is also a man fixed in the present. Whatever he knows he always knew. He did not arrive; he was not recruited; he was not trained; he did not come from this or that class; he did not go to these or those schools. We know him almost entirely by his works and his personality.[20] Except for an occasional origin myth, which tells a story about how the man got where he is, he is never a man in formation. Thus his prowess is presented as something magical. Only his understudy, the stereotypic up-and-coming young acolyte, can hope to learn what the older man knows. As for clients, they are lucky to be flattered with his attention. But lower-status professionals, though they too have come out of nowhere, are less competent. According to Michael Real (1977: 119, citing Schorr 1963) many real-life nurses wrote letters to the producer of *The Nurses*, 'complaining of the ineptness of the student nurse in the program, failure to show her in a student role, overly dramatic presentations of hospital life and the nurse's role, and portrayals of nurses as alcoholics, reactionaries, and neurotics.'

Above all, the televised professional is an idealist and an individualist. His motives are pure: to restore a warm, decent status quo ante, the symptom-free family or the crime-free neighborhood. The fee is never much of an issue, if it is mentioned at all. Perry Mason accepted a retainer with a quick flat grin, the impersonal gesture of a cash register, before getting on with the job he was born to do. Doctors have been even more exempt from the marketplace. As David W. Rintels (1974b) has said: 'Anyone who watches *Marcus Welby, M.D.*, *Medical Center*, and *The Doctors* . . . must of necessity believe . . . no doctor ever charges for his services; no hospital ever bills a patient; no one ever has to go on charity, or do without care.' A good deal of the reason is that the great majority of the patients can afford to pay their own way handsomely; Michael Real (1977: 119) has shown, for example, that almost all Welby's patients were well-to-do. Cops may occasionally grumble about their salaries: this is in keeping with the more realistic tone of the cop show. But, cops and teachers aside, the televised professional is generally a *free* professional.

We have, then, what seems at first glance distortion pure and simple. While the actual professions have become more bureaucratized and specialized, the television hero upholds the traditional image of the self-sufficient practitioner. The doctor has been either an omnicompetent general practitioner or a surgeon, that most prestigious of medical specialists, embodying a power of life and death that lends itself easily to melodrama. In either case he does not condescend to bureaucratic relations with Medicaid or Medicare or Blue Shield or the hospital administration; he is not hedged about by insurance companies; he does not politic through professional organizations because he does not need to. His hands are not dirtied by the complicated structures of his everyday world. He is free to be a household god: he is a romantic figure. Even the cop, forced to work within the confines of bureaucracy, as we have seen, is the romantic as organization man, his rebellion always incipient, always stylistic, always idealistic, always solitary. In the real America, the professional carries forward an older tradition: the frontiersman, the sawbones, the Lone Ranger. Almost everyone in the audience works for someone else; only about two per cent of the working population are unsalaried professionals (*Statistical Abstract*, 1979). But television conventions allow the audience its free-standing heroes: repositories of freedom and nurturance united, and dreams of independence for the kids.

For if television is untrue to the reality of society, it is true to a dream; it pays tribute to popular fantasy. The televised image both anchors and reinforces the prevailing aspiration toward professional status. In 1962 fewer than 2 per cent of the sons of manual laborers had entered the professions; but the aspiration persists, the luminous hope that the child will be a successful and respectable professional, will be able, as Richard Sennett (1972: 229) writes, 'to unite love and power.' So television images may fairly be criticized for lacking naturalistic accuracy, for racist and sexist and class-biased stereotyping; yet in one crucial respect the criticism misses the point. Television, like much popular culture through the ages, embodies fantasy images which speak to real aspirations. It does not simply reflect the social world; it is no mirror. The hegemonic image is an active shaping of what actually exists, but it would not take hold if it did not correspond, one way or another, to strong popular desires – as well as defenses against them (Holland 1975: ch. 4). 'False consciousness' always contains its truth: the truth of wish, the truth of illusion that is embraced with a quiet passion made possible, even necessary, by actual frustration and subordination.

But to say that the hero corresponds to a popular wish is not to say that the wish constructs the image. It is the culture industry that generates the image, often enough to tailor it to the public-relations desires of the actual profession. The networks guarantee that the professional image will not be too starkly, consistently, 'controversially' idealistic by setting up direct and indirect systems of censorship. After self-censorship has had its chance, some of the work of censorship is done in-house, by the networks' own censorship bureaus; and some is farmed out to professional associations like the American Medical Association. It is those professional associations which have first crack at approving the televised images of their professions. We have already noted the case of the FBI. And as for medicine, we have the testimony of Norman Felton (quoted in Rintels 1974b: 391) the executive producer of *Dr Kildare*, *The Eleventh Hour*, and *The Psychiatrist*, that

> on the *Dr. Kildare* series we were asked by NBC to get the approval and seal of the AMA. This meant that we submitted scripts for approval to the AMA. Although the organization gave us technical help, it goes without saying that we did not present an accurate picture of the practice of medicine, or the difficulties many people had in obtaining medical care . . .

Since 1955, the AMA has kept a Physicians Advisory Committee on Television, Radio and Motion Pictures (PAC) to – in the words of its chairman – 'maintain medical accuracy.' Toward that end, the PAC provides two on-the-spot doctors as medical advisers (Real 1977: 120-1).

But in the end it is the networks that confer censorship power and may or may not farm it out to the professional associations. They operate within a web of hegemonic institutions; their oligopoly is interlinked with the prestigious monopolies where power and knowledge interpenetrate; and the networks act in behalf of their conception of the whole. They may well relax censorship over dirty words and sexual innuendo, in order to keep up with the changing standards of their younger, hipper audiences (and of Hollywood); but they work to secure a complexly articulated version of legitimate social authority – which needs to be traced out in detail. The *NBC Radio and Television Broadcast Standards and Practices* manual reads: 'Respect for lawyers, police, teachers and clergy should not be diminished by undue and unnecessary emphasis on unfavorable aspects of members of these professions' (Rintels 1974b: 392). Bob Shanks of ABC writes (1977: 79) that 'all three networks have similar policy guidelines and adhere to the same industry and government codes.'

Again, though most hegemonic constancies remain, shifting market structures make variation possible. The near-universality of television set ownership (in 1960, 87 per cent of American households had a TV set; in 1965, 92.6 per cent; in 1970, 95.2 per cent; in 1975, 97.1 per cent) creates the possibility of a wider range of audiences than existed in the 1950s. Minority-group, working-class, age-segmented and subculturally compact audiences have proliferated. Since at least 47 per cent of American households own two or more television sets, and 10 per cent own three or more, it becomes possible to target relatively narrow bands of the population (Haight and Sterling 1978: 372). Programing becomes more centrifugal. Cable and pay television multiply, and the market becomes more segmented. The glamor standards can slacken off at times. The industry noted that the mini-series *Roots* reached people who don't normally watch TV. The homes-using-television levels during the week of *Roots* were up between 6 and 12 per cent over the comparable week a year earlier (*Broadcasting*, January 31, 1977). Untapped markets can only be brought in by unusual sorts of programing. There is room in the schedule for rebellious human slaves just as there is room for hard-hitting technological superheroes. Movies made for single showings on television also may veer toward counter-hegemonic political positions: they may sympathize with homosexuals, may criticize Senator Joseph McCarthy and the blacklist of the 1950s. ABC's 1980 version of Attica, based on Tom Wicker's *A Time to Die*, focussed its first half on the grievances of prisoners, and construed subsequent events in that light; ABC did insist that the producer splice in new footage at the last moment, showing prisoners' knives at the throats of their hostage guards, but the power of the show's reformist sympathy for the prisoners remained powerful. Such shows have prestige value, and help deflect critical opinion from the networks. On the other hand, network élites do not invest in regular heroes who will challenge, from left, right, or elsewhere, the core values of corporate capitalist society: who are, say, union organizers, or explicit socialists, or for that matter born-again evangelists. And the emergence of independently syndicated programs for independent stations does not necessarily translate into increased diversity of substance. The everyday settings and character types of television entertainment go on confirming the essential soundness of commercial values, the prerogatives of individualism, the authority of professionals (though not political leaders or business executives),[21] and the legitimacy of the national security state.

Conflict and solution

All narratives set out problems and point toward solutions. High art works its problems through with absorbing thoroughness, toward genuine resolutions; much commercial art, slapped together under pressure through formula, fails to justify its own feeble, jerry-built passes at solutions. But solutions, in either case, there must be. For it is in solution that the tensions provoked in the audience by the shaping and disguising of their desires and fears get resolved; it is through solution that the work finally produces its psychological effect. Through *happy* ending, that harmonious result which reality denies may be granted by fantasy; the irreconcilable may be reconciled.

But to say that solution is important is not to say *how* a given cultural form will frame its solutions. There must be conventions; but which will prevail? The essence of the dominant television convention is that, whatever social and psychological problems come up, they are susceptible to successful individual resolutions. However grave the problems, however rich the imbroglio, the episodes regularly end with the click of closure: an arrest, a defiant smile (now held with freeze-frame technology), an I-told-you-so explanation before the credits. As we have already seen in the discussion of character types, the convention of the star-based series requires that preserving solutions be found; it would hardly do for the hero to fail week after week, or to be killed in the line of duty. The characters with which the audience identifies must stay alive and well, ready for next week's imbroglio. (Only when there is a contract dispute, or an actor departs for more alluring horizons, or dies, does his or her character get written out of the script. The more sympathetic the character, the more gentle the departure.) However deeply the problem may be located within society, it will be solved among a few persons: the heroes must attain a solution that leaves the rest of the society untouched. Crime is solved by arrests; citizens never organize against it. Meanness is resolved by changes of heart, or the bad guy's 'come-uppance.'

Again, there are variations alongside the normal convention. There was the short-lived *East Side, West Side*, and Norman Lear's independently syndicated *Mary Hartman, Mary Hartman*, which extended soap opera conventions in the process of parodying them. (The networks would not buy it.) Beginning in 1978, CBS's successful *Dallas* signaled that the convention of daytime serial continuity – the rolling plot in which one damn thing leads to another – has become acceptable in prime time. Earlier, Norman Lear's archetypal *All in the Family* was unusual among network broadcasts in sometimes ending obliquely, softly, or ironically, on the curvature of a question mark, thus acknowledging that the Bunkers could not solve a problem whose genesis was outside their household. *Lou Grant* has been even more unusual: for a time it specialized in open rather than closed endings. One show, for example, revolved around Lou's encounter with several young black men who hung out on the street corner. Learning that one outspokenly cynical one was unemployed, Lou, the humane liberal, urged him to apply for a job at the *Tribune*. The young man, by the end of the show, has failed to get a job, and when Lou returns to the street corner and asks about him, his buddies report that he's left town. His story is still open. The problem remains; individual action cannot eliminate unemployment. Such downbeat anti-endings were fairly typical for *Lou Grant* at first, but have been cut back in later seasons. According to an informant connected with the show, the censors of CBS Standards and Practices, who had not objected to any of the anti-establishment politics implicit in many *Lou Grant* shows, had objected to the show's *open* form and were trying to regear it to orthodoxy.

So form as well as manifest content – to the extent they can be distinguished – is a matter of concern for the television élite. The concerns of minority audiences are incorporated into the dominant discourse; ideological elements are found in ethnic and subcultural communities throughout the society, and then packaged. *Roots*, television's most famous single fictional achievement, represented both the cruelty of slavery and the possibilities of resistance; it humanized blacks, and romanticized the possibility of a class alliance between slaves and poor whites. Yet the series also pointed toward the chance for upward mobility; the upshot of travail was freedom. Where Alex Haley's book was subtitled 'The Saga of an American Family,' ABC's version carried the label – and the patriotic and institutional self-congratulation – 'The *Triumph* of an American Family.' Who could say categorically whether the prevailing impression was that of the collective agony or that of the family's triumph? Both themes were there, to be taken seriously in different proportions by different audiences. Those elements conflicted within a complex hegemonic whole, and helped renew the hegemonic understanding of right relations among nation, family, and individual. The friction between agony and triumph reproduced a larger friction. Cultural bargains of this sort keep the hegemonic ideology in motion and in equilibrium at the same time.

A note on methods of study

But plainly we can proceed no further without clarifying how we are to know what a program means. Like it or not, we are thrust into methodological thickets. And methodological issues are, of course, both epistemological and theoretical, for methodology sets limits to the types of discovery that are possible, while it always contains implicit assumptions about what is worth knowing and how the knowable can be known. This is not the place to enter into a full-scale compendium of research methods and ways of knowing.[22] But a few general points are worth making. How do analysts interpret popular culture? And how do we study audience responses, and their active interpretations made by others?

The first thing to say is that the two types of interpretation are, indeed, interpretation. There are no definitive readings of cultural works, whether novels, paintings, movies, television shows, symphonies or rock records. There are more or less attentive, comprehensive, subtle, and reflexive interpretations; there are those that are more or less sensitive to the ways in which the worldview of the observer helps constitute the work as a cultural practice that is continued by its audience. There are interpretations that are more or less attuned to elements of the work's texture and style, as well as its structure and themes, that grasp its location within tradition, genre, convention, as well as its particularity (Eagleton 1976; Williams 1977). And in the end there is no way in which a neutral metacritic could survey a spread of interpretations of a given work and provide general rules by which to notify another neutral metacritic which interpretation to prefer of a given work – let alone others yet uninterpreted.

One argument about interpretation, in its pure form, pits the structuralist against the free-lance. The free-lance insists that interpretation, bringing to the work a set of analytic categories, must always risk them in the flash and heat of the analytic process. If analysis is to be more than the mobilizing of evidence to demonstrate the adequacy of prearranged analytic categories, it must remain open to the modification and subversion of those categories. The results of interpretation should not follow deductively from the initial premises, even in the initial interrogations put to the materials. Formalism is the enemy of critical interpretation – so the argument goes – for it refuses the work itself; it has already seen it. It no longer makes discoveries. Structuralist formalism of all kinds takes the cultural world as a set of permutations of fixed modules of meaning. It copes with the flux of popular culture by denying it. The bracing and truly empirical approach, by contrast, is to let one's understanding flex in the process of admitting the new material: to rethink the artifact freshly. The free-lance points out that the liveliest critical interpretations are not the most methodical, nor do they apply some fixed grid of issues to the world of cultural objects. In the second half of his *Mythologies*, Roland Barthes may have insisted on the academically obligatory general theory, but this semiological scheme is relatively thin and obvious; the real stuff is the first half, whose snippets of jovial interpretation cannot be reduced to an analytic system. Had it been so reduced, we would have a library of successor volumes by his students and epigones. The interpretive anarchist concludes that interpretive flexibility, carrying the fewest possible *a priori* assumptions, not only makes for the most reliable analytic method, it amounts to a stance in the world: it makes for the most animated existence.

And yet: against this the structuralist insists that the abandonment of *a priori* assumptions is an illusion: fresh looks are only looks that have not yet formulated the grid of their selectivity. Moreover, popular cultural commodities are themselves standardized and formulaic. They are created as formulas; they are reduced in the course of their production. Reduced objects call for reductionist analysis; reified forms require reified interpretation. A formula must be called by its proper name: 'formula.' Anything else is wishful idealism and idle connoisseurship. In effect, this was the argument of Frankfurt critical theory (Adorno 1954; Horkheimer and Adorno 1972). Confronting television entertainment, reductionism has a certain warrant, although Adorno's and Horkheimer's vitality as critics, their insistence that criticism *was* praxis, forced them to resist the stultifying implications of their own theoretical critique of stereotypy.

The problem for the structuralist argument is to determine what is the formula to which the given show should be reduced. And here the two approaches may be seen as halves of a total approach. For if the objective content of the artifact is in doubt, how shall it be ascertained? How shall the artifact be separated out from the subject-object relation which any given interpreter constitutes in the process of receiving the object and making interpretations? The answer must lie in constructing an analytic process which is itself a collaboration. The best mode of interpretation, I think, is conversation: conversation among analysts, each of whom is aware of his or her particular sensitivities and defenses, each of whom sees the object through different filters of social location and personality. Instead of formally establishing coding reliability, as in quantitative content analyses, the assembled analysts *in ensemble* 'calibrate' each others' sensibilities. Conversation brings up themes embedded in the object: indeed, a wider range of themes than the individual analyst is ordinarily aware of. Conversation then attempts to sort out aspects of individual experience – nationality, class, race, gender, age, ideology, historical encounters – which might be conditioning the varying responses of the various interpreters.[23] Analysis then triangulates the object itself, bracketing the particular frames of the observers, pointing to different – and even contradictory – layers of meaning contained within the work. It then becomes possible for individual critics to speculate more knowledgeably about what the object itself means. Subjectivity has hardly been eliminated from the critical response; but it has been, perhaps, reserved to its place. Certainly my own graduate seminar's critical conversations about television programs have generated more fruitful hypotheses about meaning than any single personal interpretations I know, not least my own.[24]

It goes without saying that audience reception needs study. However this delicate task is undertaken, let analysts not forget that audiences are made up of interpreters. People imbibe popular culture selectively, preferring cultural objects which are congenial to their own systems of understanding and defense, and interpreting them through the filters of these systems (Holland 1975: 96; Metz 1976: 81). Ascertaining the 'objective' meaning of the object is never a final process; it is always subject to the next exercise in interpretation. Moreover: the student of popular culture can never rest satisfied with armchair analysis in a controlled setting, nor with formal laboratory-style experiments. For all interpretation is interpretation in situ. We know that the experience of watching television in one's home, alone, is different from the experience of watching it in a bar, or in someone else's home among friends. We know, from sketchy sociological investigation, that people erect not only individual but small-group defenses against television (Blum 1964). One next stage in the study of popular culture must, therefore, be ethnographic: it must attend to what people do and say and look like when they consume culture *in natural settings*. When we study the meanings of popular music, we must consider not only the lyrics, but the rhythms, harmonies, and crucially the beat; we must see what people do when they dance to it (Willis, n.d. 1978). When we study the reception of television, we must pay close attention to our own responses, to our families' and friends', and to other households'. A second important project to entertain is a replication of *Mass Persuasion*, by Robert K. Merton with Marjorie Fiske and Alberta Curtis, – but this time for television. In 1945, Merton and other researchers teased out the significant themes in Kate Smith's radio war bond drive, and then interviewed a sample of listeners who had been persuaded to buy bonds alongside a sample of listeners who had not been persuaded. Skilled depth-psychological interviews got at differences in the social and psychological characteristics of the two groups, as well as the timing of the purchases of those who did buy. Such projects are expensive to finance, yet we will not learn much more about the ways in which distinct audiences respond to popular culture without careful studies of this sort.

Conclusion

The technologies of mass culture do not stand still, and they are imprinted by the structure and strategies of the political-economic system at the moment (see Williams 1975: 14-41). Radio, developed by private capital in the context of expanding consumer production, made for considerable changes in the volume of image-manufacture, and helped reconstruct the meanings of other cultural forms. Motion pictures and the form of the fiction film narrative together amounted to a historically specific social institution, with the star system anchoring a form of audience worship which reproduced the social relations of political dependency. Television broadcasting brought the spectacular image into the home, helping to undermine families' ability to withstand the fragmenting powers of the consumer economy. And the development of technology – always to be understood within the strategy of social institutions – does not stop there.

New television distribution systems loom. Cable television already enters about fifteen million American homes, pay cable about five million (*Broadcasting* 1980b). Satellites make possible low-cost production and syndication of alternative programing.[25] A fourth network becomes imaginable. Videocassette recorders and videodiscs, available at high but falling prices, open up the range of consumer choice. But what do these possibilities augur for ideological content or consequence? Only a fool guesses with great claims of certainty. As the president of the Television Bureau of Advertising reminded his National Association of Broadcasters audience in April 1980, some forecasters predicted in 1970 'that "by the end of the decade" cable penetration would be "40-60%" . . . two to three times as high as the actual penetration that has occurred. By contrast, he said, [broadcast] television's growth has been greater than anyone would have predicted' (*Broadcasting* 1980c). One thing is clear: the networks and their consultants do not anticipate losing the great bulk of their audience. RCA's Herbert S. Schlosser, former president of NBC and now in charge of videodisc programing, told the NAB that 'The total impact of the new media will be to reduce commercial television's audience somewhat, to knock the corners off that audience. But those are big corners, and new businesses can thrive in them.' He anticipated that videodisc audiences would be comparable to those of records and books rather than those of present-day television: speciality markets that would not compete with the mass markets of the networks. The effect on network programing might be ambiguous. On the one hand, more news and sports: television's coverage of the topical and live cannot be matched by other media. On the other hand, networks might amplify their access to the national market by exploiting satellite technology to produce more than a single program service (*Broadcasting* 1980b).

There are ideological rhythms in popular culture. Periods of diversity and competition alternate with periods of consolidation and market concentration (Peterson and Berger 1975). The market may serve for a while to amplify an oppositional style, as with rock music in the middle and late 1960s; oligopoly then regroups to assimilate the new forms, to flatten them and reduce them to formulae. New marginal forms, like New Wave music, spring up when the older ones have calcified. One cannot say in advance where the screw will stop turning, where a given content will prove to have gone out of bounds. Artists find out where the limits are by stepping over them.

By themselves, new forms of distribution signify nothing momentous. By no means do they guarantee that substantive alternatives will emerge; they might simply circulate new assortments of the standard ingredients. Genuine innovation can never be reduced to a technological fix. What develops in popular culture depends on the ideas of alternative producers, on the degree to which they generate culture which matches the desires of publics in distinguished ways – and not least, on the texture of political life, and the quality of demands that social groups make on the political-economic system and the culture industry within it. The sway of the culture industry presupposes audiences that it satisfies – by packaging their dissatisfaction and retailing it back – and cultural producers who are willing to work under oligopolistic constraints. To reverse Plato's formula: When the mode of the city changes, the walls of the music shake; and Plato's original tribute to the power of culture is not defunct either. The hegemonic walls can be relocated. What does not change is the existence of those walls, nor the existence of art and mind battering against them.

Acknowledgments

My great thanks to members of my Winter 1980 graduate seminar on the analysis of popular culture, at Berkeley, for wrestling with theoretical conundrums and conducting sparkling analysis of television programs; a number of their ideas find their way into this essay. Thanks especially to Jon D. Cruz, Lisa Heilbronn, Kathy Oberdeck, and Brian Powers for reading and closely criticizing an earlier draft. Thanks also to Michael Burawoy and Thelma McCormack for their thorough readings and critiques; I have not met all their objections, but hope to have set the table for more conversation. And thanks to Margaret Stetson for typing the next-to-last draft.

Notes

1 This argument follows Jameson (1979) and Holland (1975).

2 Compare Gans (1974) and Willis (1978) for different approaches to the same point.

3 These sentences partly paraphrase, partly revise the similar statement in Gitlin (1980: 253). See also Hall (1977: 332).

4 On the psychological consequences of the meritocratic principle for the working class, see Sennett and Cobb (1972); for a defense of meritocracy's central tenets, see Bell (1973).
5 The distinction is Raymond Williams's (1973: 10), and needs to be made more subtly and sharply. What exactly is alternative, what oppositional? It does not suffice to say that 'alternative senses of the world' are those 'which can be accommodated and tolerated within a particular effective and dominant culture,' since the limits of toleration may not be plain before the fact of their testing, and since even the oppositional may be 'accommodated and tolerated' through encapsulation in subcultural ghettoes. Refining the distinction, as Silvia Bizio has pointed out to me, is one of the outstanding theoretical tasks in the sociology of popular culture.
6 This is emphatically not to say that the industry 'gives people what they want.' As an oligopoly, its choices are limited to the most easily packaged commodities, and they are contained within the hegemonic forms.
7 This argument was informed by Leiss (1976).
8 On the striking continuities in American mythology, especially the myth of the hunter-hero, see Slotkin (1973).
9 The cultural capacity of the TV screen is illustrated by the work done for television by Federico Fellini and Michelangelo Antonioni in Italy, by Ingmar Bergman in Sweden, by Alain Tanner in Switzerland.
10 This point draws on Hall (1973). Compare Umberto Eco on the normality of aberrant decoding by individuals, as cited in Hall (1973) and in Fiske and Hartley (1978: 51).
11 I refer to John Brenkman's (1979) use of Sartre's concept of serialization.
12 My discussion of television conventions is a revised version of Gitlin (1979: 254-63), incorporating passages from Gitlin (1977b).
13 In 1975, CBS canceled *Gunsmoke* although it had ranked eighth and fifteenth in Nielsen ratings over the previous two seasons. The audience was primarily older and disproportionately rural, and thus not worth as much to advertisers as its numbers might have suggested. So much for the network's democratic rationale.
14 I use 'genre' loosely to refer to general categories of entertainment, like adult western, police show, black show. Genre is not an objective feature of the cultural universe, but a conventional name for a convention that exists and shifts in history, and should not be reified – as both cultural analysis and practice often do – into a cultural essence.
15 Mary Tyler Moore's *Rhoda* illustrates the sensitivity of show to audience veto. *Rhoda* built its audience when the protagonist married in 1974 and lost millions when she got separated in 1976.
16 Indeed, since there are only three networks, the oligopoly is oversensitive to success. For example, *Charlie's Angels* engendered

Flying High and *American Girls*, about stewardesses and female reporters, respectively, each on a long leash under male authority. But clones usually fail, since they replicate formula without aura; and these sank without a trace.

17 This discussion of Western and spy shows is indebted to Wright's (1975) structuralist analysis of movie Westerns and their transformations.

18 Silvia Bizio is tracing metamorphoses of police show plots, in detailed research in progress at UCLA. For preliminary notions, see Alley (1979) and Sage (1979).

19 The following discussion draws heavily on Gitlin (1977b).

20 Occasionally we see a bit of family life, or even a lot, as in *Police Story* or the more recent and startling breakthrough series, *Hill Street Blues*. I haven't the space here to discuss variations in TV treatment of the professional archetype. On styles of police show, see Alley (1979), Sage (1979), and Schneider (1977). On stylistic and structural innovations in *Hill Street Blues* see Gitlin (1981b).

21 For an impressionistic, exaggerated, but provocative argument about television's hostility to business, see Stein (1979). Stein fails to see that television can be hostile to individual businessmen and friendly to business values at the same time.

22 There is a valuable listing of ethnographic techniques in Willis (n.d.: 12-14).

23 This extrapolates from Holland (1975: 108): 'The text is fixed, but people respond to it in rather widely varying ways – just as some people will laugh at a joke and others won't. The best the critic can do, then, is consult within himself, articulate as best he can his own feelings and the reasons for them, then look for what in the poem seems to be shaping that response. If he can find form in that sense – objectively – he can then (perhaps) understand the subjective reactions of others who bring to the poem other personalities, other experiences, traits, or needs.' Caught, most likely, in the conventional individualism of the critical endeavor, Holland does not pursue this logic toward conversation as a method.

24 For a discussion of problems of method and theory in recent studies of popular culture, see Gitlin (1981a).

25 With the Federal government subsidizing ground stations for the reception of signals bounced off satellites, it becomes technically possible for independent producers to broadcast to ad hoc syndicates of local stations. Thus, in May 1979, independent producers broadcast three hours of live coverage of a Washington demonstration against nuclear power; their program was broadcast live by 15 stations and taped for later broadcast by 7 others. The satellite time cost $1,200, and a hundred people donated their services. In July 1979 this Public Interest Video Network broadcast for 90 minutes, live, from the national Right-to-Life convention in Cincinnati.

Bibliography

Adorno, T. W. (1954), 'How to Look at Television,' *Hollywood Quarterly of Film, radio and Television* (Spring), reprinted pp. 474-88 in Bernard Rosenberg and David Manning White (eds), *Mass Culture*, New York: The Free Press.

Alley, Robert S. (1979), 'Television Drama,' pp. 118-50, in Horace Newcomb (ed.), *Television: The Critical View*, 2nd edn, New York: Oxford University Press.

Altick, Richard (1978), *The Shows of London*, Cambridge, Mass.: Harvard University Press.

Barnouw, Erik (1978), *The Sponsor*, New York: Oxford University Press. versity Press.

Bernouw, Erik (1978), *The Sponsor*, New York: Oxford University Press.

Bell, Daniel (1973), *The Coming of Post-Industrial Society*, New York: Basic Books.

Benjamin, Walter (1978), 'The Author as Producer,' in *Reflections*, New York: Harcourt Brace Jovanovich. Originally published in 1934.

Blum, Alan F. (1964), 'Lower-Class Negro Television Spectators: The Concept of Pseudo-Jovial Scepticism,' pp. 429-35, in Arthur B. Shostak and William Gomberg (eds), *Blue-Collar World*, Englewood Cliffs, N.J.: Prentice-Hall.

Brenkman, John (1979), 'Mass Media: From Collective Experience to the Culture of Privatization,' *Social Text* No. 1 (Winter): 94-109.

Broadcasting (1977), 'Roots biggest event in TV entertainment history,' 31 January, p. 19.

Broadcasting (1980a), 'Researcher Fitzgibbon tells AAAA audience it will have to deal with changing social values,' March 24, pp. 56-7.

Broadcasting (1980b), 'NAB seers forecast that new media will only "knock corners" off TV's audience,' April 21, pp. 53-4.

Broadcasting (1980c), 'TVB at NAB: no need to fear the next 10 years,' April 21, p. 63.

Burawoy, Michael (1979), *Manufacturing Consent*, Chicago: University of Chicago Press.

Burke, Peter (1978), *Popular Culture in Early Modern Europe*, New York: New York University Press.

Czitrom, Danny (1977), 'Bilko: A Sitcom for All Seasons,' *Cultural Correspondence* no. 4 (Spring): 16-19.

Debord, Guy (1977), *The Society of the Spectacle*. Revised translation. Detroit: Black & Red.

Eagleton, Terry (1976), *Criticism and Ideology*, London: New Left Books.

Epstein, Edward Jay (1973), *News from Nowhere: Television and the News*, New York: Random House.

Fiske, John, and John Hartley (1978), *Reading Television*, London: Methuen.

Gans, Herbert J. (1974), *Popular Culture and High Culture*, New York: Basic Books.

Gans, Herbert J. (1979), *Deciding What's News*, New York: Pantheon.

Giedion, Siegfried (1962), *The Eternal Present*, New York: Bollingen.

Gitlin, Todd (1977a), 'Spotlights and Shadows: Television and the Culture of Politics,' *College English* 38 (April): 789-801.

Gitlin, Todd (1977b), 'The Televised Professional,' *Social Policy* (November/December), pp. 93-9.

Gitlin, Todd (1979), 'Prime Time Ideology: The Hegemonic Process in Television Entertainment,' *Social Problems* 26 (February): 251-66.

Gitlin, Todd (1980), *The Whole World is Watching: Mass Media in the Making and Unmaking of the New Left*, Berkeley, Calif.: University of California Press.

Gitlin, Todd (1981a), Review-essay of Erving Goffman, *Gender Advertisements*; John Fiske and John Hartley, *Reading Television*; and Judith Williamson, *Decoding Advertisements, Theory and Society* (January).

Gitlin, Todd (1981b), 'Make it Look Messy,' *American Film* (September).

Haight, Timothy R. and Christopher H. Sterling (1978), *The Mass Media: Aspen Institute Guide to Communication Industry Trends*, New York: Praeger Publications.

Hall, Stuart (1973), 'Encoding and Decoding in the Television Discourse,' Centre for Contemporary Cultural Studies, University of Birmingham, mimeo.

Hall, Stuart (1977), 'Culture, the Media, and the "Ideological Effect," ' pp. 315-48 in James Curran, Michael Gurevitch, and Janet Woolacott (eds), *Mass Communication and Society*, London: Edward Arnold.

Holland, Norman N. (1975), *The Dynamics of Literary Response*, New York: W. W. Norton.

Horkheimer, Max, and T. W. Adorno (1972), 'The Culture Industry: Enlightenment as Mass Deception,' pp. 120-67 in *Dialectic of Enlightenment*, New York: Seabury Press. Originally published in 1944.

Huizinga, Johan (1955), *Homo Ludens*, Boston: Beacon Press. Originally published in 1944.

Jameson, Fredric (1979), 'Reification and Utopia in Mass Culture,' *Social Text* no. 1 (Winter): 130-48.

Knutson, Pete (1974), 'Dragnet: The Perfect Crime?' *Liberation* (May), pp. 28-31.

Ladurie, Emmanuel Le Roy (1979), *Carnival in Romans*, New York: George Braziller.

Leiss, William (1976), *The Limits to Satisfaction*, Toronto: University of Toronto Press.

Lewin, David (1980), 'The Hidden Persuaders: The American Producers with the Powerful Punch,' *San Francisco Sunday Examiner and Chronicle*, Datebook (April 20), p. 42.

Lukács, Georg (1964), *Studies in European Realism*, New York: Grosset & Dunlap.

Merton, Robert, Marjorie Fiske, and Alberta Curtis (1946), *Mass Persuasion*, New York: Harper & Brothers.

Metz, Christian (1976), 'The Fiction Film and Its Spectator: A Metapsychological Study,' *New Literary History* (Autumn): 75-103.

Peterson, Richard A., and David G. Berger (1975), 'Cycles in Symbol Production: The Case of Popular Music,' *American Sociological Review* 40: 158-73.

Poulantzas, Nicos (1975), *Classes in Contemporary Capitalism*, London: New Left Books.

Real, Michael R. (1977), *Mass-Mediated Culture*, Englewood Cliffs, N.J.: Prentice-Hall.

Rintels, David W. (1974a), 'How Much Truth Does "The FBI" Tell about the FBI?' *The New York Times* March 5, 1972, reprinted in William Lutz (ed.), *The Age of Communication*, Pacific Palisades, Calif.: Goodyear Publishing Co.

Rintels, David W. (1974b), 'Will Marcus Welby Always Make You Well?' *The New York Times* March 12, 1972. Reprinted in William Lutz (ed.), *The Age of Communication*, Pacific Palisades, Calif.: Goodyear Publishing Co.

Sage, Lorna (1979), 'Kojak and Co.', pp. 151-9 in Horace Newcomb (ed.), *Television: The Critical View*, 2nd edn, New York: Oxford University Press.

Schneider, Bob (1979), 'Spelling's Salvation Armies,' *Cultural Correspondence* no. 4 (Spring): 27-36.

Schorr, Thelma (1963), 'Nursing's TV Image,' *American Journal of Nursing* 63.

Sennett, Richard, and Jonathan Cobb (1972), *The Hidden Injuries of Class*, New York: Alfred A. Knopf.

Shanks, Bob (1977), *The Cool Fire: How To Make It in Television*, New York: Vintage.

Slotkin, Richard (1973), *Regeneration Through Violence: The Mythology of the American Frontier, 1600-1860*, Middletown, Conn.: Wesleyan University Press.

Sontag, Susan (1977), *On Photography*, New York: Farrar, Straus & Giroux.

Statistical Abstract of the United States (1979), Tenth Edition, Washington, D. C.: Department of Commerce, Bureau of the Census.

Stein, Ben (1979), *The View From Sunset Boulevard*, New York: Basic Books.

Tuchman, Gaye (1978), *Making News*, New York: The Free Press.

Vidmar, Neil, and Milton Rokeach (1974), 'Archie Bunker's Bigotry: A Study in Selective Perception and Exposure,' *Journal of Communication* 24 (Winter): 36-47.

Watt, Ian (1957), *The Rise of the Novel*, Berkeley, Calif.: University of California Press.

Williams, Raymond (1973), 'Base and Superstructure in Marxist Cultural Theory,' *New Left Review* no. 82: 3-16.
Williams, Raymond (1975), *Television: Technology and Cultural Form*, New York: Schocken.
Williams, Raymond (1977), *Marxism and Literature*, New York: Oxford University Press.
Willis, Paul E. (n.d.) 'Symbolism and Practice: A Theory for the Social Meaning of Pop Music,' Centre for Contemporary Cultural Studies, University of Birmingham, mimeo.
Willis, Paul E. (1978), *Profane Culture*, London: Routledge & Kegan Paul.
Wright, Will (1975), *Sixguns and Society*, Berkeley, Calif.: University of California Press.

Chapter 8

Curricular form and the logic of technical control:

building the possessive individual

Michael W. Apple

Corporate ideologies: reaching the teacher

It does not require an exceptional amount of insight to see the current attempts by the State and industry to bring schools more closely into line with 'economic needs.' Neither side of the Atlantic has been immune to these pressures. In the UK, The Great Debate and the Green Paper stand as remarkable statements to the ability of capital in times of economic crisis to marshall its forces. As the Green Paper notes (Donald 1979: 44):

> There is a wide gap between the world of education and the world of work. Boys and girls are not sufficiently aware of the importance of industry to our society, and they are not taught much about it.

It goes on, making the criterion of functional efficiency the prime element in educational policy (Donald 1979: 36-7):

> The total resources which will be available for education and the social services in the future will depend largely on the success of the Industrial Strategy. It is vital to Britain's economic recovery and standard of living that the performance of manufacturing industry is improved and that the whole range of Government policies, including education, contribute as much as possible to improving industrial performance and thereby increasing the national wealth.

In the United States, where governmental policies are more highly mediated by a different articulation between the State, the economy, and schools, this kind of pressure exists in powerful ways as well. Often the workings of industry are even more visible. Chairs of Free Enterprise devoted to economic education are springing up at universities throughout the country. Teaching the message of industry has become a real force. Let me give one example taken from what is known as the Ryerson Plan, a corporate plan to have teachers spend their summers working mainly with management in industry so that they can teach their students 'real knowledge' about corporate needs and benefits (Ryerson and Son, Inc., no date).

> The anti-business, anti-free-enterprise bias prevalent in many parts of our American society today is very real and is growing. Unless we quit just talking about it – and do something about it now – it will prosper and thrive in the fertile minds of our youth. It will be nurtured and fed by many teachers who have good intentions but no real knowledge of how a free market operates in a free society.
>
> American business has a very positive story to tell and one of the most important places to start is with the youth of our country. The last 4,000 years of recorded history proves the interdependence of economic freedom and personal freedoms of all civilizations, countries and societies. We have a perfect example in a present day test tube. Take a look at Great Britain's decline over the last 30 years.
>
> Our response is simple and effective. Reach the high school teachers of America with the true story of American business and they will carry the message to their students and their fellow teachers. The message, coming directly from the teacher, rather than books, pamphlets or films, will have a far more telling and lasting effect. Convince one teacher of the vital importance of our free enterprise system and you're well on the way to convincing hundreds of students over a period of years. It's the ripple effect that anti-business factions have been capitalizing on for years.[1]

It is an interesting statement to say the least, one that is being echoed throughout advanced corporate economies. While it seems rather blatant, to say nothing of being historically inaccurate, we should be careful of dismissing this kind of program as overt propaganda that is easily dismissed by teachers. As one teacher said after completing it (Ryerson and Son, Inc., no date),

> My experience with the steel industry this summer has given me a positive and practical introduction to the business world that I might never had had, had it not been for the initiative of Ryerson management. Now I can pass a more positive portrayal of the industry on to my students; students who are usually very critical, very distrustful, and basically ignorant of the operation of big industry today.

This is, of course, only one of many plans for getting the ideological message across. In fact, though there has been serious resistance to this kind of material by progressive forces in the United States, the movement to 'teach for the needs of industry' is growing rapidly enough so that a clearinghouse, appropriately named The Institute for Constructive Capitalism, has been established at the University of Texas to make the material more available (Downing 1979).

Now I do not want to minimize the importance of such overt attempts at influencing teachers and students. To do so would be the height of folly. However, by keeping our focus only on these overt attempts at bringing school policy and curriculum into closer correspondence with industrial needs, we may neglect what is happening that may be just as powerful at the level of day to day school practice. One could fight the battles against capital's overt encroachments (and perhaps win some of them) and still lose within the school itself. For as I shall argue here, some of the ideological and material influences of our kind of social formation on teachers and students are not most importantly found at the level of these kinds of documents or plans, but at the level of social practice within the routine activities in schools.[2]

In essence, I want to argue that ideologies are not only global sets of interests, things imposed by one group on another. They are embodied by our commonsense meanings and practices (Williams 1977). Thus, if you want to understand ideology at work in schools, look as much at the concreta of day to day curricular and pedagogic life as you would at the statements made by spokespersons of the State or industry. To quote from Finn, Grant, and Johnson, we need to look not only at ideologies 'about' education but ideologies 'in' it as well (Finn, Grant, Johnson, and the C.C.C.S. Education Group 1978: 3-4).

I am not implying that the level of practice in schools is fundamentally controlled in some mechanistic way by private enterprise. As an aspect of the State, the school mediates and transforms an array of economic, political and cultural pressures from competing classes and class segments. Yet we tend to forget that this does not mean that the logics, discourses, or modes of control of capital will not have an increasing impact on everyday life in our educational institutions, especially in times of what has been called 'the fiscal crisis of the state' (O'Connor 1973). This impact, clearly visible in the United States (though I would hazard a guess it will become more prevalent in Europe and Latin America as well), is especially evident in curriculum, in essence in some very important aspects of the actual stuff that students and teachers interact with.

In this essay, I shall be particularly interested in curricular *form*, not curricular content. That is, my focus will not be on what is actually taught, but on the manner in which it is organized. As a number of

Marxist cultural analysts have argued, the working of ideology can be seen most impressively at the level of form as well as what the form has in it (Apple 1978; Jameson 1971; Williams 1977). As I shall argue here, this is a key to uncovering the role of ideology 'in' education.

In order to understand part of what is occurring in the school and the ideological and economic pressures being placed upon it and which work their way through it, we need to situate it within certain long term trends in the capital accumulation process. Recently these trends have intensified and have had a rather major impact on a variety of areas of social life. Among these trends we can identify certain tendencies such as (Clark 1979: 239):

> the concentration and centralization of capitals; the expansion of labour processes that are based on production-line technologies and forms of control; the continuing decline of 'heavy industry' and the movement of capital into modern 'lighter' forms of production, most notably the production of consumer durables; and major shifts in the composition of labour power – the secular tendency to 'de-skilling,' the separation of 'conception' from 'execution' and the creation of new technical and control skills, the shift of labour out of direct production and into circulation and distribution, and the expansion of labour within the state.[3]

As we shall see, the development of new forms of control, the process of deskilling, the separation of conception from execution, are not limited to factories and offices. These tendencies intrude more and more into institutions like the school. In order to unpack this, we shall have to examine the very nature of the logic of corporate deskilling and control.

Deskilling and reskilling

At first, let me speak very generally about the nature of this kind of control. In corporate production, firms purchase labor power. That is, they buy the capacity one has to do work and, obviously, will often seek to expand the use of that labor to make it more productive. There is an opposite side to this. With the purchase of labor power goes the 'right' to stipulate (within certain limits) how it is to be used, without too much interference or participation by workers in the conception and planning of the work (Edwards 1979: 17). How this has been accomplished has not stayed the same, of course. Empirically, there has been a changing logic of control that has sought to accomplish these ends.

Given this history, it is helpful to differentiate the kinds of control that have been used. I shall simplify these around basic ideal types for ease of understanding.

We can distinguish three kinds of control that can be employed to help extract more work – simple, technical, and bureaucratic. Simple control is exactly that, simply telling someone that you have decided what should go on and they should follow or else. Technical controls are less obvious. They are controls embedded in the physical structure of your job. A good example is the use of numerical control technology in the machine industry where a worker inserts a card into a machine and it directs the pace and skill level of the operation. Thus, the worker is meant to be simply an attendant to the machine itself. And, finally, bureaucratic control signifies a social structure where control is less visible since the principles of control are embodied within the *hierarchical* social relations of the workplace. Impersonal and bureaucratic rules concerning the direction of one's work, the procedures for evaluating performance, and sanctions and rewards are dictated by officially approved policy (Edwards 1979: 19-21). Each of these modes of control has grown in sophistication over the years, though simple control has tended to become less important as the size and complexity of production has increased.

The long period of experimentation by industry on the most successful modes of controlling production led to a number of conclusions. Rather than simple control where control is openly exercized by supervisors or persons in authority (and hence could possibly be subverted by blue- or white-collar workers), power could be 'made invisible' by incorporating it into the very structure of the work itself. This meant the following things. The control must come from what seems to be a legitimate over-all structure. It must be concerned with the actual work, not based on features extraneous to it (like favoritism and so on). Perhaps most importantly, the job, the process, and the product should be defined as precisely as possible on the basis of management's, not the worker's, control over the specialized knowledge needed to carry it out (Edwards 1979: 110). This often entailed the development of technical control.

Technical control and deskilling tend to go hand in hand. Deskilling is part of a long process in which labor is divided and then redivided to increase productivity, to reduce 'inefficiency,' and to control both the cost and the impact of labor. Usually it has involved taking relatively complex jobs (most jobs are much more complex and require more decision-making than people give them credit for), jobs which require no small amount of skill and decision-making, and breaking them down into specified actions with specified results so that less skilled and costly personnel can be used or so that the control of work pace and outcome is enhanced. The assembly line is, of course, one of the archetypical examples of this process. At its beginnings, deskilling tended to involve techniques such as Taylorism and various time and motion studies. Though these strategies for the division and control of labor were less than totally successful (and in fact often generated a significant amount of resistance and conflict) (Burawoy 1979; Noble 1977), they did succeed in helping to legitimate a style of control based in large part on deskilling.

One of the more effective strategies has been the incorporation of control into the actual productive process itself. Thus, machinery in factories is now often designed so that the machinist is called upon to do little more than load and unload the machine. In offices, word processing technology is employed to reduce labor costs and deskill women workers. Thus, management attempts to control both the pace of the work and the skills required, to more effectively increase their profit margins or productivity. Once again, as the history of formal and informal labor resistance documents, this kind of strategy – the building of controls into the very warp and woof of the production process – has been contested (Apple 1980b; see also Aronowitz 1973, 1978). However, the growing sophistication by management and state bureaucrats in the use of technical control procedures is apparent (Edwards 1979).

I have mentioned that deskilling is a complex process as it works its way through a variety of economic and cultural institutions. Yet it really is not that hard to grasp one of its other important aspects. When jobs are deskilled, the knowledge that once accompanied it, knowledge that was controlled and used by workers in carrying out their day to day lives on their jobs, goes somewhere. Management attempts (with varying degrees of success) to accumulate and control this assemblage of skills and knowledge. It attempts, in other words, to separate conception from execution. The control of knowledge enables management to plan;[4] the worker should ideally merely carry these plans out to the specification, and at the pace, set by people away from the actual point of production.

But deskilling is accompanied by something else, what might be called reskilling. New techniques are required to run new machines; new occupations are created as the redivision of labor goes on. Fewer skilled craftspersons are needed and their previous large numbers are replaced by a smaller number of technicians with different skills who oversee the machinery (Barker and Downing 1979). This process of deskilling and reskilling is usually spread out over the landscape of an economy so it is rather difficult to trace out the relationships. It is not very usual to see it going on at a level of specificity that makes it clear, since while one group is being deskilled another group, often separated by time and geography, is being reskilled. However, one particular institution – the school – provides an exceptional microcosm for seeing these kinds of mechanisms of control in operation.

In examining this we should remember that capitalist production has developed unevenly, so that certain areas of our social institutions will vary in the kind of control being used. Some institutions will be more resistant than others to the logic of corporate rationalization. Given the relatively autonomous nature of teaching (one can usually close one's door and not be disturbed) and given the internal history of the kinds of control in the institution (paternalistic styles of administration, often in the USA based on gender relations), the school has been partially resistant to technical and bureaucratic control, *at the level of actual practice*, until relatively recently. This 'relative autonomy' may be breaking down today (Dale 1979). For just as the everyday discourse and patterns of interaction in the family and in, say, the media are increasingly being subtly transformed by the logic and contradictions of dominant ideologies (Gitlin 1979),[5] so too is the school a site where these subtle ideological transformations occur. I shall claim that this goes on through a process of technical control. As we shall now see, these logics of control can have a rather profound impact on schools.

Controlling curricular form

The best examples of the encroachment of technical control procedures are found in the exceptionally rapid growth in the use of prepackaged sets of curricular materials. It is nearly impossible now to walk into an American classroom, for instance, without seeing boxes upon boxes of science, social studies, mathematics and reading materials ('systems,' as they are sometimes called) lining the shelves and in use.[6] Here, a school system purchases a total set of standardized material, usually one which includes statements of objectives, all of the curricular content and material needed, prespecified teacher actions and appropriate student responses, and diagnostic and achievement tests co-ordinated with the system. Usually these tests have the curricular knowledge 'reduced' to 'appropriate' behaviors and skills. Remember this emphasis on skills for it will become rather significant later on.

Let me give one example, actually taken from one of the better of the widely used curricular systems, of the numerous sets of materials that are becoming the standard fare in American elementary schools.

It is taken from *Module One* of *Science: A Process Approach*. The notion of module is important here. The material is prepackaged into cardboard boxes with attractive colors. It is divided into 105 separate modules, each of which include a set of pregiven concepts to teach. The material specifies all of the goals. It includes everything a teacher 'needs' to teach, has the pedagogical steps a teacher must take to reach these goals already built in, and has the evaluation mechanisms built into it as well. But that is not all. Not only does it prespecify nearly all a teacher should know, say, and do, but it often lays out the appropriate student responses to these elements as well.

To make this clear, here is one sequence taken from the material which lays out the instructional procedure, student response, and evaluative activity. It concerns colors (*Science: A Process Approach* 1974: 7).

> As each child arrives at school, fasten a red, yellow, or blue paper rectangle on the child's shirt or dress. . . Comment on the color of the paper and ask the child to say the name of the color he or she is wearing. . . .
>
> Put thirty yellow, red, and blue paper squares in a large bag or small box. Show the children three paper plates: one marked red, one yellow, and one blue. (See *Materials* for suggestions on marking.) These colors should closely match those in the bag. Ask the children to come forward, a few at a time, and let each child take one square from the bag and place it on the plate marked with the matching color. [A picture of this with a child picking out paper from a box and putting it on a plate is inserted here in the material so that no teacher will get the procedure wrong.] As each child takes a colored square, ask him to name the color of that square. If the child hesitates, name it for him.

In the curricular material, everything except the bag or box is included – all the plates and colored paper. (The cost by the way is $14.00 for the plan and the paper.)

I noted that not only were the curricular and pedagogical elements prespecified, but all other aspects of teachers' actions were included as well. Thus, in the 'Appraisal' of this module, the teacher is asked to (*Science: A Process Approach* 1974: 7):

> Ask each of six children to bring a box of crayons and sit together. . . . Ask each child to point to his red crayon when you say the word red. Repeat this for all six colors. Ask each child to match one crayon with one article of clothing that someone else is wearing. . . . Before each group of children leaves the activity, ask each

> child individually to name and point to the red, blue, and yellow crayon.

Even with this amount of guidance, it is still 'essential' that we know for each child whether he or she has reached the appropriate skill level. Thus, as the final element, the material has competency measures built into it. Here the specification reaches its most exact point, giving the teacher the exact words he or she should use (*Science: A Process Approach* 1974: 7):

> Task 1: Show the child a yellow cube and ask, What is the color of this cube?

This is done for each color. Then, after arranging orange, green, and purple cubes in front of a child, the material goes on.

> Task 4: Say, put your finger on the orange cube.
> Task 5: Say, put your finger on the green cube.
> Task 6: Say, put your finger on the purple cube.

I have gone on at length here so that you can get a picture of the extent to which technical control enters into the life of the school. Little in what might be metaphorically called the 'production process' is left to chance. In many ways, it can be considered a picture of deskilling. Let us look at this somewhat more closely.

My point is not to argue against the specific curricular or pedagogical content of this kind of material, though an analysis of this certainly would be interesting.[7] Rather, it is to have us focus on the form itself. What is *this* doing? For notice what has happened here. The goals, the process, the outcome, and the evaluative criteria for assessing them are defined as precisely as possible by people external to the situation. In the competency measure at the end of the module, this extends to the specification of even the exact words the teacher is to say.

Notice as well the process of deskilling at work here. Skills that teachers used to need, that were deemed essential to the craft of working with children – such as curriculum deliberation and planning, designing teaching and curricular strategies for specific groups and individuals based on intimate knowledge of these people – are no longer as necessary. With the large scale influx of pre-packaged material, planning is separated from execution. The planning is done at the level of the production of both the rules for use of the material and the material itself. The execution is carried out by the teacher. In the process, what were previously considered valuable skills slowly atrophy because they are less often required.[8]

But what about the element of reskilling that I mentioned earlier was essential to understand how ideological forms can penetrate to the heart of institutions like the school? Unlike the economy where deskilling and reskilling are not usually found operating at one and the same moment with one and the same people, in the school this seems to be exactly the case. As the procedures of technical control enter into the school in the guise of pre-designed curricular/teaching/evaluation 'systems', teachers are being deskilled. Yet they are also being reskilled in a way that is quite consequential. We can see signs of this at both teacher training institutions, in inservice workshops and courses, in the journals devoted to teachers, in funding and enrollment patterns, and not the least in the actual curricular materials themselves. While the deskilling involves the loss of craft, the ongoing atrophication of educational skills, the reskilling involves the substitution of the skills and ideological visions of management. The growth of behavior modification techniques and classroom management strategies and their incorporation within both curricular material and teachers' repertoires signifies these kinds of alterations. That is, as teachers lose control of the curricular and pedagogic skills to large publishing houses, these skills are replaced by techniques for better controlling students.

This is not insignificant in its consequences for both teachers and students. Since the material is often organized around, and employs specified outcomes and procedures, and these are built into this kind of material itself (with its many worksheets and tests often), it is 'individualized' in many ways. Students can engage in it themselves with little overt interaction on the part of the teacher or each other as they become more used to the procedures, which are usually highly standardized. The students' progress through the system can be individualized, at least according to speed, and this focus on individualizing the speed (usually through worksheets and the like) at which a student proceeds through the system is becoming even more pronounced in newer curricular systems. Since the control is technical – that is, management strategies are incorporated into it as a major aspect of the pedagogical/curricular/evaluative 'machinery' itself – the teacher becomes something of a manager. This is occurring *at the same time* that the objective conditions of his or her work are becoming increasingly 'proletarianized' due to the curricular form's logic of technical control. This is a unique situation and certainly needs further thought. The possible effect of these forms of technical control on the students is just as serious and is something to which I shall return shortly.

Yet there are important consequences besides the deskilling and reskilling that are occurring. As the literature on the labor process reminds us, the progressive division and control of labor also has an impact at the level of social relations, on how the people involved interact. While this has had a momentous effect in factories and offices, its effects will undoubtedly be felt in the school too. And as in the workplace, the impact may have contradictory results.

Let me be more specific here. With the increasing employment of pre-packaged curricular systems as the basic curricular form, virtually no interaction between teachers is required. If nearly everything is rationalized and specified before execution, then contact among teachers about actual curricular matters is minimized.[9]

If such technical control is effective, that is, if teachers actually respond in ways that accept the separation of planning from execution, then one would expect results that go beyond this 'mere' separation. One would expect, at the level of classroom practice, that it will be more difficult for teachers to jointly gain informal control over curricular decisions because of their increasing isolation. In essence, if everything is predetermined, there is no longer any pressing need for teacher interaction. Teachers become unattached individuals, divorced from both colleagues and the actual stuff of their work. However, and here is part of what I mean by a contradictory effect, while this may be an accurate estimation of one of the results of technical control on one level, it forgets that most systems of control embody contradictions within themselves. For instance, while deskilling, forms of technical control, and the rationalization of work have created isolated individuals in, say, factories, historically they have often generated contradictory pressures as well. The use of technical control has often brought unionization in its wake (Edwards 1979: 181). Even given the ideology of professionalism (an ideology that might make it difficult for collective struggles to evolve) which tends to dominate certain sectors of the teaching force, other state employees who in the past have thought of themselves as professionals have gained a greater collective sense in response to similar modes of control. Thus, the loss of control and knowledge in one arena may generate countervailing tendencies in another.

We cannot know yet how this will turn out. These contradictory results only emerge over long periods of time. In industry, it took decades for such an impact to be felt. The same will no doubt be true in schools.

Accepting technical control

So far in this essay, I have looked at teachers as if they were workers. That is, I have argued that the processes that act on blue- and white-collar workers in the large social arena will and are entering into the *cultural forms* that are considered legitimate in schools. Yet schools, because of their internal history, are different in some very important ways from factories and offices, and teachers are still very different from other workers in terms of the conditions of their work. Products are not as visible (except much later on in the rough reproduction of a labor force, in the production and reproduction of ideologies, and in the production of the technical/administrative knowledge 'required' by an economy) (Apple 1979a; Apple 1979b; Noble 1977)[10] as in offices and factories. Teachers have what Erik Olin Wright has called a 'contradictory class location' and hence cannot be expected to react in the same ways as the workers and employees of large corporations (E. Wright 1978). Furthermore, there are children who act back on teachers in ways an automobile on an assembly line or a paper on a desk cannot. Finally, teaching does not take place on a line, but goes on in separate rooms more often than not.[11]

All of these conditions do not mean that schools are immune or autonomous from the logic of capital. The logic will be mediated (in part due to the school as a *State* apparatus); it will enter where it can in partial, distorted, or coded ways. Given the specific differences of schools from other workplaces, a prime moment in its entry can be found less at the level of overt or simple controls (do this because I say so) or at the level of bureaucratic form (because individual teachers can still be relatively free from those kinds of encroachments).[12] These controls will go on, of course; but they may be less consequential than *the encoding of technical control into the very basis of the curricular form itself*. The level of curricular, pedagogic, and evaluative practice within the classroom can be controlled by the forms into which culture is commodified in schools. If my arguments are correct, then how are we to understand the acceptance and growth of this process of control?

These forms enter into schools not because of any conspiracy on the part of industrialists to make our educational institutions serve the needs of capital, as in the earlier quotes from the Green Paper and the Ryerson Plan. It occurs in large part because schools are a rather lucrative market. These sets of material are published by firms who aggressively market where there is a need, or where they can create needs. It is simply good business practice in terms of profit margins to market material of this type, especially since the original purchase of the 'system' or set of modules means increasing purchases over the years. Let me explain this by comparing it to another arena where similar techniques are employed to increase capital accumulation. Think of shaving. Large razor-blade manufacturers sell razors at below cost, or even sometimes give them away as promotional 'gimmicks,' because they believe that once you buy the razor you will continue to buy their blades and their upgraded version year after year. In the curricular systems we are considering here, the purchase of the modules (though certainly not cheap by any stretch of the imagination) with their sets of standardized disposable material means the same thing. One 'needs' to continue to purchase the work and test sheets, the chemicals, the correctly colored and shaped paper, the publishers' replacements of outmoded material and lessons, etc. Profits are heightened with every replacement that is bought. Since replacement purchases are often bureaucratically centralized, because of budget control, in the office of the administrator, the additional material is usually bought from the producer (often at exorbitant costs) not gotten from one's local store.

Thus, as with other industries, this 'good business sense' means that high volume, the standardization of each of the elements of one's product and of its form, product upgrading, and then the stimulation of replacement purchasing are essential to maintain profits (Barker and Downing 1979).[13]

Yet the notion of aggressive marketing and good business sense is but a partial explanation of this growth. In order to fully comprehend the acceptance of technical control procedures embodied in curricular form, we need to know something of the history of why these kinds of materials evolved in the first place. Let me note these briefly.

The original introduction of pre-packaged material was stimulated by a specific network of political, cultural, and economic forces, originally in the 1950s and 1960s in the United States. The views of academics that teachers were unsophisticated in major curriculum areas 'necessitated' the creation of what was called teacher-proof material. The cold war climate (created and stimulated by the State in large part) led to a focus on the efficient production of scientists and technicians as well as a relatively stable workforce; thus, the 'guaranteeing' of this production through the school curriculum became of increasing importance (Spring 1976). On top of this was the decision of the educational apparatus of the State, under the National Defense Education Act, to provide the equivalent of cash credits to local school districts for the purchase of new curricula created by the 'private sector' to increase this efficiency. At the same time, the internal dynamics within education played a part since behavioral and learning psychology – on whose principles so much of these systems rely – gained increasing prestige in a field like education where being seen as a science was critically important both for funding and to deflect criticism (Apple 1979a). In the more recent past, the increasing influence of industrial capital within the executive and legislative branches of government (O'Connor 1973) as well as in the attendant bureaucracy, no doubt was an essential element here since there is recent evidence that the federal government has backed away from the widespread production and distribution of large scale curricula, preferring to stimulate the 'private sector' to enter even more deeply into such production.[14]

This gives us a brief sense of history, but why the continued movement toward this today? A key element here is seeing the school as an aspect of the State apparatus. For the State's need for *consent* as well as control means that the forms of control in school will be encoded in particular ways (Donald 1979: 44).

The strategic import of the logic of technical control in schools lies in its ability to integrate into one discourse what are often seen as competing ideological movements, and, hence, to generate consent from each of them. The need for accountability and control by administrative managers, the real needs of teachers for something that is 'practical' to use with their students, the interest of the State in efficient production and cost savings,[15] the concern of parents for 'quality education' that 'works' (a concern that will be coded differently by different classes and class segments), industrial capital's own requirements for efficient production and so on, can be joined. It is here that one can see how two important functions of the State can be accomplished. The state can assist in capital *accumulation* by attempting to provide a more efficient 'production process' in schools. At the same time, it can *legitimate* its own activity by couching its discourse in language that is broad enough to be meaningful to each of what it perceives to be important constituencies, yet specific enough to give some practical answers to those who, like teachers, 'require' it. The fact that the form taken by these curricular systems is tightly controlled and more easily made 'accountable,' that it *is* usually individualized, that it focusses on skills in a time of perceived crisis in the teaching of 'basic skills,' etc., nearly guarantees its acceptability to a wide array of classes and interest groups.

Thus, the logic of control is both mediated and reinforced by the needs of state bureaucrats for accountable and rationale procedures and by the specific nexus of forces acting on the state itself. The curriculum form will take on the aspects which are necessary to accomplish both accumulation and legitimation.[16] As Clarke puts it (1978: 241):

> Even where institutions meet a logic required by capital, their form

> and direction are never the outcome of a simple unidirectional imposition by capital. They involve a complex political work of concession and compromise, if only to secure the legitimacy of the state in popular opinion.

This is exactly what has occurred in the use of this kind of curricular form.

The possessive individual

So far I have examined the encroachment into the work of teachers of the technical control systems embodied in curricular form. Yet, teachers are not the only actors in the setting where we find this material. There are the students as well.

A number of writers have noted that each kind of social formation 'requires' a particular kind of individual. Williams and others, for instance, have helped us trace the growth of the abstract individual as it developed within the theoretic, cultural, and economic practices of capitalism (Macpherson 1962; Williams 1961). These are not simply changes in the definition of the individual, but imply changes in our actual modes of material and cultural producing, reproducing, and consuming. To be an individual in our society signifies a complex interconnection between our day to day meanings and practices and an 'external' mode of production. While I do not mean to imply a simple base/superstructure model here, it is clear that in some very important ways there is a dialectical relationship between economic and ideological form. As Gramsci and others would put it, ideological hegemony sustains class domination; subjectivities cannot be seen as unrelated to structure. Yet the questions remain: How are they related? Where are the sites where this relationship is worked out? The school provides a critical point at which one can see these things working out. As Richard Johnson (1978: 232) notes, 'It is not so much a question that schools . . . *are* ideology, more that they are the sites where ideologies are produced in the form of subjectivities.'

But what kind of subjectivity, what kind of ideology, what kind of individual may be produced here? The characteristics embodied in the modes of technical control built into the curricular form itself are ideally suited to reproduce the possessive individual, a vision of oneself that lies at the ideological heart of corporate economies.

The conception of individualism located in the material we have been examining is quite similar to those found in other analyses of aspects of the cultural apparatus in our society. As Will Wright has demonstrated, for example, in his recent investigation of the role of cultural artifacts like film as carriers and legitimators of ideological changes, important aspects of our cultural apparatus represent a world in which the society recognizes each member as an individual; but that recognition is dependent almost entirely upon technical skills. At the same time, while heightening the value of technical competence, these films direct the individual to reject the importance of ethical and political values through their form. They portray an individualism, situated in the context of a corporate economy, in which 'respect and companionship are to be achieved only by becoming a skilled technician.' The individual accepts and does any technical job that is offered and has loyalty to only those with similar technical competence, not primarily 'to any competing social and community values' (W. Wright 1975: 187).

An examination of these curricular 'systems' illuminates the extent to which this kind of ideological movement is occurring in increasingly dominant curricular forms. Here, the *rate* at which a student proceeds is individualized; however, the actual product as well as the process to be accomplished are specified by the material itself.[17] Thus, it is not 'just' the teacher who faces the encroachment of technical control and deskilling. The students' responses are largely pre-specified as well. Much of this growing arsenal of material attempts as precisely as possible to specify appropriate student language and action as well, often reducing it to the mastery of sets of competencies or skills. Here Wright seems correct.

The notion of reducing curriculum to a set of skills is not unimportant in this regard since it is part of the larger process by which the logic of capital helps build identities and transforms cultural meanings and practices into commodities (Aronowitz 1973: 95). That is, if knowledge in all its aspects (of the logical type of that, how, or to – i.e., information, processes, and dispositions or propensities) is broken down and commodified, like economic capital it can be accumulated. The mark of a good pupil is the possession and accumulation of vast quantities of skills in the service of technical interests. As an ideological mechanism in the maintenance of hegemony this is rather interesting. In the larger society, people consume as isolated individuals. Their worth is determined by the possession of material goods or, as Will Wright noted, of technical skills. The accumulation of such goods or of the 'cultural capital' of technical competence – here atomistic bits of knowledge and skills measured on pre-tests and post-tests – is a technical procedure, one which requires only the mastery of the prior necessary technical skills and enough time to follow the rules, at one's own pace, to their conclusion. It is the message of the new petty bourgeoisie writ large on the ideological terrain of the school.

In fact, one might hypothesize just this, that this kind of movement speaks to the increasing importance in the cultural apparatus of the ideologies of class segments with contradictory class locations, in particular what I have called the new petty bourgeoisie – those groups who make up middle management and technical occupations (E. Wright 1978: 79). The particular kind of individualism we are witnessing here is an interesting shift from an ideology of individual autonomy, where a person is his or her own boss and controls his or her destiny, to a careerist individualism. Here the individualism is geared towards organizational mobility and advancement by following technical rules. As Eric Wright puts it, for the new petty bourgeoisie, 'individualism is structured around the requirements of bureaucratic advancement' (E. Wright 1978: 59). It may also be a coded 'reflection' of the increasing proletarianization of white-collar work. For, while previously individualism signified some serious sense of autonomy over how one worked and what one produced, for a large portion of white-collar employees autonomy has been trivialized (E. Wright 1978: 81; Braverman, 1974). The rate at which one works may be individualized, but the work itself, how it is accomplished, and what the exact specifications of the final product will be, are increasingly being specified.

At this stage, we are left with many questions. When technical control means that the form that the curriculum takes is highly specified, that it is individualized to such an extent that there is little required interaction among the students so that each activity is by necessity viewed as an individual intellectual act of skill, that answers often take the form of simple physical activities (as we saw in the module I discussed earlier), that answers are either correct or incorrect based on the application of technical rules, and this kind of form is what one follows throughout one's elementary school life, what impact does it have on the teachers and students who interact with it at the level of practice each day?

We do have evidence to suggest what procedures of this type do to workers in industry and in offices.

Increasing rationalization and a more sophisticated level of control tend to encourage people to manifest an interesting array of traits: a 'rules orientation' – that is, an awareness of rules and procedures and a habit of following them; greater dependability – that is, performing a job at a relatively consistent level, being reliable and getting the job done even when rules have to be modified a bit to meet changing day to day conditions; and, the 'internalization of the enterprise's goals and values' – that is, conflict is minimized and slowly but surely, there tends to be a homogenization of interests between management and employees (Edwards 1979: 150-1).[18]

Will this happen in schools as well? This clearly points to the significance of engaging in analyses of what actually happens within the black box of the school. Do teachers and students accept this? Will the gradual introduction of the logic of technical control generate resistances, if only on a cultural level? Will class and work cultures contradict, mediate, or even transform the expected outcomes? (Apple 1980a, 1980b, 1981a, 1981b). It is to this that we shall now turn.

Resistances

I have not presented an optimistic appraisal here. As the activities of students are increasingly specified, as the rules, processes, and standard outcomes are integrated through and rationalized by the materials themselves, so too are teachers deskilled, reskilled, and anonymized. Students work on material whose form both isolates individuals from each other and establishes the conditions of existence for the possessive individual; the form of the material and the embedded nature of the technical control process does nearly the same for the teacher. Surrounded by a specific logic of control, the objective force of the social relations embodied in the form itself tends to be quite powerful.

Yet I am not arguing for a crude kind of functionalist perspective, where everything is measured by, or is aimed toward, its ability to reproduce an existing static society. The creation of the kind of ideological hegemony 'caused' by the increasing introduction of technical control is not 'naturally' pre-ordained. It is something that is won or lost in particular conflicts and struggles (Johnson 1979: 70).

On the one hand teachers will be controlled. As one teacher said about a set of popular material even more integrated and rationalized than the ones I have pointed to here, 'Look, I have no choice. I personally don't like this material, but everyone in the district has to use this series. I'll try to do other things as well, but basically our curriculum will be based on this.'

On the other hand, resistances will be there. This same teacher who disagreed with the curriculum but used it, also was partially subverting it in interesting ways. It was employed only three days a week instead of the five days which were specified. As the teacher put it, 'Listen, if we worked hard we'd finish this stuff in two or three months and besides it's sometimes confusing and boring. So I try to go beyond it as often as possible, *as long as I do not teach what is in the material to be covered by this series next year.*' Thus, as we can see from this last part of her comment, internal conditions make such overt resistances more difficult.

Yet these internal conditions need not preclude teachers from also making these commodified cultural forms their own, to generate their own creative responses to dominant ideologies, in a manner similar to what the counter-cultural groups studied by Marxist ethnographers have done to commodified culture. These groups transformed and reinterpreted the products they bought and used so that they became tools for the creation of alternative pockets of resistance (Willis 1978). Students and teachers may also find ways of creatively using these systems in ways undreamed of by state bureaucrats or corporate publishing. (I must admit, however, that my repeated observations in classrooms over the last years make me less than totally optimistic that this will always or even very often be the case.)

Other elements in the environment may provide the site for different meanings and practices to evolve, though, even within the curricular form itself. For we should remember that there may be progressive elements within the *content* of the curriculum that contradict the messages of the form.[19] And it is in the interaction between the content, the form, and the lived culture of the students that subjectivities are formed. No element in this set of relations can be ignored.

While I have focussed on the form of the material here, it is important to specify in somewhat more detail what is entailed in analyzing the possible contradictions between form and content. An ideological 'reading' of any material is not a simple matter. Such a reading in fact cannot be limited to content analysis, to what a 'text' simply and openly 'says,' especially if we are interested in the grounds upon which resistance may be generated. In this regard, our analyses could profit immensely from the incorporation of the work of people such as Barthes, Macherey, Derrida, and other investigators of the process of signification and impact of ideology on cultural production. Thus, to complete our analyses of content, we would need to engage in a semiological reading of the cultural artifact to 'extract the structure of significations within the object which provides the parameter' for possible readings of it (Sumner 1979: 134). This is not to imply that all possible readings can be specified. One must still be aware, as Derrida argues for instance, that reading a text is an active process of signification. As one commentator puts it, this active process 'decentres the orthodox, customary meaning of the discourse by its invocation of other, less orthodox, private meanings and references' (Sumner 1979: 149). Thus, every discourse, all content, may have a 'surplus of meaning.' This surplus can create a 'play' in the process of signification, so that while each element in the text may have 'normal' ways in which it is used, it also refers to other possible meanings at the same time.

I want to stress this point. Interrogation of the content itself is important, not just to see what ideologies are 'expressed' or 'represented' in the material itself (the notion of representation being an inherently complex and difficult one in the first place), but so that we can begin to both unpack the way any content 'is itself part of an active process of signification through which meaning is produced' (Hill 1979: 114) and understand the possible contradictions within the content, the text, itself.

In his discussion of the lack of analyses of contradiction in studies of the content of cultural products like the media, Hill makes a similar point (1979: 115).

> If the media do not merely express ideologies, they must then be considered as actively constitutive of ideologies. That is to say, ideologies are not merely ingredients to be detected in the media, but also its products. And again, as active productions, ideologies are not merely to be seen as sets of positivities but also as processes of exclusion – with these 'exclusions' potentially being able to feed back to disturb or deform their progenitive system (and thereby furnishing our analysis with a notion of 'contradiction' retrieved from both a reductionism which would merely place it as a reflection of contradictions determined at the level of the economic and the homeostasis of a reproduction-oriented Marxist fuctionalism).

As Hill implies in the above quote, the 'meaning' of the content is not only to be found in the text or cultural product itself, in its codes and regularities (though such a reading is an essential part of a complete analysis). The meaning is also constituted 'in the interaction between the text and its users' (Hill 1979: 122), in our own case between curriculum content and student.

This still is incomplete, though. As Hill also states, a key is the notion of exclusion. Cultural products not only 'say,' but they 'don't say' as well. The fact that one needs to investigate not only 'what material says' and its surplus of meaning, contradictions, and structures of signification but also what it excludes is brought home by people such as Macherey and Eagleton. As both have noted, any text is not necessarily constituted by readily evident meanings – those positivities that Hill talked about in the prior quote from him – that are easily seen by an observer. Rather, a text 'bears inscribed within it the marks of certain determinate absences which twist its significations into conflict and contradiction.' The *not said* of a work is as important as the *said* since 'ideology is present in the text in the form of its eloquent silences' (Eagleton 1976: 89).

In brief, then, to adequately examine the possible contradictions between form and content in these curricular materials we would be required to unpack what is present and missing within the content itself, what structures provide the parameters for possible readings of it, what 'dissonances' and contradictions exist within it that provide for alternate readings, and finally the interactions between content and the lived culture of the reader.[20]

This last point about the lived culture of the actors, the students themselves, needs to be stressed. One would expect resistances to the ideological practices I have discussed in this essay on the part of the students as well as teachers, resistances that may be *specific by race, gender, and class*. My earlier quote from Johnson is correct here. The formation of ideologies – even those of the kind of individualism I have examined in this analysis – is not a simple act of imposition. It is produced by concrete actors and embodied in lived experiences that may resist, alter, or mediate these social messages (Johnson 1978). As Willis demonstrates in his ethnography of working-class culture, for instance, segments of working-class youth partially defeat the ideology of individualism. The same may be true for many women and 'minority' students. While we can and must focus on these resistances, though, their actual meaning may be unclear. Do they, like those of the lads in Willis' study, also reproduce at an even deeper level ideological meanings and practices that provide quite powerful supports to relations of domination (Willis 1977)?

Take teachers, for example. While technical controls could possibly lead to unionization, within the school most resistances that occur will be, by necessity, on an individual not a collective level because of the very social relations generated by the curricular form itself (Edwards 1979: 154). The effects, hence, can be rather contradictory.

We must remember as well that, as I mentioned earlier, these more 'invisible' modes of control may be accepted if they are perceived as coming from a legitimate over-all structure. The fact that curriculum selection committees give teachers a say in the curriculum they will employ means that some of the prior conditions for the consent necessary for this kind of control to be successful have already been laid. The choice is made, in part, by the teachers themselves. It is hard to argue in the face of that. This affects the level of content once again. While the ideology of choice remains, teachers and even parent advisory groups are usually limited in their choices to sets of textual or prepackaged curricular material published by the relatively few major corporate publishing concerns which aggressively market their products.

While numerically one's choices may be high, often there will be little difference among the curricular materials from which one can choose. At the level of content, especially in elementary schools, perceived ideological differences over race, sex, and class in the communities in which publishers want to sell their products will provide substantial limits on what is considered 'legitimate' (or safe) knowledge. After all, the production of these curricular materials *is* a business. In the United States, as well, most pre-designed curricular materials are produced with state adoption policies in mind.That is, a number of states maintain approved lists of material. Those districts purchasing from the approved list will have their costs partially reimbursed by the State. Getting one's products on that list is quite important, therefore, since a substantial profit is nearly guaranteed.

Conspiracies to eliminate provocative or honest material are not necessary here. The internal working of an educational apparatus, in conjunction with both the political economy of publishing and the fiscal crisis of the state, is sufficient to homogenize the core of the curriculum. This is not to deny the power of industry in making its case the fundamental problem schools are to face or to deny capital's power in comparison to other groups. Rather, it is to claim that this power is highly mediated and works its way through schooling in ways that are not always identical to its original intent. The effect may be relative ideological homogenization, but to say that this is ultimately what industry wants is to substitute a logic of cause and effect for what is, instead, a particular conjuncture of ideological, cultural, political, and economic forces and conflicts which 'creates' the conditions of existence of the material.

Yet this very process of determination can be contradictory, in part because of the fiscal crisis faced by school systems. Once the curriculum is in place, the original subsidized costs become fixed costs assumed by the local school district. As school budgets are voted down more and more, money is not made available to purchase new material or replace outdated ones. Any 'surplus' money tends to go into the ongoing purchase of the consumable material required by the pre-packaged curriculum. One is slowly left with expensive 'dinosaurs.' The economics of this are essential if we are to see the contradictory pressures this will evoke. Since the state apparatus has expanded the range of participation in curriculum decision-making by selection committees (which sometimes now include parents as well as teachers), and the selected material can often not be replaced because of its expense later on, the State opens up new spaces of opposition (Donald 1979). The growth of the discourse of rights of selection (a right which now cannot be acted upon in any significant way) is objectively at odds with the economic context in which the State currently finds itself, thereby transforming the issue into a potentially volatile one.[21]

These potential conflicts, however, may be mitigated by rather powerful economic and ideological conditions that may seem all too real to many of the individuals employed within the State. And the very same pressures may have important and similar implications for those teachers who may in fact recognize the impact that rationalization and control are having on them.

It is easy to forget something: that this is not a good time, ideologically or economically, for teachers who engage in overt resistances. Given a difficult ideological climate and given the employment situation among teachers today – with thousands having either been laid off or living under the threat of it – the loss of control can progress in a relatively unthreatened way. Deskilling and reskilling, progressive anonymization and rationalization, the transformation of educational work, somehow seem less consequential than such economic concerns as job security, salary, etc., even though they may seem to us to clearly be part of the same dynamic.

When all this is said, though, we must recognize that these powerful social messages, while embedded in the actual experiences of teachers and students as they go about their day to day lives in classrooms, *are* highly mediated by other elements. The fact that individual teachers like most other workers may develop patterns of resistance to these patterns of technical control at the informal cultural level alters these messages. The contradictory ideologies of individualism and cooperativeness that are naturally generated out of the crowded conditions of many classrooms (you can't be an isolated individual all the time when there are twenty or thirty other people around with whom one teacher must cope) also provide countervailing possibilities. And lastly, just as blue- and white-collar workers have constantly found ways to retain their humanity and continually struggle to integrate conception and execution in their work (if only to relieve boredom) so too will teachers and students find ways, in the cracks so to speak, to do the same things. The real question is not whether such resistances exist – Aronowitz, myself, and others have claimed at length elsewhere that they are never far from the surface (Apple 1980b; Aronowitz 1978; Burawoy 1979) – but whether they are contradictory themselves, whether they lead anywhere beyond the reproduction of the ideological hegemony of the most powerful classes in our society, whether they can be employed for political education and intervention.

Our task is first to find them. We need somehow to give life to the resistances, the struggles. What I have done here is to point to the terrain within the school (the transformation of work, the deskilling and reskilling, the technical control, and so on) over which these struggles will be fought. The resistances may be informal, not fully organized or even conscious; yet this does not mean that they will have no impact. For as Gramsci (1971) and Johnson (1979) remind us, hegemony is always contested. Our own work should help in this contestation.

Notes

(An earlier version of this essay will appear in the *Journal of Economic and Industrial Democracy*)

1 I wish to thank Linda McNeil for bringing this material to my attention.
2 This is not to deny the importance of analyzing official documents, especially those emanating from the State. Donald (1979) provides an excellent example of the power of discourse analysis, for example, in unpacking what these documents mean and do.
3 See also the impressive discussion in Braverman (1974) and Burawoy (1979).
4 I have discussed the school's role in producing this knowledge in Apple (1979b).
5 The work of Philip Wexler (in press) of the University of Rochester on the commodification of intimate relations is important here.
6 This is not only an American phenomenon. The foreign subsidiaries of the companies who produce these materials are translating and marketing their products in the third world and elsewhere as well. In many ways it is similar to the cultural imperialism of Walt Disney Productions (see, e.g., Dorfman and Mattelart 1975).
7 See, for example, my analysis of science curricula in Apple (1979a).
8 I do not mean to romanticize that past, however. Many teachers probably simply followed the textbook before. However, the level of specificity and the integration of curricular, pedagogical, and evaluative aspects of classroom life into *one* system is markedly different. The use of the system brings with it much more technical control of every aspect of teaching than previous text-based curricula. Obviously, some teachers will not follow the system's rules. Given the level of integration, though, it will undoubtedly be much more difficult to ignore it since many systems constitute the core or only program in that curricular area in the entire school or district. Thus, accountability to the next grade level or to administrators makes it harder to ignore. I shall return to this point later on.
9 This may be similar to what happened in the early mills in New England, when standardized production processes drastically

reduced the contact among workers (see Edwards 1979: 114).

10 One could also claim that schools operate to produce use value, not exchange value (Erik Olin Wright, personal conversation).

11 Therefore, any outcomes of schooling must be analyzed as the products of cultural, political, and economic resistance as well as determinations (see Willis 1977 and Apple 1980a).

12 I do not want to ignore the question of the relationship between capitalism and bureaucracy. Weber and others were not wrong when they noted that there are needs for rationalization specific to bureaucratic forms themselves. However, neither the *way* bureaucracy has grown in corporate economies nor its *effects* have been neutral. This is treated in considerably more detail in Clawson (1978) (see also Wright 1978).

13 See also Noble (1977) for his account of standardization and its relationship to capital accumulation.

14 Among the reasons for the fact that the State has slowly but surely backed away from such production and distribution is the controversy surrounding 'Man: A Course of Study' and, no doubt, the intense lobbying efforts on the part of publishing firms. Corporations will let the government socialize the costs of development, but obviously would prefer to package and distribute the curricula for themselves (see Apple 1977).

15 This is not meant to imply that the State always directly serves the needs of industrial capital. It, in fact, does have a significant degree of relative autonomy and is the site of class conflict as well (see Dale (in press), Donald 1979 and E. Wright 1978).

16 We should remember, however, that accumulation and legitimation may be in conflict with each other at times. See E. Wright (1978) for a discussion of these possible contradictions and for an argument about the importance of understanding the way the State and bureaucracies mediate and act back on 'economic determinations.' Though I have not specifically noted it here, the transformation of discourse in schools is similar to, and needs to be analyzed in light of, the process described by Habermas in his discussion of the constitutive interests of purposive/rational action. I have dealt with this at length elsewhere in Apple (1979a).

17 Bernstein's work on class and educational codes is interesting here. As he notes, 'The pacing of educational knowledge is class based' (Bernstein 1975: 113).

18 This does not mean that important resistances and countervailing practices do or will not occur. But they usually occur on the terrain established by capital.

19 Geoff Whitty has been particularly helpful in enabling me to see this point. It should also be recognized that the very fact that industrialists *are* interested in content speaks to the import of content as a contested area.

20 These 'internalistic' readings can be taken too far, of course.

For to only focus our attention on the contradictions and ideologies produced by the relationship between form and content, has a serious danger. We may forget how very important are the forces which 'determine' the actual production of curricular material in this way, a point I made earlier in my discussion of the way the school has become a rather lucrative market (see Golding and Murdock 1979: 220).

21 An interesting discussion of the contradictory relationship between the liberal discourse of rights and the 'needs' of advanced capitalism can be found in Gintis (1980).

Bibliography

Apple, Michael W. (1977), 'Politics and National Curriculum Policy,' *Curriculum Inquiry* 7 (number 4), 351-61.

Apple, Michael W. (1978), 'Ideology and Form in Curriculum Evaluation,' in G. Willis (ed.), *Qualitative Evaluation*, Berkeley: McCutchan Publishing Corp., pp. 495-521.

Apple, Michael W. (1979a), *Ideology and Curriculum*, Boston: Routledge & Kegan Paul.

Apple, Michael W. (1979b), 'The production of knowledge and the production of deviance in schools,' in Len Barton and Roland Meighan (eds), *School, Pupils and Deviance*, Driffield, England: Nafferton Books, pp. 113-31.

Apple, Michael W. (1980a), 'Analyzing Determinations: Understanding and Evaluating the Production of Social Outcomes in Schools,' *Curriculum Inquiry* 10 (Spring), 55-76.

Apple, Michael W. (1980b), 'The other side of the hidden curriculum: correspondence theories and the labor process,' *Journal of Education* 162 (Winter), 47-66.

Apple, Michael W. (1981a), 'Class, crisis and the state in educational interventions,' in R. Everhart (ed.), *The Public School Monopoly*, Cambridge, Mass: Ballinger.

Apple, Michael W. (1981b), 'Social Structure, Ideology and Curriculum,' in Martin Lawn and Len Barton (eds), *Rethinking Curriculum Studies*, London: Croom-Helm.

Aronowitz, Stanley (1973), *False Promises*, New York: McGraw-Hill.

Aronowitz, Stanley (1978), 'Marx, Braverman and the Logic of Capital,' *The Insurgent Sociologist* 8 (Fall), pp. 126-46.

Barker, Jane and Hazel Downing (1979), 'Word Processing and the Transformation of Patriarchal Relations,' Unpublished paper, Birmingham, England: University of Birmingham Centre for Contemporary Cultural Studies.

Bernstein, Basil (1977), *Class, Codes and Control* vol. 3, 2nd edn, Boston: Routledge & Kegan Paul.

Braverman, Harry (1974), *Labor and Monopoly Capital*, New York:

Monthly Review Press.

Burawoy, Michael (1979), 'Toward a marxist theory of the labor process: Braverman and beyond,' *Politics and Society* 8 (number 3/4).

Clarke, J. (1979), 'Capital and culture: the post-war working class revisited,' pp. 238-53, in J. Clarke, C. Critcher, and R. Johnson (eds), *Working Class Culture*, London: Hutchinson.

Clawson, Daniel C. (1978), 'Class struggle and the rise of bureaucracy,' PhD dissertation, Stony Brook: State University of New York at Stony Brook.

Dale, Roger (1979), 'The politicization of school deviance,' in L. Barton and R. Meighan (eds), *Schools, Pupils and Deviance*, Driffield, England: Nafferton Books, pp. 95-112.

Dale, Roger (in press), 'Education and the capitalist state: contributions and contradictions,' in M. Apple (ed.), *Cultural and Economic Reproduction in Education*, Boston: Routledge & Kegan Paul.

Donald, James (1979), 'The green paper: noise of a crisis,' *Screen Education* 30 (Spring), 13-49.

Dorfman, Ariel and Armand Mattelart (1975), *How to Read Donald Duck*, New York: International General Editions.

Downing, Diane (1979), 'Soft choices: teaching materials for teaching free enterprise,' Austin: The University of Texas, Institute for Constructive Capitalism, mimeo.

Eagleton, Terry (1976), *Criticism and Ideology*, London: New Left Books.

Edwards, Richard (1979), *Contested Terrain*, New York: Basic Books.

Finn, Dan, N. Grant, Richard Johnson, and the C.C.C.S. Education Group (1978), 'Social democracy, education and the crisis,' Birmingham, England: University of Birmingham Centre for Contemporary Cultural Studies, mimeo.

Gintis, Herbert (1980), 'Communication and politics: marxism and the "problem" of liberal democracy,' *Socialist Review* 10 (March-June), 189-232.

Gitlin, Todd (1979), 'Prime time ideology: the hegemonic process in television entertainment,' *Social Problems* 26 (February), 251-66.

Golding, Peter and Graham Murdock (1979), 'Ideology and the mass media,' in M. Barrett, R. Corrigan, A. Kuhn and J. Wolff (eds), *Ideology and Cultural Production*, New York: St Martin's Press, pp. 198-224.

Gramsci, Antonio (1971), *Selections from the Prison Notebooks*, London: Lawrence & Wishart.

Hill, John (1979), 'Ideology, economy and the British cinema,' in M. Barrett, R. Corrigan, A. Kuhn and J. Wolff (eds), *Ideology and Cultural Production*, New York: St Martin's Press, pp. 112-34.

Jameson, Fredric (1971), *Marxism and Form*, Princeton: Princeton University Press.

Johnson, Richard (1978), 'Three problematics: elements of a theory of working class culture,' in J. Clarke, C. Critcher and R. Johnson

(eds), *Working Class Culture*, London: Hutchinson, pp. 201-37.
Johnson, Richard (1979), 'Histories of culture/theories of ideology: notes on an impasse,' in M. Barrett, R. Corrigan, A. Kuhn and J. Wolff (eds), *Ideology and Cultural Production*, New York: St Martin's Press, pp. 49-77.
MacPherson, C. B. (1962), *The Political Theory of Possessive Individualism*, New York: Oxford University Press.
Noble, David (1977), *American By Design: Science, Technology and the Rise of Corporate Capitalism*, New York: Alfred A. Knopf.
O'Connor, James (1973), *The Fiscal Crisis of the State*, New York: St Martin's Press.
Ryerson, J. and Son, Inc. (no date), 'The Ryerson plan: a teacher work-learn program,' Unpublished advertisement, Chicago: Joseph T. Ryerson and Son, Inc.
Science: a Process Approach (1974), *Module One*, Lexington: Ginn.
Spring, Joel (1976), *The Sorting Machine*, New York: David McKay.
Sumner, Colin (1979), *Reading Ideologies*, New York: Academic Press.
Wexler, Philip (in press), *Critical Social Psychology*, Boston: Routledge & Kegan Paul.
Williams, Raymond (1961), *The Long Revolution*, London: Chatto & Windus.
Williams, Raymond (1977), *Marxism and Literature*, New York: Oxford University Press.
Willis, Paul (1977), *Learning to Labour*, Farnborough, England: Saxon House.
Willis, Paul (1978), *Profane Culture*, Boston: Routledge & Kegan Paul.
Wright, Will (1975), *Sixguns and Society*, Berkeley: University of California Press.
Wright, Erik (1978), *Class, Crisis and the State*, London: New Left Books.

Chapter 9

Structure, text, and subject: a critical sociology of school knowledge

Philip Wexler

> This is why it is essential at all times to demonstrate the futility of mechanical determinism: for, although it is explicable as a naive philosophy of the mass and as such, but only as such, can be an intrinsic element of strength, nevertheless when it is adopted as a thought-out and coherent philosophy on the part of the intellectuals, it becomes a cause of passivity, of idiotic self-sufficiency.
>
> Antonio Gramsci

In the early 1970s we applied the sociology of knowledge to education and attacked the surface of liberal knowledge. We rejected idealism, objectivism and privatism in favor of a social and historical analysis of educational forms and school knowledge. It appears that we succeeded. There is now a 'new' sociology of education (Karabel and Halsey 1977), a revisionist educational history (Karier, Violas and Spring 1973), studies of curriculum as ideology (Apple 1979), and even reflexive analyses of the sociology of education and of curriculum studies (Franklin 1974; Wexler 1976). This shift in assumptions was part of a general crisis in the social sciences. The critical models that emerged from the crisis included categories of Marxist social analysis, like capital accumulation, alienation, exploitation, labor process, hegemony, and even contradiction, which were new to the social study of schooling (Apple 1979a; Bowles and Gintis 1976; Carnoy 1974; Wexler 1979).

Yet despite these new terms and the apparent academic success of critical models, we remain trapped in the grip of the dominant culture. Take, for example, three categories which have been especially influential in the social study of schooling. In opposition to the socially abstracted study of the communication of facts and values – curriculum, educationalists discovered the existence of social relations in the classroom – hidden curriculum. Instead of seeing the school as the stable repository of cumulative truth, it is increasingly studied as a social site for the presentation of partial knowledge – ideology. The older individual voluntarism of learning is displaced by an emphasis on imposed knowledge – socialization. These concepts are part of a critical way of analyzing schools. They replace an earlier idealist, objectivist and privatist educational analysis with a social one. They question appearances. But they also represent the practical concerns of the present corporate society. Hidden curriculum asserts the primacy of social relations over knowledge and technology in the same way that human relations replace technicism as a managerial strategy (Edwards 1979). The concept of ideology relativizes knowledge in a social context where cultural relativism and cognitive pluralism have the effect of confirming apathy and serving as sustaining rationales for sociopolitical inaction. The category of socialization affirms the powerlessness of the individual against a reified collectivity, a system, which purportedly reproduces itself. Critical scholars of education do not, of course, accept managerialism, social apathy, and individual powerlessness. In the hidden curriculum they find social control. In ideology they see the display of economic and political inequalities, and in socialization, training for the reproduction of a class system. The significantly different critical interpretation, notwithstanding, these topics and ways of thinking still belong to the present corporate administered society. The combined use of the concepts hidden curriculum and system reproduction is an unintended reinforcement of reification (Lukács 1971). Conscious rational human activity is dissolved between the poles of manipulative human relations and iron-like systems laws. The popularity of the hidden curriculum concept has the effect of replacing knowledge with interpersonalism. The system reproduction perspective leads to forgetting that social structures are the result of human activity, and not its source. The analysis of ideology has traditionally been a critical, unmasking activity (Mannheim 1936). When, however, social domination works through the symbolic and the analyst portrays the symbolic as secondary, translates it away into something else – some privileged anterior material base, then critique becomes affirmation. The concept of socialization surrenders in advance the human capacity for appropriation and transformation to the needs of a system for which individuals are merely structural supports.

A critical sociology of school knowledge questions these deeper assumptions which we critics still share with the intellectuals of the corporate order. Instead of relegating knowledge and information to the personal relations of hidden curriculum, knowledge is brought to the fore of educational analysis. Instead of allowing a social analysis of knowledge to be exhausted by hypotheses about system needs and subsumed in the magical metaphor of cultural reproduction, socially structured processes of knowledge production are described. Instead of reducing ideology to antecedent material causes, the power of symbols is acknowledged, and school knowledge is analyzed as a meaningful text. Instead of accepting the alienated social psychology of role socialization, the student is seen as a person, a subject, making and being made, within the history of discourse and production.

Structure: representation and transformation

The sociology of knowledge is the basis for most social analyses of school knowledge or curriculum. This sociology is built on a theory of representation or naming. One thing stands for another, usually an idea for a social position. Naming, or representation, is already an audacious act against the autonomy of the object. It is a claim of ownership, in which one set of words, objects or relations is subsumed and repossessed by another. Representation destroys the integrity and aura of the object, which is why the most sacred objects of knowledges are so resistant to naming (Benjamin 1969). In the sociology of knowledge, representation means the translation of knowledge into a social matrix, ordinarily that of classes, system requisites, social statuses, and patterns of social organization. Since knowledges are stratified, social translations are selectively applied, depending upon the power of the knowledge-bearers and the closeness of knowledge to the core of the sacred.

In this culture, scientific knowledge resists social representation. The sociology of science, particularly in the United States, avoids social translations of scientific knowledge. Sociologists of science analyze instead the social relations of science, using the models of normative consensus, competition and social mobility which are characteristic of American sociology generally (Ben-David 1978). There is a minority interest among British (Whitley 1974) and American (Brown 1979) sociologists of science in a social analysis of the content of scientific knowledge. But even Marxists respect the 'purity of science', and usually exempt scientific concepts from sociological representation (Young 1973). The less prestigious knowledge domain of literature is more likely to be translated as a representation of the social. Plekhanov, Caudwell, Fox, and Goldmann depict literature as a reflection of a more fundamental social reality (for a summary see Eagleton, 1976b; also Fox 1945; Goldmann 1976). The familiar base-structure model may be modified so that form rather than content mirrors social reality; the representation of the social in knowledge is not seen as direct, but mediated; culture may represent social contradiction in addition to social unity (Brown 1979; Goldman 1976; Young 1973). But, as Eagleton (1976a: 65) observes: 'One does not escape from reflectionist models by imagining a somewhat more complicated mirror.'

Sociologists of school knowledge use this qualified representational sociology of knowledge. School knowledge reflects class interest (Anyon 1979: 379):

> A whole range of curriculum selections favors the interests of the wealthy and powerful. Although presented as unbiased, the historical interpretations provide ideological justification for the activities and prerogatives of these groups and do not legitimize points of view and priorities of groups that compete with these established interests for social acceptance and support.

School knowledge is the unequal representation of the experience and culture of social classes (Bourdieu 1973: 84):

> By making social hierarchies and the reproduction of these hierarchies appear to be based upon the hierarchy of 'gifts', merits, or skills established and ratified by its sanctions, or, in a word, *by converting social hierarchies into academic hierarchies* (emphasis added), the educational system fulfills a function of legitimation which is more and more necessary to the perpetuation of the 'social order' as the evolution of the power relationship between classes tends more completely to exclude the imposition of a hierarchy based upon the crude and ruthless affirmation of the power relationship.

School knowledge is an organizational representation of different class languages (Bernstein 1975: 11, 22):

> Thus from this point of view, power and control are made substantive in the classification and framing which then generate distinctive forms of social relationships and thus communication, and through the latter initially, but not necessarily finally, shape mental structures.
>
> The class assumptions, of elaborated codes are to be found in the classification and framing of educational knowledge, and in the ideology which they express.

School knowledge develops as cultural representation in response to the system needs of capitalism (Apple 1979b: 118):

> We shall need to look at schools as aspects of the productive apparatus of a society in two ways: first, as institutions that help produce

agents for positions outside of the school in the economic sector of society; and second, as institutions that produce the cultural forms directly and indirectly needed by this same economic sector.

I think that this work is an important contribution to the analysis of school knowledge. It is currently replacing an earlier portrayal of knowledge in schools as a socially transcendant, taken-for-granted occasion for invidious individual differentiation. This new sociology of school knowledge and curriculum demonstrates that social power is culturally represented, and that knowledge and culture are essential moments in the process of social domination and capital accumulation. The selective transmission of class culture as common culture silences the cultures of the oppressed, and legitimates the present social order as natural and eternal.

Like their counterparts in the sociologies of science and literature, the new sociologists of school knowledge are also increasingly aware of limitations in the reflectionist perspective. Apple writes about the pitfalls of reflection and correspondence models, notes the importance of contradiction and resistance in the school and in the work place, and urges the use of '. . . metaphors describing other modes of determination such as mediation and transformation,' to 'complement' the metaphor of reproduction (Apple 1980: 18-19).

Critical qualified representational analysis is still representation. It moves away from the object or the knowledge toward its context. It tells a story of how one thing fits in with another, how, for example, school knowledge contributes to social legitimation. The problem, however, is that representation and reflection are themselves the modes of thought, the ideologies which sustain the present. They challenge the autonomy of the object, but quickly reposition it within social structure. They are ways of thinking which put things in their place, and permit the flow of present thoughts and social relations. The representational mode of thought is naturalizing. It prevents awareness of tenuousness, disjunction, interruption, and possibility. 'History,' as Aronowitz (1979: 110) declares, 'is not and can never become a seamless narrative.' A critical analysis which hides uncertainty and disjunction in a coherent story is also ideology.

A critique of ideology requires a mode of analysis which makes the tenuousness of the object apparent, not by contextualizing it, but by deconstructing it. To deconstruct the object, whether it is school knowledge, film, or social organization, means to show how it is itself an outcome of its own composition, a result of its own internal production, and not an entity among other self-generating entities. Objects, knowledge, and relations are not simply representations of something else, but stabilized moments of the internal processes out of which they are made, and which it is the task of ideology to naturalize by freezing the present into a convenient snapshot. The language of class interest, class reflection and cultural reproduction emphasizes the role of school knowledge in a broader social context, but neglects the continuous human activity, the production, which makes knowledge possible. This language relates knowledge to social structure while ignoring the internal construction which gives knowledge its appearance as natural fact. It leads to a strategy of social change that demands systemic change, while overlooking strategies for changing the course of everyday perception and action.

Knowledge can be analyzed as a process of transformation. It is made by a series of transformative activities which end at the point where knowledge is a recognizable commodity. The end point, the labelling of activity as knowledge, and the process of transformation which leads to that, is socially patterned. The source of knowledge, human labor, the transforming activities which constitute it, and the definition and distribution of the product are socially variable. Artisanal knowledge is different from bureaucratically made knowledge. Schoolbooks written by a single author present a different meaning from schoolbooks produced through editorial collage and organizationally prescribed formulae, even when they are about the same event (Fitzgerald 1979). The apparatus which makes the reality that we experience is more complex than a mirror. Describing the operation of that apparatus as a mediation between anterior reality and final product places the process of knowledge production into the background. But, to paraphrase McLuhan, the mediation may be the message. The socially organized process by which knowledge is produced makes its own reality. The more that we live in the world of constructed knowledge, the more does the translation of knowledge into something other than its own production lead us away from understanding what shapes our lives. The informationally overloaded subject is propelled toward a secure external code. Representational translation offers a handle on the present, but only at the hidden cost of affirming it.

The early Russian film-makers, who insisted that conscious assemblage, editing and montage make a new reality (Henderson 1976) offer us an alternative to the device of the mirror and the concept of cultural reproduction. If we ask about the process of assembling knowledge, instead of horizontally mapping its relation to exterior domains, we can begin to think about knowledge production as a series of editings and recodings. During this process, raw materials are continuously transformed until they reach the social definition of a product. Although this is a humanly directed series of activities, in contrast to individual auteur theories, we can suggest that the directed activity which makes each knowledge frame, and its subsequent assemblage and transformation, is social rather than private. Social montage, and not representation, reflection or reproduction, may be the more appropriate metaphor with which to pursue a sociology of school knowledge.

The montage metaphor would lead us beyond system mapping or qualified reflectionism to trace the social archeology of knowledge. This would not be, as it is for Foucault (1970) a history of discourse, but rather an effort to reconstruct the series of socially organized labors through which knowledge is made. This labor includes representation, as part of knowledge-making, but it emphasizes transformative translation – how knowledge is constantly re-worked and made anew. What I have in mind is not a simple process of selection, but a process of transformative selection, of recoding as knowledge is pushed through the apparatus – the social organization of meaning production. Empirically, this may require working backward from a description of the internal structure of the finished product, to the history of its coding and recoding. One research strategy is to assume an hierarchical process, in which official, socially hegemonic knowledge is a recoding of popular knowledge. The production of knowledge is then seen as systematic exploitation, in which the social relations of knowledge production not only make official knowledge, but remove from its earliest producers any claim or awareness of ownership. In this familiar cycle of fetishized production-consumption, recoded knowledge is then sold back to the producers, now acting as consumers. They are taught by ideology that what they are buying is an opaque object, and not one which has a history of production, a history to which they are themselves attached by their own labor. From this assumption, a history of science, for example, could be written as a series of socially organized transformations of popular cultural beliefs and practices.

In my cultural history of American sociology of education, I tried to show how the basic assumptions of mainstream sociology of education were related to the ideals of a particular social movement, Progressivism (Wexler 1976). Similarly, Forman (1971) has documented how the fundamental acausal assumption of quantum mechanics was developed by physicists in Weimar Germany, as an adaptation to a cultural milieu of *Lebensphilosophie*, in which determinist causality was strongly and popularly criticized. Both of these studies lack, however, sufficient attention to the social organization through which the coding was accomplished and a new knowledge produced. A second research strategy emphasizes precisely this organizational aspect, while ignoring a transformational history of cultural traces. Epstein underlines his thesis that the apparatus alone makes knowledge by entitling his book, *News From Nowhere* (1973). The content and form of the official knowledge which we recognize as television news is not made, according to Epstein, through a biased representation or reflection. Rather, the news is made according to organizational criteria based on internal organizational social routines, technologies and formulized definitions of what constitutes a saleable product or commodity. Epstein quotes a network executive (1973: 4):

> Every news story should, without any sacrifice of probity or responsibility display the attributes of fiction, or drama. It should have structure and conflict, problem and denouement, rising action and falling action, a beginning, a middle and an end. These are not only the essentials of drama; they are the essentials of narrative.

Both these emphases, the way that the knowledge-producing apparatus and the transformation of popular cultures make official knowledge, have not been central interests of the sociology of school knowledge. The new sociologists of education have been rightfully busy breaking the spell of idealism. Perhaps now we may begin to break the spell of realism through narrative and the reification of human activity which are the additional ingredients of objectivism. In the sociology of school knowledge we are just starting to take knowledge seriously again, and to see it as a human social activity.

There are already critical social content analyses of texts. Fitzgerald (1979) for example, working outside the academy, has written an account, full of insight, of the changing content and style of American history books, suggesting how the rationalization of the textbook industry has affected the texts. Anyon (1979) has closely examined history textbooks, showing how economic change, labor unions and social problems are presented from a conservative point of view. We need more content analyses of curricula, study guides and instructor manuals, in addition to textbooks. These content analyses should, I think, include examination of the form as well as content of knowledge, and of the symbolic methods which create in a knowledge or text an appearance of completeness, and hence, of matter-of-factness. The organizational production of these school knowledges has hardly been studied. There are some chatty descriptions of the school textbook industry. Black (1967) for example, provides brief anecdotes about corporate consolidation and conglomeration in the textbook industry, and the interlocking network of corporate, educational and government élites who have initiated curricula reforms. Boyd's discussion of professional and local curriculum politics provides another link in the series of transformative practices which result in official knowledge. The production of school knowledges involves also a politics of distribution, which Boyd (1978) has begun to explicate. Descriptions of the politics of distribution, the organization of the knowledge producing industry, the internal structure and content of school knowledges and texts, and their relation to broader cultural formations, are not yet assembled into an analysis of the socio-historical processes through which school knowledge is produced. Such an analysis does not deny the realities of systematic structured social power. On the contrary, it attempts to demonstrate how exploitation, accumulation and fetishized consumption occur within the domain of knowledge. Those who own the knowledge apparatus and control the routines which produce and transform popular knowledge for sale as specialized privately owned official knowledge, increasingly own reality.

The view of knowledge as a process of transformative social activity, rather than a system reproduction of entities, has implications for critical pedagogy. First, it implies that the perception of the opaqueness and immovability of 'the system' is partly our own doing. In efforts to describe 'the system', we have used a language which sews together and obscures the seams of a series of potentially disjunctive and transformable knowledge producing activities. Opening the seams to public view destroys the appearance of integrated totality, and makes it easier to see that there are a number of possible points of active public entry into the transformation series. To change school knowledge, it may not be necessary to wait for the last gasping crisis of capital. Second, the technical aesthetics of film montage (and I have been using the term broadly) and literary and dramatic production (Benjamin 1978; Henderson 1976) suggests how we might increase our control of knowledge through the forms that we favor, and the modes of communication which we practice. New unalienated knowledge can be created by opening up and disturbing the narrative. Brecht, for example, forced the audience away from inclusion toward a stance of distance and participation. Reflexive knowledge which bares the device of its own assemblage, helps blast through the misleading façade of verisimilitude. I am underlining that transformation and deconstruction are practical activities, and not just research metaphors. Modes of knowledge production which open the text to interpretation, and force a moment of estrangement and critical distance, invite participation in the making of knowledge. The text which convinces by its emotional and conceptual fluidity, which paralyzes by drawing on intertextual familiarity and glossy self-advertisement (Coward and Ellis 1977: 54), locks us out from recognizing the fruits of our labor and from realizing the horizons of our capacities.

Philip Wexler

Text: semiotics and class consciousness

'Hunger', Jung wrote, 'makes a god of food.' The power of meaning rests on our need for it. At the same time that symbolic products are widely distributed, meaning is dissolved into the rationalized practices of state and economic bureaucracies and predictable packages of human relations. Mass culture moves to the fore as the arena of potential self-integration, but only tantalizes us (Horkheimer and Adorno 1972), increasing even further our desire for a personally transcendant grid of meaning in which to locate personal identity. Analyses which leave this psychocultural process unattended for macrosystem political economy and human relations, enable the tantalizing domination of culture to continue unquestioned. When the sociologist of school knowledge studies knowledge in the language of system needs and reproduction, or makes interpersonal relations, hidden curriculum, primary targets for analysis, she/he recapitulates the social denial of meaning which adds to its controlling effectiveness. If the older false consciousness among educational researchers entailed a reduction of the social to the objective and the private, the newer false consciousness translates the cultural entirely into the social structural and the interpersonal. For this reason, it is important to consider the school text, the curriculum, in its own terms, and to avoid the hurry of translating it out of analytical sight.

Assertions of the importance of non-reductive internal analyses of knowledge are typical of the New Criticism in literature, and of the broader intellectual trends of formalism, structuralism, and semiotics. New Criticism insisted on analysis of the literary work itself, the 'words on the page', without any antecedent or exterior points of reference. It is an analysis of literary technique which, according to Hawkes (1977: 152) 'never goes "beyond" the work to validate its arguments.' Russian Formalists share with the New Criticism what Jameson (1972: 43) characterizes as a 'stubborn refusal to be diverted from the "literary fact" to some other form of theorization.' They are different because they are less concerned with exemplifying tradition, balance and 'intelligence', and aim instead toward the critical goal of textual work through *ostranenie* – making strange or defamiliarizing perception. Structuralism, the diffuse intellectual movement which spans linguistics, literary analysis and anthropology, may be briefly described as a synchronic (rather than historical) study of the internal relational rules of difference which constitute language, literature, and (for Lévi-Strauss) mind and society. Semiotics builds on Peirce's pragmatic philosophy and on Saussure's analysis of language, which posits a system of signs made possible by a set of rules, a *langue*. Semiotics is an attempt to create a general science of signs, of all meaning or message systems. Each of these traditions suggests methods for analyzing school knowledge. According to Jameson (1972: 101): 'We may therefore understand the Structuralist enterprise as a study of superstructures, or in a more limited way, of ideology.' It is, however, a study of ideology – not as a collection of entities, ideas, but as itself a production, a set of practices, structures, or methods which make meaning. The value of structuralism and semiotics for a study of school knowledge is that by viewing curriculum as a set of rules or symbolic practices, it enables us to avoid reducing knowledge to a static representation of social process – a representation which subverts its critical intent by reifying symbolic activities. Ideas are the result of the symbolic practices which make them, just as cultural reproduction is the contingent outcome of collective social practices or activities. Deconstructing concepts and facts of curriculum into the patterned methods out of which they are made, attacks the opaqueness of knowledge as object. This covering over of process, the naturalizing of dynamic, internal relational production as solid appearance, is, for the critical analyst, what constitutes ideology as activity.

A decomposition of coherent curriculum stories into their constituent practices, or structures, might take a variety of paths. Analyses developed from Lévi-Strauss' studies of myths would analyze school knowledges as myth, and as bundles of binary oppositions, the elemental differences, which are their bases (Lévi-Strauss 1972). To take an example from formalism, in Propp's analysis of fairy-tales there are a limited number of functions. Hawkes (1977: 68) defines textual function as 'an act of a character defined from the point of view of its significance for the course of action.' Wright (1975), who borrows from Lévi-Strauss, and more directly from Propp, has analyzed Hollywood Western film as a set of sixteen functions that define a classic Western plot (e.g. the hero is unknown to society; the hero is revealed to have an exceptional ability). The functions are expressed through a narrative which includes the use of elemental binary oppositions (good/bad, inside society/outside society, strong/weak, civilization/wilderness). The semiotician, Umberto Eco, analyzes the 'Myth of Superman' (1979), which he sees as organizing time so as to destroy the concept of historical time, creating an 'immobile present' (1979: 116-17):

> In growing accustomed to the idea of events happening in an ever-continuing present, the reader loses track of the fact that they should develop according to the dictates of time. Losing consciousness of it, he forgets the problems which are at its base, that is, the

existence of freedom, the possibility of planning, the necessity of carrying plans out, the sorrow that such planning entails, the responsibility that it implies, and finally, the existence of an entire human community whose progressivism is based on making plans.

Jameson (1972), in his critical interpretation of formalism and structuralism, describes the formalist literary techniques which defamiliarize (1972: 60-1). He emphasizes their method of 'laying bare the device' by choosing a text which '. . . takes itself for its own subject matter, and presents it own techniques as its own content (1972: 76).' Eco (1979: 120-1) in his analysis of popular culture, describes the structural practice of redundance, which reassures the consumer-reader, and itself becomes an expectation. The pleasure of repetition blocks the possibility of using a text as an occasion for imagining possibilities for change.

In the field of curriculum studies, there is already evidence of what we might broadly call a semiotic interest. In his analysis of children's Revolutionary War fiction, Taxel (1980), for example, uses Wright's model, though with somewhat different findings, to analyze historically changing textual structures. Apple (1981) stresses that it is the form of curriculum modules used in science education which acts as a mode of technical control. His description of how pre-packaged school materials eliminate the need for conscious planning, parallels Eco's (1979) semiotics of the redundance and timelessness of a popular culture which eliminates the imagination of planning. Pinar's (1979) work makes its own production a topic and bares the experience behind the text. By doing that, he violates the seemingly natural form of the academic narrative. All of this work, in different ways, moves from base-superstructure representationalism toward meaning production, and toward an analysis of the activities and practices which constitute the school text. I think that much more of this type of work needs to be done in all areas of curriculum. A semiotics of school text, descriptions of the operation of structure to produce textual effects, counters the reification of knowledge as a solid, though socially reflective, object. In this sense, it supports opposition against the pervasive commodifying processes (Lukács 1971: 81) that incorporate even such critical analyses as those of cultural reproduction. It makes it possible to understand knowledge production as a chain or series of transformative activities which range from the social organization of text industries, to the activities of text producers, through the symbolic transformations of the text itself, and to the transformative interaction between text and reader, or school knowledge and student. Various kinds of remakings can be traced across the boundaries that we conventionally label the social, the cultural, and the personal. The problem of textual analysis may itself become reified, abstracted and frozen. A graphical scholasticism of textual structural diagramming merges with computer onanism. Such a formalism may lead us, in Nietzsche's oft-quoted phrase, to forget why we ever began. The 'text' replaces the system, and, before that, the soul. If cultural reproduction theory can become a new objectivism, semiotics can become a new idealism.

We began because we had faith in the power of knowledge. And then, we began again because we saw that faith betrayed. We discovered that the knowledge which we thought was universal and disinterested, was partial and socially interested. The sociology of knowledge is one response to that discovery. It is an analytical move toward class consciousness, toward the reclamation of appropriated knowledge. The intellectual path toward class consciousness begins by demonstrating how the representation of events is partial and class-based. Anyon's (1979) analysis of American history texts is a good example. However, the specific 'bias' of selective historical representation is itself the product of a conceptual apparatus that operates within the text. That apparatus is built from more general concepts. It structures, often silently, the organization of social relations and history in ways which make the more specific interpretations possible. Bringing these implicit structuring concepts to the surface is, I think, a next step toward showing how class consciousness is conceptually embodied in school knowledge.

First, class consciousness means the location of human activity in history. It is obviously difficult for history texts to avoid some such consideration, even if it is only a portrait of history as the passage of time, an uninterrupted flow of events underlined by chronology. The teaching of science, however, like current scientific thought itself, increasingly abstracts scientific activity from any history (Brown 1979; Taylor 1979). When English curriculum in the current 'back-to-basics' reaction against 'humanities' (Reininger 1979) is presented as a set of timeless norms of expression, and literary works taught as exemplars of fixed form, any awareness of historicity is silenced. Class consciousness also means the ability to situate the individual and the immediate within a larger frame, to have a view of the social totality. Compartmentalizing the entire curriculum, and separating instruction into tightly bound units, teaches fragmentation as a mode of thought, and blocks the potential for synthetic integration, and the capacity to imagine totality (Bernstein's (1975) findings are seen as an aspect of class consciousness). Class consciousness includes not only an awareness of conflict (Apple 1979a), but of conflict rooted in opposing interests. The curriculum which teaches differences as cultural pluralism, reads difference as an attitudinal, cultural misunderstanding. The source of difference in opposing interests is ignored. The silent problem, exploitation, can then be resolved through understanding, goodwill and common values. History, totality, and exploitation are not only static concepts which are largely absent in ordinary school knowledge. They are also modes of relation, practices of making sense which stand behind and structure specific representations. They are at once descriptions of social relations and rules of information processing. A critical semiotics of school knowledge would take the constituents of class consciousness as the organizing practices, whether present or significantly absent, with which to deconstruct the text. The most important of these operations, the human social making of relations and products, is perhaps the most general of these rules. It is the assumption required for confidant action, and it is the relational rule, the organizing principle, without which knowledge is reified. A critical semiotics based on class consciousness must show how the text symbolically shuts out awareness of collective human labor as the continuing source of what we are and of what we have. The construction of causality, like the text's production of a seemingness of time, stands behind particular textual discussions of whether entrepreneurs or labor unions are more potent historical determinants. Certainly such differences of representation offer the student significantly different narrative accounts. For critical textual analyses to become more than revisionist chronologies, and alternatively, for semiotics to become more than pure formalism, the symbolic practices which, together, produce as effect the constituent categories of class consciousness, must be considered. Conceptual elements such as history, totality, exploitation and human production (and, of course, others like class and contradiction) which make specific representations likely are also themselves the result of more microscopic textual practices. To describe these transformations within the text, what stands behind, or more precisely, operates to produce these concepts (or to omit them) within the school text, would be the task of a critical semiotics of school knowledge.

Beyond class consciousness as the recognition of biased historical representation, and beyond class consciousness as a deeper conceptual structure which stands between representation and the methods of the text, there is the class consciousness which is still another degree removed from reification – class consciousness as more actively and materially realized, class consciousness as a participatory remaking of the text. Bernstein's analysis of codes of curriculum structure (1975: 79-84) suggests that the structure of the curriculum makes possible different types of social actions. In another textual domain, Eco (1979: 47-66) differentiates between open and closed works in music and in literature. Describing the classical composition (1979: 48-9):

> He converted his idea into conventional symbols which more or less oblige the eventual performer to reproduce the format devised by the composer itself. Whereas the new musical works referred to above reject the definitive, concluded message and multiply the formal possibilities of the distribution of their elements. They appeal to the initiative of the individual performer, and hence they offer themselves, not as finite works which prescribe specific repetition along given structural coordinates, but as 'open' works, which are brought to their conclusion by the performer at the same time as he experiences them on an aesthetic plane.

The open text invites participation. It refuses the assumption of a reproduction of fixed forms as the basis of expression and communication. The open text is class consciousness because its incompleteness underlines that the work is a process of activity rather than a dead object. Eco calls it 'a work in movement.' It is class consciousness not only because its form serves as a reminder that the work has been made, but also because it calls for further making, for the interpretive and constructive activity which characterizes transformation, as opposed to reproduction. Texts can be open to the continuing work of transformation, which is a form that teaches activity rather than passive consumption as its message. Even highly structured musical compositions can demand nonreproduction by the performer through the use of extensive pauses, just as works of literature may have what Iser (1978: 169) calls the 'blanks', the less narratively enclosed spaces, which stimulate the participation of the reader. The text which contains its own internally stated negation, communicates contradiction, and makes it more likely that the reader or 'addressee' can stand 'in relation' (Iser 1978: 169) to the text, instead of being captured and included in it. The presentation of ambiguity, of a text which remains unexhausted even after systematic interpretative grids are placed over it, 'structurally prefigures' a world of indeterminancy, of possibility, and itself makes possible interpretive activity. A Brechtian play refuses to close contradiction with an advance resolution: 'A solution is seen as desirable and is actually anticipated, but it must come from the collective enterprise of the audience. In this case the "openness" is converted into an instrument of revolutionary pedagogics.' (Eco 1979: 55). Barthes (1974) applies the open work to the whole text. The 'readerly text' is the closed, classic text, literature, but the 'writerly text' is the openness to transformative activity generalized (1974: 5):

> the writerly text is not a thing, we would have a hard time finding it in a bookstore. Further, its model being a productive (and no longer a representative) one, it demolishes any criticism which, once produced, would mix with it. . . . The writerly text is a perpetual present, upon which no *consequent* language (which would inevitably make it past) can be superimposed, the writerly text is *ourselves writing.*

If class consciousness is fundamentally the opposite of reification, then the texts which reveal and produce further transformation, rather than those which absorb and hide production, affirm class consciousness as an activity, and not just a set of conceptual entities. Ironically, an ahistorical semiotics leads us toward class consciousness through an emphasis on the internal practices of textual production, while a representational commitment to class consciousness leads us toward its denial in reification.

I am suggesting three levels of analyzing school knowledge as class consciousness. The first level of analysis is the study of representational bias, class-specific narratives, which are naturalized as History, Science, Literature and Truth. The second level requires a digging out of the concepts which order and stand behind specific representations. These concepts constitute a social theory of class consciousness and can be seen as the textual functions of history, totality, exploitation, class and contradiction which comprise the curriculum story. Third, an analysis of school knowledge as ideology or reification – to examine whether and how production is hidden, underlined or made possible by the school text. False-consciousness, in this model, is more than class misidentification or historical onesidedness. False consciousness is, increasingly, *pseudo-participation*. The inquiry curriculum which promises activity but communicates a redundant formula like exploration-invention-discovery as its constant theme is false consciousness (Taylor 1979). Applied to textual research, this means an analysis of time, causality, human agency, freedom, and social production, not as abstract concepts, but as themselves the products of the structured text of school knowledge.

The imagery of the open work in practical activity and in research, does not end with the school text. The process of transformation that begins in the wider organization of social production, in commodity-fetishism and capital accumulation, and works in and through the domain of knowledge-production and the internal methods of the text itself, also includes the subject. The open-text makes the 'addressee' into a collaborative producer rather than an object. Although we may affirm transformative activity as a goal, through our choice of research metaphors, and though we may see the open works of modernism as exemplars of that goal, in the school the closed text is even more the norm, and the elusive subject is an easily mapped object. Even the term 'subject' seems an old-fashioned concept which belongs to the moralizing humanism that lies adjacent to the discourse of the representational narrative. Why then ask about the subject?

Subject: socialization and conditional action

At the very time that we begin to see the text as productive activity, and the open work as an opportunity for transformative human action, structuralism proclaims the death of the subject (Althusser 1971; Foucault 1970). This death, the 'end of man' is, however, closely bound to its opposite, the doctrine of the free individual. For like individualism, this type of structuralism denigrates the conditional capacity for human transformative action. Individualism ignores social and historical conditions to assert the market relations of the bourgeoisie as human freedom. Structuralism, recoiling against this misrepresentation, dissolves the human being into conditioning structures of discourse and society. The assumption of solidity in individualism is of the person as subject, and in structuralism is of the person as object. In both cases, internal and contradictory processes of conditional transformative action are ignored and reified, either as freedom or as determinism. The reproduction metaphor slights the process of social production. Representationalism misses the internal productive practices of the text. Similarly, individualism and structuralism divide between them and obscure the transformative production of the subject.

In the current sociology of school knowledge, the language of structural reproduction discourages interest in transformative activity as practice. An earlier functionalist sociology eliminated the possibility of imagining a transformative subject through its naturalization of historical alienation as social role. Normative role performance keeps the fixed grid of the division of labor in place. Socialization to socially required values and skills insures role performance. Marxist structuralist sociology of education opposes the society which schooling helps sustain. School reproduces a society of the alienated social relations, social control, and the class structure of capital (Bowles and Gintis 1976). This account does not, however, oppose conceptualizing reproduction as 'socialization'. The activity of the subject is seen as an enactment of a script written to meet the needs of the system. In structuralist sociology, the economic apparatus writes the subject, as does the text in literary structuralism. In the model of socialization, whether as transmission of social values and roles, or as textual positioning, the subject becomes the object of a social or cultural system.

I agree that the social apparatus *can* make the subject. Goffman (1962) and Lifton (1961) describe how a person can be destroyed and remade according to the routines and ideals of social organization. Literary structuralists also argue persuasively that the narrative text *can* constitute the subject (Coward and Ellis 1977: 50):

> Narration rather sets the subject in place as the point of intelligibility of its activity: the subject is then in a position of observation, understanding, synthesizing. The subject of narration is a homogenous subject, fixed in a relation of watching. It is precisely this relationship of specularity that becomes clear in the analysis of films.

The inmate and the spectator may indeed be the social types of our times. Advertising becomes the paradigm of a culture in which transformative labor is reduced to the acquiescent roles of employee and consumer. We should add the human commodity to the social gallery of inmate and spectator (Horkheimer and Adorno 1972: 167):

> The most intimate reactions of human beings have been so thoroughly reified that the idea of anything specific to themselves now persists only as an utterly abstract notion: personality scarcely signifies anything more than shining white teeth and freedom from body odor and emotions.

This critical vision is only possible from the vantage point of an opposing theory. If, however, the absence of a subject is not a problem, but a research assumption, it is unlikely that an active subject will even be seen as a possibility. The socialization model affirms as natural fact the processes by which the subject is eliminated.

In both sociology of education and in cultural studies, the socialization model in which the subject is the object of social routines and relational rules has recently been qualified. Working-class youths can resist accepting the impositions or socialization of the middle-class school, although such resistance may ultimately result in the reproduction of social classes (Willis 1977). It is now commonplace to acknowledge that resistance is possible, and that the socialization model is incomplete. But the concept of resistance, like the categories of mediation and contradiction, when used as addenda, only qualifies the model. It does not go far enough to challenge the assumption of the subject as object. Similarly in cultural studies, discussions of the avant-garde literary text, the film montage, the ambiguous and the incomplete in music and theater – the open work – are all assertions that the subject is not fully positioned by the text. The open work is also a qualification. The exceptions confirm the ordinary rule of the text, and the production of the solid object-subject of structuralism. Both concepts, resistance and open work, can challenge objectivism, for they point to the tenuousness of the apparently closed and hegemonic. They remind us that realistic narrative, like role socialization, is a contingent accomplishment. The qualifications begin to make it possible to see that the center as well as the periphery of social structural or cultural text is constituted by the subject. Openness and disjunction rupture the naturalness of the objective. They force us to consider all the signifying practices of the text and the structures of social relations as traces of human activity. The avant-garde subject, who makes the rupture, and so brings human action back to awareness, is not the bourgeois subject whose death structuralism announces. She/he is not the market actor who assimilates profit to conscience. No, the avant-garde subject of modernism is different. She/he is a self-parody, an ephemeral self in movement, a multidimensional, decentered and decentering subject. The social apparatus creates not only the inmate, who is the paradigmatic object-subject of socialization theory, but also the spectator and the human commodity. And, in its contradictoriness, the apparatus also produces the contradictory decentered divided subject. To this subject the false sanity of the inmate, tolerance of the spectator, and rationality of the human commodity are the result of narratives of repression (Cooper 1971; Deleuze and Guattari 1977). This new decentered subject perceives socially rationalized repression, and recognizes that behind the text stands transformative human activity. In the brief moment when the divided subject appears, the solid positioned subject of socialization models is revealed as the subjective aspect of the ideology of reification. The dialectic of fragmentation diffuses and weakens the integrated bourgeois subject, while making possible the unexpected and disjointed activity of the decentered subject, who in turn, dramatizes and reaffirms the possibility of human action.

Each of these social types, the inmate, the spectator, the human commodity and the divided subject, has a different relation to knowledge. Each is adapted to a different text. To the veteran inmate, knowledge can only be read as a command. The habit of acquiescence to instruction generalizes to all information, and the inmate's social context, the asylum (whether mental hospital, school or society), is organized in ways that accommodate and reinforce this need. The bureaucratic announcement/memo is the form of the closed text to which the inmate is accustomed. The spectator awaits excitement.

Conditioned to the narrative of suspense, the time between the tantalizing opening and the overcoded reassuring closing passes without notice. It is the limbo in which the extra dream-work of surplus repression operates. The spectator rises to every icon of beginning, and breathes easier with every demarcation of sequence. Intertextuality, connotation, bringing the familiar to each event, affords protection from new experience and feeds addiction to pleasing redundance. The spectator loves to cry, 'foul! density! incomprehensibility!' at every violation of the encratic code (Barthes 1975: 40):

> Now, encratic language (the language produced and spread under the protection of power) is statutorally a language of repetition: all official institutions of language are repeating machines: school, sport, advertising, popular songs, news, all continually repeat the same structure, the same meaning, often the same words: the stereotype is a political fact, the major figure of ideology.

The human commodity wants knowledge that will buy and sell easily, even offering itself for the same price. Efficiency is its watchword, and condensation and commonality are its practices. The best knowledges are emptied of content, since commensurability is what the commodity market requires (Horkheimer and Adorno 1972: 7):

> Bourgeois society is ruled by equivalence. It makes the dissimilar comparable by reducing it to abstract qualities. To the Enlightenment, that which does not reduce to numbers, and ultimately to the one, becomes illusion; modern positivism writes it off as literature.

The divided subject seeks over-interpretation and under-interpretation, eschewing the norm of moderation. Knowledge which is elusive, associational, and complexly connotative enables the fragmented decentered subject to push forward, interiorly, toward realizing a residual desire for integration. Knowledge which requires no interpretation, the pop-art of the everyday, that blares itself out from every node of the communication network, permits a disconnected wandering. In its midst, the decentered subject asserts itself through short spurts of deafening and stylized activity.

The interaction between text and subject is not ordinarily conceived of in this way. In the more familiar interactionist perspective, the activity of the subject realizes the text of school knowledge. Resistance is only a point which indicates that there is an interaction between text and subject. Realization of the text depends not only on inevitable response to its cues, but also on the history and predisposition of the subject. In the study of school knowledge, the new sociology of education describes how the class history of the student can lead either to an acceptance of the middle-class text and its interpretation of the students' differences as failures (Bernstein 1975; Bourdieu and Passeron 1977), or to a class-based resistance (Willis 1977). Interpretive sociology emphasizes the interactionally produced constructions through which the official text is made sense of and transformed (Keddie 1977; Mehan 1979). Developmentalists describe how students at different points on the continua of cognitive development construct different meanings of the same text (Waxman 1980). The existential theorist sees life-history as the source of selective underlinings and individually different uses of common texts and knowledges (Pinar 1979). For literary phenomenologists (Iser 1978) reading is an act of appropriation, a transformation of meanings that takes cues from the text, but adapts them differently, according to the subject's schemata of meaning. In scanning social types, I have suggested that there are a variety of ideal typical subjects, who have different expectations and definitions of knowledge. The inmate has learned to prefer the directive to the mystery, while the human commodity dismisses the divided-subject's text as nonlinear and, sneeringly, as poetic. In all these examples the text is viewed as an interactive invitation to interpretive activity, rather than as the socializing imposition of behavioral rules. Nevertheless, not all texts leave open the same space in which the transformative action of the subject can occur. Despite my affirmation of potential transformative activity as practice and as research assumption, the subject is not always able to appropriate the presented text. Between a structuralism which permits little room for transformative action, and an individualism which sees repression beyond the needs of the unconscious, lies the terrain of conditional action.

The text and the subject are moving in opposite directions: one to closure, the other to opening. The press toward capital accumulation and the rationalization of economic production is a broad social tendency which affects the process of knowledge production. Knowledge which is produced in every domain (while each has its own rules and practices) is unified by the overriding social logic of the commodity (Lukács 1971: 83). Its attributes are standardization and calculation. Its requirement of saleability implies an intensification of exploitation to increase profit. It includes making the social relations of production invisible, through agglomeration, dispersion and opaque governance by bureaucratic rule. Commodity-logic is extended to language, meaning and perception by the generalization of a specific organization of human labor, and not as a magical response to the needs of capital (Marcuse 1964). The technology of production is adapted to social organization. Its use is socially limited and prevents questioning the social form which contains it. The potential of media technology for reciprocal human discourse is, for example, only peripherally realized. Illich's (1970) learning network is unlikely in a centralized system of knowledge commodity production. Cultural commodities as market-fetishes are not reflections but fixed, frozen transformations. Culture is made continuous and homologous with the social organization of production by being forced into a commodity form. The means of production, including the most powerful means of the mass production of signification, are privately owned and controlled (Golding and Murdock 1979). Signification, like every other commodity, is made for sale. It is made through commodified social relations. The knowledge or culture which is produced through such relations, whether television, film, or school and academic knowledge, is an extension of the commodifying practices that characterize labor in other spheres of production. The labor of signification is also commodified. That is why knowledge and culture appear as the textual practices which occlude the transformative activity of the subject – redundance, reduction, simplification, and self-advertisement. In the school this takes the form of the bureaucratically made history text of 'forces' without human actors (Fitzgerald 1979), or the routinizing pre-packaged instructional model of science education (Apple 1981). The text, then, is not an object, but a set of commodifying signifying practices. It invites the participation of the subject, but as a human commodity. Such participation carries over the commodity experience of other areas of social life (Aronowitz 1973) to symbolic work. This guarantees the appearance of objectivity and closure.

There are at least two potential challenges to the cycle of knowledge commodity production. First, each point in the currently rigid series of transformations – from the appropriation of cultural traces, through routinized organizational production, to the constitution of the text through distribution and its appropriation by the subject – is potentially open to the collective action of the producers. Oppressed groups can recognize and reclaim their knowledge as it is being made unrecognizably official. Workers within the apparatus of knowledge production can, by changing their social relations of production, affect also the character of their products. Selective distribution of school texts is accomplished by pressure-group politics (Boyd 1978; Fitzgerald 1979). In boycotts against cultural consumption, a collective subject reaches back behind the text to challenge its production. There are also alternative knowledge-producing organizations, like collectively produced community newspapers. Second, competition can squash innovation in an effort to keep market and work routines stable and predictable. But, in competing for consumers the apparatus encourages an 'aura of the new.' The cultural research and development necessary to maintain newness may increasingly follow the tamed in-house pattern of corporate industrial research (Apple 1979b; Noble 1977). The promise of marketability allows a commercial avant-garde. This avant-garde is poised between commodifying and demystifying, through reflective cultural work, the apparatus that supports it. The spread of knowledge production into new areas (e.g., video education), in search of profitable new markets, can result in cultural expressions, which in the moment before their incorporation and routinization, permit a glimpse of symbolic alternatives. Yet, these are still only peripheral possibilities. Currently, the prevailing social knowledge, including school knowledge, is produced as a commodifying and closed text.

Commodity production has a different effect on the subject. Faced simultaneously with powerlessness in production, decay of earlier bases of identity in family and community, and a continuing ethos of individualism, the integrated ideal subject of early capitalism becomes the new decentered subject (Turner 1976; Wexler 1977). Potentially collectivizing tendencies within production, which include centralization and the use of human relations techniques to regulate the social relations of production, press toward a new sociality. The social character of the subject changes from the earlier interiority of conscience to an anchoring meaning in others. But this outwardness is not solidified by collective social power. Instead, the field-dependence, which results from the habit of communication without power, combines with the ethos of individualism to make the subject hungry for symbolic affirmations of selfhood (Dannefer 1980; Wexler 1980). The norm of self-realization is underlined without the economic and social resources necessary for its accomplishment. In these circumstances, the subject is pushed toward the arena of consumption as the site for self-affirmation. Simultaneously, self-realization through the control of productive labor recedes from the horizon of imagined possibility. Denuded of the centering bourgeois virtues, needful of social validation, yet without social power, the subject becomes open to vicarious sociality. The subject attains a sense of social participation through the imagined activity that mass culture provides (Brenkman 1979). The outcome is that as commodity-production encapsulates knowledge within commodifying practices, and closes the text to the open work of transformative activity, the subject stands open, awaiting the newest symbolic product to provide confirmation of his/her existence. If the text, even the closed commodifying text, is an invitation to transformative activity rather than an imposed socialization, it is an invitation with few takers. The passivity of the subject, that is assumed by the socialization model, is not a natural but an historically social condition. The relation between subject and text, as between text and social structure, is a contingent, conditional relation. Each of these relations seems automatic, reflective or natural because conditional transformative action is ordinarily neither imagined nor realized. The subject is not absent, but only presently immobilized. The open subject faces the closed text. It is this particular historical conjuncture which gives power to the text, both in theory and in practice.

Although ascendant knowledge texts may be closed, history is not. The mass production of cultural commodities, of which school knowledge is an instance, bases its claim for consumption on individualism. Even while consumption is practiced as imitation, the advertised commodity promises that individual differentiation can be accomplished through ownership. Individualism remains also a buttressing incentive in the world of work. Within the homogenizing bureaucratic organization, career advancement stands in for the earlier rule of morality. Compliance is offered because estimations of self-worth are attached to organizational conformity. Achievement complements consumption. Both require some appeal to the self-referential and self-directive power of the individual. Industrial systems management requires the ideal of self-direction in the middle, as well as in the higher places. It generates a self-regulating subject as a device within a cybernetic system. In schooling, also, we have valued the self-directed learner, although we rarely question how the learning materials of the school text position that self-direction. But the individualism which serves commodity production is also a basis for opposition to it. Production-required autonomy and the ethos of freedom can pass beyond expected bounds of organizational containment. The subject learns to want more space. When she/he is included in planning, even if it is in the pseudo-participation of human relations management, she/he may recognize that his/her autonomy is defined by a larger and constraining apparatus. Acceptance of limited self-direction in production is challenged also by the unbounded egoism which commodity consumption urges upon the subject. A combined taste of power and hunger for meaning can induce the subject to ask who controls the production of meaning. In this scenario, the cybernetically controlled robots want the controlling tapes. Knowledge text is that tape, not as object, but as a regulative series of information-processing operations, or alternatively, symbolic practices. In education the fight against secrecy (e.g., testing) is an example of how an individualism, fostered by work achievement and consumer freedom, pushes out from within the commodity society to seek greater control of the means of knowledge production.

The decentered field-dependent subject is the vulnerable object of closed mass culture. The fragmentation of the nineteenth century bourgeois ego enables the commodity-as-symbol to replace the personal authority of the familied society as the locus of individual regulation. The new subject is, however, still caught in a spin, looking to human and object passers-by for a directional clue. The decenteredness, in which the older cathexis of family attachment is loosened, is not thoroughly absorbed and redomesticated by the commodity it now serves. A labile decentered condition makes possible a recentering, in newer forms of association. Self-help organizations, consciousness-raising groups, food and learning co-operatives, may become locations for the recentering which lies between and against privatism and commodity. These scant and dispersed social forms prefigure a process of recentering from which a new social subject emerges. This still unformed new subject learns the habit of collective action, which provides a method for realizing the ambitions that individualism encourages. To control the text, the signifying process through which the transformative subject becomes self-constituting, requires collective action to control the social process of its production. A combination of defamiliarization and organization is required to develop the desire and the capacity to control the apparatus of meaning-production, of which school knowledge is one aspect. In every act of remaking the text, the subject is affirmed. The social subject exemplifies conditional transformative action and invalidates the myth of a social system and a cultural text without a subject.

In the absence of the practical and intellectual work which makes the subject possible, Horkheimer and Adorno's assertion will stand as our epitaph (1972: 38):

> In their eyes, their reduction to mere objects of administered life, which preforms every sector of modern existence including language and perception, represents objective necessity, against which they believe there is nothing they can do.

Bibliography

Althusser, Louis (1971), 'Ideology and Ideological State Apparatuses,' in Louis Althusser, *Lenin and Philosophy and Other Essays*, London: NLB, pp. 123-73.

Anyon, Jean (1979), 'Ideology and United States History Textbooks,' *Harvard Educational Review* 43 (August), 361-85.

Apple, Michael W. (1979a), *Ideology and Curriculum*, London: Routledge & Kegan Paul.

Apple, Michael W. (1979b), 'The Production of Knowledge and the Production of Deviance in Schools,' in Len Barton and Roland

Meighan, (eds), *Schools, Pupils and Deviance*, Driffield, England: Nafferton Books, pp. 113-31.

Apple, Michael W. (1980), 'The Other Side of the Hidden Curriculum: Correspondence Theories and the Labor Process,' *The Journal of Education* 162 (Winter), 47-66.

Apple, Michael W. (1981), 'Curriculum Form and the Logic of Technical Control: Building the Possessive Individual,' in Michael W. Apple (ed.), *Cultural and Economic Reproduction in Education*, London: Routledge & Kegan Paul, chapter 8.

Aronowitz, Stanley (1973), *False Promises: the Shaping of American Working-Class Consciousness*, New York: McGraw-Hill.

Aronowitz, Stanley (1979), 'Film – the Art Form of Late Capitalism,' in *Social Text* 1 (Winter), 110-29.

Barthes, Roland (1974), *S/Z*, New York: Hill & Wang.

Barthes, Roland (1975), *The Pleasure of the Text*, New York: Hill & Wang.

Ben-David, Joseph (1978), 'Emergence of National Traditions in the Sociology of Science: the United States and Great Britain,' in Jerry Gaston (ed.), *Sociology of Science*, San Francisco: Jossey-Bass, pp. 197-218.

Benjamin, Walter (1969), 'The Work of Art in the Age of Mechanical Reproduction,' in Walter Benjamin, *Illuminations*, New York: Schocken.

Benjamin, Walter (1978), 'The Author as Producer,' in Walter Benjamin, *Reflections: Essays, Aphorisms, Autobiographical Writings*, New York: Harcourt, Brace Jovanovich, pp. 220-8.

Bernstein, Basil (1975), *Class, Codes and Control, Vol. 3: Towards a Theory of Educational Transitions*, London: Routledge & Kegan Paul.

Black, Hillel (1967), *The American Schoolbook*, New York: William Morrow.

Bourdieu, Pierre (1973), 'Cultural Reproduction and Social Reproduction,' in Richard Brown (ed.), *Knowledge, Education and Cultural Change*, Birkenhead: Tavistock Publications, pp. 71-112.

Bourdieu, Pierre and Jean Claude Passeron (1977), *Reproduction in Education, Society and Culture*, London: Sage.

Bowles, Samuel and Herbert Gintis (1976), *Schooling in Capitalist America*, New York: Basic Books.

Boyd, William Lowe (1978), 'The Changing Politics of Curriculum Policy-making for American Schools,' *Review of Educational Research* 48 (Fall), 577-628.

Brenkman, John (1979), 'Mass Media: From Collective Experience to the Culture of Privatization,' *Social Text* 1 (Winter), 94-109.

Brown, Theodore M. (1979), 'Putting Paradigms into History,' unpublished MS, Department of History, University of Rochester.

Carnoy, Martin (1974), *Education as Cultural Imperialism*, New York: David McKay.

Cooper, David (1971), *The Death of the Family*, New York: Pantheon Books.
Coward, Rosalind and John Ellis (1977), *Language and Materialism: Developments in Semiology and the Theory of the Subject*, London: Routledge & Kegan Paul.
Dannefer, William Dale (1980), 'Rationality and Passion in Private Experience: Modern Consciousness and the Social World of Old Cars,' *Social Problems* (in press).
Deleuze, Gilles and Felix Guattari (1977), *Anti-Oedipus: Capitalism and Schizophrenia*, New York: Viking Press.
Eagleton, Terry (1976a), *Criticism and Ideology: A Study in Marxist Literary Theory*, London: New Left Books.
Eagleton, Terry (1976b), *Marxism and Literary Criticism*, Berkeley: University of California.
Eco, Umberto (1979), *The Role of the Reader: Explorations in the Semiotics of Texts*, Bloomington: Indiana University Press.
Edwards, Richard (1979), *Contested Terrain: The Transformation of the Workplace in the Twentieth Century*, New York: Basic Books, Inc.
Epstein, Edward Jay (1973), *News from Nowhere: Television and the News*, New York: Random House.
Fitzgerald, Frances (1979), *America Revised*, Boston: Little Brown.
Forman, Paul (1971), 'Weimar Culture, Causality and Quantum Theory, 1918-1927: Adaptation by German Physicists and Mathematicians to a Hostile Intellectual Environment,' in Russell McCormmack, (ed.), *Historical Studies in the Physical Sciences*, Philadelphia: University of Pennsylvania, vol. 3, pp. 1-115.
Foucault, Michel (1970), *The Order of Things: An Archaeology of the Human Sciences*, New York: Random House.
Fox, Ralph (1945), *The Novel and the People*, New York: International Publishers.
Franklin, Barry M. (1974), 'The Curriculum Field and the Problem of Social Control, 1918-38: A Study in Educational Theory,' PhD dissertation, University of Wisconsin, Madison.
Goffman, Erving (1962), *Asylums*, Chicago: Aldine.
Golding, Peter and Graham Murdock (1979), 'Ideology and the Mass Media: The Question of Determination,' in Michele Barrett, Philip Corrigan, Annete Kuhn and Janet Wolf, *Ideology and Cultural Production*, New York: St Martin's Press, pp. 198-224.
Goldmann, Lucien (1976), *Cultural Creation in Modern Society*, Saint Louis: Telos.
Gramsci, Antonio (1971), *Selections from the Prison Notebooks*, New York: International Publishers.
Hawkes, Terence, (1977), *Structuralism and Semiotics*, London: Methuen.
Henderson, Brian (1976), 'Two Types of Film Theory,' in Bill Nichols, (ed.), *Movies and Methods: An Anthology*, Berkeley: University

of California, pp. 388-400.

Horkheimer, Max and Theodore W. Adorno (1972), *Dialectic of Enlightenment*, New York: Herder & Herder.

Illich, Ivan (1970), *De-Schooling Society*, New York: Harper & Row.

Iser, Wolfgang (1978), *The Act of Reading: A Theory of Aesthetic Response*, Baltimore: Johns Hopkins University Press.

Jameson, Frederic (1972), *The Prison-House of Language: A Critical Account of Structuralism and Russian Formalism*, Princeton: Princeton University Press.

Karabel, Jerome and A. H. Halsey (eds) (1977), *Power and Ideology in Education*, New York: Oxford University Press.

Karier, Clarence J., Paul C. Violas and Joel Spring (eds) (1973), *Roots of Crisis: American Education in the Twentieth Century*, Chicago: Rand McNally.

Keddie, Nell (1977), 'Classroom Knowledge,' in Arno Bellack and Herbert Kliebard (eds), *Curriculum and Evaluation*, Berkeley: McCutchan, pp. 280-316.

Lévi-Strauss, Claude (1972), 'The Structural Study of Myth,' in Richard and Fernandez de George (eds), *The Structuralists: From Marx to Lévi-Strauss*, New York: Anchor, pp. 169-94.

Lifton, Robert Jay (1961), *Thought Reform and the Psychology of Totalism*, New York: W. W. Norton.

Lukács, Georg (1971), *History and Class Consciousness*, Cambridge: MIT Press.

Mannheim, Karl (1936), *Ideology and Utopia*, New York: Harcourt, Brace & World.

Marcuse, Herbert (1964), *One-Dimensional Man*, Boston: Beacon Press.

Mehan, Hugh (1979), *Learning Lessons*, Cambridge: Harvard University Press.

Noble, David (1977), *America by Design*, New York: Alfred A. Knopf.

Pinar, William F. (1979), 'The Abstract and the Concrete in Curriculum Theorizing,' unpubished MS. Graduate School of Education and Human Development, University of Rochester.

Reininger, Meredith E. (1979), 'An Historical Overview of Central School's English Curriculum,' unpublished paper, Graduate School of Education and Human Development, University of Rochester.

Taxel, Joel (1980), 'The Depiction of the American Revolution in Children's Fiction: A Study in the Sociology of School Knowledge,' PhD dissertation, University of Wisconsin.

Taylor, Deborah T. (1979), 'Science, History, and Inquiry Curricula,' unpublished paper, Graduate School of Education and Human Development, University of Rochester.

Turner, Ralph H. (1976), 'The Real Self: From Institution to Impulse,' *American Journal of Sociology* 81 (March), 989-1014.

Waxman, Barbara (1980), 'Children's Understanding of Literature,' unpublished MS. Graduate School of Education and Human Development, University of Rochester.

Wexler, Philip (1976), *The Sociology of Education: Beyond Equality*, Indianapolis: Bobbs-Merrill.

Wexler, Philip (1977), 'Comment on Ralph Turner's, "The Real Self: From Institution to Impulse,"' *American Journal of Sociology*, 83 (July), 178-85.

Wexler, Philip (1979), 'Educational Change and Social Contradiction: An Example,' *Comparative Education Review* 23 (July), 240-55.

Wexler, Philip, (1980), 'Commodification, Self and Social Psychology,' *Social Text* (in press).

Whitley, R. D. (1974), *Social Processes of Scientific Development*, London: Routledge & Kegan Paul.

Willis, Paul (1977), *Learning to Labour: How Working Class Kids Get Working Class Jobs*, Farnborough, England: Saxon House.

Wright, Will (1975), *Six Guns and Society: A Structural Study of the Western*, Berkeley: University of California Press.

Young, Robert (1973), 'The Historiographic and Ideological Contents of the Nineteenth Century Debate on Man's Place in Nature,' in Mikulas Teich and Robert Young (eds), *Changing Perspectives in the History of Science: Essays in Honour of Joseph Needham*, London: Heinemann, pp. 344-438.

Chapter 10

Codes, modalities and the process of cultural reproduction:

a model

Basil Bernstein

Foreword

This paper follows closely the analyses developed in part II of *Class, Codes and Control*, vol. III, revised edition, Routledge & Kegan Paul 1977, particularly chapter 8, 'Aspects of the relation between education and production'. Indeed this paper is a re-ordering, development and refinement of a model presented in Note 'c', and a further elaboration of Note 'a' to that paper.

Introduction

Class relations will be taken to refer to inequalities in the distribution of power and in principles of control between social groups which are realised in the creation, distribution, reproduction and legitimation of physical and symbolic values which have their source in the social division of labour. In terms of the particular problem of the relationships between class and the process of its cultural reproduction, as developed in this thesis, what has to be shown is *how* class regulation of the distribution of power *and* of principles of control generates, distributes, reproduces and legitimates dominating and dominated principles regulating the relationships within and between social groups and, so, forms of consciousness. What we are asking here is how the distribution of power and principles of control are transformed, at the level of the subject, into different, invidiously related, organising principles, in such a way so as *both* to position subjects and to create the possibility of change in such positioning. The broad answer given by this thesis is that class relations, generate, distribute, reproduce and legitimate, distinctive forms of communication, which transmit dominating and dominated codes; and that subjects are differentially positioned by these codes in the process of their acquisition. Positioning is used here to refer to the establishing of a specific relation to other subjects *and to* the creating of specific relationships within subjects *In general*, from this point of view, codes are culturally determined positioning devices. More specifically, class regulated codes position subjects with respect to dominating and dominated form of communication *and* to the relationships between them. Ideology is constituted, through and in, such positioning. From this perspective ideology inheres in and regulates *modes of relation*. Ideology is not so much a content but a *mode of relation for the realising of contents*. The skeleton of the thesis can now be exposed diagrammatically (Figure 10.1).

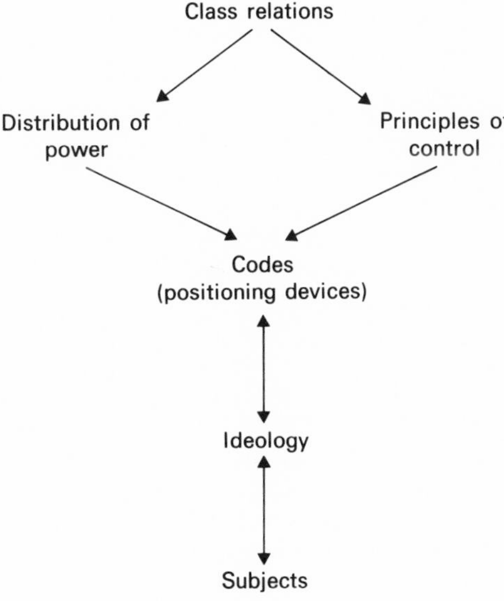

Figure 10.1

Codes – general

The first step towards filling out the entailed relationships in Figure 10.1 is to define codes, and the second step will be to derive from that definition propositions which will facilitate the defining of *specific* codes. In the postscript to *Class, Codes and Control* vol. I, revised edition 1971, there are a series of definitions of code which represent the evolution of the concept. Basically there has been a movement from the giving of definitions in terms of linguistic indices to definitions in terms of their underlying semantic. In both cases the underlying semantic was considered to be the regulator of *specific* linguistic realisations. Specific linguistic usages were taken in the earlier definitions as indices of a specific *semantic* organisation. The process of giving *explicit primacy* to the semantic systems is continued here. We shall now give the general definition of code.

A code is a regulative principle, tacitly acquired, which selects and integrates:

(a)	relevant meanings	meanings
(b)	form of their realisation	realisations
(c)	evoking contexts	contexts

(1) It follows from this definition that the unit for the analysis of codes is not an abstracted utterance nor a single context but relationships *between* contexts. Code is a regulator of the relationships *between* contexts and, through that relationship, a regulator of the relationships *within* contexts. What counts as a context depends not upon relationships *within*, but *relationships between*, contexts. The latter relationships, *between*, create boundary markers whereby specific contexts are distinguished by their specialised meanings and realisations. Thus if code is the regulator of the relationships *between* contexts *and* through that, the regulator of the relationships *within* contexts, then code must generate principles for *distinguishing* between contexts and principles for the *creation and production* of the specialised relationships within a context. We have previously called these principles, respectively, ground rules and performance rules.[1] However, in order to avoid confusion and irrelevant associations, the names of these two sets of rules will here be changed to *recognition rules* and *realisation rules*. Recognition rules create the means of distinguishing between and so *recognising* the speciality which constitutes a context and *realisation* rules regulate the creation *and* production of specialised relationships internal to that context. At the level of the subject, differences in code entail differences in recognition and realisation rules. Later in this essay we shall be concerned to explicate *how* code generates recognition and realisation rules.

(2) It follows from the definition that if code selects and integrates relevant meanings then code presupposes a concept of irrelevant or illegitimate meanings; that if code selects forms of realisation, then

code presupposes a concept of inappropriate or illegitimate forms of realisation; that if code regulates evoking contexts, then again this implies a concept of inappropriate, illegitimate contexts. The concept of code is inseparable from concepts of legitimate and illegitimate communications and thus it presupposes a hierarchy in forms of communications and in their demarcation and criteria (see note I; app.1).

Specific codes

The first step towards writing specific codes will require a rewriting of the original definitions so that it is possible to make specific empirical relationships. The rewriting will also make explicit the causal chain of relevant meanings, realisations, context. *Relevant meanings* (a) will be rewritten as *orientations to meanings*. (Orientations to meaning may be glossed as privileged/privileging referential relations.) *Forms of realisation* (b) will be rewritten as *textual productions*. *Evoking contexts* (c) will be rewritten as *specialised interactional practices*. Thus we now obtain the following causal chain. The features which create the speciality of the interactional practice (that is, the *form* of the social relationship) regulate orientation to meanings, and the latter generate through *selection* specific textual productions.[2] From this perspective, the specific text is but a transformation of the specialised interactional practice; the text is the form of the social relationships made visible, palpable, material. It should be possible to recover the original specialised interactional practice from an analysis of its text(s) in its context. Further, the selective creation, production and changing of texts is the means whereby the positioning of subjects is revealed, reproduced and changed. We can now fill in a little more detail in the inner structure of the thesis which is shown in Figure 10.2. What is required is to show the means whereby it is possible to perform the following transformations:

(1) Class relations and positioning (via power and control)
(2) Positioning and codes
(3) Codes and communication

If such transformations can be accomplished then the invisible can be recovered from the visible.

Elaborated and restricted codes

(a) Orientations
(b) Location

(c) Distribution
(d) Realisations

First we shall start by examining 'orientations to meanings' remembering that these look backward to specialised interactional practices and look forward to textual productions. Our first approach is to attempt to recover specialised interactional practices from orientations to meaning. We shall then try to account for (b) and (c) – the conditions for the *location* and *distribution* of such orientations.

We shall begin with a brief description of an enquiry into the social basis of classifications carried out by the Sociological Research Unit[3] (Holland 1980). The SRU was concerned to create a means whereby it would be possible to discover children's orientation to principles of classification and the means of their change. The sample consisted of thirty middle-class boys and girls and thirty lower-working-class boys and girls aged eight *and* eleven. We wished to use as the basis for classification, materials which would be equally familiar to all the children, although we expected the *reading* of the materials in the experimental context would be different, according to the class background of the children. The children were presented with coloured pictures of food, for example, bread, cheese, bacon, hamburger, fish fingers, sardines, soup, butter, several vegetables, etc. Many of these items the children would have eaten in their lunch at school as the majority of primary school children at the time of the experiment ate their lunch at school. Although the *individual food items* would be a common experience for all children, clearly their grouping in *specific* dishes is likely to vary between the classes, and the relation between dishes is also likely to vary. Further the frequency of certain groupings is likely to vary between the social classes, and the social context of the meal would be yet another source of class variation between the children. In the first stages of the experiment we were concerned with the principle the children used when invited to make groups of the food items which they considered went together. Accordingly the children were asked 'Do you think you could put these together in groups? Do it any way you like. Just put together the ones that seem to go together. You don't have to use all of them if you don't want to'.

Then, after the children had made their groups, they were asked why they had made each group. It was possible for the children to give at least two broad principles for their groups. They could give a principle which had a direct relation to a specific, local, context of their lives and which took its significance from local activities and local meanings. In which case the classification would relate to everyday life in the family, for example, 'it's what we eat at home', 'what we have for

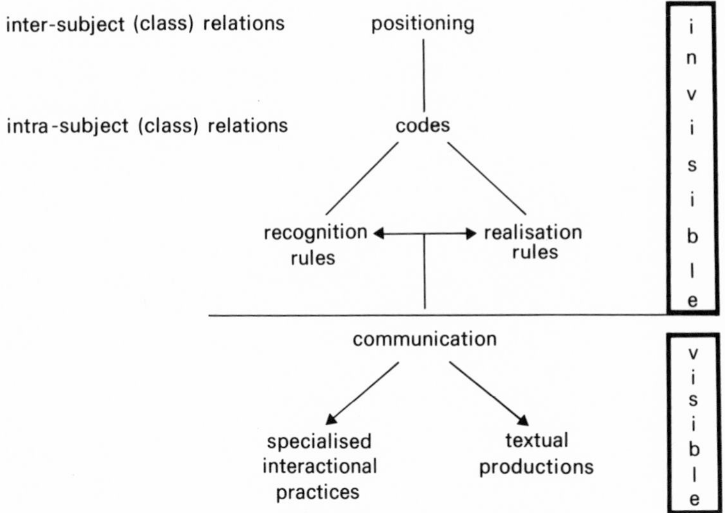

Figure 10.2

breakfast', 'what Mum makes', etc. In this case we propose that the principle of classification has a relatively *direct* relation to a specific local material base (a gloss on 'material base' will be given in the section (d) 'realisations'). However, the children could give a principle of classification which related *less* to the specific, local context of their everyday experience of food and its attendant social relations and practices, e.g. 'these come from the ground', 'these come from the sea', 'these all have butter in them', etc. It is not that the later examples do not relate to a material base, for they do, but the relationship is more indirect and less specific. We found as we expected that the modal principle of classification of the middle-class children was relatively independent of a specific context, whereas the modal principle of classification of the lower-working-class was relatively dependent upon a specific context.[4] In other words, the crucial difference between the groups of children lay in the relation of the classificatory principle to a material base; in one case the relation was direct and specific, in the other the relation was more indirect and less specific. The children were then asked 'Can you do it a second time? Can you try to put them together in a different way this time?' This time many middle-class children (a statistically significant number) switched their principle of classification and produced principles *similar to those produced by the lower-working-class children*, whereas the lower-working-class continued to use the principle they had used before. (However, almost one third of the lower-working-class changed their principle by the end of the experiment.) What is interesting is that the middle-class children showed that they held *two* principles *and* that these children held priority rules with respect to these principles such that those which had a relatively direct relation to a specific material base were given *second* that is, had a lower priority. Indeed we would argue, that in the first four minutes, the middle-class children created orientations to meanings based upon a *hierarchy of principles* each of which had a *different* relation to a material base, such that the principle which related to *a specific, local material base* in the *experimental context* was the dominated principle, that is, the *second*.

We have discussed the first section of the experiment in order to prepare the ground for defining the *location* of elaborated and restricted orientations to meaning. In previous papers we have located these orientations in different modes of social solidarity, mechanical and organic, which regulate different interactional practices and we argued that class relations regulated *how* these orientations were made available in formal education and how different class groups were differently placed with respect to their *formal* acquisition in the school. This formulation will now be modified, so as to make more explicit the power relationships under-pinning the location of these orientations and the distinctive feature of their materiality.

(1) General definition of the location of elaborated and restricted orientation

The simpler the social division of labour and the more *specific and local the relation between an agent and its material base*, then the more direct the relation between meanings and a specific material base *and* the more restricted the coding orientation.

The more complex the social division of labour, the less specific and local the relation between an agent and its material base, then the more indirect the relation between meanings and a specific material base and the more elaborated the coding orientation.

It is important to point out that in each case *we are regarding the social division of labour from the specific location of one of its agents*. For example, if one were a peasant working on a sugar-cane plantation, then from the point of view of that peasant he/she would physically see himself/herself as part of a simple division of labour and such an agent's interactional practices would have as their centre of gravity interactions within a simple division of labour regulating practices with respect to a local, specific material base. Whereas in the case of the patron he (historically not *she*) would physically see himself as part of a complex division of labour which would include the total *local* division of labour of the plantation, the local market and circulation of capital, and which would also include national and international markets with their entailed capital circulations. The patron's centre of gravity would lie within a complex division of labour regulating practices with respect to a *generalised* material base.

Thus the most *primitive* conditions for *location* of coding orientations is given by the location of agents in the social division of labour. Different locations generate different interactional practices *which realise different relations to the material base* and so different coding orientations. At this point it is important to state that we are here stating the *location* of different coding orientations not their origins.[5]

(2) Distribution

The conditions for the distribution of coding orientations in this model are clear. If agents become specialised categories of the social division of labour, and their location is fixed and so non-transposable, then coding orientations become specialities of position within the social division of labour. The conditions for these conditions is the *principle of the social division of labour itself*. The group which dominates the principle of the social division of labour determines the extent to which positions in the social division of labour give access to specialised coding orientations. These coding orientations are in no sense inevitable consequences of any position. Coding orientations are not intrinsic to different positions. Whether they become so depends upon the distribution of power. Thus the distribution of *coding orientations* depends upon the distribution of power created by the principles regulating the social division of labour.

Performance: classification and framing

Introduction

In the following sections we shall be concerned to develop a model showing how the distribution of power and principles of control regulate the *realisations* of orientation to meaning. We shall be concerned to make explicit the modes of regulation of specialised interactional practice which define specific recognition and realisation rules. For only if these practices can be defined, can *specific* codes be determined. We have so far only indicated the location and distribution of elaborated and restricted orientations, which in our model have their origin in the class regulation of the principle of the social division of labour. This creates differential access to meanings having different degrees of dependency upon a specific material base. Thus access to orientations is regulated by the principle constituting the social division of labour of production which in turn directly transforms and reproduces differential orientations in the family. However, access to elaborated orientations is available through agencies of defence, challenge and opposition, for example, trade unions, political parties. The institutional availability, distribution and realisation of elaborated codes is established through the modality of education.[6] We see education as a fundamental reproducing and producing agency crucial to, but not in a close correspondence relation with, the class regulation of the mode of production, and crucial to the class regulation of modes of social control.

We shall develop a model for generating codes regulating the class production of physical resources and class reproduction and production of discursive resources.[7] The difference between physical and discursive resources does not lie in the materiality of one and the non-materiality of the other. Discourse as we shall see, has a material base, albeit it is less obvious and its relation to its materiality is more opaque. Despite differences in the dissimilarities of the realisations of production and education, the social basis of these realisations is structurally similar. In both cases (physical/discursive resources) we have a social division of labour with specialised categories of agents *and* their interrelations *together* with their social relations. The former consists of the *relations* between social categories (agents) and the latter consists of the *specific realisations* of these categories (*agents*), that is, their specific practices/activities. Thus, any production or reproduction has its social basis in *social categories* and *practices*. In the production of physical resources we have sets of differently specialised categories, with their sets of differently specialised practices, and in the production/reproduction of discursive resources we have sets of specialised categories (such as teachers), and sets of specialised practices (pedagogy). This can be illustrated with reference to a family, which is a primary discourse reproducing agency. Here the social division of labour is constituted by the category set of the kinship, whilst the social relations are the specific practices *between* the categories (for example, between parents, between parents and children, between children, between gender categories). We can apply the same analysis to a school. Here the basic social division of labour is constituted by the set of categories of transmitters (teachers) and the set of categories which constitute acquirers; the social relations refer to practices between transmitters *and* acquirers, and practices *between* transmitters and practices *between* acquirers.[8]

Classification and social division of labour

Basic to the mode of production and modality of education are categories and practices which are regulated by the principles of a social division of labour and its internal social relations. Practices are the realisation of categories. The form taken by these practices, that is, their degree of specificity, the extent to which practices are specialised to categories, depends entirely upon the relation *between* these categories. (Relation '*between*' regulates relation '*within*'.) Once the categories are specialised it necessarily follows that their realisation and their practices are also specialised. The practice can be regarded as the 'message' of the category and *means of its acquisition*. At this stage we shall simply state that specialised categories necessarily entail specialised 'voices', but we are as yet in no position to say anything about what is 'voiced'. We shall disconnect 'voice' from 'message'. For purposes of exposition, we shall disconnect our analysis of the principles regulating the relation between categories, from principles regulating their associated practices. We shall see later that there are also good analytic reasons for making such a separation. If categories either of agents or discourse are specialised, then each category necessarily has its own specific identity and its own specific boundaries. The speciality of each category is created, maintained and reproduced *only* if the relations *between* the categories of which a given category is a member, is preserved. What is to be preserved? – *The insulation between the categories*. It is the strength of the insulation which creates a space in which a category can become specific. If a category wishes to increase its specificity, it has to appropriate the *means* to produce the necessary insulation, which is the prior condition to its appropriating specificity. The stronger the insulation between categories, then the stronger the boundary between one category and another and the more defined is the space that any category occupies, and to which it is specialised. It follows that as the strength of the insulation between categories varies, so will the categories vary in their relation to each other and so will their space, their identity and 'voice'. Thus the *degree of insulation* is a crucial regulator of the relations between categories and the specificity of their 'voices'.[9] We can begin to see that the degree of insulation regulates criteria of demarcation between categories and so the *rules of their recognition*.

We are now in a position to state the fundamental principle regulating the relations between categories, that is, the fundamental principle regulating the social division of labour of production/reproduction. Different degrees of insulation between categories create different principles of the relations between categories and so different principles of the social division of labour.[10] If there is strong insulation between categories then we shall say that there is a principle of strong classification, whereas if there is weak insulation between categories we shall say that this gives rise to a principle of weak classification. (Classification refers to the relations *between* categories, not to *what* is classified.) Any change in the principle of the classification will require a change in the degree of insulation. Alternatively, the maintenance of a given principle depends upon preserving the strength of the insulation. In order for insulations to be maintained there must be insulation maintainers (and a consequent division of labour, of reproducers, repairers and surveyors) who work at constituting, sharpening, clarifying, repairing, defending boundaries. The principle of the classification is created, maintained, reproduced and legitimated by insulation maintenance. Any attempt to change the classification necessarily involves a change in the degree of insulation between categories, which in itself will provoke the insulation maintainers (reproducers, repairers, surveyors) to restore the principle of the classification and themselves as the dominating agents. In order for this to be accomplished the insulation maintainers must have power and the conditions to exert it. Thus insulation presupposes *relations of power* for its creation, reproduction and legitimation.

We have shown, formally, that power relations regulate principles of classification, by preserving or changing degrees of insulations between categories. In terms of our earlier analysis, power relationships establish the 'voice' of a category (subject/discourse) but *not* the 'message' (the practice). Power relations, in establishing the 'voice' of a category, necessarily establish demarcation markers and recognition procedures/rules. *Power relations position subjects through the principles of the classifications they establish*. If power relations are regulated by class relations then class relations position subjects through the principles of classification they establish.

We can give examples of the relations between power, classification and 'voice' by examining the division of labour according to gender. When this division of labour generates strong classification then there is a strong insulation between each category and each category has its own specialised 'voice' and necessarily 'voice' will be specialised to gender. Further any attempt to weaken the classification, that is to reduce the insulation so as to change 'voice' (discourse), will provoke the power relationship to re-establish the relations between gender categories by restoring the insulation.

We can see in this example another implication of insulation. Insulations are intervals, breaks, de-locations, which establish categories of similarity and difference; the equal and the unequal; punctuations written by power relations which establish as the order of things distinct subjects through distinct voices. Indeed, insulation is the means whereby the cultural is transformed into the natural, the contingent into the necessary, the past into the present, the present into the future. In Bourdieu's terms, symbolic violence is accomplished *not* by communication but by *de-locations which regulate differences between voices*. In as much as the insulation of strong classification of gender categories produces an arbitrary (contingent) specialisation of gender 'voices', it has created imaginary subjects whose voices are experienced as real, as validating and constituting of the specialised category.[11] Here the insulation attempts to suppress the arbitrariness of the principle of classification, by suppressing the contradictions and dilemmas which inhere in the very principle of the classification. We can see that power relations can accomplish their reproduction by establishing a principle of classification which suppresses its own contradictions and dilemmas through the insulation it creates, maintains and legitimates.

We can take another example from education. We can regard the social division of labour of a school to be composed of categories of agents (transmitters and acquirers) and categories of discourses ('voices'). If the coding principle is one of strong classification, then there is strong insulation between educational discourse ('voice') and non-educational discourse ('voices'). Discourses are strongly insulated from each other, each with their own specialised 'voice' so that transmitters and acquirers become *specialised categories* with *specialised 'voices'*. Within the category transmitter there are various 'sub-voices' and within the category acquirer there are various 'sub-voices'; age, gender, 'ability', ethnic. In the process of acquiring the demarcation markers of categories (agents/discourse), the acquirer is constituted as a specialised category with variable sub-sets of voices depending upon age, gender, 'ability', ethnicity. In the same way that a strong classification of gender attempts to justify itself in terms of its being a natural, non-arbitrary order, so the strong classification of educational agents/discourse attempts to justify itself in terms of a 'natural order' within discourse (logical), a 'natural order' of acquisition (biological), a 'natural order' of the relation between educational and non-educational discourse (specialised/lay).

It could be argued that whereas the principle of the classification of gender categories and that of the categories of the mode of production have an arbitrary base, the principle of the classification of discourse ('voices') of education, derives from features *intrinsic* to the specialised discourse and is therefore non-arbitrary. This may be the case. We need, however, to distinguish between the distinctive features of a form of discourse which give it its speciality *and* the social division of labour created for its transmission and reproduction, and it is the *latter* which is the object of our concern.

From the point of view of the social division of labour of reproduction, we can distinguish the following classificatory features each constituted by its own arbitrary insulation features and power relations:

(1) Extra-discourse relations of education

Educational discourse as a whole, may be strongly or weakly insulated from non-educational discourse.

(2) Intra-discourse relations of education

Administrative context

(a) Strong insulation between agents and strong insulation between discourse. In this situation agents and discourses are specialised to departments which are stongly insulated from each other.
(b) Insulation between discourses but not between agents. Here agents and discourses are not specialised to departments but share a common administrative context.

(3) Transmission context

(a) Educational discourses may be related to each other in the process of transmission whilst retaining their specific distinguishing features. Here discourse is *subordinate to principles of relation* within the total discursive field and there can be variation in the number of discourses so related.

(4) System context

Education may be wholly subordinate to the agencies of the State or it may be accorded a relatively autonomous space with respect to discursive areas and practices.

We can, therefore, distinguish classificatory principles between the category of educational discourse and the category of non-educational discourse, classificatory principles internal to educational discourse, and classificatory principles regulating the context of the system. In all of the above (1), (2), (3), (4), the question of the definition of discourse in terms of internal criteria is not of issue. What is of issue, is the social basis of the insulation, the principle(s) of classification created by the insulation and the power relations which maintain insulations (whatever their degree) and so the principle of the classification.

It may well be useful to make explicit the language used to discuss reproduction/production. We have earlier argued that production and reproduction have their social basis in categories and practices; that categories are constituted by the social division of labour and that practices are constituted by social relations *within* production/reproduction; that categories constitute 'voices'; practices constitute their 'message'; 'message' is dependent upon 'voice'; the subject is a dialectical relation between voice and message. In this section we have dealt with the relation between the social division of labour, classification and 'voice'. Our view is that the social division of labour is a relation between categories established by a principle of classification. The principle of classification establishes the degree of specificity of the 'voices' of the categories through the insulation it establishes. The insulations are the de-locations produced by the distribution of power and through which power relations are given their voice. The subject is established by the silence through which power speaks.

Classification, voice reproduction and acquisition

We can present in diagrammatic form the structure of the arguments we have so far offered in our explication of the realisation rules for the defining of specific codes. The sets of relationships displayed in Figure 10.3 are external to the subject and initially position the subject with respect to the social division of labour. The positioning of the subject creates the 'voice' of the subject but *not* the specific message. The 'voice' sets the *limits* on what can be a legitimate message. To create a message beyond these limits is to change 'voice'. Such a change entails changing the degree of insulation which initially was the condition for the speciality of the original 'voice'. A change in the insulation produces a change in the principle of the classification, which in turn indexes a change in the social division of labour, which will then move its dominating categories (agents) to exert their power through the hierarchy(ies) they regulate to induce a return to the original 'voice'. We have also argued for a further set of relationships which are the conditions for the *acquisition* of the 'voice' by the subject. We shall give those in Figure 10.4.

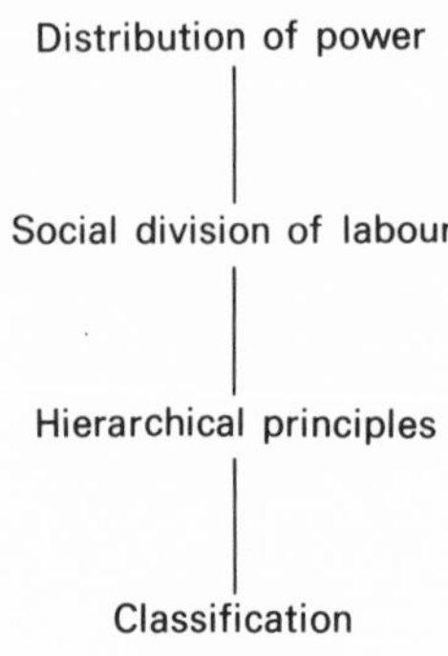

Figure 10.3

The principle of the classification generates through its insulations the speciality of the categories *and* the marking of that speciality. The marking of the categories, from the point of view of the acquiring subject, provide a set of demarcation criteria for recognising the categories in the variety of their presentations. The sets of demarcation criteria provide a basis for the subject to infer recognition rules. The *recognition rules* regulate what goes with what; *what meanings may be legitimately put together*, what referential relations are privileged/privileging. The recognition rules regulate the principles for the generating of legitimate meaning and in so doing create what we have called the *syntax of generation* of meaning. We can now trace a relation between the distribution of power external to the subject and the syntax of generation internal to the subject via the classificatory principle of the social division of labour. The subject creates, maintains, reproduces and legitimises the *distribution of power* through the development and establishing of the syntax of generation. This syntax

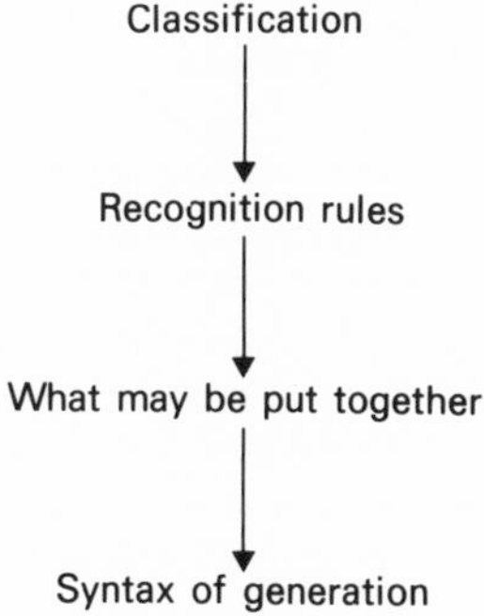

Figure 10.4

is tacitly acquired, in the sense that it develops through inferences the subject makes from the surface features of her/his on-going everyday inter-actions. We shall refer to this process as tacit practice. We can distinguish two modalities of tacit practice generated by two related arbitrary classificatory principles.

(1) The modality of culture

Every culture specialises principles for the creation of a specific reality through its distinctive classificatory principles and, in so doing, necessarily constructs a set of procedures, practices, and relations from a range of such sets. As a consequence, each modality can be regarded as an arbitrary angling of a potential reality. There may well be features in common to *modalities of culture* which have their source in general features of the cultural subject (see app. 2).

(2) Modalities within culture

Within each culture there are classificatory principles which are generated by the *specific* form of the social division of labour, produced and reproduced by the distribution of power, regulating the relations between its categories (agents) which establish its distinctive classificatory principles. We are here concerned with classificatory principles regulating the social division of labour for the production and reproduction of physical and discursive resources. In this lies the source of a second arbitrary order.

Both modalities, (of and within culture), can be, and have been, regarded as ideological representations.[12] A crucial question is the nature of the dynamic relations between them. This question cannot be developed here. Modality *within* culture, unlike the modality *of* culture, does not so much have its source in general features of the cultural subject, except in the last instance, but in a specific distribution of power which creates, maintains, reproduces and legitimates a specific syntax of generation of meaning. We shall assert that, in its tacit acquisition, not only are dominating and dominated 'voices' produced, but equally an oppositional 'yet to be voiced', whose syntax is constituted by *insulations* created by the classificatory principle. We have argued that these insulations necessary for the preservation of the classificatory principle and the dominant *or* dominating order

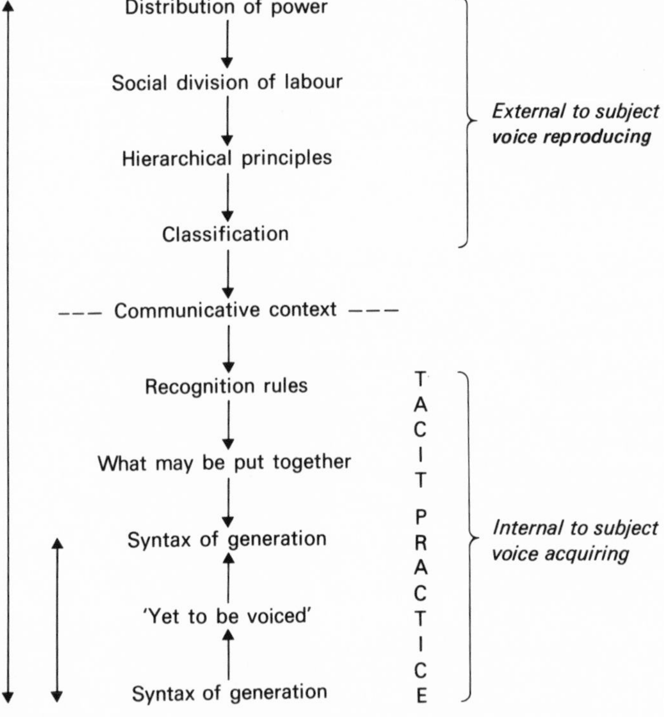

Figure 10.5

it legitimates, suppress potential cleavages, contradictions and dilemmas. The latter are a source of change in 'voice' but, in an important sense, they can only be the source of a change in 'voice' if they are already a feature of that 'voice'. We shall argue that these features are the 'unvoiced', 'yet to be voiced' components of the 'voice' and constitute a stratum of tacit practice.

We do not want to give the impression that the stratum of tacit practice 'yet to be voiced' and its underlying condensed syntax necessarily creates in each subject a potential theory of change. It should, however, provide a potential source of the arbitrary nature of the dominating classificatory principles and the power relations which speak through them. From this point of view it could provide the basis for anomie and so could speak to either order or change, or to the tension of their relations. It may well be that for those dominating the power relations it would speak to anomie, whereas for those dominated it may well speak to change. The tension between order and change may be the distinguishing feature of the new agents of symbolic control.[13]

We can extend our diagrammatic illustration of our argument with reference to classification, 'voice' production and acquisition (see Figure 10.5).

Summary

It may be useful at this stage to indicate what has been so far proposed. In order to specify specific codes, we are required to show how the distribution of power and principle of control are realised in the relationship within and between, meanings, realisation and contexts. We rewrote the latter as interactional practices, orientation to meanings (privileged and privileging referential relations) and textual productions. Orientation to meanings (privileged and privileging referential relations) are seen as generated by different locations within the social division of labour of the production of physical resources (relations between dominant and dominated locations). *Realisation* of these meanings are specified in terms of specialised interactional practices, i.e., the categories and social relations *within* production. It was argued that the codes of education consist of elaborated orientations to meanings because of the indirect relation of these meanings to a *specific material base*. The *realisation* of these meanings is considered to be a function of the *specific* form taken by the interactional practices of education. The next step involved an analysis of interactional practices. Our analysis distinguished two crucial features, a category relation and a message. We considered that the category relation is created by the principle of the relation between categories, a classificatory principle, which in turn, is regulated by the social division of labour constituted by a given distribution of power. We then examined the relation between the classificatory principle and 'voice' and, in this way, we examined interactional practices in terms of 'voices'. We then made explicit the relations between the classificatory principle, 'voice', recognition rules, syntax of generation, and the distribution of power. In other words we specified a relation between *relations between categories* and *that which it is legitimate to mean*. We have as yet not specified the regulation upon *the making public of this meaning*. We have not yet analysed *how* what it is legitimate to mean comes to form a *specific message*. It is essentially through this specific message that the specific code is acquired. The specific message is the form of the socialisation into the code. Briefly, the code regulates the *what* and *how* of meanings: what meanings may legitimately be put together *and* how these meanings may be legitimately realised. We have so far concentrated upon the 'what', and shown the relationship between the distribution of power and the regulation of the 'what' (see Figure 10.5). We shall now turn to the analysis of the regulation of the 'how', that is, to the relationships between principles of control and specific 'hows'. Here we shall be concerned with social relations, and their regulation of 'message' and its contextualisation.

As we are going to discuss 'message' with reference to the primary acquisition of discursive resources, we shall be referring to the social relations within reproduction, that is, to pedagogical relations essentially in education. However, we can extend the model to consider the social relations within production and the principles of their realisation, that is, the message. We have in fact carried out such an analysis in note 3, but we suggest that it is read after the completion of the discussion of framing.

Social relations, practice and message

In the previous section we discussed the relations between the distribution of power, the social division of labour, the principle of its classification, the degree of specificity of categories, 'voice', recognition rules and the syntax of generation of privileged and privileging relations. We shall now turn to an analysis of social relations, practices, and 'message'. There are difficulties in this discussion because 'message' is both dependent on 'voice' and yet is the potential instrument of change of voice.

'Message' is dependent upon 'voice', for the latter limits the range of the legitimate potential of the message. Yet the cleavages, contradictions, and dilemmas, which are latent in the 'voice' are a potential of the realisation of the message. Put in a less metaphoric way, the principle of the social division of labour necessarily limits the *realisation* of its practices, yet the practices contain the possibility of change in the social division of labour and thus of their own change. The dynamic potential of the relation between 'voice' and 'message', between social categories and practices, between the social division of labour and its social relations, should be born in mind throughout the subsequent analysis. Empirically it is not possible to separate out 'voice' from 'message'. 'Voice', implicitly or explicitly, is always announced, realised in 'message'. In an important sense the *classificatory principle* is continuously present in every pedagogical relation. All the 'voices' are invisibly present in any one 'voice'. Socialisation into *one* 'voiced-message' involves socialisation into all, that is, into the principle of the classification.

Crucial to our perspective here is the analytic distinction between power and control; that is, between what is to be reproduced *and* the form of its acquisition. The latter directs our attention to the specific practices between transmitters and acquirers which create the local context of reproduction. Social relations refer to the specific practices regulating the relationships between transmitters and acquirers which constitute the context of acquisition. Essentially these social relations regulate the form of the pedagogic practice, and so the specific category-message. *The fundamental message of a pedagogic practice is the rule for legitimate communication.* Thus the social relations within reproduction control principles of communication, and in so doing, regulate what we shall call the communicative context.

The communicative context

If the degree of insulation is the crucial feature of the classificatory principle generated by the social division of labour, then the *form* of the communicative context is the crucial feature generated by their social relations, through the pedagogic practices which they regulate. These practices constitute, relate and regulate the possibilities of *two* communicational principles.

(a) Interactional:

This principle regulates the selection, organisation (sequencing), and pacing of communication – oral/written/visual – together with the position, posture, and dress of the communicants.

(b) Locational:

This principle regulates physical location and the form of its realisation, that is, the range of objects and their attributes, their relation to each other and the space in which they are constituted.

Basically, these two principles represent the spatial and temporal features of the communicative context; the spatial feature is given by the locational principle, and the temporal feature is given by the interactional principle. We may well find that under certain conditions these two features are tied to each other in a one-to-one figure/ground relation, for example, teacher/school, teacher/class, but this need not necessarily be the case. The interactional features may not be tied to a particular space. If we consider parents/children the interactional feature is not necessarily tied to a particular space or sub-space. Thus there is a classificatory regulation of the communicative context. The stronger the tie between the temporal (interactional) and spatial (locational) features of the communicative context, the stronger will be its classification. The stronger its classification, the more likely that the array of objects, attributes and their relation within the communicative context stand in a fixed relation to each other and so are specialised to that context.

We should note also that the possibilities of a communicative context include the marking of the relation between the locational and interactional features. It is possible for a specific practice to mark the locational feature more strongly than the interactional, or vice versa.

The *interactional principle* is the dominating feature of the communicative context, for it is this principle which establishes, relates, regulates and *changes* the possibilities of the two principles.

We can see how recognition rules and realisation rules are features of the communicative context. The classificatory principle, through its insulations, constitutes the degree of speciality of the communicative context, and so provides the limits of its legitimate potential. In so doing, the classificatory principle creates *specific recognition rules*. The *interactional* principle *within* the communicative context, creates the specific message; that is, the specific rules for generating what counts as legitimate communication/discourse and so the range of its possible texts. The interactional principle creates the specific realisation rules. Thus we can say that the communicative context provides access to both recognition and realisation rules, or more explicitly and more generally, the social relations, through their regulation of the communicative context, provide access to recognition and realisation rules. Realisation rules, which establish what counts as a legitimate text, presuppose and are limited by, recognition rules. Classificatory principles determine the limits and legitimate potential of communicative principles and are reproduced through them. Yet the 'message' is also the means of change of 'voice' and so of itself. In general, social relations, although initially dominated by the classificatory principle, are also the means of change of principle.

Framing

We have so far discussed the inter-relations between social relations, principles of communication, and the communicative context. We now need to distinguish between various forms of social relations and so various forms of the principles of communication. We shall use the concept of 'framing' to describe these variations. *Framing* stands in the same relation to *principle of communication*, as *classification* stands in relation to the *principles of the relation between categories*. In the same way as relations between categories can be governed by strong or weak classification, so principles of communication can be governed by strong or weak framing. From this point of view, it does not make sense to talk about weak or strong principles of communication. Principles of communication are to varying degrees acquired, explored, resisted, challenged, and their vicissitudes are particular to a principle. *Control* is always present, *whatever the principle*. What varies is the *form* the control takes. The *form* of control is described here in terms of its framing.

Changes or variations in the classificatory principle produce changes or variations in the '*voices*' of categories; changes or variations in framing produce changes or variations in '*message*'; changes or variations in framing produce variations or changes in *pedagogic practices*, which in turn, produce changes or variations in *principles of communication* (temporal and spatial – interactional/locational) and so changes or variations in the communicative context; variations or changes in framing produces variations or changes in the rules regulating what counts as legitimate communication/discourse and its possible texts. In the same way that the distribution of power regulates the classificatory principle via the social division of labour, so principles of control regulate framing via its social relations.

Definition of framing

Framing refers to the principle regulating the communicative practices of the social relations within the reproduction of discursive resources; that is, between transmitters and acquirers. Where framing is strong, the transmitter explicitly regulates the *distinguishing features* of the interactional and locational principles which constitute the communicative context. Where framing is weak, the acquirer has a greater degree of regulation over the distinguishing features of the interactional and locational principles which constitute the communicative context. (This may be more apparent than real.)

Variations in the degree, and change, of framing regulate variations and change in realisation rules. In order to give a more precise definition of framing, we need to make explicit the phrase 'the distinguishing features of the communicative context'. These distinguishing features will vary according to whether the communicative context is generating physical or discursive resources (see app. 3). If it is the latter, then the distinguishing features would be constituted by:
the *selection*, *organisation* (sequencing) *pacing*, of the communication and the position, posture and dress of the communicants, *together with the features of the physical location.*

Strong framing:

The transmitter controls the selection, organisation, pacing, and the position, posture and dress and the features of the space.

Weak framing:

The acquirer has more control over selection, organisation, pacing and the position, posture and dress and the features of the space.

We can distinguish at a greater level of delicacy between the *internal* values of the strength of framing (F(i)) and the *external* values of the strength of framing (F(e)). If we consider a school where F(e) is strong, then the transmitter regulates what features of non-school communication and practice can be realised within the school's specific pedagogic context, such as the classroom or equivalent F(i). Where F(e) is weak, then the acquirer has more regulation over what features of *non-school communication and practice* may be realised within the classroom or equivalent F(i). It is possible for F(e) to be weak and F(i) still to be relatively strong. Further the relations between F(i) and F(e) may change over the time-span of the transmission. When the acquirers are young in age F(e) may be relatively weak, whereas with advancing age F(e) may increase in strength for one group of acquirers such as the successful, whereas F(e) may be weakened or remain weak for the unsuccessful (social education, community projects, education for work, etc.). We can summarise our discussion in Figure 10.6.

In the previous section devoted to classification, 'voice' reproduction, and acquisition, we indicated in Figure 10.5 in setting out the ordering of those relations, a level of relation we called the 'yet to be voiced', which we argued was a potential of the contradictions, cleavages, and dilemmas generated by the classificatory principle itself. In Figure 10.6, we have distinguished a level of relation we have called the 'yet to be realised', which is a potential message of the 'yet to be voiced'. It is a matter of some importance to distinguish between the *reactions to, or the challenge of, the realisation rule* imposed by a given framing *and* the level we have called the 'yet to be realised'.

Any framing carries with it the procedures of its disturbance and challenge. Consider an elaborated code with values +C +F, that is, realised in a communicative context of a secondary school, in which the pedagogical relations are between a teacher and a class of pupils who have been disabled by the code. The strategies for challenging the code are given by the code's principles. If the pupils are to challenge the code effectively this cannot be done by *one* pupil. It requires changing the basic unit of acquisition, which is that of an isolated, privatised, competitive pupil, to communal, non-competitive, classroom relations. There must be a change in the pupils' principles of social integration. Given this change then the new group can substitute its own norm of production for that of the teacher's norms. The group can now impose its own realisation rules. These may well include sabotaging the means of the pedagogy, subverting its rules, assuming aggressive postures. These disturbances and challenges are resistances called out by the specific code; they do not *necessarily* index a move even to de-classify, let alone to re-classify. Challenge of, or resistance to, the framing of pedagogic practice by transmitters *or* acquirers may be *within* the terms of the classificatory principles.

The level of tacit practice we have called 'yet to be realised' operates

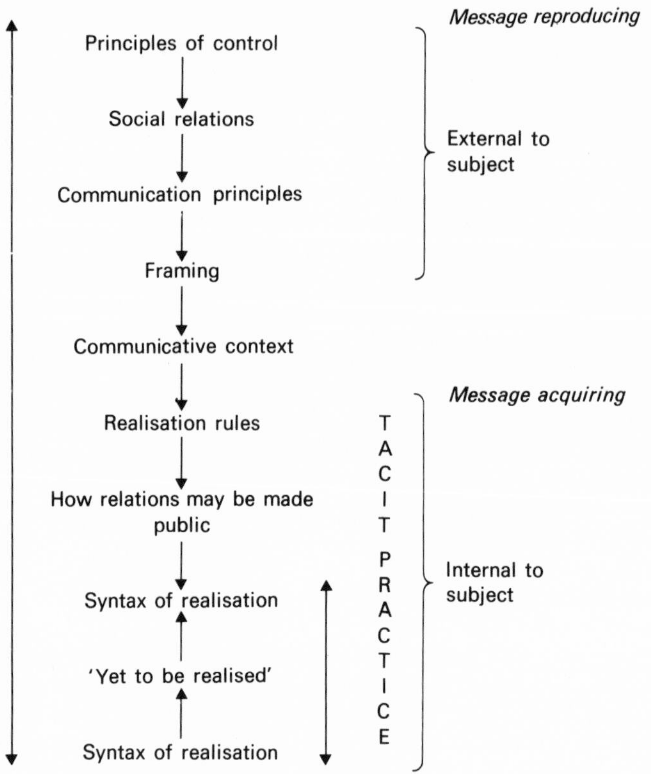

Figure 10.6

at a deeper level. It is the 'message' of the 'yet to be voiced'. The 'yet to be voiced' is a potential answer to the distribution of power and varies with its principles; the 'yet to be realised' is a potential answer to the principles of control and varies with those principles. Just as the classificatory principle may be realised by, and acquired through different principles of communication ('message') so the 'yet to be voiced' may be realised through different principles of communication ('message'). Its 'message' is a function of the dominating principle of control, acting through a specific framing. What are the realisations of the 'yet to be realised'? The realisations, at this level, are not the product of a process of selection and orderings which can be consciously varied; they are unsolicited and gratuitous and take the form of metaphors of new possibilities. To say this is to say that they are unregulated, for they are the potential of a *code* and of its change or variation.

We have distinguished two levels of tacit practices:

(1) A level which is subject to conscious selection and ordering within the possibilities of a given syntax of generation and realisation.
(2) A level which is not subject to conscious selection and orderings but which is derivable from the first level.

These two levels are similar to the distinction between conscious and preconscious. It might be possible to show the relation between the levels of tacit practice and that of unconscious practice through the writings of Lacan (see Figure 10.7).

Specific codes and their modalities

We began this analysis with the statement that to write specific codes it is necessary to state orientation and specific realisation conditions. In class societies *in general*, the distribution of orientations (elaborated/restricted) is created and legitimised by the social division of labour of the mode of production and transferred to the family. However, such transfer is not necessarily automatic, as it may be transposed by countervailing (oppositional) agencies arising out of the social matrix of the mode of production (trade unions, political parties) *and* mediations of particular families. Whilst the distribution of power creates the strength of the classification between elaborated and restricted orientations, the principles of control regulate the realisations of these orientations, that is, the classification and framing values. From this point of view, dominating principles of control select classification and framing values, which will permit the reproduction of the distribution of power. These principles of control are dependent upon the principles of the forces of production (technology) and the principle by which agents relate to these forces, so as to constitute practices and interactions. Increasingly, the principles creating and legitimising forces and practices have their origin in education, in its productive, not reproductive levels. Education necessarily is predicated upon, *irrespective* of the dominating principles of a social formation elaborated orientations; but the dominating principle of the social

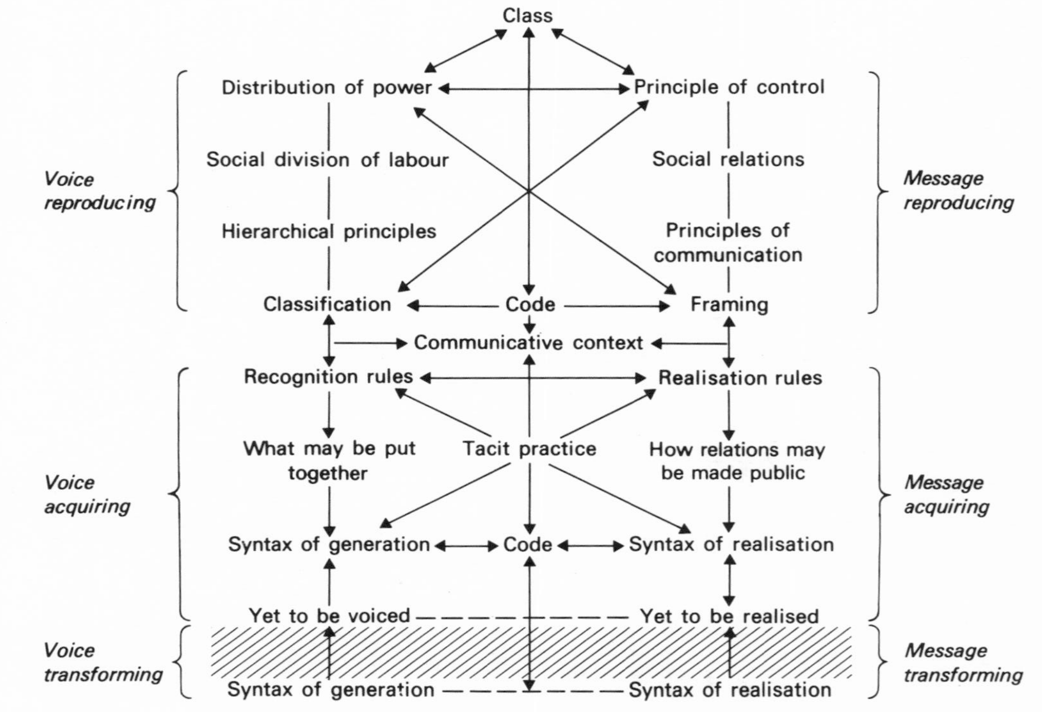
Class
Distribution of power
Principle of control
Social division of labour
Social relations
Voice reproducing
Message reproducing
Hierarchical principles
Principles of communication
Classification
Code
Framing
Communicative context
Recognition rules
Realisation rules
What may be put together
Tacit practice
How relations may be made public
Voice acquiring
Message acquiring
Syntax of generation
Code
Syntax of realisation
Yet to be voiced
Yet to be realised
Voice transforming
Message transforming
Syntax of generation
Syntax of realisation

Figure 10.7

formation regulates their realisations; that is the classification and framing values and so the code/codes (see app. 4).

On page 330 we have put together the two halves of our model which our exposition separated. The distribution of power and principle of control, are realised in the social division of labour and its social relations. These establish the classificatory and framing values, which define the mode of transmission/acquisition or practice in basic communicative contexts for the production of discursive and physical resources. The classificatory principles regulate recognition rules, what is legitimate to put together, and so what we have called the syntax for the generating of legitimate meaning. Framing principles regulate realisation rules, how relations may be made public and so what we have called the syntax of realisation. From this point of view, the distribution of power and principle of control translate into classificatory and framing principles, regulating the structure (organisation), interactions and communicative contexts of agencies for the production and reproduction of discursive and physical resources. What the subject acquires is classification and framing principles, which create for the subject, and *legitimise*, the speciality of his/her voice and message (see app. 5).

The unbroken vertical line of the model (Figure 10.7) shows the imposition of what is to be reproduced and the process of its acquisition. Codes enable subjects not only to read and create texts which are legitimately available to be so constructed, but also to read and create texts which are within the possibilities of the syntax of generation/realisation as potential orthodox/heterodox texts. The diagonal lines show the process of resistance, challenge or opposition. The shading indicates the process shaping the response to the cleavages, contradictions, and dilemmas suppressed by the insulations of the classification. We do not want to give the impression that we are operating with a theory of variation, resistance, and opposition which is based upon an isolated individual realisation. Of course, variation, resistance, challenge, opposition and struggle, arise out of the structural relations produced by class itself. We are concerned to show the regulations of its reading and readings.

We can now write specific codes regulating the reproduction/production of physical and discursive resources in terms of orientation to meanings and their realisations, created by specialised interactional practices constituting communicative contexts. Codes can be specified by the following formula:

$$\frac{O}{(\pm)\,C \quad F\,(\pm)^{i/e}}$$

where

O refers to orientation to meanings elaborated/restricted (privileged/ privileging referential relations)

C refers to the principle of classification

F refers to the principle of framing

(±) refers to the values of C & F with respect to strength (strong/weak)

i/e i refers to the *internal* values of F *within* a communicative context, for example, family, school and work.
e refers to the *external* values of F, that is the regulation on communicative relations *between* communicative contexts, for example, family/community and school, school and work.

We can talk about the *modality* of a code and its change. The modality of a code or its change is given by the values of classification and framing. The values of classification and framing can vary independently of each other. Any *one* set of values for classification and framing constitutes the modality of the code.

Change of code

A change of code involves a change in the strength of a *basic classification*. We consider that there are two basic classifications which may or may not be interrelated, in the sense that changing the value of one does not necessarily lead to changing the value of the other. We consider that the basic classificatory principle is created by the distribution of power – constituting, reproducing and legitimising the social division of labour of physical production. A change in this classificatory principle from strong to weak involves not a change in, but a change of, class relations. However, we must add immediately that, whilst not diminishing the significance of such a change, it would not, in itself, necessarily produce a change of institutionalised elaborated codes and therefore a change in the principle of cultural reproduction. In order (in the terms of this paper) for there to be a change in institutionalised elaborated codes and thus in the principles of cultural reproduction, then the classificatory relation between the category education and the category production must be fundamentally weakened. This is the necessary condition for weakening the second basic classification; that between mental and manual work. In class societies the strength of these two classifications are causally related. However, in societies dedicated to a change in the mode of production, there are few indeed which have even attempted to institutionalise a weakening of the classificatory relation between education and production. On the contrary, such societies are as pre-occupied as class societies with the *systemic* relations between education and production.[14]

Code modalities

Code modalities are essentially variations in the means and focii of symbolic control on the basis of a given distribution of power. Although modalities do not change fundamentally the principles of cultural reproduction or material production, their effects are, on the whole, confined to changes in the process whereby the principle is transmitted/acquired, it would be inappropriate to dismiss variations in modalities as superficial phenomena. It is useful to classify such variations in modalities according to the location and code value of the modality.

(1) Location

(a) The variation may regulate an agency/agencies *within* a field, for example, symbolic control, production or the various agencies of the State.
(b) The variation may regulate relations *between* agencies in different fields.
(c) The variation may be specific to a dominating or dominated modality or both.

(2) Code value

The variation may effect only the principle of the classification, or only the framing, or it may effect both.

Classification

(a) *Within* a given principle of classification there may be variations in different historical periods in the *number* of categories (the set) regulated by the classification. (The social division of labour.)
(b) There may be a *substitution* of categories within an existing set, e.g. 'applied' for 'pure', more for less specialised.

(c) The strength of the classification may undergo a change with or without reference to (1) and (2).

Framing

Variation may effect only the internal values of the framing *or* it may effect the external values or both values. Any variation *within* a code which effects the classification will create a conflict *not* over the general principle of the distribution of power but over the distribution *within* the general principles. We can give examples of the relations between location and values of code modalities.

We shall use the distinctions made on the previous page based upon locations and code values *within and between fields* in order to give a more formal and concrete presentation of code modalities.

Code modalities

(a) Within agencies/fields

(1) *Variation within a dominating modality*
Examples of such variations would be historical variations in dominating *academic* curricula and practice in the various levels and departments of the educational system; historical variations in the administrative/management/practices of material production.[15]

(2) *Variations within a dominated modality*
Examples of such variation would be historical variations in curricula and practice for non-élite pupils; shop-floor practices of material production.

(3) *Opposition within a dominating modality*
Examples of such opposition would be orthodox-heterodox, conservative-progressive practices with respect to agencies within the field of symbolic control or the field of production – or the State.

(4) *Opposition between modalities*
A crucial and fundamental opposition here is the opposition between *codes* elaborated and restricted within education and within material production.

(b) Between agencies/fields

(1) *Variations in the relation between different agencies*
Framing relations *within* education may be relatively weakened in order to accommodate the requirements for different categories of labour so as to strengthen the *systematic* or correspondence relation between the output of education and the requirements of work.[16]

(2) The degree of regulation (classification) by agencies of the State, of agencies within the field of symbolic control or material production or both may vary. Variation in the strength of this classification regulates the degree of autonomy of the fields with respect to the State.

In the process of distinguishing locations of variations and change of elaborated codes we have utilised Bourdieu's concept of field and distinguished three related fields. We would say that code modalities establish and reproduce the practices specific to a field and, again in Bourdieu's terms, create the specificity of a habitus. We have distinguished the field of symbolic control whose ideologies and agencies regulate the means, contexts and legitimate possibilities of cultural reproduction, the field of production whose ideologies and agencies regulate the social basis for the means, contexts and possibilities of physical resources and the field of the State whose various agencies and ideologies define, maintain, vary and change what counts as legitimate order and the use of legitimate force. The educational system today is a crucial producer and reproducer of discursive resources within the field of symbolic control. What is of interest is the process whereby productions of the educational system, theories, become de-contextualised and re-contextualised in other fields of practice including different levels and functions of education. Theories in the natural sciences may alter the forces of production but code modalities select, vary or change their social relations. Theories in the social sciences establish an empirical basis for symbolic control but code modalities regulate their selection, variation and change. The issue is more complex. The positioning of theories within the intellectual field has itself to do with the relations between the principles of that field and the fields of specialised practice, especially that of the State. It is important to understand the social principles regulating the re-contextualising of theories in the fields of practice. This requires study both of re-contextualising agencies *and* agents. In order to understand how it is that theories become dominating we need to understand dominating code modalities (see Appendix 6).

Conclusion

We have been concerned in this paper with the following:

(1) To systematise developments which have been adumbrated in previous papers.
(2) To create a model capable of generating class regulated modalities of elaborated codes.
(3) To show how the model may be used to write specific codes regulating agencies of cultural reproduction or agencies of production.
(4) To show the specific principles regulating modes of transmission and acquisition.
(5) To enable the possibilities of diachronic and synchronic comparison.

Our primary distinction is between power and control. At the most abstract level we have argued that power constitutes relations 'between' and control relations 'within'; that power, constitutes the principle of the relations between categories and control the principle of the realisation of these relations. From this perspective, codes are transformations into specific semiotic principles/grammars of the relations and realisations of categories, where category relations represent the paradigmatic and realisations represent the syntagmatic. Class codes and their modalities are specific semiotic grammars which regulate the acquisition, reproduction and legitimation of fundamental rules of exclusion, inclusion and appropriation, by which and through which subjects are selectively created, positioned and oppositioned. These rules, whilst having their origin in the social division of labour and its social relations of material production, do not necessarily have the conditions of their cultural reproduction located in such a division and relations.

There are today under conditions of advanced capitalism many different sites of unequal relations between social groups, gender, ethnic, religious, regional, each having its own particular context of reproduction, generating in the language of this paper its specific 'voiced message'. This paper has concentrated upon the development of a model for understanding the process, whereby what is regarded as a basic classification (class relation), is transmitted and acquired by codes which differentially, invidiously and oppositionally position subjects, with respect to both discursive and physical resources. Whether gender, ethnic or religious categories (or any combination) are considered, it is held that these, today, speak through class regulated modes, and it is the manner of the cultural reproduction of the latter that has been the concern of this paper. We would emphasise that despite the abstract language of the model we have proposed, it is not the intention to create a representation of a process ruled by some determination which inexorably fulfills some inner law. On the contrary, variation, opposition and change inhere in the possibilities of code.

Appendix 1

Code, competence and dialect

Although we have distinguished between the above concepts (Bernstein 1971) it is unfortunately necessary to repeat the basis of the distinctions.

Code and competence

Theories which operate with a concept of competence (linguistic or cognitive) are theories in which the conditions for acquisition of the given competence require some innate facility *together* with interaction with a culturally *non*-specific other who also possesses the competency. In other words, the crucial communication necessary for the acquisition of the competence is with a culturally non-specific other. Of course, no other who possesses a given competence can be culturally non-specific. There is no way of being a cultural subject without being culturally specific. Be that as it may, and it inevitably is, theories of competence necessarily abstract the non-culturally specific from the culturally specific. Code is transmitted and acquired in interactions which are *culturally specific*. Codes therefore pre-suppose *specialised* others. It is crucial to distinguish between theories which differ in the location of their problematic. The concept code presupposes competencies (linguistic/cognitive) which all acquire and share, therefore it is not possible to discuss code with reference to cognitive/linguistic deficiencies located at the level of competence. Code refers to a specific cultural regulation of the realisation of commonly shared competencies. Code refers to specific semiotic grammars regulated by specialised distributions of power and principles of control. Such grammars will have amongst other realisations, specific linguistic realisations.

Code and dialect

The term dialect refers to a variety of language which can be marked-off from other varieties by phonological, syntactic, morphological, lexical features. The term is descriptive. It should give the demarcation rules for a specialised usage of a language and the special rules of its internal orderings. In the same way that *every* language carries the same potential for generating codes as defined in this thesis, language varieties, dialects, have the same potential. There is no reason to believe that in our terms any language variety can generate only one code. It is therefore highly misleading and inaccurate to equate a standard variety with an elaborated code and a non-standard variety with a restricted code, even though there may well be a class distribution of language varieties. Codes and dialects belong to different theoretical discourses, to different theories and address fundamentally different problematics.

Appendix 2

Modality of culture and gender

Perhaps we can give an example of modality of culture and what we mean by general features of the cultural subject through the consideration of gender relations. Cultural subjects are generated by a distinct and highly specialised reproductive device. This device consists of reproducers (R) and reproduced (r). Reproducers may consist of a large set of categories (Kinship) or a very small set. There are three distinctive features of this device which are culturally non-specific.

(1) The communicative principle, language, consists of a finite rule system capable of generating 'N' number of other rule systems.
(2) Communication principles between similars is different from communication principles between dissimilars as a consequence of the recognition of similarity and difference.
(3) Sex markers are read off, usually and normally, with the birth of 'r' by 'R'.

If we apply the above to the relations between 'R' and 'r' we obtain Figure 10.8.

Communication principles between RM and rm are different from communicative principles between Rm and rf, and similarly for RF and rm and RF and rf. Gender marking by communication is a feature intrinsic to the reproductive device. However, and it is a crucial 'how-

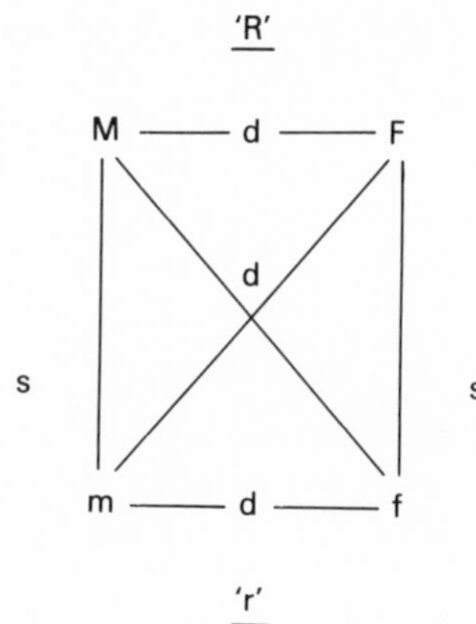

Categories

Where M refers to Reproducer Male
Where m refers to reproduced male
Where F refers to Reproducer Female
Where f refers to reproduced female

Communication

Where s refers to communication between similars
where d refers to communication between dissimilars

Figure 10.8

ever', the form the markings take, that is *their realisations are always culturally specific*. In our model we have given 'R' as a male and a female and 'r' as a male and a female, but the same argument would hold if we limited the model to 'R' Male and 'r' male or 'R' Female or 'r' female. It is also not necessary for 'R' to be biologically responsible for 'r'.

Appendix 3

Classification and framing of the codes of production

We can use the concepts of classification and framing to write the codes for the production of physical resources. We can consider the social relationships constituted by the mode of production in terms of classification and framing. We can ask what are the relationships between the various categories of production: that is, the relationships between the various agents, unskilled, technologists, managers, administrators, etc. The relationships between these categories can be strongly or weakly classified. If the former, then the relationships are stable and sharply distinguished, the functions well insulated from each other, and the agents are not interchangeable. If the latter, then the relationships between agents are less sharply distinguished, there is reduced insulation between functions and agents are more interchangeable between categories. In the same way, we can consider the framing of the mode of production. This refers to the regulation on the realisation of the categories: that is, to the form of communication constituted by the category system of the mode of production.

If the primary unit of production is a repetitive, individually performed, strongly paced, explicitly sequenced divisive act, we can say that this is strong framing. If the primary unit of production is relatively co-operative, group based, where there is opportunity to vary the conditions and perhaps sequencing and pacing, where the outcome is less a fraction of the total object of production but bears a more direct relation to it, we can say that this represents weak framing.

We shall consider the basic unit of production, the basic social relations of production, the level of the shop-floor. We have distinguished between the form of the productive act – what is made, what a worker produces – and the form of the relation between agents of production (workers). We distinguish between what is made and the relationships between those who are involved in making it. We call what is made, what is produced – that is, the social act of production – a realisation of an agent. We examine the act in terms of the degree of fragmentation or divisiveness it entails. The degree of fragmentation or divisiveness refers to the relationship between the act and the final product. The more fragmented or divisive the act(s), the less like the final product is its realisation. The more integrated the act, the more like the final product is its realisation, that is, its consequence. The act is a socially regulated realisation of a category (agent). The act of production is a communicative consequence of an agent. We can therefore consider the regulation of the act in terms of framing. The more fragmented or divisive the act, the stronger the framing; the less fragmented or divisive, the weaker the framing.

The form of the social relationship between agents of the basic unit of production can be referred to the concept classification, because here we are considering the principle of the relationships between the categories (agents) of the social division of labour. The relationships between agents have two features, horizontal and vertical. The horizontal feature refers to the relationship between agents who share membership of a common category – e.g. unskilled, skilled, supervisory, managerial. The vertical feature refers to the relationship between agents who are members of different categories. The vertical feature may, but not necessarily always, create a hierarchical ordering of the relationships between the categories. We can generate the following relationships between the primary agents of production in terms of the principle of their classification.

Very strong classification (++C)

The primary act of the result of an isolated agent.
The unit is an isolated agent.

Strong classification (+C)

The primary act is the result of related agents within a category, for example, a group of workers who are members of a common category. The unit is a group.

Less strong classification (C)

The primary act is the result of related agents between adjacent categories. The unit is a team of workers: skilled, semi-skilled, various skilled.

Weak classification (–C)

The primary act is the result of integrated agents across categories. The unit entails an integration of workers of various skills, and levels of supervision/management in policy and practice of production.

Now if we put together the nature of the primary act in terms of its framing (divisive/integrated) and the form of the relation between agents in terms of the principle of their classification (isolated/integrated), we can obtain at least five forms of regulation of the basic unit of production.

Codes of production

(1)	Isolated agents; divisive act.	++C++F
(2)	Related agents within a category; divisive act.	+C +F
(3)	Related agents between adjacent categories; integrated act.	C –F
(4)	Integrated agents across categories; divisive act.	–C +F
(5)	Integrated agents across categories; integrated act.	–C –F

We can now identify four forms of ideological control over the mode of production in class societies.

We can identify a historical process in the development of these production codes, from entrepreneurial to corporate capitalism, from code 1 to code 3. We would argue that codes 4 and 5 would constitute a qualitative change in the production code were they to be fully implemented and generalised throughout the system of production. A necessary condition for this would be a change in the dominant cultural category – that is a change in class structure.

We could link theories of control, which both legitimise and provide a scientific basis for exploitation of production, to the codes.

(1) We might connect Taylorism with (1)
(2) We might connect the Human Relation School with (2)
(3) We might connect the Socio-Technical System theory with (3)
(4/5) We might connect industrial democracy as a worker-based theory in opposition to the others.

As we move from (1) to (5) there is an important qualitative change occurring in the code value regulating the primary unit of production. Codes (1), (2) and (3) are variations of a restricted code, the capitalist relation of production, whereas codes (4) and (5) are variations of an elaborated code, realising collective relations of production.

Appendix 4

Class assumption of pedagogic codes

We shall give here a brief analysis of the class assumptions of a dominating modality of an elaborated code with strong classification and strong framing values (+C/+F). Such a code is transmitted through what we have called a visible pedagogy whereas where there is a major weakening of classification and framing (–C/–F) the code is transmitted through what we have called an Invisible Pedagogy. (See *Class, Codes and Control*, ch. 6, vol. III, revised edn, 1977).

We shall here be concerned with modes of transmission at the level of the primary/secondary school. The secondary school in our terms may well contain a dominating code in which the values of C and F are strong and dominated codes where the values are weaker.

We distinguish between modes of transmission/acquisition in terms of rules regulating hierarchy, rules regulating sequence and pacing, and rules regulating criteria.

(1) Hierarchical rules:

(a) *Explicit*: where such rules are explicit, the power basis of the social relation is undisguised and visible.
(b) *Implicit*: where such rules are implicit, the power basis of the social relation is masked, hidden, obscured by strategies of communication.

(2) Seqential rules and pacing:

(a) *Explicit*: where such rules are explicit, the principles and signs of the progression of the transmission are explicit, and made public. The educand has some awareness of his/her future state of expected legitimate consciousness and practice.
(b) *Implicit*: where such rules are implicit, the principles and signs of the progression are known only to the transmitter. The educand can have no knowledge (at least for some period of time) of the principles of his/her progression.

Pacing: refers to the rate of expected acquisition of the sequencing rules.

(3) Criteria rules:

(a) *Explicit*: where rules are explicit, criteria to be transmitted are explicit, and specific.
(b) *Implicit*: where rules are implicit, criteria to be transmitted are implicit, multiple, and diffuse.

Visible pedagogies can be defined as transmissions regulated by explicit hierarchy, explicit sequencing rules, strong pacing and explicit criteria. There are a variety of such pedagogies. We can distinguish two main forms with respect to their autonomy of, or dependency upon recruitment, selection, training for relations of production.

We will now give a *brief* analysis of the class assumptions and consequences of visible pedagogies at the school level (primary/secondary). Visible pedagogies are the forms of transmission/acquisition of elaborated codes (+C/+F).

(1) Context of Reproduction (Ideal)

(a) A group of homogeneous with respect to some or all of the following attributes: age, gender, ability.
(b) The act of acquisition will be solitary, privatised, and competitive.

(2) Progression

(a) It is crucial to read early in order to acquire the written code for beyond the book is the textbook which is the crucial pedagogical medium and social relation.
(b) Strong pacing regulates acquisition of sequencing rules; failures to acquire sequencing rules are difficult to redeem. Usually visible padegogies have to create a vast, often inadequate, repair system for those who cannot meet the sequencing rules.
(c) The sequencing rules regulate the temporal ordering of the content such that initial stages are concerned with the concrete and the learning of rote operations and relationships and later stages are concerned with the abstract and the learning of principles. Thus visible pedagogies separate 'concrete' and 'abstract' in time which becomes the basis for the separation (strong classification) of manual and mental labour. Visible pedagogies create and distribute different forms of consciousness.

Criteria

The pedagogical intention is to show the child what is *missing* in his or her product; as a consequence the criteria are explicit and specific. The latter create the possibility of 'objective' assessment and measurement and so facilitate the ideology of pedagogic neutrality.

Sites of reproduction

(a) Visible pedagogies usually require two sites of acquisition; the school and the home. Two sites are possible because the medium of the textbook enables their transfer. Not all homes can operate as second sites and in as much this does not occur, failure is highly likely.
(b) The relation between the two sites are regulated by strong framing; that is the school is selective of communications, practices, events

and objects, which may pass from the home into the pedagogical context.

Communication

See above. Communication between transmitters and acquirers is specially constituted by the strong classification and strong framing (especially with respect to sequencing rules and pacing). Time is scarce and discourses are strongly bounded. These affect the rules regulating spoken and written texts, question and answer format and their contexts.

Economics

Although the cost of the building is higher for a visible than an invisible pedagogy, the cost of the transmission is relatively low. The space occupied by the learner is relatively small, the pacing is such that often as much time must be spent in the home as in the school. The hidden costs of visible pedagogies are the attributes of the home, physical, discursive, interactional, which enable children to manage or fail to manage the class assumptions of the *context* and *sites of reproduction*, *progression* and *communication*.

Modes of transmission ideologically create and position subjects.

Appendix 5

Code values and experimental contexts

The model we have developed may be used to generate relations between agencies, and relationships within agencies, whether these be at so-called 'macro' or 'micro' levels. The latter would refer to what we have called the communicative context. This context is regulated by framing values on the basis of a given classificatory value. The classificatory principle is often invisibly present in the sense that it is presupposed. If we examine the communicative context established in the 'food' experiment we discussed in the main text, from the perspective of our model, we may be able to suggest an explanation of the differences between the middle-class and the lower-working-class children. We shall begin by indicating the apparent opposition between the *implicit* dominant code values constituting the communicative context and the spoken text or apparently *explicit* code values. The implicit dominant code values in our terms would be $\frac{E}{+C/+F^{+e}}$ which we will now elaborate.

Classification

Recognition rule

(i) This context is a sub-context of a specialised context; school (+C)
(ii) This sub-context is specialised adult, instructional evaluative, *elaborate orientation* (E)

Framing

Realisation rule

(i) Select interactional practice and text in accordance with recognition rule; (+F)
(ii) Create specialised text; exhaustive principle, no narrative, no isolated situational exemplars or lists

There are, of course, many other features of the communicative context regulated by framing values but on the whole these resulted in practices shared by the children (sex, class).

However, when we look at the spoken text the code values are in apparent opposition. The instructions to elicit groupings and principles were of the order –C/–F. 'Group the pictures any way you want' (–C) with no indication of the spoken text required (–F). The middle-class children in the *first* request to group, ignored the –C –F instruction and transposed it into its opposite +C/+F, whereas the lower-working-class children read the instruction at its surface value and read it as the dominant code value. There can be little doubt that the lower-working class were aware of the classifying principles used by the middle-class children and indeed, towards the end of the experiment some lower-working-class children used these principles as dominating principles. The difference between the children is therefore not a difference in cognitive facility but a difference in the recognition and realisation rules used by the children to read the context and to create their texts; a code difference. (See also 'open question', Foreword to *Code in Context*, Adlam, D., Routledge & Kegan Paul, 1977).

It is possible from this analysis to make explicit a variety of sources of difference in children's contextual practices.

(1) Inappropriate recognition rules therefore inappropriate realisation rules.
(2) Appropriate recognition rules but inadequacy of realisation rules either in creating the specific text or in the social relations of the performance or both.

We can give other examples of the selective effect of the formal setting upon the recognition and realisation rules used by seven-year-old children from middle-class and lower-working-class family backgrounds matched for 'intelligence' ('IQ') (See Adlam, D. *et al.* (1977), *Code in Context*, Routledge & Kegan Paul, Chapters 2, 3 and 4.)

The children were given reproductions about the size of a postcard of a Belgian naive painter, Trotin, and asked to talk about the cards. The probe/s was

'What is going on in the picture?'
'What are the people doing?'
'What is the picture all about?' (Last probe after the child had finished talking about the card).

Such probe/s could be understood as a request for (a) narrative, or (b) a description of persons, objects, events, relationships depicted in the card, i.e. a verbal demography.

We found that in general the focus of the child's speech was more a function of the child's class background than the child's 'IQ'. The middle-class child, irrespective of gender, produced a text similar to, or approximating (b) whereas the lower-working-class child produced a text *either* orientated to (b) or, although orientated to (a), was imbedded in the context, in the sense that it was less likely to be understood without the original picture card. Other researchers or critics have interpreted this finding as showing no more than the fact that the lower-working-class children were aware that both the researcher and the researched were looking at the picture card, and, as a consequence, there was no need to make verbally explicit a context which was shared. This 'explanation' is both *ad hoc* and selective as it signally fails to explain:

1 Why the middle-class children produced little narrative. Only 6 out of a total of 64 children.
2 Why the lower working class produced narrative.
3 Why it was the girls in the lower working class who were mainly responsible for narrative texts.
4 Why the lower-working-class children's speech orientation was

similar in *other* situations presented to the child in which the presumption of a shared perspective between researcher and researched could not be postulated. (Instructional and control situations.)

Another situation offered to the children in the same interview required them to explain the rules of a game (hide and seek) to a child who did not know how to play, after first indicating to the researcher knowledge of the rules. We again found that the social class family background was more important that the child's 'IQ' in accounting for the orientation of the child's speech and referential relations. In general middle-class children (but not uniformly) created a relatively context-independent text, in the sense that the text was not imbedded in a local context/practice; whereas the text created by the lower-working-class children (but not uniformly) was relatively context dependent *compared* with the text of the middle-class children in that it was more imbedded in a local context/practice and assumed knowledge of that context/practice. It does not necessarily follow that the middle-class child's text was a more effective instruction. Indeed there may well be grounds to believe otherwise (Adlam, D. *et al.* (1977), *Code in Context*, Routledge & Kegan Paul).

The children were given a third situation based upon one created for their mothers two years earlier. The mothers were given six hypothetical situations in which their own child had done something wrong and they were asked what they would do or say. These same situations were presented to the children as if they (the children) were the mothers and were faced with *their* child who had done something wrong. In general (independent of 'IQ') there were marked differences in the focus of the control used by the children in terms of their family class background. Whilst all the children tended to give imperative forms of control and forms which announced simple rules, the middle-class children used these forms less and gave forms which allowed for options and contingencies.

In general the opening question to the children in the above situations had the same general form as the opening question in the 'food' inquiry referred to earlier. It did not stipulate any particular relation between categories of referential relation nor did the question explicitly direct the children to realise a *particular* text. We can account for the texts by the following recognition and realisation rules.

Middle-class children

Recognition rule

In all three situations the same rule would hold.

(i) This context is a sub-context of a specialised context: school.
(ii) The sub-context is specialised adult, instructional, evaluative; elaborated orientation.

Thus the *modal* orientation of the middle-class children across the three contexts was elaborated, whereas the modal orientation of the lower-working-class children was restricted which does not mean that there was *no* variation. (Indeed lower-working-class *girls* produced more variation than lower-working-class boys.)

1 Trotin picture card text

Middle-class children

Realisation rule

(i) Use criteria True/False. Given this rule there could be *no* narrative *and very few* middle-class children gave any narrative. Further, given the above rule, there would be a need to use modals (might be, could be) and other forms indicating uncertainty. More middle-class children used such forms.
(ii) Make all referential relations explicit and specific.

The rules (i) and (ii) are sufficient to generate the structure of the modal middle-class text.

Lower-working-class children

Recognition rule

Relative to the middle-class child the lower-working-class child did not mark the context with the same speciality, therefore their modal orientation across the three contexts was restricted. In other words the context was for the middle-class child *relative* to the lower-working-class child *strongly classified* (+C) whereas for the lower-working-class child relative to middle-class child it was weakly classified (–C).

Lower-working-class children
Realisation rule

Given that the *context was weakly classified* we could expect a range of texts all selected from informal everyday practices and modes.

i. Narrative
ii. Implicit referential relations.

2 Hide-and-seek text
Realisation rules

Middle-class children
Make all sequencing rules, reference sets and criteria, explicit, specific and unambiguous.

Lower-working-class children
Similar to Trotin realisation rule.

In both of the above situations the middle-class transformed an opening question generated by apparent –C –F rules to +C +F. The lower-working-class children carried out this transformation significantly less frequently.

3 Mother-child control

Here we have a situation very different from the above two situations. The child is taking on the role of the mother and what we expect here are differences in the recognition rules and realisation rules, which are less a function of the *particular formal interview setting* but more a function of the recognition and realisation rules used by the child's major controller in the family. Indeed we know this to be the case (Cook-Gumperz, J., *Social Control and Socialization*, Routledge & Kegan Paul, 1973).

Middle-class children's recognition and realisation rules were of the form +C –F relative to the lower-working-class children's +C +F. The difference between the children at seven years of age showed only in the strength of the framing, i.e. middle-class children accorded more options/contingencies to the controlled than did the lower-working-class children.

Conclusion

We have here extended our analysis to show how classification and framing values act selectively on recognition and realisation rules which we *infer* are used by middle-class and lower-working-class children in the production of texts in a formal interview setting *and* in the *reproduction* of familial texts (of control) in that setting.

Appendix 6

Primary, recontextualising and secondary contexts

We shall here make rather more explicit the importance of the recontextualising field, and of its agents, in the selective movement of texts from the intellectual field created by the educational system, to that system's fields of reproduction.

Definitions: primary, secondary and recontextualising contexts

Primary context: production of discourse

We shall distinguish three crucial, interdependent contexts of educational discourse, practice and organisation. The first of these we shall call the *primary* context. The process whereby a text is developed and positioned in this context we shall call primary contextualisation. The latter refers to the process whereby new ideas are selectively created, modified and changed, and where specialised discourses are developed, modified or changed. This context creates, appropriating Bourdieu, the intellectual field of the educational system. This field and its history is created by the positions, relations and practices arising out of the *production* rather than the reproduction of educational discourse and its practices. Its texts, today, are dependent partly *but by no means wholly* on the circulation of private and state public funds to research groups and individuals.

Secondary context: the reproduction of discourse

This context, its various levels, agencies, positions and practices refers to the selective *reproduction* of educational discourse. We shall distinguish four levels, tertiary, secondary, primary and preschool. Within each level there may be some degree of specialisation of agencies. We shall call these levels and their interrelations, together with any specialisation of agencies within a level, the secondary context of the reproduction of discourse. This context structures the *field of reproduction*. We can ask here questions referring to the classificatory and framing principles regulating the relations between and within levels and regulating the circulation and location of codes and their modalities.

Recontextualising context: relocation of discourse

Between these two fundamental contexts and the fields they structure we shall distinguish a third context which structures a field or subset of fields, whose positions, agents and practices are concerned with the movements of texts/practices from the primary context of discursive production to the secondary context of discursive reproduction. The function of the position, agents and practices within this field and its subsets, is to regulate the circulation of texts between the primary and secondary context. Accordingly we shall call the field and the subset structured by this context, the *recontextualising field*. The *recontextualising context* will entail a number of fields.

1 It will include specialised departments and sub-agencies (School Council) of the state and local educational authorities together with their research and system of inspectors.
2 It will include university departments of education, polytechnics and colleges of education together with their research.
3 It will include specialised media of education, weeklies, journals, etc. and publishing houses together with their readers and advisers.
4 It may extend to fields *not* specialised in educational discourse and its practices which are able to exert influence both on the state and its various arrangements and/or upon special sites, agents and practices within education.

When a text is appropriated by recontextualising agents, operating in positions of this field, the text usually undergoes a transformation prior to its relocation. The form of this transformation is regulated by a *principle of decontextualising*. This process refers to the change in the text as it is first *delocated* and then *relocated*. This process ensures that the text is no longer the same text:

1 The text has changed its position in relation to other texts, practices and positions.
2 The text itself has been modified by selection, simplification, condensation and elaboration.
3 The text has been repositioned and refocused.

The decontextualising principle regulates the new ideological positioning of the text in its process of relocation in one or more of the levels of the field of reproduction. Once in that field the text undergoes a *further* transformation or repositioning as it becomes active in the pedagogic process within an agency within a level. It is crucial to distinguish between and analyse the relations between the two transformations (at least) of a text. The first is the transformation of the text within the *recontextualising field* and the second is the transformation of the *transformed* text in the pedagogic process as it becomes active in the process of the reproduction of acquirers. *It is the recontextualising field which generates the positions and oppositions* of pedagogic theory, research and practice. It is a matter of some importance to analyse the role of departments of the state in the relations and movements within and between the various contexts and their structuring fields.

Acknowledgment

I am very indebted to seminars held in a number of universities for constructive criticism and especially so to the University of Lund (Pedagogical Institute) and to the University of New York (Department of Sociology). I am very grateful to students of the Department of the Sociology of Education, University of London Institute of Education, for lively discussion and debate.

Bibliography and Notes

* Bernstein, B. (1977), *Class, Codes and Control*, vol. III, 2nd edn, Routledge & Kegan Paul. See 'Introduction', pp. 30-2.

1 Ground rule was first used in 'Postscript: A brief account of the theory of Codes in "Social Relationships and Language" ', Block 3 of the Educational Studies Second Level course Language and Learning, The Open University, 1973. Performance rules were distinguished from ground rules in the Foreword to Adlam *et al.*, *Code in Context*, Routledge & Kegan Paul 1977.

2 This formulation of the general definition of code was developed by Ms Antonella Castelnuovo, PhD student of the Department of the Sociology of Education, University of London Institute of Education.

3 Holland, J. (1980), 'Social class and changes in orientations to meanings', *Sociology* (in press forthcoming).

4 This formulation follows closely earlier formulations (*Class, Codes and Control*, vol. I, Introduction, Routledge & Kegan Paul 1971) in terms of context dependent and context independent. The latter is independent, clearly not in any absolute but in a relative sense.

5 It is important to make a distinction between the *location* of these orientations and their *origins*. Whilst historically we can locate orientations in different positions of the mode of production, these orientations may not originate in this mode. In non-literate

small-scale societies with a simple division of labour (called 'primitive' by nineteenth century anthropologists) elaborate orientations are found less in the social relations of material production but more in the *religious cosmologies*. This is not to say that these religious cosmologies have no relation to a material base; indeed, they often legitimated the categories and social relations of material production. Similarly, restricted orientations are likely to be found in relations of intimacy and close proximity. Elaborated orientations (where there is an indirect relation to a specific material base) are, *however*, always subject to strong regulation and surveillance; for these orientations have the potential of creating alternative realities, possibilities, and practices. Elaborated orientations are potentially dangerous and those acquiring them have to be made safe.

6 Historically the institutionalising of, access to, and distribution of elaborated codes was regulated by the Church's control of formal education. See *Evolution of Pedagogy in France*, Durkheim, E., Alcan Press, 1938, translated by Peter Collins and published as *The Evolution of Educational Thought*, Routledge & Kegan Paul, 1977.

We do not wish to transpose the technical term 'mode' as in the concept 'mode of production' to education. However, we wish to distinguish between the various possibilities of a given elaborated code institutionalised as a dominant code in education. Modality refers to the specific values of a given elaborated code (its classification and framing values). See later discussion.

7 There is a problem in making a distinction between physical and discursive resources. For it implies that the latter is qualitatively different from the former. We do not take this view, indeed, on the contrary, we would hold that discursive resources/practices are a condition for, and are constituted in, physical resources. We are using these terms simply as low level descriptions.

8 See Bernstein, B. (1977), *Class, Codes and Control*, vol. III, revised edn, ch. 8, Routledge & Kegan Paul.

9 Torode, B., and Silverman, D., in their impressive book *The Material Word*, Routledge & Kegan Paul, 1980, first drew my attention to the possibilities of 'voice'. I have, however, with apologies put the concept to a rather different use.

10 From now onwards we shall use social division of labour to refer to both production and to agencies of cultural reproduction, in particular the agencies of education and the family.

11 Althusser, L. (1971), 'Ideology and the ideological state apparatus' in *Lenin and Philosophy*, translated by Brewster, B., New Left Books.

12 Bourdieu, P. and Passeron, J. C. (1977), *Reproduction in Education, Society and Culture*, translated by Nice, R., Sage Publications.

13 See Bernstein, B. (1977), 'Aspects of the relation between educa-

tion and production', *Class, Codes and Control*, vol. III, revised edn, ch. 8, Routledge & Kegan Paul.

14 See ibid.

15 Bourdieu, P. and Boltanski, L. (1978), 'Changes in social structure and changes in the demand for education' in *Contemporary Europe, Social Structures and Cultural Patterns*, ed. Giner, S., and Scotford Archer, M.

16 See Bernstein, op. cit.

Index

American spellings, e.g. 'labor', are used throughout this index